Studies in Virtual Communities, Blogs, and Modern Social Networking:

Measurements, Analysis, and Investigations

Subhasish Dasgupta
George Washington University, USA

An Imprint of IGI Global

Managing Director:	Lindsay Johnston
Editorial Director:	Joel Gamon
Production Manager:	Jennifer Yoder
Publishing Systems Analyst:	Adrienne Freeland
Assistant Acquisitions Editor:	Kayla Wolfe
Typesetter:	Christina Henning
Cover Design:	Jason Mull

Published in the United States of America by
Information Science Reference (an imprint of IGI Global)
701 E. Chocolate Avenue
Hershey PA 17033
Tel: 717-533-8845
Fax: 717-533-8661
E-mail: cust@igi-global.com
Web site: http://www.igi-global.com

Library of Congress Cataloging-in-Publication Data

Studies in virtual communities, blogs, and modern social networking : measurements, analysis, and investigations / Subhasish Dasgupta, editor.
       pages cm
  Includes bibliographical references and index.
  Summary: "This book provides a cross-cultural perspective of social networking, including ethical considerations and business implications"--Provided by publisher.
  ISBN 978-1-4666-4022-1 (hardcover) -- ISBN (invalid) 978-1-4666-4023-8 (ebook) -- ISBN 978-1-4666-4024-5 (print & perpetual access) 1. Social networks. 2. Electronic villages (Computer networks) 3. Blogs. I. Dasgupta, Subhasish, 1966- editor of compilation.
  HM741.S784 2013
  302.3--dc23
                                                     2013001598

British Cataloguing in Publication Data
A Cataloguing in Publication record for this book is available from the British Library.

The views expressed in this book are those of the authors, but not necessarily of the publisher.

Table of Contents

Detailed Table of Contents

The ability to generate innovative products and services is a critical success factor for organizations. The trend of open innovation has brought about many-faceted, IT-based tools (e.g., lead user method or online tool kits), among these, the innovation contest seems particularly promising and continuously gains in importance as a corporate practice. However, a deep understanding of this online innovation practice is still lacking. Contrary to other methods used to realize open innovation, research in the field of online innovation contests displays a growing, but only rudimentarily intertwined body of publications. This paper provides the quintessential systematization of the field by integration of academic knowledge and business deployment. Juxtaposing 33 relevant journal and conference publications with empirical basis and an analysis of 57 real-world innovation contests, interesting disruptions are pointed to and six pathways for future research are described. These cover the optimal degree of elaboration, the interplay of competition and community, the importance of community applications, the trajectory toward open evaluation, and the identification of additional design elements.

Chapter 2

Virtual communities are an increasingly popular way to conduct business over the Internet. However, from the service provider's point of view they pose special challenges. In particular, unless the provider itself engages in content or service provision, the service relies entirely on its members for provision of services. The members should thus be seen as resources for service provision. This type of networked service production system implies challenges in terms of service quality management and, subsequently, value creation for community members. This paper explores these issues by revisiting service marketing and service operations literature on service quality. Analysis of the literature indicates that firms facilitating virtual communities need to ensure the quality of their service by not only ensuring technical quality but also by nurturing the social aspects of the community that have an impact on the willingness of community members to provide service to each other.

As the young generations grow up using applications like Facebook and as fans of social networking technologies, understanding the presentations of self in a virtual community becomes a worthwhile topic to be addressed. Drawing on the theory of dramaturgical theory (Goffman, 1959), this interpretive research was conducted to observe the self presentation of the participants in a virtual community to analyze their online behaviors and interactions. The observations found that only in the early stage of interaction, people can have a high degree of control over the ideal images creation; however, the clues to reveal actual images are accumulated over time and across cyberspaces. This research suggested that personal control over image delivery in a virtual community weakens over time, which challenged the assumption made by prior literature regarding how people have greater control in creating ideal images in the virtual community. The findings of this research could provide insight for people who use virtual community to search for credible personal information or to build ideal images. Besides, this research suggested that although Internet technologies facilitate access to a rich source of information, the convenience in information acquisition and verification comes at the expense of personal privacy.

Chapter 4

The nature of the enterprise and the way people work is changing rapidly. The enabling power and competitive advantage of new social and participative technologies will benefit those that recognize the way work is changing. Web 2.0, the "second phase" of the Web, is the foundation of a new and improved Enterprise 2.0. Enterprise 2.0 provides, through a web of interconnected applications, services, and devices, the capabilities for enterprise employees and vendors to be more competitive and productive and for enterprise customers to be more engaged and loyal by accessing the right information from the right people at the right time. This paper describes Enterprise 2.0 management challenges and issues identified by Chief Information Officers, which include the unauthorized use of services and technologies, the integration of a myriad of technologies and capabilities, and the potential compliance and security implications. The authors have proposed a conceptual framework that explores the relationships of three Enterprise 2.0 dimensions – technology, its use, and how resulting user-generated content may lead to business value – with management implications affecting IT culture and policies within the enterprise. This paper provides observations and suggestions for future research.

The purpose of this study is to develop an integrated model designed to examine users' continuance of Facebook based on the unified theory of acceptance and use of technology (UTAUT), the expectation disconfirmation model (EDM), and flow theory. Empirical data collected from 482 users who have experience with Facebook are subjected to structural equation modeling based on the proposed research model. Results show that users' continuance intention of Facebook is determined by social influence, performance expectancy, effort expectancy, flow experience, and satisfaction. Satisfaction is significantly affected by flow experience and disconfirmation. Results also suggest that effort expectancy is positively related to flow experience. Based on the findings, managerial implications are discussed in this paper and directions for future research are also highlighted.

Purnendu Karmakar, Indian Institute of Technology Kharagpur, India
Rajarshi Roy, Indian Institute of Technology Kharagpur, India

Distributed network researchers are trying to address one important issue concerning networked structures and how the network came into existence, i.e., dynamics of network evolution. From the knowledge of social science it is observed that trust is one such metric that evolves with the network particularly where human interaction is involved. This work presents a "trust" model of the authors' studies and its various properties. In virtual (and "real") communities (chat rooms, blogs, etc.) behavioral segregation over time is observed. Differences in identities of interacting agents result in evolution of various degrees of "trust" (and "distrust") among them over a period of time. This process ultimately leads to emergence of self-segregation in behavioral kinetics and results in formation of preference clusters.

Chingning Wang, National Sun Yat-Sen University, Taiwan

"Social shopping" (or social commerce), combining shopping and social networking, is an application of Web 2.0 in electronic commerce to benefit from users' social networks. This paper explores the development of the emergent "social shopping" and related perspectives. It incorporates comparisons between social shopping marketing and search engine marketing. For example, search engine marketing assumes shoppers are certain of their shopping goal; social shopping marketing assumes shoppers are uncertain of their shopping goals and gather shopping ideas from their peers. In this paper, the challenges in social shopping development are identified, including governing shopper communities and retrieving content from social networking sites. The author concludes that social shopping and e-commerce are not dichotomous concepts. Social shopping can be an evolutionary concept, meaning a singular EC site advancing with social networking functions, or a synergistic concept, meaning EC sites connecting with the other social networking sites to form strategic alliance.

Guoying Zhang, Midwestern State University, USA
Alan J. Dubinsky, Midwestern State University, CALIMT Learning and Innovation Research
    Center, USA & Purdue University, USA
Yong Tan, University of Washington, USA

In this study, blog data were collected and network parameters were captured to represent three common measurements of online Word-Of-Mouth: intensity, influence level, and dispersion. These parameters were then analyzed using a General Estimating Equation (GEE) model to test their effects on average weekly movie box office receipts. Findings indicated that all three parameters were significant in the model. The aggregated degree, representing WOM intensity, was positively significant, which was consistent with results from extant research. Further, diameter of a network, representing WOM dispersion, was observed to be positively significant, which validated the importance of spreading WOM as far as possible. Counter-intuitively, the aggregated size node, representing WOM influence level, was ascertained to be negatively significant, which might be explained by the possible negative stance from opinion leaders with high influence level. Applying network analysis methodology to blog entries, the present work differentiated itself from extant WOM literature that has focused chiefly on content analysis. The findings also provided managerial insights to companies interested in utilizing blogs as online WOM for marketing initiatives and implications for future research.

Kanna Al Falahi, United Arab Emirates University-Al Ain, UAE

Saad Harous, United Arab Emirates University-Al Ain, UAE

Yacine Atif, United Arab Emirates University-Al Ain, UAE

Clustering is a major problem when dealing with organizing and dividing data. There are multiple algorithms proposed to handle this issue in many scientific areas such as classifications, community detection and collaborative filtering. The need for clustering arises in Social Networks where huge data generated daily and different relations are established between users. The ability to find groups of interest in a network can help in many aspects to provide different services such as targeted advertisements. The authors surveyed different clustering algorithms from three different clustering groups: Hierarchical, Partitional, and Density-based algorithms. They then discuss and compare these algorithms from social web point view and show their strength and weaknesses in handling social web data. They also use a case study to support our finding by applying two clustering algorithms on articles collected from Delicious.com and discussing the different groups generated by each algorithm.

Niyoosha Jafari Momtaz, K. N. Toosi University of Technology, Iran

Abdollah Aghaie, K. N. Toosi University of Technology, Iran

Somayeh Alizadeh, K. N. Toosi University of Technology, Iran

Recently, the impact of social networks in customer buying decision is rapidly increasing due to effectiveness in shaping public opinion. This paper helps marketers analyze social network's members based on different characteristics and choose the best method for identifying influential people among them. Then, marketers can use these influential people as seeds to market products/services. Considering the importance of opinion leadership in social networks a comprehensive overview of existing literature has been done. Studies show, different titles (such as opinion leaders, influential people, market mavens and key players) are used to refer to the influential group in social networks whom we know as opinion leaders. The study shows all the properties presented for opinion leaders in the form of different titles are classified into three general categories including structural, relational and personal characteristics and based on studying opinion leader identification methods; appropriate parameters are extracted in a comprehensive chart to evaluate and compare these methods accurately.

Norshuhada Shiratuddin, Universiti Utara Malaysia, Malaysia

Shahizan Hassan, Universiti Utara Malaysia, Malaysia

Nor Laily Hashim, Universiti Utara Malaysia, Malaysia

Mohd Fo'ad Sakdan, Universiti Utara Malaysia, Malaysia

Mohd Samsu Sajat, Universiti Utara Malaysia, Malaysia

Although weblogs are a popular medium of communication, their influence on society is unclear. In particular, studies that investigate the impact and influence of blogosphere on the community and government have not been fully exploited. Such studies are important especially to the government in reshaping and realigning the policies related to new media. This article presents the outcomes of a study to identify measures on how to assess the influence of weblogs. At least four dimensions are critical for measuring weblog influence, which are recognition (number of in links and number of visitors), activity generation (number of comments and number of posts), novelty (number of out links), and credibility of a blog (number of information presentation type, number of factual errors, and number of hyperlink citations). It is hereby proposed that these dimensions make up a measure called the Blog Influence Index.

Leila Esmaeili, University of Qom, Iran

Mahdi Nasiri, Iran University of Science and Technology, Iran

Behrouz Minaei-Bidgoli, Iran University of Science and Technology, Iran

Analysis of data in social networks is very important for researchers, sociologists, and academics. Given the size and diversity of web data in a Web 2.0 environment, analyzing this data has been a challenge. Since data act as inputs in such projects, the accuracy of the output is directly related to the input. Good data allows for extraction of valuable knowledge. In this article, the authors present their experiences with preparation and preprocessing of data in a Persian social network. The authors also report on the analysis of the data and findings.

*Nana Adu-Pipim Boaduo, Walter Sisulu University, South Africa, & University of the Free
State-Bloemfontein Campus, South Africa*

Contextually, all tertiary institutions have four major responsibilities – teaching, research, publication, and community service. The adage "publish or perish" has become a thorn in the flesh of many university academic staff who rest on their laurels and do nothing about research, publication, and community engagement. Practising university academic staff are required by the nature of their profession to engage in regular research be it in their daily lecturing and supervision of students' research thesis or writing for publication. Currently, research has become the buzz-word in all tertiary institutions but not all of them take the pains to school academic staff in the practice of research in terms of the virtual communities where the institution is located. In the context of this paper, the author looks at action research through the eyes of teachers of all categories in virtual communities and how their involvement can complement successful social networking. The approaches used in this discussion are purely from empirical and exploratory perspectives and provide detailed discussion with emphasis on the application of action research for effective and efficient social networking considering the social, cultural, organizational and human cognitive perspectives.

Sandra A. Vannoy, Walker College of Business, Appalachian State University, USA
B. Dawn Medlin, Walker College of Business, Appalachian State University, USA
Charlie C. Chen, Walker College of Business, Appalachian State University, USA

The trust of members is essential to the sustainability of e-business. Unlike other business models, the success of online social networks is highly dependent upon the growth rate of social network size. In order to accelerate and continue the growth rate, online social networks need to be able to continuously roll out diversified services and use them to interest existing and new members. However, the nature of this business model can expose online social networks to ubiquitous security threats such as spam, viral marketing and viruses. In order to convince users to adopt social network services, cultivation of brand equity and trust in the online social networks is essential. This study integrates technical and marketing perspectives to examine the potential influence of website quality and brand equity on user satisfaction, thereby influencing users' formation of trust. A survey was conducted with 385 subjects to understand the causal relationships between the studied constructs. Regression analysis indicates that website quality, brand loyalty, brand association, and brand quality have a positive influence on user satisfaction, thereby increasing the trust of members in online social networks. Brand awareness shows no significant influence on user satisfaction. These findings lead us to derive theoretical and practical implications on the sustainable operation of online social networks.

Kamna Malik, U21Global Graduate School, Singapore, Singapore

Research conferences provide an important platform for idea exchange and validation as well as for social networking and talent hunt. Online social networks and collaborative web tools can make conferences budget friendly for sponsors, flexible for attendees, and environment friendly for the society without loss of effectiveness. While many conferences have adopted such tools during pre and post conferencing stages, their use during actual meeting hours is very limited. This paper deliberates on the current and potential use of such technologies on various stages of a conference. It then presents the case of a pure virtual conference in comparison with a face to face conference with an aim to analyze the immediate benefits that virtual conferencing brings for organizers and participants. Perceived deterrents and potential benefits for various stakeholders are discussed. Suggestions are made for educational institutions to review their norms for conference sponsorships.

Chapter 16

    Demosthenes Akoumianakis, Department of Applied Information Technology & Multimedia,
        Technological Education Institution of Crete, Greece

    Giannis Milolidakis, Department of Applied Information Technology & Multimedia,
        Technological Education Institution of Crete, Greece

    George Vlachakis, Department of Applied Information Technology & Multimedia,
        Technological Education Institution of Crete, Greece

    Nikolas Karadimitriou, Department of Applied Information Technology & Multimedia,
        Technological Education Institution of Crete, Greece

    Giorgos Ktistakis, Department of Applied Information Technology & Multimedia,
        Technological Education Institution of Crete, Greece

The present work rests and elaborates on the assumption that social technologies are increasingly turned into computer-mediated virtual settlements, thereby allowing the excavation of a variety of enacted cyber-phenomena such as ad hoc online ensembles, informal social networks and virtual communities, on the grounds of "digital" traces or remains. In this vein, the authors motivate and present a method for virtual excavations that is tightly coupled to a transformational technology such as knowledge visualization. The analytical and explanatory value of the method is assessed using two case studies addressing representative genres of social technologies, namely web sites augmented with social plug-ins and social networking services. Analysis reveals intrinsic aspects of "digital" traces and remains, the form they take in today's social web and the means through which they can be excavated and transformed to useful information. It turns out that such virtual excavations, when organized and conducted carefully, can be of benefit to enterprises, service organizations and public sector institutions. In addition, their tight coupling with knowledge visualization eliminates extensive data analysis as much of this work can be done using the visualization. On the other hand, and depending on the size of digital trace data, the choice of visualizations and the underlying toolkit are of paramount importance.

Preface

As social networks continue to expand, their importance in professional as well as personal settings is becoming abundantly clear. The chapters within this compilation of theory, research, and application will provide researchers, practitioners, and users with the information necessary to make the most of virtual communities and social networks in their everyday activities. This book explores topics as diverse as Peer-to-Peer (P2P) networking systems, enterprise 2.0, social shopping, blogging, management, etc. The following paragraphs describe what readers should expect from each chapter in this crucial reference source.

The book opens with "Innovation Contests: Systematization of the Field and Future Research" by Angelika C. Bullinger and Kathrin Moeslein. The ability to generate innovative products and services is a critical success factor for organizations. The trend of open innovation has brought about many-faceted, IT-based tools (e.g., lead user method or online tool kits), among these, the innovation contest seems particularly promising and continuously gains in importance as a corporate practice. However, a deep understanding of this online innovation practice is still lacking. Contrary to other methods used to realize open innovation, research in the field of online innovation contests displays a growing but only rudimentarily intertwined body of publications. This chapter provides the quintessential systematization of the field by integration of academic knowledge and business deployment. Juxtaposing 33 relevant journal and conference publications with empirical basis and an analysis of 57 real-world innovation contests, interesting disruptions are pointed to and six pathways for future research are described. These cover the optimal degree of elaboration, the interplay of competition and community, the importance of community applications, the trajectory toward open evaluation, and the identification of additional design elements.

Next, Aku Valtakoski, Juhana Peltonen, and Mikko O. J. Laine describe "Peer-to-Peer Service Quality in Virtual Communities." Virtual communities are an increasingly popular way to conduct business over the Internet. However, from the service provider's point of view they pose special challenges. In particular, unless the provider itself engages in content or service provision, the service relies entirely on its members for provision of services. The members should thus be seen as resources for service provision. This type of networked service production system implies challenges in terms of service quality management and, subsequently, value creation for community members. This chapter explores these issues by revisiting service marketing and service operations literature on service quality. Analysis of the literature indicates that firms facilitating virtual communities need to ensure the quality of their service by not only ensuring technical quality but also by nurturing the social aspects of the community that have an impact on the willingness of community members to provide service to each other.

Following this is "Unfolding the Diminishing Image Control in Online Self Presentation: An Investigation of Virtual Community" by Chien-Nai Lin, Yu-Tzu Lin, and Ching-Cha Hsieh. As the young generations grow up using applications like Facebook and as fans of social networking technologies, understanding the presentations of self in a virtual community becomes a worthwhile topic to be addressed. Drawing on the theory of dramaturgical theory, this interpretive research was conducted to observe the self-presentation of the participants in a virtual community to analyze their online behaviors and interactions. The observations found that only in the early stage of interaction, can people have a high degree of control over the ideal images creation; however, the clues to reveal actual images are accumulated over time and across cyberspaces. This research suggested that personal control over image delivery in a virtual community weakens over time, which challenges the assumption made by prior literature regarding how people have greater control in creating ideal images in the virtual community. The findings of this research could provide insight for people who use virtual community to search for credible personal information or to build ideal images. Besides, this research suggests that although Internet technologies facilitate access to a rich source of information, the convenience in information acquisition and verification comes at the expense of personal privacy.

In "Enterprise 2.0 Management Challenges," Karen P. Patten and Lynn B. Keane describe how the nature of the enterprise and the way people work is changing rapidly. The enabling power and competitive advantage of new social and participative technologies will benefit those that recognize the way work is changing. Web 2.0, the "second phase" of the Web, is the foundation of a new and improved Enterprise 2.0. Enterprise 2.0 provides, through a Web of interconnected applications, services, and devices, the capabilities for enterprise employees and vendors to be more competitive and productive and for enterprise customers to be more engaged and loyal by accessing the right information from the right people at the right time. This chapter describes Enterprise 2.0 management challenges and issues identified by Chief Information Officers, which include the unauthorized use of services and technologies, the integration of a myriad of technologies and capabilities, and the potential compliance and security implications. The authors have proposed a conceptual framework that explores the relationships of three Enterprise 2.0 dimensions—technology, its use, and how resulting user-generated content may lead to business value—with management implications affecting IT culture and policies within the enterprise. This chapter provides observations and suggestions for future research.

The purpose of the next chapter, "Understanding Users' Continuance of Facebook: An Integrated Model with the Unified Theory of Acceptance and Use of Technology, Expectation Disconfirmation Model, and Flow Theory," by Chia-Lin Hsu and Cou-Chen Wu, is to develop an integrated model designed to examine users' continuance of Facebook based on the Unified Theory of Acceptance and Use of Technology (UTAUT), the Expectation Disconfirmation Model (EDM), and flow theory. Empirical data collected from 482 users who have experience with Facebook are subjected to structural equation modeling based on the proposed research model. Results show that users' continuance intention of Facebook is determined by social influence, performance expectancy, effort expectancy, flow experience, and satisfaction. Satisfaction is significantly affected by flow experience and disconfirmation. Results also suggest that effort expectancy is positively related to flow experience. Based on the findings, managerial implications are discussed in this chapter and directions for future research are also highlighted.

Chapter 6

Distributed network researchers are trying to address one important issue concerning networked structures and how the network came into existence, i.e., dynamics of network evolution. From the knowledge of social science, it is observed that trust is one such metric that evolves with the network particularly where human interaction is involved. "Evolution of Trust and Formation of Preference Clusters in Distributed Networked Structure" by Purnendu Karmakar and Rajarshi Roy presents a "trust" model of the authors' studies and its various properties. In virtual (and "real") communities (chat rooms, blogs, etc.) behavioral segregation over time is observed. Differences in identities of interacting agents result in evolution of various degrees of "trust" (and "distrust") among them over a period of time. This process ultimately leads to emergence of self-segregation in behavioral kinetics and results in formation of preference clusters.

Next, Chingning Wang writes about "social shopping" (or social commerce), combining shopping and social networking to create an application of Web 2.0 in electronic commerce to benefit from users' social networks. "Social Shopping Development and Perspectives" explores the development of the emergent "social shopping" and related perspectives. It incorporates comparisons between social shopping marketing and search engine marketing. For example, search engine marketing assumes shoppers are certain of their shopping goal; social shopping marketing assumes shoppers are uncertain of their shopping goals and gather shopping ideas from their peers. In this chapter, the challenges in social shopping development are identified, including governing shopper communities and retrieving content from social networking sites. The author concludes that social shopping and e-commerce are not dichotomous concepts. Social shopping can be an evolutionary concept, meaning a singular EC site advancing with social networking functions, or a synergistic concept, meaning EC sites connecting with the other social networking sites to form strategic alliance.

In the next chapter, "Impact of Blogs on Sales Revenue: Test of a Network Model," Guoying Zhang, Alan J. Dubinsky, and Yong Tan collected blog data and captured network parameters to represent three common measurements of online Word-Of-Mouth: intensity, influence level, and dispersion. These parameters were then analyzed using a General Estimating Equation (GEE) model to test their effects on average weekly movie box office receipts. Findings indicated that all three parameters were significant in the model. The aggregated degree, representing WOM intensity, was positively significant, which was consistent with results from extant research. Further, diameter of a network, representing WOM dispersion, was observed to be positively significant, which validated the importance of spreading WOM as far as possible. Counter-intuitively, the aggregated size node, representing WOM influence level, was ascertained to be negatively significant, which might be explained by the possible negative stance from opinion leaders with high influence level. Applying network analysis methodology to blog entries, the present chapter differentiated itself from extant WOM literature that has focused chiefly on content analysis. The findings also provided managerial insights to companies interested in utilizing blogs as online WOM for marketing initiatives and implications for future research.

Kanna AlFalahi, Saad Harous, and Yacine Atif then present "A Comparative Study of Clustering Algorithms." Clustering is a major problem when dealing with organizing and dividing data. There are multiple algorithms proposed to handle this issue in many scientific areas such as classifications, community detection, and collaborative filtering. The need for clustering arises in Social Networks where huge data generated daily and different relations are established between users. The ability to find groups of interest in a network can help in many aspects to provide different services such as targeted advertisements. The authors surveyed different clustering algorithms from three different clustering groups: Hierarchical, Partitional, and Density-based algorithms. They then discuss and compare these algorithms from Social Web point view and show their strength and weaknesses in handling Social Web data. They also use a case study to support our finding by applying two clustering algorithms on articles collected from Delicious.com and discussing the different groups generated by each algorithm.

Chapter 10

Recently, the impact of social networks in customer buying decision is rapidly increasing due to effectiveness in shaping public opinion. "Identifying Opinion Leaders for Marketing by Analyzing Online Social Networks" by Niyoosha Jafari Momtaz, Abdollah Aghaie, and Somayeh Alizadeh helps marketers analyze social network's members based on different characteristics and choose the best method for identifying influential people among them. Then, marketers can use these influential people as seeds to market products/services. Considering the importance of opinion leadership in social networks, a comprehensive overview of existing literature has been done. Studies show different titles (such as opinion leaders, influential people, market mavens, and key players) are used to refer to the influential group in social networks whom we know as opinion leaders. All the properties presented for opinion leaders in the form of different titles are classified into three general categories including structural, relational, and personal characteristics, and based on studying opinion leader identification methods; appropriate parameters are extracted in a comprehensive chart to evaluate and compare these methods accurately.

Norshuhada Shiratuddin, Shahizan Hassan, Nor Laily Hashim, Mohd Fo'ad Sakdan, and Mohd Samsu Sajat have developed the "Blog Influence Index: A Measure of Influential Weblog." Although Weblogs are a popular medium of communication, their influence on society is unclear. In particular, studies that investigate the impact and influence of blogosphere on the community and government have not been fully exploited. Such studies are important, especially to the government in reshaping and realigning the policies related to new media. This chapter presents the outcomes of a study to identify measures on how to assess the influence of Weblogs. At least four dimensions are critical for measuring Weblog influence, which are recognition (number of in links and number of visitors), activity generation (number of comments and number of posts), novelty (number of out links), and credibility of a blog (number of information presentation type, number of factual errors, and number of hyperlink citations). It is hereby proposed that these dimensions make up a measure called the Blog Influence Index.

In the next chapter, "Analyzing Persian Social Networks: An Empirical Study," Leila Esmaeili, Mahdi Nasiri, and Behrouz Minaei-Bidgoli explain how analysis of data in social networks is very important for researchers, sociologists, and academics. Given the size and diversity of Web data in a Web 2.0 environment, analyzing this data has been a challenge. Since data act as inputs in such projects, the accuracy of the output is directly related to the input. Good data allows for extraction of valuable knowledge. In this chapter, the authors present their experiences with preparation and preprocessing of data in a Persian social network. The authors also report on the analysis of the data and findings.

Nana Adu-Pipim Boaduo then investigates "Action Research in Virtual Communities: How Can This Complement Successful Social Networking?" Contextually, all tertiary institutions have four major responsibilities – teaching, research, publication, and community service. The adage "publish or perish" has become a thorn in the flesh of many university academic staff who rest on their laurels and do nothing about research, publication, and community engagement. Practising university academic staff are required by the nature of their profession to engage in regular research be it in their daily lecturing and supervision of students' research thesis or writing for publication. Currently, research has become the buzzword in all tertiary institutions, but not all of them take the pains to school academic staff in the practice of research in terms of the virtual communities where the institution is located. In the context of this chapter, the author looks at action research through the eyes of teachers of all categories in virtual communities and how their involvement can complement successful social networking. The approaches used in this discussion are purely from empirical and exploratory perspectives and provide detailed discussion with emphasis on the application of action research for effective and efficient social networking considering the social, cultural, organizational, and human-cognitive perspectives.

In Chapter 14, "Enhancing the Trust of Members in Online Social Networks: An Integrative Technical and Marketing Perspective," Sandra A. Vannoy, B. Dawn Medlin, and Charlie C. Chen explore an element of social networking essential to the development of e-business: trust between members. Unlike other business models, the success of online social networks is highly dependent upon the growth rate of social network size. In order to accelerate and continue the growth rate, online social networks need to be able to continuously roll out diversified services and use them to interest existing and new members. However, the nature of this business model can expose online social networks to ubiquitous security threats such as spam, viral marketing, and viruses. In order to convince users to adopt social network services, cultivation of brand equity and trust in the online social networks is essential. This study integrates technical and marketing perspectives to examine the potential influence of Website quality and brand equity on user satisfaction, thereby influencing users' formation of trust. A survey was conducted with 385 subjects to understand the causal relationships between the studied constructs. Regression analysis indicates that Website quality, brand loyalty, brand association, and brand quality have a positive influence on user satisfaction, thereby increasing the trust of members in online social networks. Brand awareness shows no significant influence on user satisfaction. These findings lead us to derive theoretical and practical implications on the sustainable operation of online social networks.

Research conferences provide an important platform for idea exchange and validation as well as for social networking and talent hunt. Online social networks and collaborative Web tools can make conferences budget friendly for sponsors, flexible for attendees, and environmentally friendly for the society without loss of effectiveness. While many conferences have adopted such tools during pre and post conferencing stages, their use during actual meeting hours is very limited. "Virtual Research Conferences: A Case-Based Analysis" by Kamna Malik deliberates on the current and potential use of such technologies on various stages of a conference. It then presents the case of a pure virtual conference in comparison with a face-to-face conference with an aim to analyze the immediate benefits that virtual conferencing brings for organizers and participants. Perceived deterrents and potential benefits for various stakeholders are discussed. Suggestions are made for educational institutions to review their norms for conference sponsorships.

The final chapter of this book, "Retaining and Exploring Digital Traces: Towards an Excavation of Virtual Settlements" by Demosthenes Akoumianakis, Giannis Milolidakis, George Vlachakis, George Vlachakis, and Giorgos Ktistakis, elaborates on the assumption that social technologies are increasingly turned into computer-mediated virtual settlements, thereby allowing the excavation of a variety of enacted cyber-phenomena such as ad hoc online ensembles, informal social networks, and virtual communities on the grounds of "digital" traces or remains. In this vein, the authors motivate and present a method for virtual excavations that is tightly coupled to a transformational technology such as knowledge visualization. The analytical and explanatory value of the method is assessed using two case studies addressing representative genres of social technologies, namely Websites augmented with social plug-ins and social networking services. Analysis reveals intrinsic aspects of "digital" traces and remains, the form they take in today's Social Web, and the means through which they can be excavated and transformed to useful information. It turns out that such virtual excavations, when organized and conducted carefully, can be of benefit to enterprises, service organizations, and public sector institutions. In addition, their tight coupling with knowledge visualization eliminates extensive data analysis, as much of this work can be done using the visualization. On the other hand, and depending on the size of digital trace data, the choice of visualizations and the underlying toolkit are of paramount importance.

Subhasish Dasgupta
George Washington University, USA

Chapter 1

Innovation Contests:
Systematization of the Field and Future Research

Angelika C. Bullinger
University of Erlangen-Nuremberg, Germany

Kathrin Moeslein
University of Erlangen-Nuremberg, Germany

ABSTRACT

The ability to generate innovative products and services is a critical success factor for organizations. The trend of open innovation has brought about many-faceted, IT-based tools (e.g., lead user method or online tool kits), among these, the innovation contest seems particularly promising and continuously gains in importance as a corporate practice. However, a deep understanding of this online innovation practice is still lacking. Contrary to other methods used to realize open innovation, research in the field of online innovation contests displays a growing, but only rudimentarily intertwined body of publications. This paper provides the quintessential systematization of the field by integration of academic knowledge and business deployment. Juxtaposing 33 relevant journal and conference publications with empirical basis and an analysis of 57 real-world innovation contests, interesting disruptions are pointed to and six pathways for future research are described. These cover the optimal degree of elaboration, the interplay of competition and community, the importance of community applications, the trajectory toward open evaluation, and the identification of additional design elements.

INTRODUCTION

From a company perspective, the ability to generate innovative products and services is a critical success factor in a dynamic market environment (Christensen, 1997). Intensified global competi-tion, technological advance, and the emergence of the knowledge economy force companies to focus more strongly on innovation. The ability to bring novel products and services to the market is necessary to improve an organization's com-petitiveness or just maintain its current position

DOI: 10.4018/978-1-4666-4022-1.ch001

(Lawson & Samson, 2001). Moreover, from a macro-economic perspective, innovation is crucial for economic welfare and societal advance (von Hayek, 1968, 1971).

The loss of expert knowledge is particularly dangerous as innovative capability strongly depends on employees' ability to deploy knowledge resources (Subramaniam & Youndt, 2005). Accordingly, the innovation process has been described as a *knowledge management process* (Madhavan & Grover, 1998) and innovative companies as *knowledge creating companies* (Nonaka & Takeuchi, 1995; Subramaniam & Youndt, 2005). More specifically, a company's ability to deploy *external knowledge resources* is considered crucial (Cohen & Levinthal, 1990).

Thus, parallel to companies' increasing need to innovate, there is a change in managing innovation: the opening of traditionally closed innovation processes to the environment and the integration of external actors. This approach is often referred to as *Open Innovation* (Chesbrough, 2003; Von Hippel, 2005). Especially customers and users can be a valuable external knowledge resource (Enkel et al., 2005; Neyer et al., 2009; Thomke & Von Hippel, 2002). Open innovation goes beyond obtaining information from (potential) customers by using common methods of market research. In contrast to these traditional methods, which are usually concluded before the innovation process starts, open innovation approaches have the potential to integrate so-called *outside innovators* (Neyer et al., 2009) into every innovation process step. Typically, open innovation focuses on the early stages, like idea generation or conceptualisation, but in the later stages, like development or prototyping, integration is also possible. This kind of customer integration helps a company gather the necessary information as well as solution information (Reichwald & Piller, 2009; Von Hippel, 1978, 1994).

Among the many-faceted tools that enable open innovation (e.g., lead user method or online tool kits), the *innovation contest* seems particularly promising and interesting. Innovation contests are increasingly used in practice and are also attracting growing academic attention (Bullinger & Moeslein, 2010; Ebner et al., 2010; Piller & Walcher, 2006). Innovation contests have proved useful in different contexts and might be an appropriate means to deal with the mentioned challenges.

Competition can be found in various aspects of life: in the evolution of creatures as well as in sports, business, arts and science (Von Hayek, 1971). It is the underlying principle of the free market economy. In "The Wealth of Nations", Adam Smith concludes that in a competitive environment, individuals' endeavour to maximize utility is conducive to societal welfare (Smith, 2009). Similarly, Von Hayek (1968) considers competition beneficial for the development of innovations and technological as well as societal progress.

Besides a competitive economic system, history has many examples in which a call for solutions in the form of a competition lead to a variety of answers, even from unexpected (external) sources. Innovation contests in their basic structure have a long-standing tradition and have influenced industries or even societies. For example, in 1869, Emperor Louis Napoleon III of France offered a prize to anyone who could make a "satisfactory substitute for butter, suitable for use by the armed forces and the lower classes." Still, neither Michel-Eugene Chevreul nor Hippolyte Mege-Mouris (historians are uneven about the inventor) were paid when they came up with margarine, since Napoleon died before. In the 19th century, innovation contests leave the realm of political organizers as they are increasingly adopted by industrialists as a powerful means of problem solving. Famous examples of this period include the "Rainhill trials" (1829) which were used by the directors of the Liverpool and Manchester Railway Company to decide whether hauling trains should be powered by stationary engines or locomotives. During the next century, realization of innovation contests slowly entered average business: An early example can be identified in 1997, when the "Fredkin Prize for Computer Chess" granted USD 100'000 for building the first computer to beat world chess champion Garry Kasparov.

The deployment of innovation contests took off, however, with the development of information and communication technology, in particular the internet, which allows for online competitions. Nowadays, highspeed internet access allows individuals as well as firms, public organizations, and non-profit organizations, to act as *organizers* of innovation contests (Piller & Walcher, 2006). Accordingly, innovation contests have continuously gained in number and multitude for about twenty years. Some of them, e.g., the platform Innocentive (founded in 2001), where companies publish open challenges for scientists, or the t-shirt company Threadless (founded in 2000), entirely based on the submission and evaluation of designs by users, have gained quite a reputation among research and practice. However, there are many more innovation contests currently running. At the moment of writing, 77'800 hits at google.com when searching for the term "innovation contest".

Whereas innovation contests can thus be attributed to continuously gain in importance as an innovation practice among companies, a deep understanding of this instrument is still lacking. Contrary to other methods used to realize open innovation, research in the field displays a growing, but only rudimentarily intertwined body of publications on the topic. This paper provides the essential systematization of the field and goes beyond academic knowledge by juxtapositioning business deployment. We present at first the methodological approach chosen to unite academic knowledge and practical deployment of innovation contests (cf. Method). Subsequently, the results of the systematic review of literature and practice are presented (cf. Findings from the reviews) and discussed (cf. Discussion: Juxtaposing research and practice). Following this presentation of interesting disruptions between academia and practice and the identification of six pathways for future research, a conclusion section closes the paper.

METHOD

We define an innovation contest[1] as a web-based competition of innovators who use their skills, experiences and creativity to *provide a solution* for a particular contest *challenge* formulated by an organizer (cf. Piller & Walcher, 2006; Ebner et al., 2010). To better assess the current state of innovation contests in research and practice, we chose a two-fold methodological approach subsequently explained.

Systematic Literature Review

We performed first a systematic literature review following the guidelines of Creswell (2002). The literature was reviewed by two researchers in innovation management and an *outside judge* specialized in information systems.

The step "keyword search" (1) encompassed search terms derived from the combination "*a + b*", where *a* equals *idea, ideas, concept, innovation* or *design* and *b* equals *contest, competition, jam, tournament* or *prize*. Search began with the terms *idea, ideas* and *competition, contest*, as suggested prior expert interviews. The list was continuously amplified when a new term appeared for the *third time* in publications, typically in the reference section (step (3) of the literature review). This evolving approach was chosen to grasp the multiplicity of terms currently used to describe the topicality. The search process led to the identification of $n1_{bsc}=2'411$ articles within the *Business Source Complete* database which were published in the last 50 years (April 1959 to July 2009). We used Business Source Complete as database as its focus on *management* publications fits our perspective on innovation contests as tools for managing open innovation. Drilling down results to articles in academic publications and selected magazines, in which innovation contests (or one of the many synonymous terms) were in the *focus*, e.g., title or abstract enclosed the term led to $n1_{IC}=38$ articles. The same procedure was applied to search with *Google Scholar*

(2). We added Google Scholar as the relatively novel topicality is covered also in outlets which are accessed via Google Scholar but not included in Business Source Complete. In particular, we wanted to include work in progress on the topic, if available. We included the subject areas *Business, Administration, Finance,* and *Economics; Engineering, Computer Science,* and *Mathematics;* as well as *Social Sciences, Arts,* and *Humanities* since the topic is covered by these strands of research mostly. The initial sample from the search terms "*a + b*" (as indicated) resulted in $n2_{gs}=15'661$ hits. Again, by two steps of limitation, $n2_{IC}=82$ relevant contributions were selected. Bringing together the 38 articles from Business Source Complete and the 82 publications identified by Google Scholar, we set a third delimiter and included only papers with an empirical basis (i.e., at least one case study). This choice was made to fulfill our research goal to amalgamate academia and practice in the field and led to a final sample of $n3_{data}=33$ articles. Articles integrated in the sample are marked by an asterisk in the reference section of this paper.

Systematic Field Review

Our systematic field review on innovation contest was performed in two overlapping phases: First, *identification and selection* of innovation contests to be included in the sample. Innovation contests were chosen according to the information needed (Glaser & Strauss, 1967). Thus, the final sample is not meant to be a representative one. We focused on those contests which are characterized by a set of pre-defined criteria. Second, *analysis* of the sample in the light of the design elements we distilled from literature was performed.

In phase one "identification and selection", we identified innovation contests via *Google*; search terms were derived from the combination "*a + b*" as in the review of literature. Using awareness level as first criterion, we selected innovation contests which scored highest in page rank (state of December 2008); ($n4_{google}=73$). To relate

our review of practice to extant knowledge, we chose a subset of contests based on the following limiters: *online* innovation contest; provision of *rewards*; medium to very long term *contest period* within the last 4 years; representation of *different industries*; majority of organizers active in the *business-to-consumer* field; and *openness* to a broad public[2]. These characteristics apply to most of the publications identified in the review of literature. Limitation led to a set of $n4_{start}=45$ innovation contests. In the course of the *analysis phase* (phase 2), we have been continuously adding contests until saturation was reached in June 2009 ($n4_{end}=57$) and additional innovation contests have provided only marginal information (Glaser & Strauss, 1967). Details on the analyzed innovation contests are in appendix.

During phase two, we analyzed whether and how the innovation contests in our sample integrate the design elements derived during the systematic literature review. Analysis was done by *3 independent raters* who were asked to state: "Is [name of innovation contest] considering [specific design element]?", with response possibility limited to *binary* responses. If two of the raters agreed that an innovation contest integrates a particular design element, this design element was marked as being *given*; otherwise it was marked *not given*.

FINDINGS FROM THE REVIEWS

Overall, the literature review shows that extant publications are dominated by *single case studies*. Even if multiple case studies are used, they are typically used side by side (e.g., Ogawa & Piller, 2006). This methodological trend leads to in-depth knowledge silos on individual cases with only limited possibilities for generalization. When analyzing the 33 articles, however, we found that a common and unifying trend across the majority of publications is the *recommendation of design elements* for innovation contests.

We collected the different design elements mentioned within our sample and distilled a set of ten which were most often referred to. With the design elements, the papers typically list attributes which we hence unified for each design element in order to reach a holistic framework. In the following, we condense the results of our literature review by presenting the ten design elements and their attributes as distilled from the literature. To ease readability, we use only pertinent articles out of the sample.

Concerning *media*, innovation contests can be run online, offline or mixed mode (Boudreau et al., 2008; Brabham, 2009). They are run by an *organizer*, herewith encompassing companies, public organizations, individuals as well as non-profit organizations, e.g., museums (Ebner et al., 2010; Klein & Lechner, 2009; Smith et al., 2003). Usually, the organizer dedicates the contest to a specific *topic*; details of which vary extensively. The topic indicates *specificity* of the *task/topic* (ranging between *low* if the task is very open and *high* if the task is highly specific) and the desired *degree of elaboration*. The contest might call for simple textual descriptions of rough *ideas, sketches,* more elaborated *concepts*, or even *prototypes* and fully functional *solutions* (Ebner et al., 2010; Klein & Lechner, 2009; Smith et al., 2003). Also evolving potential innovations that get refined during a number of contests are an option. By definition of the topic, the organizer also indicates the interesting *target group* of participants. Literature identifies a distinction between an *unspecified target group,* i.e,. participation is open to everybody and a *specified target group*, when participation is e.g., limited to a country or qualified by age or interest (Brabham, 2009; Bullinger et al., 2009; Carvalho, 2009). In addition, the organizer indicates whether participation is required by an *individual,* in *teams* or *both* (Boudreau et al., 2008; Carvalho, 2009; Smith et al., 2003). Each innovation contest runs for a limited period of time; during this *contest period* participation is allowed. *Contest periods* range from *very short term* (some hours to a maximum of 14 days), *short term* (15 days to 6 weeks) to *long term* (6 weeks to four month) or even *very long term* (more than four months/ongoing) (Boudreau et al., 2008; Bullinger et al., 2009; Ebner et al., 2010). To foster participation, the organizer establishes a *reward system* to *motivate* the participation of the target group – adapted to its needs (Boudreau et al., 2008; Bullinger et al., 2009; Ogawa & Piller, 2006). Motivation can be induced via extrinsic motivators (awards and prizes), intrinsic motivators (enjoyment) or mixed mode. As for extrinsic motivators, literature reports them to cover both monetary awards (prize money) and non-monetary awards (e.g., valuable goods) (Brabham, 2009; Bullinger et al., 2009; Piller & Walcher, 2006). Intrinsic motivation is stressed in combination with social motivation, covering positive community feedback, reputation among relevant peers, and self-realization (Fueller, 2006). Fostering intrinsic and social motivation and simultaneously supporting interaction of participants are *community functionalities* (Brabham, 2009; Piller & Walcher, 2006). They enhance information exchange, topic related discussion, and – if allowed – collaborative design of products. Applications belonging to the field of social software are well suited to foster community building, e.g., a fanpage of the contest on *facebook.com*, messaging services and personal profiles. Once submissions are made, their evaluation can be made along to three basic pathways which can be freely combined: *self-assessment* by the participant, *peer review* by the (other) participants of the innovation contest and evaluation by a *jury of experts* (Carvalho, 2009; Ebner et al., 2010; Klein & Lechner, 2009).

Table 1 illustrates the state of knowledge on design elements of innovation contests. It subsumes the 10 design elements with synonyms, a definition (left column), and common attributes (right column).

Table 1. Design elements for innovation contests (IC) as derived from systematic literature review

Design Element *(synonyms): definition*	Attributes					
1. Media (-): environment of IC	Online		Mixed		Offline	
2. Organizer (-): entity initiating IC	Company	Public organization	Non-profit		Individual	
3 Task/Topic Specificity *(problem specification)*: solution space of IC	Low (Open Task)		Defined		High (Specific task)	
4. Degree of Elaboration *(elaborateness, eligibility, degree of idea elaboration):* required level of detail for submission to IC	Idea	Sketch	Concept	Proto-type	Solution	Evolving
5. Target Group *(target audience, target participants, composition of group):* description of participants of IC	Specified			Unspecified		
6. Participation as *(eligibility)*: number of persons forming one entity of participant	Individual		Team		Both	
7. Contest Period *(timeline)*: runtime of IC	Very short term		Short term	Long term		Very long term
8. Reward/Motivation (-): incentives used to encourage participation	Monetary		Non-monetary		Mixed	
9. Community Functionality *(community application, communication possibility, tools):* functionalities for interaction within participants	Given			Not given		
10. Evaluation *(ranking)*: method to determine ranking of submissions to IC	Jury evaluation		Peer review	Self assessment		Mixed

DISCUSSION: JUXTAPOSING RESEARCH AND PRACTICE

Putting side by side the review of literature and the 57 cases, we identify a set of disruptions of which we derive pathways for future exploration of the fascinating field of innovation contests. Generally, we observe that academic literature allows to distill ten design elements with their attributes. While literature has so far not focused on distribution of attributes across multiple cases or likely combinations, the 57 cases indicate preferences in the design and implementation of online innovation contests. In addition, practice is contradictory to some of the design elements mentioned in the literature; these differences will subsequently be highlighted for each design element. From most relevant differences, we derive propositions for future research in the field.

As the focus of our research is on *online* innovation contests, we included 46 contests which are purely online and a set of eight which include

offline parts, e.g., a presentation in front of a jury (e.g., *Sony Ericsson Content Award 2008*, *Brown Shoe Student Design Contest*). For reasons of comparison, we integrated three contests without online component (*First Lego League*, *Advertising & Circulation Idea Contest 2009* and *Innovation & Entrepreneurship contest 2009*).

In our sample, we found an overwhelming majority of 43 contests to be conducted by *firms*. Only 9 *public organizers* (e.g., London's Victoria and Albert Museum with its *Shoe Design Competition*) and 5 *non-profit* organizers like the Advantan Foundation which initiated an idea exchange platform for entrepreneurs (*Ideablob*) could be identified. The predominance of innovation contests initiated by *companies* expands on Walcher (2007) who describes a continuum of organizers.

Closely related to the *organizer* is the topic of the idea contest, defined by *specificity* of the *task/topic* and the required *degree of elaboration*. Interestingly, a medium amount of *specificity* prevails (41 contests); this can be easily illustrated for the area of fashion, where organizers often purport a specific theme, like the "original origins" of the *CEC Shoe Design Contest*. The *degree of elaboration*, on the other hand, is nearly equally distributed among the attributes *ideas, sketches, concepts, prototype, solution* and *evolving*. This result is interesting, as e.g., Walcher (2007) and Piller and Walcher (2006) suggest in their paper near equal distribution of the attributes. Therefore, we judge prevailing degrees – *low (idea)* or *high (solution)* – as insufficiently precise. Accordingly, we *propose to research (1)* the design element *elaboration* in more detail in order to specify the optimal degree of elaboration depending on the type of contest (e.g., task/topic specificity).

Concerning the addressed *target group*, a design element closely related to *specificity* and *degree of elaboration*, our sample shows a strong trend towards *specified* (n=36), while criteria used for specification of participants range widely. For instance, innovation contests in the field of *ICT* explicitly target software developers or very technically interested people. A similarly strong tendency has been identified for *participation as individual or team*. While two thirds (n=31) of the examined innovation contests allow submissions only by *individuals*, nine focus explicitly on *teams* (e.g., *Sony Ericsson Content Award 2008*). In 17 contests, for instance the *A1 Innovation Days*, participation both as team and as individual has been accepted.

Results concerning the *contest period* show a predominance of *long* and *very long term* contests (18 respectively 22). Innovation contests comprising of a complex task in combination with a high *degree of elaboration*, as *BraunPrize 2009* and *Sony Ericsson Content Award 2008*, have a duration of more than four months in each stage; they are representatives of the attribute *very long term*[3]. This shows a change since Walcher (2007) put forward an average duration of six weeks and calls for alteration of attributes.

When it comes to *reward/motivation*, we identified 20 innovation contests basing solely on monetary rewards, while the biggest group – 30

contests – combined both reward schemes. Monetary assets thereby include assets like notebooks (*MTV Engine Room*), cell phones, or voyages (*A1 Innovation Days*) as well as money prizes; these start with EUR 500 for a third place in *Tchibo Ideas* and can reach up to EUR 500'000 (*Scoop!*). *Non-monetary motivation* has been explicitly integrated for instance in the reward scheme of the *NoAE Innovation Competition* where winners take part in workshops with experts. Given the discussion on account *of intrinsic and extrinsic motivation* for participation in an online environment which stress the importance of intrinsic and social motivation (e.g., Fueller, 2006; Lakhani & von Hippel, 2003), it is surprising that our sample shows such a strong predominance of extrinsic reward schemes. Given this state, we *propose to research (2)* the link between *intrinsic motivators* and *community applications* in more detail.

Community functionality can be found in 31 cases. Commenting functions and forums are frequently occurring applications, but limited to innovation contests that comprise any kind of peer review; an outstanding example is *Osram's LED emotionalize your light* contest which provides a set of social networking applications comparable to *facebook.com*. Given the majority of *individual* participants while community functionality is increasingly realized, we *propose to research (3)* how the elements of competition among participating individuals and their community-building is orchestrated.

In addition, given the surge of social software applications, community applications seem particularly interesting to explore in the context of innovation contests. We *propose to research (4)* the impact of *community applications* on participants' behavior in innovation contests.

Which submission wins is by a vast majority of contests decided by a *jury of experts* (35 innovation contests). We judge this to be a standard procedure for contests in the area of apparel – only the *CEC Shoe Design* contest and *Iqons x Nike ID* explicitly *also* ask for peer review. The prominent exception from the rule is *Threadless* which outsources the entire evaluation of submitted t-shirt designs to potential customers (Ogawa & Piller, 2006). The trend towards jury voting is surprising, as first, literature is ambiguous whether cross-functional juries, with a broad scope of experience are at all suitable for evaluation (pro: McDermott & O'Connor, 2002; contra: Galbraith, DeNoble, & Ehrlich, 2008); and second, as the integration of larger (external) groups in the evaluation of innovations seems to generate better results (Piller & Walcher, 2006; Soukhoroukova, 2007). We derive a pressing need to better understand evaluation and *propose to research (5)* in-depth the different forms of *evaluation*, e.g., by comparison of the results of peer review during and after the contest period.

All in all, our review of the online innovation contests has shown a set of design elements not included in the extant literature, e.g., the goal an organizer has when initiating a contest. We consequently *propose to research (6)* which additional design elements should be added to the list in order to better identify and purposely design an online innovation contest.

CONCLUSION

Based on a systematic review of literature and juxtapositioning of research and practice, this paper has distilled ten design elements for online innovation contests and illustrated their real-life deployment. Discrepancies between research and practice have led to the proposition of six pathways for further research on innovation contests.

The strengths of our study, however, must be tempered with recognition of its limitations. Given the qualitative nature of the review of current practice, the integrated systematization of design elements of innovation contests should be seen as a structured analysis of reality, and not as reality itself. First, we do not claim to have identified the comprehensive set of design

elements and according attributes in sufficient detail. We see a need to further and in more detail explore a number of *design elements*. Second, whereas our findings present the design elements as stand-alone elements, further research could increase the knowledge on their *relations and interdependencies*.

ACKNOWLEDGMENT

This research was partially supported by the German Federal Ministry of Education and Research (project EIVE, 01FG09006). An earlier version of this article has been presented at the 16th Americas Conference on Information Systems 2010. We thank the reviewers and the trackchair for their insightful comment.

REFERENCES

Ahonen, M., & Lietsala, K. (2007). Managing service ideas and suggestions – Information systems in innovation brokering. In *Proceedings of the Tekes Haas Conference of Service Innovation*, Berkeley, CA.

Bjelland, O. M., & Wood, R. C. (2008). An inside view of IBM's 'Innovation Jam'. *MIT Sloan Management Review, 50*(1), 31–40.

Boudreau, K. J., Lacetera, N., & Lakhani, K. R. (2008). Incentives versus diversity: Re-examining the link between competition and innovation. In *Proceedings of the Wharton Technology Conference*.

Brabham, D. C. (2009). *Moving the crowd at Threadless: Motivations for participation in a crowdsourcing application*. Paper presented at the Annual Meeting of the Association for Education in Journalism & Mass Communication, Boston, MA.

Bretschneider, U., Huber, M., Leimeister, J. M., & Krcmar, H. (2008). Community for innovations: Developing an integrated concept for open innovation. In León, J., Bernardos, A. M., Casar, J. R., Kautz, K., & DeGross, J. I. (Eds.), *Open IT-based innovation: Moving towards cooperative IT transfer and knowledge diffusion*. New York, NY: Springer. doi:10.1007/978-0-387-87503-3_28.

Bullinger, A. C., Haller, J., & Moeslein, K. (2009). Innovation mobs – Unlocking the innovation potential of virtual communities. In *Proceedings of the Fifteenth Americas Conference on Information Systems*, San Francisco, CA.

Bullinger, A. C., & Moeslein, K. M. (2010). Online innovation contests – Where are we? In *Proceedings of the 16th Americas Conference on Information Systems*, Lima, Peru.

Bullinger, A. C., Neyer, A.-K., & Koelling, M. (2009). Is open innovation really open: A cross-cultural perspective. In *Proceedings of the 20th ISPIM Conference*, Vienna, Austria.

Carvalho, A. (2009). *In search of excellence - Innovation contests to foster innovation and entrepreneurship in Portugal*. Évora, Portugal: University of Évora.

Chesbrough, H. W. (2003). *Open innovation: The new imperative for creating and profiting from technology*. Boston, MA: Harvard Business School Press.

Christensen, C. M. (1997). *The innovator's dilemma: When new technologies cause great firms to fail*. Boston, MA: Harvard Business School Press.

Cohen, W. M., & Levinthal, D. A. (1990). Absorptive capacity: A new perspective on learning and innovation. *Administrative Science Quarterly, 35*(1), 128–152. doi:10.2307/2393553.

Creswell, J. W. (2002). *Research design: Qualitative, quantitative, and mixed methods approaches* (2nd ed.). Thousand Oaks, CA: Sage.

Ebner, W., Leimeister, J.-M., Bretschneider, U., & Krcmar, H. (2010). Leveraging the wisdom of crowds: Designing an IT-supported ideas competition for an ERP software company. *Information Systems, 49*(89).

Ebner, W., Leimeister, J. M., & Krcmar, H. (2010). Community engineering for innovations: The ideas competition as a method to nurture a virtual community for innovations. *R&D Management Journal, 40*(4), 342–356.

Enkel, E., Perez-Freije, J., & Gassmann, O. (2005). Minimizing market risks through customer integration in new product development: Learning from bad practice. *Creativity and Innovation Management, 14*(4), 425–437. doi:10.1111/j.1467-8691.2005.00362.x.

Fueller, J. (2006). Why consumers engage in virtual new product developments initiated by producers. *Advances in Consumer Research. Association for Consumer Research (U. S.), 33*(1), 639–646.

Fueller, J., Bartl, M., Ernst, H., & Mühlbacher, H. (2006). Community based innovation: How to integrate members of virtual communities into new product development. *Electronic Commerce Research, 6*(1), 57–73. doi:10.1007/s10660-006-5988-7.

Galbraith, C. S., DeNoble, S. B., Ehrlich, A. F., & Kline, D. M. (2008). Can experts really assess future technology success? A neural network and Bayesian analysis of early stage technology proposals. *The Journal of High Technology Management Research, 17*(2), 125–138. doi:10.1016/j.hitech.2006.11.002.

Glaser, B. G., & Strauss, A. L. (1967). *The discovery of grounded theory: Strategies for qualitative research*. Chicago, IL: Aldine.

Gregson, P. H., & Little, T. A. (1998). Designing contests for teaching electrical engineering design. *International Journal of Engineering Education, 14*(5), 367–374.

Hackbert, P. H. (2009). Idea contests: A model for stimulating creativity and opportunity recognition. In *Proceedings of the 17ᵗʰ American Society of Business and Behavioral Sciences Annual Conference*, Las Vegas, NV.

Helander, M., Lawrence, R., & Liu, Y. (2007). Looking for great ideas: Analyzing the innovation jam. In *Proceedings of the 9th WebKDD Workshop on Web Mining and Social Network Analysis* (pp. 66-73).

Hong, J., Lin, C., & Lin, Y. (2005). Operating a successful PowerTech creativity contest. *Journal of Technology Studies*, 25-31.

Klein, D., & Lechner, U. (2009). The ideas competition as tool of change management – Participatory behaviour and cultural perception. In *Proceedings of the 20ᵗʰ ISPIM Conference*, Vienna, Austria.

Lakhani, K. R., & von Hippel, E. (2003). How open source software works: "free" user-to-user assistance. *Research Policy, 32*, 923–943. doi:10.1016/S0048-7333(02)00095-1.

Lawson, B., & Samson, D. (2001). Developing innovation capability in organisations: A dynamic capabilities approach. *International Journal of Innovation Management, 5*(3), 377–400. doi:10.1142/S1363919601000427.

Leimeister, J.-M., Huber, M., Bretschneider, U., & Krcmar, H. (2009). Leveraging crowdsourcing - Theory-driven design, implementation and evaluation of activation-supporting components for IT-based idea competitions. *Journal of Management Information Systems, 26*(1), 1–44.

Limited, Q. E. (2008). Competing for defence ideas: Looking wider for innovation. *Strategic Direction, 24*(1), 35–37. doi:10.1108/02580540810839359.

Madhavan, R., & Grover, R. (1998). From embedded knowledge to embodied knowledge: New product development as knowledge management. *Journal of Marketing, 62*(4), 1–12. doi:10.2307/1252283.

Malone, T. W., Laubacher, R., & Dellarocas, C. (2009). *Harnessing crowds: Mapping the genome of collective intelligence* (pp. 1–20). Cambridge, MA: MIT Press.

McDermott, Ch. M., & O'Connor, G. C. (2002). Managing radical innovation: An overview of emergent strategy issues. *Journal of Product Innovation Management, 19*(6), 424–438. doi:10.1016/S0737-6782(02)00174-1.

Murphy, R. R. (2000). Using robot competitions to promote intellectual development. *AI Magazine, 21*(1), 77–90.

Nasar, J. L., & Kang, J. (1989). A post-jury evaluation: The Ohio State University design competition for a center for the visual arts. *Environment and Behavior, 21*(4), 464–484. doi:10.1177/0013916589214005.

Neyer, A.-K., Bullinger, A. C., & Moeslein, K. M. (2009). Integrating inside and outside innovators: A sociotechnical systems perspective. *R&D Management Journal, 39*(4), 410–419. doi:10.1111/j.1467-9310.2009.00566.x.

Nonaka, I. A., & Takeuchi, H. A. (1995). *The knowledge-creating company: How Japanese companies create the dynamics of innovation*. New York, NY: Oxford University Press.

Ogawa, S., & Piller, F. T. (2006). Reducing the risks of new product development. *MIT Sloan Management Review, 47*(2), 65–71.

Piller, F. T., & Walcher, D. (2006). Toolkits for idea competitions: A novel method to integrate users in new product development. *R & D Management*, *36*(3), 307–318. doi:10.1111/j.1467-9310.2006.00432.x.

Plaisant, C., & Grinstein, G. (2007). Promoting insight based evaluation of visualizations: From contest to benchmark repository. *IEEE Transactions on Visualization and Computer Graphics*, 1–18.

Poetz, M. K., & Schreier, M. (2009). *The value of crowdsourcing: Can users really compete with professionals in generating new product ideas?* Paper presented at the Druid Summer Conference, Copenhagen, Denmark.

Randolph, G. B., & Owen, D. O. (2008). Attracting communities and students to IT with a community service web contest. *Information Systems*, 77–80.

Reichwald, R., & Piller, F. (2009). *Interaktive Wertschoepfung: Open Innovation, Individualisierung und neue Formen der Arbeitsteilung* (2nd ed.). Wiesbaden, Germany: Gabler.

Schepers, J., Schnell, R., & Vroom, P. (1999). From idea to business - How Siemens bridges the innovation gap. *Research-Technology Management*, *42*, 26–31.

Sheng, L., Li, S., & Zhu, J. (2008). *Using the IBM innovation factory idea management solution to focus your company on innovation and ideation for strategic issues*. Armonk, NY: IBM.

Smith, A. (2009). *An inquiry into the nature and causes of the wealth of nations (reproduction)*. BiblioLife.

Smith, A., Banzaert, A., & Susnowitz, S. (2003). The MIT ideas competition: Promoting innovation for public service. In *Proceedings of the 33rd IEEE Annual Conference on Frontiers in Education* (Vol. 3).

Soukhoroukova, A. (2007). *Produktinnovation mit Informationsmärkten*. Unpublished doctoral dissertation, University of Passau, Passau, Germany.

Subramaniam, M., & Youndt, M. A. (2005). The influence of intellectual capital on the types of innovative capabilities. *Academy of Management Journal*, *48*(3), 450–463. doi:10.5465/AMJ.2005.17407911.

Terwiesch, C., & Ulrich, K. (2008). *Innovation tournaments: Creating, selecting, and developing exceptional opportunities*. Philadelphia, PA: The Wharton School.

Thomke, S., & Von Hippel, E. (2002). Customers as innovators: A new way to create value. *Harvard Business Review*, *80*(4), 74–81.

Tidd, J., Bessant, J., & Pavitt, K. (1997). *Managing innovation: Integrating technological, market, and organizational change*. Chichester, UK: John Wiley & Sons.

Von Hayek, F. A. (1968). Der Wettbewerb als Entdeckungsverfahren. Kiel, Germany: Institut für Weltwirtschaft an der Universität Kiel.

Von Hayek, F. A. (1971). *Die verfassung der freiheit*. Tübingen, Germany: Mohr.

Von Hippel, E. (1978). Successful industrial products from customer ideas. *Journal of Marketing*, *42*(1), 39–49. doi:10.2307/1250327.

Von Hippel, E. (2005). *Democratizing innovation*. Cambridge, MA: MIT Press.

Walcher, D. (2007). *Der Ideenwettbewerb als Methode der aktiven Kundenintegration: Theorie, empirische Analyse und Implikationen fuer den Innovationsprozess*. Wiesbaden, Germany: Gabler.

Wallmark, J. T. (1986). Innovation by contest. Innovation 83 – An Inter-Scandinavian innovation contest. *International Journal of Management Science*, *14*(3), 251–257.

ENDNOTES

[1]   We use "*innovation* contest" (IC) instead of "*idea* contest" to illustrate that a contest is able and suited to cover the entire innovation process from idea creation and concept generation to selection and implementation (Tidd et al. 1997).

[2]   Consequently, we excluded innovation contests as presented by Innocentive (www. innocentive.com) where, for most of the challenges, participants need expert knowledge to submit an idea.

[3]   Continuous innovation contests like *Threadless* are classified according to their smallest module.

APPENDIX

ANALYZED INNOVATION CONTESTS (IN ALPHABÉTIC ORDER)

- A1 Innovation Days
- Advertising & Circulation Idea Contest 2009
- ASICS Design Competition 200
- Bata Shoe Design Competition
- Braun Prize 2009
- Brown Shoe Student Design Contest
- CEC Shoe Design Contest
- Change.org
- Comic Book Challenge
- Dein Wille geschehe
- First Lego League 2008
- Go! Animate
- Google Android Developer Challenge
- Google Lunar X Prize
- Google's Project 10 to the 100
- Ideablob
- Ideenwettbewerb der Region Cham
- Imagine Cup 2009
- Information Systems Contest
- Innovation & Entrepreneurship Contest 2009
- Intelchallenge
- IntelliJ IDEA(L) Plugin Contest 2006
- Iqons x Nike ID
- IT Services for Tomorrow's Data Center
- Juicy Ideas Competition
- LED emotionalize your light contest
- Light on Gesu
- Live Edge Contest
- Malaysia Footwear Design Competition
- MTV Engine Room
- Netflixprice
- Next Generation 2009
- NoAE Innovation Competition
- NoAE Innovationswettbewerb
- PLW Design Competition
- Progressive Automotive X Prize
- Project 10^100
- Samsung "How deep is your love?"
- Scoop!

- Sennheiser SoundLogo
- Shoe Design Competition
- Shoe Star
- Shoeperstar
- Sony Ericsson Content Award 2008
- StartUp Impulse
- Swatch MTV Playground
- Tchibo Ideas
- The Saltire Prize
- The Sims 2 H&M Fashion Runway
- Threadless
- Usable
- Virgin Earth Challenge
- Vodafone Wireless Innovation Project
- WePC.com
- What's your crazy green idea?
- WindSCAPE

This work was previously published in the International Journal of Virtual Communities and Social Networking, Volume 3, Issue 1, edited by Subhasish Dasgupta, pp. 1-12, copyright 2011 by IGI Publishing (an imprint of IGI Global).

Chapter 2
Peer–to–Peer Service Quality in Virtual Communities

Aku Valtakoski
Aalto University School of Science, Finland

Juhana Peltonen
Aalto University School of Science, Finland

Mikko O. J. Laine
Aalto University School of Science, Finland

ABSTRACT

Virtual communities are an increasingly popular way to conduct business over the Internet. However, from the service provider's point of view they pose special challenges. In particular, unless the provider itself engages in content or service provision, the service relies entirely on its members for provision of services. The members should thus be seen as resources for service provision. This type of networked service production system implies challenges in terms of service quality management and, subsequently, value creation for community members. This paper explores these issues by revisiting service marketing and service operations literature on service quality. Analysis of the literature indicates that firms facilitating virtual communities need to ensure the quality of their service by not only ensuring technical quality but also by nurturing the social aspects of the community that have an impact on the willingness of community members to provide service to each other.

DOI: 10.4018/978-1-4666-4022-1.ch002

INTRODUCTION

Leading firms in the Web 2.0 phenomenon such as Facebook, Twitter, MySpace, Habbo and YouTube draw hundreds of millions of users to participate in virtual communities. These communities depend on a service provider to develop and maintain a technological platform, which enables communication between the members of the community, as well as other services. However, virtual communities often rely heavily on the content and services provided by the community itself. Different purposes for virtual communities include collaboration (e.g., SourgeForge, Skype), creation and maintenance of contacts (e.g., LinkedIn, Plaxo), gaming (e.g., World of Warcraft), sharing information (e.g., Wikipedia, Google Earth), and enabling consumer-to-consumer retailing (e.g., eBay, Amazon) (Messerschmitt, Peltonen, Laine, & Oza, 2008).

From the perspective of the service provider, building a commercially successful virtual community poses a specific challenge. The value of the community to its members often depends on the services provided by members of the community to other members, and subsequently has a direct impact on the value of the community to potential advertisers and third-party content creators. Yet, the service provider cannot directly affect the quality of services – the general satisfaction of the members of a virtual community with the community. As indicated by Hofacker et al. (2006), much of the extant research on e-services has been directed towards e-services which are complements or substitutes to existing offline services, for example e-commerce. In such a setting, the service provider has much more control over the quality of the service compared to virtual community services.

Additionally, despite the extensive research on service quality in the Internet context, most of it has mostly concentrated on the technical aspects of web sites (Kuo, 2003; Santos, 2003; Yang & Jun, 2002; Zhang & Prybutok, 2005). Furthermore, most of the papers have considered service quality in commercial web sites, and online purchasing or "e-tailing" (Parasuraman, Zeithaml, & Malhotra, 2005; Zeithaml, 2002; Zeithaml, Parasuraman, & Malhotra, 2002). The quality of community-based services has been analyzed only in relation to these commercial communities (Wiertz & de Ruyter, 2007; Wasko & Faraj, 2005). Thus, in contrast to Wiertz and de Ruyter (2007) and Yen and Hsu (2006), who discuss communities related to B2C and B2B e-commerce sites, we analyze service quality of a commercial virtual community, In other words, we are interested in communities that provide value to its own members, which is facilitated by web sites managed by a service provider. In these cases, consumer-to-consumer (C2C) service actually becomes the core offering of the firm. In summary, what is missing is an analysis of determinants of perceived service quality of a virtual community when viewing them as networked service production systems (Hofacker et al., 2006).

This paper explores the issues of service quality and value creation in a virtual community where the community members bear the main responsibility of providing the service instead of the service provider itself. To explore these issues, we assess how the factors impact an incumbent service quality framework, ES-QUAL (Parasuraman et al., 2005), which is based on the assumption that the service provider has nearly complete control over service quality. In addition, we identify mechanisms the service provider can use to indirectly manage the quality of the service and thus regain some control over service quality. Although we argue that the community plays a critical role in determining service quality, the web site must obviously still meet the technical, tangible quality requirements of community members (Parasuraman et al., 2005). In other words, the service provider must also ensure that the quality of the technical platform is satisfactory or potential members of the community may not see the community as valuable enough for further contribution.

The remainder of this paper is organized as follows. First, we review the literature on virtual communities, service quality, and e-service quality. Based on this review, we propose a framework on the antecedents of service quality in community networked services, and the consequences of this service quality perceived by the members of the virtual community. Furthermore, we also identify mechanisms that the service provider may use to manage the quality of service provided by the members of the community.

LITERATURE REVIEW

Virtual Communities and Service Production

Due to virtual community being a relatively new concept, multiple definitions exist for it in the literature, with no common consensus (Leimeister & Krcmar, 2004). Another reason for this is that a virtual community is a multi-disciplinary concept (Preece, 2000), and researchers tend to define the concept from the perspective of their own discipline. The most straightforward way to define a virtual community is to consider it as a special case of a conventional community. However, sociologists struggle to define even the conventional community (Preece, 2000). To explore the areas of common agreement on the definition of a community, Hillery (1955) studied a wide number of community definitions and found that researchers agree that a community (1) is a group of people who (2) share social interaction and (3) share some common ties amongst themselves and the other members of the group and who (4) share the same space for at least a part of the time. For the purpose of this paper, we consider virtual communities to fulfill the criteria with the special case that the shared space is virtual. Examples of the virtual space range from simple web forums to 3D virtual worlds.

From a business perspective, virtual communities are claimed to present lucrative business opportunities for firms that facilitate them (Hagel & Armstrong, 1997). Indeed, this has been indicated by success stories such as Facebook and MySpace. However, recent research has shown that management research on virtual communities is still very scarce and topically scattered (Laine, 2009). Therefore, virtual communities in general are a valid and important area of research from both practitioner and academic standpoints.

In this paper, we concentrate on virtual communities where the service provider adopts a passive role as a platform developer and maintainer, and relies on community members to provide value through the provision of various services. We define these services as *activities carried out by community members for the benefit of other community members*. In particular, these services are based on the application of specialized competences, such as knowledge and skills possessed by community members (cf. service-dominant logic, Vargo & Lusch, 2004). This dependence on customers to provide service makes service production more challenging, because customers as service production resources are less easily manageable than employees (Chase, 1978; Kelley, Donnelly, & Skinner, 1990). This makes designing and implementing the service production system particularly challenging, as the service provider has less control over production resources to ensure the quality of these services.

As the services available in virtual communities are fully based on the contributions of the members of the community, we also conceptualize virtual communities as *networked service production systems*. The networked nature of these communities means that service production is not arranged in a hierarchical way but instead is decentralized. This conceptualization is compatible with the notion of service systems, defined by Spohrer et al. (2008) as: "A dynamic value co-creation configuration of resources, including people, organizations,

17

shared information (language, laws, measures, methods), and technology, all connected internally and externally to other service systems by value propositions".

Considering customers as part of service production systems is not a new idea. This was first conceptualized in the 1970s as part of the emerging service marketing stream (Bowen, 1986; Chase, 1978; Lovelock & Young, 1979). This perspective suggests that customers should be understood as the co-producers of service (Bettencourt, Ostrom, Brown, & Roundtree, 2002; Xue & Field, 2008) or as human resources available for service production (Bowen, 1986), and hence be managed similarly to managing the internal human resources of the service provider. Furthermore, customers engage in value co-creation (Spohrer & Maglio, 2008; Prahalad & Ramaswamy, 2004) either with the technical platform, as in self-service, or with other customers, as in the case of virtual communities.

As indicated in the service operations management literature, the distinctive feature of service production systems is the involvement of customer in production (Sampson & Froehle, 2006; Kellogg & Nie, 1995). In other words, customer input in terms of information or resources is required before service production can take place. Furthermore, as the quality of these customer inputs into service production is often more variable and harder to control, management of quality is more difficult in service operations (Mills, Chase, & Marguiles, 1983; Correa, Ellram, Scavarda, & Cooper, 2007; Johnston, 1999; Johnston & Morris, 1985; Sampson & Froehle, 2006; Roth, & Menor, 2003; Fließ & Kleinaltenkamp, 2004; Goldstein, Johnston, Duffy, & Rao, 2002).

Service Quality in Virtual Communities

Service quality has been studied extensively in the context of online service settings (Zeithaml et al., 2002; Rowley, 2006). Most of this literature is

based on the notion of service quality originating in the service marketing literature (Parasuraman, Zeithaml, & Berry, 1985) and augmented by research on quality in information systems research (Pitt, Watson, & Kavan, 1995; van Dyke, Kappelman, & Prybutok, 1997). Much of research on service quality is based on the SERVQUAL framework, which relies on customer perceptions (Parasuraman, Zeithaml, & Berry, 1988). This framework conceptualizes service quality as a five-dimensional construct, with dimensions of *tangibles, reliability, responsiveness, assurance* and *empathy*. Although the SERVQUAL framework has been criticized in both service marketing (Cronin & Taylor, 1994) and information systems literature (van Dyke et al., 1997), it still forms the basis of much of service quality research.

A common extension of the service quality discussion is to consider the quality of e-services or online services (Zeithaml, Parasuraman, & Malhotra, 2000, 2002; Parasuraman et al., 2005). However, much of this literature is concentrated on the technical aspects of quality in e-services, such as website design and availability of information (Moraga, Calero, & Piattini, 2006). Furthermore, most of the studies have been conducted in an e-commerce context. As the role of human-provided service is often limited to user support provided by the e-commerce site provider (Parasuraman & Zinkhan, 2002; Bauer, Falk, & Hammerschmidt, 2006; Cai & Jun, 2003), these frameworks have limited applicability to virtual communities.

Service quality has also been discussed in more networked fashion, in the context of virtual communities (Kuo, 2003, 2004; Lin, 2008; Oh, Choi, Lee, & Jung, 2003; Santos, 2003; Chen, 2007; Lin, 2007) and peer-to-peer networks (Kwok, Lang, & Tam, 2002; Lui, Lang, & Kwok, 2002). Most of these contributions have still largely been based on the traditional notion of service quality, exemplified by the SERVQUAL framework. Furthermore, many of the developed quality models are still biased towards technological factors of quality (Lin, 2007). However, many papers on virtual community service quality have explicitly considered problems specifically associated with networked service production, namely the public good nature of knowledge and the possibility of free riding it entails (Kwok et al., 2002). In other words, service provision in networked environment is dependent on the willingness of users to provide their service to the system without direct compensation, i.e., "the kindness of strangers" (Wiertz & de Ruyter, 2007; Wasko & Faraj, 2000, 2005; Constant, Sproull, & Kiesler, 1996). Knowledge sharing and service provision in networked service production systems thus requires a level of social norms to form in the community (Wiertz & de Ruyter, 2007; Wasko & Faraj, 2005, 2000). The service provider must be able to nurture a "sense" of virtual community that will increase the willingness to participate in networked service production (Blanchard & Markus, 2004; Blanchard, 2007a). We also point out that since the virtual community is based on voluntary collaboration, it can only be directly managed to a limited degree (Lechner & Hummel, 2002).

Assessing Peer-to-Peer Service Quality in the Virtual Community

To elaborate more on the limitations of contemporary service quality frameworks, we discuss the applicability of the e-service quality framework (Santos, 2003; Zeithaml et al., 2002; Parasuraman et al., 2005) in a virtual community service context. This e-service quality framework is divided into two main dimensions: *incubative* and *active*. The incubative dimension is concerned with the proper design of a web site (Santos, 2003), which has traditionally been under the strict control of the service provider. This dimension may be further divided into ease of use, appearance, linkage, structure and layout, and content (Santos, 2003; Zeithaml et al., 2002). By contrast, the active dimension relates to functional aspects of web sites, and consists of reliability, efficiency, support, communication, security and incentive.

We contend that in the virtual community context, the service provider still retains great control of the incubative dimension, yet in some areas the responsibility has shifted towards the community. For example, many virtual community sites use interactive discussion boards to provide customer support. Effective means of communication provide value for the community, but the technical features used for communication can be easy to mimic. For these reasons, the quality of communication resides predominantly in the hands of the community. We argue that the same also applies to incentives in a virtual community context, as indicated by literature on the determinants of contribution (Wang & Fesenmaier, 2004; Lin, 2006).

As with traditional e-commerce services, security and efficiency belong to the responsibilities of the service provider, though policies toward third party extensions also fall into this category, particularly if hosted outside the service provider. Security in a virtual community context must also be viewed from a non-technical perspective. Privacy-related issues are highly sensitive topics in the area of social networking, and sites are increasingly adding features to give users more control over the visibility of their data. Clearly defined privacy policies may also increase the user's perceived quality of the service.

The notion of reliability in the virtual community context also captures aspects of the user-to-user interaction and extends beyond the technical platform. For instance, if a technical discussion forum is used only by individuals with low technical skills, the reliability of the content of the site can be low. One of the key ways service providers can influence the quality of their content is through setting governance policies and providing features to enforce them. As an example, on-line trust and reputation systems have received much interest among researchers.

TOWARDS A VIRTUAL COMMUNITY SERVICE QUALITY MODEL

Based on the assessment of literature on e-service and virtual community service quality, we propose a tentative high-level model of service quality in virtual communities, depicted in Figure 1. Our model, quite similar to the model proposed by Lin (2007), suggests that the overall quality of service perceived by the members of the virtual community is dependent on the system quality, information quality and service quality. However, in comparison to Lin's model, we suggest that features of the networked service production system are antecedents rather than consequences of the various dimensions of virtual community service quality. Furthermore, as the service provider cannot directly affect the service quality or information quality dimensions, indirect measures must be taken to manage them.

Information quality refers to the extent to which the knowledge and information provided within the virtual community fulfills the needs of community members. This dimension is related to information availability and content (Zeithaml et al., 2002), or the usefulness of content (Yang, Cai, Zhou, & Zhou, 2005). As this dimension is fully dependent on the actions of community members, the service provider cannot directly affect information quality. However, the provider may attempt to indirectly improve it, for example by providing easy content creation mechanisms, utilizing spell-checkers or using administrators to control contributions.

Figure 1. Components of virtual community service quality

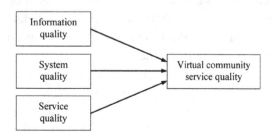

System quality refers to the technical quality of the web site used to serve the virtual community (Lin, 2007). Unlike the other two dimensions of virtual community service quality, the service provider as the provider of the technological platform of the community can directly affect this dimension of service quality through technical and user interface design of the technological platform. Specific components of system quality include ease of use/usability (Santos, 2003; Yang et al., 2005; Zeithaml et al., 2002), reliability (Santos, 2003), availability of the system (Parasuraman et al., 2005), efficiency of using the platform (Santos, 2003; Parasuraman et al., 2005), and privacy/security issues (Zeithaml et al., 2002; Yang et al., 2005).

Service quality refers to the perceived level of personal service received and provided by community members. Unlike Lin (2007), we consider this aspect of virtual community service quality to be increasingly dependent on the actions of community members the more passive role the service provider assumes. Here we refer to the original SERVQUAL framework and propose that this aspect of virtual community service quality depends on the reliability, assurance, responsiveness and empathy displayed by the community members towards each other when communicating in the virtual community.

As the service provider does not contribute to the provision of services in a community based purely on the interaction of community members, it can only affect the service quality component indirectly. This requires fostering a "sense of community" (Blanchard & Markus, 2004; Koh & Kim, 2003; Blanchard, 2007b), and the norms of the community, for example through setting explicit rules for using the system. As indicated by Yen and Hsu (2006), virtual community management can have a positive impact on the norms and motivation to participate in networked service production. Hence, the service provider should actively seek to identify mechanisms by which it can indirectly contribute to the service quality perceived by community members.

CONCLUSION

In this paper, we have conceptualized virtual communities as networked service production systems where the online service is predominantly provided by the members of the community instead of a central commercial service provider. Seeing the members of the community as resources for service production has significant implications for managing the quality of service perceived by community members. In particular, the service provider cannot directly affect the quality of service but instead must rely on several indirect strategies for ensuring the service quality for the members of the community. However, since the quality of service perceived by community members is directly related to the perceived value of the community, and hence the performance of the commercial service provider, we have argued that ensuring service quality is a key priority for the service provider.

However, we have considered only one kind of virtual community, namely a community where the service provider's role is limited to the provision of a technological platform, and where the members of the community provide most of the services. As there are also other kinds of communities, in which the role of the service provider is more significant, the implications of this study may not directly apply.

In addition, we have assumed that the members of the community are a homogeneous group. Obviously, in many virtual communities this is not the case. For example, the providers and consumers of service may be sharply divided groups. In some other communities, some members may specialize in developing new features to the technological platform. A full model of virtual community service quality would require addressing the heterogeneous nature of the members of a virtual community.

Furthermore, we have only provided anecdotal support for the developed framework. Thus, the developed framework of networked service production system and service quality should be considered tentative. In addition, as the overall value of a virtual community is also dependent on the size of the community due to network externalities, the economic analysis of the impact of community size should be incorporated in future development of the framework on the value of the virtual community to its members.

REFERENCES

Bauer, H. H., Falk, T., & Hammerschmidt, M. (2006). eTransQual: A transaction process-based approach for capturing service quality in online shopping. *Journal of Business Research*, *59*(7), 866–875. doi:10.1016/j.jbusres.2006.01.021.

Bettencourt, L. A., Ostrom, A. L., Brown, S. W., & Roundtree, R. I. (2002). Client co-production in knowledge-intensive business services. *California Management Review*, *44*(4), 100–128.

Blanchard, A. L. (2007a). Testing a model of sense of virtual community. *Computers in Human Behavior*.

Blanchard, A. L. (2007b). Developing a sense of virtual community measure. *Cyberpsychology & Behavior*, *10*(6), 827–830. doi:10.1089/cpb.2007.9946.

Blanchard, A. L., & Markus, M. L. (2004). The experienced "sense" of a virtual community: Characteristics and processes. *ACM SIGMIS Database*, *35*(1), 64–79. doi:10.1145/968464.968470.

Bowen, D. E. (1986). Managing customers as human resources in service organizations. *Human Resource Management*, *25*(3), 371–383. doi:10.1002/hrm.3930250304.

Cai, S., & Jun, M. (2003). Internet users' perceptions of online service quality: A comparison of online buyers and information searchers. *Managing Service Quality*, *13*, 504–519. doi:10.1108/09604520310506568.

Chase, R. B. (1978). Where does the customer fit in a service operation? *Harvard Business Review*, *56*(6), 137–142.

Chen, I. Y. L. (2007). The factors influencing members' continuance intentions in professional virtual communities - A longitudinal study. *Journal of Information Science*, *33*(4), 451. doi:10.1177/0165551506075323.

Constant, D., Sproull, L., & Kiesler, S. (1996). The kindness of strangers: The usefulness of electronic weak ties for technical advice. *Organization Science*, *7*(2), 119–135. doi:10.1287/orsc.7.2.119.

Correa, H., Ellram, L., Scavarda, A., & Cooper, M. (2007). An operations management view of the services and goods offering mix. *International Journal of Operations & Production Management*, *27*(5), 444–463. doi:10.1108/01443570710742357.

Cronin, J. J., & Taylor, S. A. (1994). SERVPERF versus SERVQUAL: Reconciling performance-based and perceptions-minus-expectations measurement of service quality. *Journal of Marketing*, *58*(1), 125–131. doi:10.2307/1252256.

Fließ, S., & Kleinaltenkamp, M. (2004). Blueprinting the service company - Managing service processes efficiently. *Journal of Business Research*, *57*(4), 392–404. doi:10.1016/S0148-2963(02)00273-4.

Goldstein, S. M., Johnston, R., Duffy, J. A., & Rao, J. (2002). The service concept: The missing link in service design research? *Journal of Operations Management*, *20*(2), 121–134. doi:10.1016/S0272-6963(01)00090-0.

Hagel, J. III, & Armstrong, A. (1997). *Net gain: Expanding markets through virtual communities*. Cambridge, MA: Harvard Business School Press.

Hillery, G. A. (1955). Definitions of community: Areas of agreement. *Rural Sociology*, *20*(2), 111–123.

Hofacker, C. F., Goldsmith, R. E., Bridges, E., & Swilley, E. (2006). E-services: A synthesis and research agenda. *Journal of Value Chain Management, 1*.

Johnston, R. (1999). Service operations management: Return to roots. *International Journal of Operations & Production Management*, *19*(2), 104–124. doi:10.1108/01443579910247383.

Johnston, R., & Morris, B. (1985). Monitoring and control in service operations. *International Journal of Operations & Production Management*, *5*(1), 32–38. doi:10.1108/eb054730.

Jøsang, A., Ismail, R., & Boyd, C. (2007). A survey of trust and reputation systems for online service provision. *Decision Support Systems*, *43*(2), 618–644. doi:10.1016/j.dss.2005.05.019.

Kelley, S. W., Donnelly, J. H. Jr, & Skinner, S. J. (1990). Customer participation in service production and delivery. *Journal of Retailing*, *66*(3), 315–335.

Kellogg, D., & Nie, W. (1995). A framework for strategic service management. *Journal of Operations Management*, *13*(4), 323–337. doi:10.1016/0272-6963(95)00036-4.

Koh, J., & Kim, Y. G. (2003). Sense of virtual community: A conceptual framework and empirical validation. *International Journal of Electronic Commerce*, *8*(2), 75–94.

Kuo, Y. F. (2003). A study on service quality of virtual community websites. *Total Quality Management and Business Excellence*, *14*, 461–474. doi:10.1080/1478336032000047237a.

Kuo, Y. F. (2004). Integrating Kano's model into web-community service quality. *Total Quality Management & Business Excellence, 15*(7), 925–939. doi:10.1080/14783360410001681854.

Kwok, S. H., Lang, K. R., & Tam, K. Y. (2002). Peer-to-peer technology business and service models: Risks and opportunities. *Electronic Markets, 12*(3), 175–183. doi:10.1080/101967802320245947.

Laine, M. O. (2009). Bibliometric analysis and systematic review of management literature on virtual communities. In *Proceedings of the 9th European Academy of Management Conference*, Liverpool, UK.

Lechner, U., & Hummel, J. (2002). Business models and system architectures of virtual communities: From a sociological phenomenon to peer-to-peer architectures. *International Journal of Electronic Commerce, 6*(3), 41–53.

Leimeister, J. M., & Krcmar, H. (2004). Revisiting the virtual community business model. In *Proceedings of the 10th Americas Conference on Information Systems*, New York, NY (pp. 2716-2726).

Lin, C. F. (2008). The cyber-aspects of virtual communities: Free downloader ethics, cognition, and perceived service quality. *Cyberpsychology & Behavior, 11*(1), 69–73. doi:10.1089/cpb.2007.9932.

Lin, H. F. (2006). Understanding behavioral intention to participate in virtual communities. *Cyberpsychology & Behavior, 9*(5), 540–547. doi:10.1089/cpb.2006.9.540.

Lin, H. F. (2007). The role of online and offline features in sustaining virtual communities: An empirical study. *Internet Research, 17*(2), 119–138. doi:10.1108/10662240710736997.

Lovelock, C. H., & Young, R. F. (1979). Look to consumers to increase productivity. *Harvard Business Review, 57*(3), 168–178.

Lui, S. M., Lang, K. R., & Kwok, S. H. (2002). Participation incentive mechanisms in peer-to-peer subscription systems. In *Proceedings of the 35th Annual Hawaii International Conference on System Sciences* (pp. 3925-3931).

Messerschmitt, D. G., Peltonen, J., Laine, M. O. J., & Oza, N. (2008). *Community networked services: Learning from Web 2.0*. Retrieved from http://papers.ssrn.com/sol3/papers.cfm?abstract_id=1320947

Mills, P. K., Chase, R. B., & Marguiles, N. (1983). Motivating the client/employee system as a service production strategy. *Academy of Management Review, 8*(3), 475–485.

Moraga, A., Calero, C., & Piattini, M. (2006). Comparing different quality models for portals. *Online Information Review, 30*(5), 555–568. doi:10.1108/14684520610706424.

Oh, S., Choi, J., Lee, S., & Jung, S. (2003). Toward an integrated framework for assessing website performance: Depending on presence of virtual community. In *Proceedings of the Annual Meeting of the Decision Sciences Institute* (pp. 955-960).

Parasuraman, A., Zeithaml, V. A., & Berry, L. L. (1985). A conceptual model of service quality and its implications for future research. *Journal of Marketing, 49*(4), 41–50. doi:10.2307/1251430.

Parasuraman, A., Zeithaml, V. A., & Berry, L. L. (1988). SERVQUAL: A multiple-item scale for measuring consumer perceptions of service quality. *Journal of Retailing, 64*(1), 12–40.

Parasuraman, A., Zeithaml, V. A., & Malhotra, A. (2005). ES-QUAL: A multiple-item scale for assessing electronic service quality. *Journal of Service Research*, *7*(3), 213. doi:10.1177/1094670504271156.

Parasuraman, A., & Zinkhan, G. M. (2002). Marketing to and serving customers through the Internet: An overview and research agenda. *Journal of the Academy of Marketing Science*, *30*(4), 286. doi:10.1177/009207002236906.

Pitt, L. F., Watson, R. T., & Kavan, C. B. (1995). Service quality: A measure of information systems effectiveness. *Management Information Systems Quarterly*, *19*(2), 173–187. doi:10.2307/249687.

Prahalad, C. K., & Ramaswamy, V. (2004). Co-creating unique value with customers. *Strategy and Leadership*, *32*(3), 4–9. doi:10.1108/10878570410699249.

Preece, J. (2000). *Online communities: Designing usability and supporting sociabilty*. New York, NY: John Wiley & Sons.

Roth, A. V., & Menor, L. J. (2003). Insights into service operations management: A research agenda. *Production and Operations Management*, *12*(2), 145–164. doi:10.1111/j.1937-5956.2003.tb00498.x.

Rowley, J. (2006). An analysis of the e-service literature: Towards a research agenda. *Internet Research*, *16*(3), 339–359. doi:10.1108/10662240610673736.

Sampson, S. E., & Froehle, C. M. (2006). Foundations and implications of a proposed unified services theory. *Production and Operations Management*, *15*(2), 329–343. doi:10.1111/j.1937-5956.2006.tb00248.x.

Santos, J. (2003). E-service quality: A model of virtual service quality dimensions. *Managing Service Quality*, *13*(3), 233–246. doi:10.1108/09604520310476490.

Spohrer, J., & Maglio, P. P. (2008). The emergence of service science: Toward systematic service innovations to accelerate co-creation of value. *Production and Operations Management*, *17*(3), 238–246. doi:10.3401/poms.1080.0027.

Spohrer, J., Vargo, S. L., Caswell, N., & Maglio, P. P. (2008). The service system is the basic abstraction of service science. In *Proceedings of the 41ˢᵗ Hawaiian International Conference on Systems Sciences* (pp. 7-10).

van Dyke, T. P., Kappelman, L. A., & Prybutok, V. R. (1997). Measuring information systems service quality: Concerns on the use of the SERVQUAL questionnaire. *Management Information Systems Quarterly*, *21*(2), 195–208. doi:10.2307/249419.

Vargo, S. L., & Lusch, R. F. (2004). Evolving to a new dominant logic for marketing. *Journal of Marketing*, *68*(1), 1–17. doi:10.1509/jmkg.68.1.1.24036.

Wang, Y., & Fesenmaier, D. R. (2004). Towards understanding members' general participation in and active contribution to an online travel community. *Tourism Management*, *25*(6), 709–722. doi:10.1016/j.tourman.2003.09.011.

Wasko, M. M. L., & Faraj, S. (2000). "It is what one does": Why people participate and help others in electronic communities of practice. *The Journal of Strategic Information Systems*, *9*, 155–173. doi:10.1016/S0963-8687(00)00045-7.

Wasko, M. M. L., & Faraj, S. (2005). Why should I share? Examining social capital and knowledge contribution in electronic communities of practice. *Management Information Systems Quarterly*, *29*(1), 35–57.

Wiertz, C., & de Ruyter, K. (2007). Beyond the call of duty: Why customers contribute to firm-hosted commercial online communities. *Organization Studies*, *28*(3), 347–376. doi:10.1177/0170840607076003.

Xue, M., & Field, J. M. (2008). Service coproduction with information stickiness and incomplete contracts: Implications for consulting services design. *Production and Operations Management*, *17*(3), 357–372. doi:10.3401/poms.1080.0024.

Yang, Z., Cai, S., Zhou, Z., & Zhou, N. (2005). Development and validation of an instrument to measure user perceived service quality of information presenting web portals. *Information & Management*, *42*(4), 575–589. doi:10.1016/S0378-7206(04)00073-4.

Yang, Z., & Jun, M. (2002). Consumer perception of e-service quality: From internet purchaser and non-purchaser perspectives. *The Journal of Business Strategy*, *19*(1), 19–41.

Yen, H. J., & Hsu, H. Y. (2006). Consumer co-production in product-related virtual community - Does community management matter? In *Proceedings of the 11ᵗʰ Annual Conference of Asia Pacific Decision Sciences Institute*, Hong Kong (pp. 14-18).

Zeithaml, V. A. (2002). Service excellence in electronic channels. *Managing Service Quality*, *12*(3), 135–138. doi:10.1108/09604520210429187.

Zeithaml, V. A., Parasuraman, A., & Malhotra, A. (2000). *A conceptual framework for understanding e-service quality: Implications for future research and managerial practice* (Report No. 00-115). Cambridge, MA: Marketing Science Institute.

Zeithaml, V. A., Parasuraman, A., & Malhotra, A. (2002). Service quality delivery through web sites: A critical review of extant knowledge. *Journal of the Academy of Marketing Science*, *30*(4), 362–375. doi:10.1177/009207002236911.

Zhang, X., & Prybutok, V. R. (2005). A consumer perspective of e-service quality. *IEEE Transactions on Engineering Management*, *52*(4), 461–477. doi:10.1109/TEM.2005.856568.

This work was previously published in the International Journal of Virtual Communities and Social Networking, Volume 3, Issue 1, edited by Subhasish Dasgupta, pp. 13-22, copyright 2011 by IGI Publishing (an imprint of IGI Global).

Chapter 3
Unfolding the Diminishing Image Control in Online Self Presentation:
An Investigation of Virtual Community

Chien-nai Lin
National Taiwan University, Taiwan

Yu-Tzu Lin
National Taiwan University, Taiwan

Ching-Cha Hsieh
National Taiwan University, Taiwan

ABSTRACT

As the young generations grow up using applications like Facebook and as fans of social networking technologies, understanding the presentations of self in a virtual community becomes a worthwhile topic to be addressed. Drawing on the theory of dramaturgical theory (Goffman, 1959), this interpretive research was conducted to observe the self presentation of the participants in a virtual community to analyze their online behaviors and interactions. The observations found that only in the early stage of interaction, people can have a high degree of control over the ideal images creation; however, the clues to reveal actual images are accumulated over time and across cyberspaces. This research suggested that personal control over image delivery in a virtual community weakens over time, which challenged the assumption made by prior literature regarding how people have greater control in creating ideal images in the virtual community. The findings of this research could provide insight for people who use virtual community to search for credible personal information or to build ideal images. Besides, this research suggested that although Internet technologies facilitate access to a rich source of information, the convenience in information acquisition and verification comes at the expense of personal privacy.

DOI: 10.4018/978-1-4666-4022-1.ch003

INTRODUCTION

A virtual community is not only a space for people to seek information and solve problems, but also a space for them to meet other people, obtain support and build up friendships (Chiu, Hsu, & Wang, 2006). Past studies have mostly suggested that a virtual community can serve as a platform which is especially applicable to construct ideal images. People tend to convey ideal projections of their own images in a virtual community in order to obtain and enjoy recognition and support within the community. Those studies postulated that textual interaction allows more time for people to consider the content they are writing. Moreover, text-based communication in a virtual community is free from social cues embedded in body language, such as facial expressions and bodily movements. Therefore, in a virtual community, people have greater control in creating ideal self images by presenting appropriate texts following a process of thorough thinking. Those confronting these images do not have many clues to identify whether the persons they are viewing in are consistent with their personas in the real world (Bowker & Tuffin, 2002; Dominick, 1999; Ellison, Heino, & Gibbs, 2006; Papacharissi, 2002a, 2002b; Trammell & Keshelashvili, 2005; Vaast, 2007).

Contrary to the past studies, this paper argues that only in the early stage of interaction, people have a high degree of control over the establishment of their ideal images in a virtual community. As time goes by, more and more cues are accumulated across cyberspace so that others can obtain a truer picture. As the internet serves functions in regard to searches and connections, the hidden identity and idealized personality of a person in a virtual community can be easily connected to the real world through search engines and cross reference functions. Such background information is fairly helpful for others to understand the scenarios in which a person places himself/herself. It also helps in discriminating the degree of truthfulness of the comments made by a person in a virtual community. Therefore, the image of a person that takes extensive efforts to create in a virtual community may be completely destroyed via an accidental link made by others which reveals contradictions or inconsistencies in presented images. Nonetheless, people usually do not have the corresponding control over factors that violate their ideal personal images.

This is an interpretive research and draws on the views of "give" and "give off" in dramaturgical theory (Goffman, 1959) as its theoretical foundation. A virtual community, Mommy's Circle (alias), is unobtrusively observed and the data analyzed according to three stages of hermeneutic circles, by iterating between the interdependent meaning of parts and the whole (Klein & Myers, 1999; Myers 2004). In addition to focusing on thick description of presenting ideal images in a virtual community and the violations of those ideal images, this research proposes an alternative view to investigate the creation and violation of personal images in a virtual community.

The remainder of this paper is organized as follows. The next section reviews the "give" and "give off" concepts in dramaturgical theory and the studies related to self presentation in the virtual community and in the other cyberspace. The following section then describes the research setting and method used for data collection and analysis. The findings regarding the creation and the violation of the ideal images in virtual community are discussed, and the conclusion is presented in the final section.

LITERATURE REVIEW

Dramaturgical Theory and the Views of "Give" and "Give Off"

Dramaturgical theory (Goffman, 1959) interprets the face-to-face interaction in daily life by using the metaphor of theatrical performance. Many studies also observe online interaction in the light of dramaturgical theory (Bowker & Tuffin, 2002; Broom, 2005; Correll, 1995; da Cunha & Orlikowski, 2008; Ellison et al., 2006; Fayard, 2006; Ross, 2007; Vaast, 2007). In this theory, various social situations and their settings are viewed as stages and everyone on a stage is an actor as well as the audience of other actors. Actors play their roles based upon different scripts which may include: the norms, rituals, obligations or expectations in their particular social settings.

According to dramaturgical theory, the actors and the audience start to define the situation of their interaction the first moment they meet. The audience refers to the messages provided by the actors in order to decide the appropriate manner for subsequent interactions. Meanwhile, the audience pays extra attention to the cues that the actors may reveal unintentionally. Those unintended cues weight even more for the audience in judging if the situation involves an appropriate interaction. On the other hand, the actors often aggressively "give" personal information to influence the definition of the situation. Because the actors are aware that the unintended cues are more critical for the definition of the situation, they sometimes pretend to unintentionally "give off" necessary messages. In the definitions of dramaturgical theory, the information which one "gives" in an interaction "involves verbal symbols or their substitutes which he uses admittedly and solely to convey the information that he and the others are known to attach to these symbols", while the information which one "gives off" is "a wide range of action that others can treat as symptomatic of the actor, the expectation being that the action was performed for reasons other than the information conveyed in this way" (Goffman, 1959, p. 2). The way in which the actors "give" and "give off" personal information in the interactions constitutes the process of impression management or self presentation.

The Presentation of Self in a Virtual Community

Most past studies argue that individuals have great control over self presentation in a virtual community. They consider that people can be free from unexpected or embarrassing situations which may often occur in face-to-face interactions. Individuals have sufficient time and space to hide or polish their physical shortcomings or personality traits in a virtual community. In addition, as far as the lack of social cues is concerned in the text-based interactions, some scholars suggest that readers usually determine the creditability of delivered images by referring to visual cues which individuals reveal in their text, such as: spelling, punctuation, wording, sentence flow, tone, content, and special symbols. These visual cues make up for the gap of social cues manifested with facial expressions and body movements in face-to-face communication (Dominick, 1999; Ellison et al., 2006; Kock, 1998; Papacharissi, 2002a, 2002b; Ramirez, Walther, & Sunnafrank, 2002; Taylor & MacDonald, 2002; Walther 1992; Weisband, Schneider, & Connolly, 1995). Therefore, the use of visual cues to support text-based interactions in a virtual community will enhance the credibility in the projections of idealized images.

Drawing on the dramaturgical theory, text-based interactions in a virtual community provides individuals, the actors, with a beneficial environment in which to control the timing, methods and content of the information which they want to "give" or "give off". People can create their ideal images without worrying about the gap between ideal images and real images being easily identified. For example, someone who likes to act as an expert in a virtual community usually aggressively "gives" his/her professional perspectives on the issues or his/her qualifications in providing recommendations (Galegher, Sproull, & Kiesler, 1998; Panteli & Duncan, 2004). Alternatively, people may also choose specific nicknames with strong hints or connotations, display their guest books in personal blogs or link with specific websites to "give off" their identities, tastes or the folks with whom they associate (Dominick, 1999; Papacharissi, 2002a, 2002b; Trammell & Keshelashvili, 2005). On the other side, readers also examine the hints and cues between the lines to determine whether the images people "give" and "give off" are reliable. For example, members in a virtual community often estimate the education level of a person who makes comments, based on his/her typos or sentence flow in the text (Ellison et al., 2006).

In his studies on the presentation of self in personal web pages or blogs, Papacharissi (2002a) proposed that personal web pages or blogs cannot be completely anonymous like other interactions in cyberspace because the presentation is individual-centered. Readers can easily trace the authenticity of personal information through the clues in guest books or external links. However, individuals retain great control over their self presentation by choosing not to "give" certain background information or purposely "give off" visual cues. Papacharissi (2002b) found that sometimes they unfortunately fail to establish ideal images due to insufficiency of webpage techniques or personal experience in cyber world communication. Dominick (1999) also supported the argument that individuals have great control in expressing ideal images in the web pages. His research focuses on the study of "give" information and proposes that most self presentation in personal web pages is rather the performance by an actor than the real images of a person. Interestingly, Trammell and Keshelashvili (2005) examined blogs with high hit rates and find that these blogs tend to establish personal images by actively providing personal background information instead of using "give off" cues. Besides providing information such as personal email address or work place for readers' reference, the hosts of these blogs seldom ignore or delete unfriendly responses from readers but

rather try again to communicate with them. This research proposes that by actively releasing background information, the hosts of these blogs are more persuasive in expressing the ideal images than those who like to pretend to unintentionally "give off" information in their blogs.

In sum, all of the previously mentioned researches agree that people have great control over their ideal images in a virtual community or in the other cyberspace either by "give" or "give off" messages. However, these researches overlook the fact that readers can also test the creditability of the image delivered by someone in the virtual world by external linkages or cross references. Do people still have high degree of control over their self presentation in these web sites? Will people still retain control of the projection of their ideal images in a virtual community if factors such as online cross references are included? Unfortunately, all of the previous researches rarely mention these concerns. Thus, this issue is explored in this research.

RESEARCH SETTING AND METHOD

Mommy's Circle (alias) which was founded in June 2003 by 12 females, was observed. These women possess expertise in media, law, finance, IT and social work. This virtual community aims to offer authentic knowledge on nutrition and medicine for women during their pregnancy and breastfeeding periods as well as social support during all the years of their child care. In addition to the online forum, Mommy's Circle intensively cooperates with government and medical professionals to promote friendly environments for breastfeeding and has established support groups for career women. Mommy's Circle is open to the general public without any obligations. However, given that the majority of hardware, software and technical support are provided by volunteer workers, the community encourages but does not reinforce payment of annual fees to facilitate the day-to-day operations. The community also accepts donations or sponsorships from individuals or businesses. According to the data provided by the community, Mommy's Circle possesses the world's largest Chinese-language database of information on nutrition, medicine and healthcare for breastfeeding mothers and babies. By July 2008, the number of effective registered members exceeded 20,000. The official statistics indicate that a majority of the members are the women who are pregnant, breastfeeding or new parents. Nearly 1.2 billion clicks hit the website each month.

This research selected Mommy's Circle as its research setting because one of the researchers has been a member of this virtual community for four years and has in-depth understanding of the community culture, which would enhance the data collection and analysis. Although unconscious and unintended bias might exist for a researcher with long membership in this community, the three researchers regularly triangulate the findings to avoid obvious misinterpretation. The researchers unobtrusively observed Mommy's Circle and conducted data analysis by hermeneutic circle. Since the observed targets might modify their online behavior once they find out that they are being observed, the data were collected by unobtrusive observation, and only a few members were cognizant of the research progress. Regarding the research ethics related to unobtrusive observation, Allen et al. (2006) suggested that "Manual, non-automated access of information on publicly available web pages should be acceptable without special permissions or actions" (p. 607). This research fully adhered to the principles of research ethics. Moreover, in this paper, the real name of the virtual community and the personal online nicknames were replaced by aliases because of privacy concerns.

Data collection and analysis were conducted between September 2006 and April 2009. The researchers had logged onto the community at least five times per week and at least three hours each time. This research defines each posting under a single heading (the first message after the heading, possibly in the form of a question, a comment, a description, an announcement or forwarding of an article, in order to trigger follow-up discussions) and the subsequent responses to the posting as the interactions of the same round. The implications presented in relation to the creation of ideal images and revelations of true images were observed during each round of interactions. Over 10,000 interaction rounds were observed.

This was an interpretive research which involves three hermeneutic circles by iterating between the interdependent meaning of parts and the whole (Klein & Myers, 1999; Myers, 2004). In the first hermeneutic circle, the researchers deployed dramaturgical theory as a theoretical lens to observe the phenomena at the research site, at the same time, no specific research focus were identified. Interestingly, this research found that the same person in the observed virtual community might present very differently in other cyberspaces. For example, one that has very positive image in the virtual community may have a negative reputation in another cyberspace, according to other bloggers' criticisms. Those criticisms could indeed conflict with what one intended or wish to be perceived in the virtual community. Thus, the finding was noted and led to the second hermeneutic circle. In the second hermeneutic circle, the researchers focused on the situations which personal image in the Mommy's Circle and in other cyberspace were found incongruent. Each posting in the community was examined to identify several speakers with distinctive images for further personal investigation. The researchers linked to other personal blogs or virtual communities outside Mommy's Circle to review their postings, and looked for comments of their postings. It was found that, when a person is using the same nickname as the one used for Mommy's Circle, often time, his/her image presentation is consistent. However, when a person enters another cyberspace which holds different nature of purpose, he/she tends to enter with a different nickname and speaks with a different voice tone. In addition, although a person tends to present a consistent image with the same nickname across cyberspace, the effort usually fails according to the criticisms posted outside of Mommy's Circle. This phenomenon was duly noted and resulted in the next hermeneutic circle. In the third hermeneutic circle, the researchers interpreted phenomena by the lens of "give" and "give off" views in dramaturgical theory. As each interacting participant in any cyberspace is both an audience and an actor at the same time, a person is still engaged in the process of presenting himself/herself even when he/she responds the postings made by others, or when he/she leaves messages on others' blogs. Therefore, this research modified the assumption made by past studies that any individual would become an audience as long as he/she is in the cyberspace possessed by others.

FINDINGS AND THEORETICAL INTERPRETATION

This research agrees that individuals usually take every opportunity to "give" and "give off" messages in order to create ideal personal images. Meanwhile, readers pay more attention and trust more to those unintended "give off" messages. However, despite those "give" and "give off" messages, the creation of ideal images and the revelation of true images in the virtual community can be affected by various contexts.

Style Consistency

In the target case, it is found that most community members leave messages with the same nicknames in other online spaces and choose to interact with others with personal images which are consistent with the ones which they project in the community. For example, Susan (alias) always plays the role of a peacekeeper in the community. However, the researchers personally believed that Susan chooses to play such a role not only because she

is compassionate, but also because she is eager to create a superior image, namely, that she is able to consider disputes dispassionately and keep a clear head in the process of her analysis. She likes to use professional jargon and often compares community arguments to similar phenomena in politics and sociology. This writing style usually does little to calm dispute within the community. Instead, other members sarcastically agree that people can finally understand messages left by other members thanks to the instruction and guidance provided by Susan. Susan maintains her own consistent style when she visits other online space and uses the same nickname when visiting other blogs. In the discussion on domestic movies with the blog owner, she leaves a comment whose style is consistent with the style she expresses in the community.

In this example, for people who both post comments and reply to comments, (both hosts and visitors of the website or blogs), everyone could be an actor and an audience at the same time, as long as they take part in interactions. They create their own ideal images as well as review the images released by others. Thus, one must maintain a consistent style across cyberspace instead of restriction to a specific online space to establish an ideal image.

However, past studies on self presentation in cyberspace, in the use of the metaphors of theatre performance, specify neither who the actors are nor who their audiences are. The implied assumption is that the owners of personal web pages or blogs are the subjects, and it goes without saying that they are also the actors. The actors usually actively "give" and "give off" messages in order to construct their ideal images. The visitors who leave messages on the web pages or blogs are classified as the audience, who need to determine the truthfulness of the images and messages released by actors. Those studies that simply apply the roles of actors and audience in dichotomy, based on dramaturgical theory, fail to reflect the reality of online communities.

Clues for True Self

The prior statement indicates that the establishment of ideal images in a virtual community is by no means restricted to the scope of any specific community. It also includes any other cyberspace that the same nicknames (persons) access. Similarly, the channels used by the audience to differentiate fact from falsehood are not limited to any specific community. They also include all the Internet information traceable to the same nicknames. It is interesting that although both actors and audience can create or validate images with the same Internet identifications across cyberspace, the audience seems to have a large pool of clues to verify the truthfulness of the performances. The extra clues are mostly hidden in the cyberspace where the actors have never visited or simply cannot access.

For example, Marian (alias) is one of the leaders of the volunteer workers for the community. She often provides appropriate consolation and assistance when members seek help online. She indicated that she wishes to always be a comfortable and non-aggressive person. However, in a member's personal blog, the member aggressively accused "the conservative school of the administrative team led by Marian": "it is cruel to treat a founder by stopping her membership, given that the founder had spent considerable time and efforts over the past 7 years" and "it forces out the people who really make contributions". These clues are definitely possible keys to destroying the ideal image which Marian has tried hard to deliver in the community.

The evidence in the previous example makes the past studies argument that actors have great control over image creations, less credible. In our opinion, the actors can "give" and "give off" abundant messages to establish ideal images only in the cyberspace which they can access. The audience will expand their cross reference which includes the cyberspace which the actors never visit in order to validate the messages. It is difficult to categorically state who has a higher level of control in the process.

The Law of Diminishing Control

Whenever willing, actors can choose to access different online spaces with the same nickname in a short period of time and establish their ideal images by "giving" and "giving off" a large amount of personal messages. But the expansion of clue collected by the audience requires good timing and opportunities. This may explain why the actors do have a higher level of control in the initial days of online community interactions when it comes to the establishment of ideal images. However, the audience gains more opportunities to gather messages over time by which to validate or undermine the images presented. As time goes by, an increasing number of clues in cyberspace can be found to verify whether the images the actors release are close to the true picture. As a result, the control over image creation possessed by the actors lessens over time.

For example, the researchers were unaware of the blog that posted the statement accusing Marian in the right beginning. It was one day that one of researchers was reading through discussions on abortions in the Mommy's Circle community and stumbled onto the links provided by a member in her response message. Then, the researcher visited those sites out of curiosity. More than one year after the first access to the blogs that the researcher came across the attacks on Marian.

CONCLUSION

This research unobtrusively observed the text-based interactions of a virtual community by drawing on the perspectives of dramaturgical theory, analyzed the data by hermeneutic circle, and focused on the issue of the creation of ideal images and the revelation of true images in virtual communities. While the conventional research approach usually examines the "give" or "give off" messages that individuals use to create their ideal images or the clues to which readers pay attention in seeking to verify the authenticity of images, this research proposed that the scope of previous approaches in the study of the creation and the violation of personal images in a virtual community was limited. In this paper, such images are considered as a result of presentations across cyberspace rather than just in one specific virtual community. Moreover, while past studies seldom explore the causations to the violation of ideal images, this research advanced the concept that the key is the cyberspaces that individuals have no access or simply never been to. Meanwhile, this paper argues that the personal control over image delivery in a virtual community weakens over time. This research, drawing on dramaturgical theory, also concluded that every interacting participant in any cyberspace is both audience and actor at the same time. This statement modifies the assumption made by past studies that any individual becomes audience as long as he/she is in the cyberspace possessed by others.

As virtual communities have been used more frequently by organizations to support changes or to unify employees, the findings of this research provide profound insight for managers who use virtual community to search for highly credible personal information, as well as for persons who build ideal images for job seeking or social connections through virtual communities. For website service providers, this research demonstrates that although Internet technologies facilitate access to a rich source of information, the convenience in information acquisition and verification comes at the expense of personal privacy.

REFERENCES

Baym, N. K. (1995). The performance of humor in computer-mediated communication. *Journal of Computer-Mediated Communication*, *1*(2). Retrieved from http://jcmc.indiana.edu/vol1/issue2/baym.html.

Bowker, N., & Tuffin, K. (2002). Disability discourses for online identities. *Disability & Society*, *17*(3), 327–344. doi:10.1080/09687590220139883.

Broom, A. (2005). The eMale: Prostate cancer, masculinity and online support as a challenge to medical expertise. *Journal of Sociology (Melbourne, Vic.)*, *41*(1), 87–104. doi:10.1177/1440783305050965.

Chiu, C. M., Hsu, M. H., & Wang, E. T. G. (2006). Understanding knowledge sharing in virtual communities: An integration of social capital and social cognitive theories. *Decision Support Systems*, *42*(3), 1872–1888. doi:10.1016/j.dss.2006.04.001.

Correll, S. (1995). The ethnography of an electronic bar: The lesbian café. *Journal of Contemporary Ethnography*, *24*(3), 270–298. doi:10.1177/089124195024003002.

Da Cunha, J. V., & Orlikowski, W. J. (2008). Performing catharsis: The use of online discussion forums in organizational change. *Information and Organization*, *18*(2), 132–156. doi:10.1016/j.infoandorg.2008.02.001.

Dominick, J. R. (1999). Who do you think you are? Personal home pages and self-presentation on the World Wide Web. *Journalism & Mass Communication Quarterly*, *76*(4), 646–658.

Ellison, N., Heino, R., & Gibbs, J. (2006). Managing impressions online: Self-presentation processes in the online dating environment. *Journal of Computer-Mediated Communication, 11*(2), 415–441. doi:10.1111/j.1083-6101.2006.00020.x.

Fayard, A.-L. (2006). Interacting on a video-mediated stage: The collaborative construction of an interactional video setting. *Information Technology & People, 19*(2), 152–169. doi:10.1108/09593840610673801.

Galegher, J., Sproull, L., & Kiesler, S. (1998). Legitimacy, authority, and community in electronic support groups. *Written Communication, 15*(4), 493–530. doi:10.1177/0741088398015004003.

Goffman, E. (1959). *The presentation of self in everyday life*. New York, NY: Anchor Books.

Joinson, A. N. (2001). Self-disclosure in computer-mediated communication: The role of self-awareness and visual anonymity. *European Journal of Social Psychology, 31*(2), 177–192. doi:10.1002/ejsp.36.

Joinson, A. N., & Dietz-Uhler, B. (2002). Explanations for the perpetration of and reactions to deception in a virtual community. *Social Science Computer Review, 20*(3), 275–289.

Klein, H. K., & Myers, M. D. (1999). A set of principles for conducting and evaluating interpretive field studies in information systems. *Management Information Systems Quarterly, 23*(1), 67–93. doi:10.2307/249410.

Kock, N. (1998). Can communication medium limitations foster better group discussion? An action research study. *Information & Management, 34*(5), 295–305. doi:10.1016/S0378-7206(98)00066-4.

Myers, M. D. (2004). Hermeneutics in information systems research. In Mingers, J., & Willcocks, L. (Eds.), *Social theory and philosophy for information systems* (pp. 103–128). Chichester, UK: John Wiley & Sons.

Panteli, N., & Duncan, E. (2004). Trust and temporary virtual teams: Alternative explanations and dramaturgical relationships. *Information Technology & People, 17*(4), 423–441. doi:10.1108/09593840410570276.

Papacharissi, Z. (2002a). The self online: The utility of personal home pages. *Journal of Broadcasting & Electronic Media, 46*(3), 346–368. doi:10.1207/s15506878jobem4603_3.

Papacharissi, Z. (2002b). The presentation of self in virtual life: Characteristics of personal home pages. *Journalism & Mass Communication Quarterly, 79*(3), 643–660.

Ramirez, A. Jr, Walther, J. B., & Sunnafrank, M. (2002). Information-seeking strategies, uncertainty, and computer-mediated communication toward a conceptual model. *Human Communication Research, 28*(2), 213–228.

Ross, D. A. R. (2007). Backstage with the knowledge boys and girls: Goffman and distributed agency in an organic online community. *Organization Studies, 28*(3), 307–325. doi:10.1177/0170840607076000.

Sannicolas, N. (1997). Erving Goffman, dramaturgy, and on-line relationships. *Cybersociology Magazine, 1*. Retrieved from http://www.cybersociology.com/files/1_2_sannicolas.html

Tayor, J., & MacDonald, J. (2002). The effects of asynchronous computer-mediated group interaction on group processes. *Social Science Computer Review, 20*(3), 260–274.

Trammell, K. D., & Keshelashvili, A. (2005). Examining the new influencers: A self-presentation study of a-list blogs. *Journalism & Mass Communication Quarterly, 82*(4), 968–982.

Vaast, E. (2007). Playing with masks: Fragmentation and continuity in the presentation of self in an occupational online forum. *Information Technology & People, 20*(4), 334–351. doi:10.1108/09593840710839789.

Walther, J. B. (1992). Interpersonal effects in computer-mediated interaction: A relational perspective. *Communication Research, 19*(1), 52–90. doi:10.1177/009365092019001003.

Walther, J. B. (1996). Computer-mediated communication: Impersonal, interpersonal, and hyperpersonal interaction. *Communication Research, 23*(1), 3–43. doi:10.1177/009365096023001001.

Weisband, S. P., Schneider, S. K., & Connolly, T. (1995). Computer-mediated communication and social information: Status salience and status differences. *Academy of Management Journal, 38*(4), 1124–1995. doi:10.2307/256623.

Wynn, E., & Katz, J. E. (1997). Hyperbole over cyberspace: Self-presentation and social boundaries in internet home pages and discourse. *The Information Society, 13*(4), 297–327. doi:10.1080/019722497129043.

This work was previously published in the International Journal of Virtual Communities and Social Networking, Volume 3, Issue 1, edited by Subhasish Dasgupta, pp. 23-31, copyright 2011 by IGI Publishing (an imprint of IGI Global).

Chapter 4
Enterprise 2.0 Management Challenges

Karen P. Patten
University of South Carolina, USA

Lynn B. Keane
University of South Carolina, USA

ABSTRACT

The nature of the enterprise and the way people work is changing rapidly. The enabling power and competitive advantage of new social and participative technologies will benefit those that recognize the way work is changing. Web 2.0, the "second phase" of the Web, is the foundation of a new and improved Enterprise 2.0. Enterprise 2.0 provides, through a web of interconnected applications, services, and devices, the capabilities for enterprise employees and vendors to be more competitive and productive and for enterprise customers to be more engaged and loyal by accessing the right information from the right people at the right time. This paper describes Enterprise 2.0 management challenges and issues identified by Chief Information Officers, which include the unauthorized use of services and technologies, the integration of a myriad of technologies and capabilities, and the potential compliance and security implications. The authors have proposed a conceptual framework that explores the relationships of three Enterprise 2.0 dimensions – technology, its use, and how resulting user-generated content may lead to business value – with management implications affecting IT culture and policies within the enterprise. This paper provides observations and suggestions for future research.

INTRODUCTION

The evolution of more social and participatory Web 2.0 services and applications is challenging chief information officers (CIOs) to transform traditional enterprise IT services and applications planning, implementation and adoption into new services that support new applications by enterprise employees, vendors, and customers. David Armano speculated that by 2009 CIOs would learn from early trials of Web 2.0 social media services and be able to transition from a "what" is Web

DOI: 10.4018/978-1-4666-4022-1.ch004

2.0 mentality to a "how" social media initiatives should be implemented and supported within the enterprise (Kim, 2008). Preliminary research by the authors has shown that this transition has occurred in several industries – hospitality, tourism, entertainment, but CIOs in other industries are still struggling with how to support social media within their enterprises.

Considered by some to be the "second phase" of the Web, Web 2.0 is a new and improved Web (Anderson, 2007; O'Reilly, 2005). Enterprise 2.0 therefore is the new and improved way for the enterprises to use Web 2.0 services and technologies throughout its supply chain and value-added services. As a result, enterprise Intranet and Extranet services and applications should also be new and improved. For example, some consider the current enterprise Extranet (1.0) to be primarily a functional backbone network that focuses on transactions and is connected to backroom enterprise resource systems (ERPs) and customer-facing relationship management (CRM) applications. A new and improved Extranet (2.0) is formed by merging social media, personalization, and segmentation capabilities with user-generated content, which leads to a more engaging and valuable experiences for users. Web 2.0 principles defined by O'Reilly (2005) could be implemented by the enterprise IT organization executives to better manage this new and improved Extranet 2.0 (Vignette, 2009). Applying these same principles to the enterprise Intranet (2.0) would also enhance employee communications and collaboration, which could lead to increased employee investment and retention.

Three key issues emerge for CIOs as they integrate Web 2.0 technologies and services within the enterprise. The first is that if CIOs do not embrace Web 2.0 services and manage their policies and implementations, employees who currently use these services for their personal use will begin using similar social media and communication channels within their work environment without IT executive involvement (Ward, 2009).

The second is that Web 2.0 is a generic concept. It is not simply a new type of technology, nor is it just services. It covers a wide range of media and practices with a wide range of definitions and benefits. For example, employees have adopted different terms for social media connectivity such as "social networking," "open space," "personal space," and "online communities" (Eccleston & Griseri, 2008). Finally, Preston (2009) points out that the enterprise IT executive compliance and security responsibilities will continue to increase, the third major Web 2.0 key issue. Today, CIOs are responsible to ensure that their companies comply with financial reporting, privacy, and security regulations. Social media services increase concerns for the protection and safety of personal and corporate data including intellectual property as well as the unintended consequences of these new services and cyber-risk assessment and protection (Barkiewicz, 2009; Preston, 2009).

This paper describes an Enterprise 2.0 Management Framework for CIOs developed by the authors to summarize what is known and understood about Web 2.0 and to define what is meant by the term "Enterprise 2.0." The authors discuss enterprise business implications and issues comparing old Enterprise 1.0 to new Enterprise 2.0 services. This framework focuses on the relationships of three dimensions of Enterprise 2.0: What are different Enterprise 2.0 *technology tools?* How do employees, customers, and vendors *use these tools?* What new *user-generated information content* is created? By considering the organizational culture and management policies implications, these new Enterprise 2.0 services can be used to create business value. Based on theories and practices identified in the literature, this framework can be used to identify issues regarding the use and management of Enterprise 2.0 services and technologies as they affect the IT culture and policies within the enterprise. Additionally, this framework can be used to create a future research agenda.

ENTERPRISE 2.0 BUSINESS MANAGEMENT DILEMMA

The "new" web, Web 2.0, enables non-technical users to digitally publish and evaluate content, to socialize anywhere in the world, and to communicate instantly with hundreds of people. Mrkwicka, Kiebling, and Kolbe (2009) described in their analysis of Web 2.0 applications for television viewer retention, that the business concept of Web 2.0 is controversial because there is no one specific technical innovation. However, because of the potential to transform the way business is conducted through interactivity, social networking, and user integration, enterprise IT executives need to identify, understand, and integrate a wide range of existing and new technologies, applications, and functions. New technologies and services are being developed on a rapid rate as users, themselves, create new applications.

Advocates for the enterprise adoption of Web 2.0 services and technologies argue that "new" Enterprise 2.0 services will create business value by increasing revenues, improving productivity, improving customer relationships, and lowering costs (Bicknell, 2008). Plus, social networking tools such as Facebook, YouTube, MySpace, and Google are already being used by enterprise employees for both personal and business applications. As early as 2008, according to Bicknell (2008) over 20,000 employees from IBM, 17,000 employees from Microsoft, and 13,000 employees from Accenture had Facebook accounts. By 2010, IBM had over 53,000 employees on IBM's own SocialBlue (IBM's Facebook for employees), over 200,000 employees on LinkedIn, and over 100,000 with internal blogs (Hibbard, 2010).

A series of articles from *CIO.com* described implications from how CIOs introduce and manage Enterprise 2.0 services and technologies within the enterprise. Daniel (2007) pointed out that the promise of Enterprise 2.0 would be its capability to make critical information available to the people who need the information through the use of blogs and wikis that could store institutional information. Early enterprise adopters of these tools were newspapers, ad agencies, and consumer brands, who recognized the potential communications and advertising benefits. Today, enterprise employees are using social media technology tools such as text, audio, and video for online conversations, information sharing, and community building (Teich, 2008). Gartner calls Web 2.0 social networking tools a new form of "social enhancement technology" as they track the impact of the socializing of business on the performance of the enterprise. One impact is that introducing these tools into the enterprise is not simply implementing the next round of web development technologies. It is a change in the way technology is delivered and managed (Bicknell, 2008). Another implication is that social media services will increase concerns for the protection and safety of personal and corporate data including intellectual property (Barkiewicz, 2009; Preston, 2009). Web 2.0 risks from unsanctioned employee use include security, licensing, information reliability, and policy compliance (Bicknell, 2008). How will CIOs, who are responsible to ensure that the enterprise complies with financial reporting, privacy, and security regulations, be able to reduce the risk of the unintended consequences of these new services and cyber-risk assessment and protection? The next section describes a review of the current academic research literature along with a review of the trade press reports about Web 2.0 services and technologies, the use of Enterprise 2.0 within the enterprise, and implications and issues of using user-generated content.

REVIEW OF THE LITERATURE

The term "Web 2.0" evolved from a brainstorming session with Dale Dougherty and Tim O'Reilly in 2003 about what companies that survived the 2001 dot-com bubble burst had in common. They concluded the Web was more important than ever and that a new era was beginning – hence – Web 2.0 (O'Reilly, 2005). Anderson (2007, p. 53) summarized this new Web as "the network as platform, spanning all connected devices; Web 2.0 applications…through an 'architecture of participation'… to deliver rich user experiences."

O'Reilly (2005) visualized Web 2.0 as a set of principles and practices, several of which can be applied by CIOs to the Enterprise 2.0, the new and improved way for the enterprise to use Web 2.0 services and technologies throughout its supply chain. The first principle is that the "Web is a platform," where the service automatically gets better the more people use it! New Web 2.0 technology tools such as Wikipedia, tagging, viral marketing, blogging, and RSS (Really Simple Syndication) will "harness the collective intelligence of the masses," O'Reilly's second principle. The collective intelligence of social networking is already changing the way information is shared in the enterprise. Most companies that survived the dot.com bubble crash had a specialized data base such as Google's web crawl, Yahoo's directory, Amazon's database of products, and eBay's database of products, which leads to the third principle, that "data is the next *Intel Inside*."

The fourth O'Reilly principle is the "end of the software release cycle." When software is delivered as a service rather than a product or artifact, the business model for enterprises that develop software for internal applications must fundamentally change. Applications software operations should become a core competency, which is maintained on a daily basis rather than a periodic release cycle. Also, end users should be treated as co-developers. Finally, CIOs must recognize that their employees should have "software above the level of a single device," because they need multiple services to be accessible from anywhere at any time by a single device. This requires an integrated form of services and applications.

Anderson (2007) described how Web 2.0 is changing the way people interact. Two of the most powerful Web 2.0 ideas are the potential business benefits of individual production and user-generated content and the concept of architecture of participation, where through normal use of an application or service, the application or service gets better. Google Search is an example of a system that is designed to take user interactions and use them to improve itself (Anderson, 2007). This also represents the "net effect," where the value of a service increases to existing users when there is some form of interaction with others, such as when more people start to use it (Klemperer, 2006). Two examples of this are when a new user joins a phone network and everyone already on the network has a new person to call, or when a new person joins a social network and everyone else on the site benefits from the interaction of a new person. Once the network effect begins to build, people become aware of the services, the services increase in popularity, and the products take off very rapidly.

Anderson (2007) also identified three implications for how Web 2.0 potentially may transform the enterprise. The importance of the "crowd" and its "power" will increase as the concept of new communities and groups increase from Web tools. The interactivity and integration capabilities will enable user participation, provide additional information about customer needs, and strengthen business relationships (Mrkwicka et al., 2009). Another implication is the growth of user-generated content (UGC) on the part of enterprise employees, but especially from engaged customers who discuss the positives and negatives of enterprise services and products. This capability moves the use of the Internet from primarily a broadcast business-to-consumer (B2C) medium to one where information flows in three directions, business-to-consumer, consumer-to-consumer (C2C), and consumer-to-business (C2B) (Eccleston & Griseri, 2008). Finally, intellectual property debates will increase over the ownership of Web 2.0 data that is being generated, aggregated, and processed (Anderson, 2007).

Although the new Web 2.0 is receiving much attention, it doesn't mean that the old Web 1.0 services and technologies are being replaced. Eccleston and Griseri (2008) compared the "new" and the "old" Internet to identify the use of Web 2.0 tools by "influencers," those who are responsible for creating "word of mouth (WOM)" influence on purchasing decisions. They found that the enterprise needed to integrate both the new with the old depending on the business needs. The old Internet consists of low-engagement and traditional online activities such as Web-surfing, sending/receiving emails. The study found that influencers predominantly use "old" Internet as well as Web 2.0 applications. For example, both Internet 1.0 and 2.0 technologies were used by

influencers to "discuss products and/or services with other people" and to "recommend products and services." Owyang (2009) predicted that there will be a fundamental shift in using customer reviews from Web 2.0 connective technologies such as FacebookConnect, Google FriendConnect, or OpenID. Through Web 2.0 connective technologies, since consumers "know" the people who are posting the reviews, experiences, and critiques, they will probably also "trust" those people (Kim, 2009).

Table 1 summarizes information from the literature review, comparing the business "use" of the "old" Enterprise 1.0 tools with the "new" Enterprise 2.0 tools. The Table also provides benefits of the new services.

Table 1. Comparison of Enterprise 1.0 and the Enterprise 2.0 technology tools and uses

Use	Enterprise 1.0 Tools	Enterprise 2.0 Tools	Benefits	References
Authoring	Word processing	Wiki Blog	Time saving Individual production User-generated content Wisdom of crowds Social capital	Blinn, Lindermann, Fäcks, and Nüttgens (2009) Anderson (2007) O'Reilly (2005) Tan, Ngyuen, Oo, Tha, and Yu (2009)
Business Communication	Memo Email	Email Instant messaging Texting	Less formal Time saving Cost saving No postage Multi-tasking Efficiency of communication Increased productivity Social capital	Wang and Gallivan (2009) Blinn et al. (2009) Tan et al. (2009)
Collaboration	Travel Meetings Teleconferencing	Adobe-Connect WebEx Instant messaging Wiki	Time saving Cost saving React to situations on the fly	Blinn et al. (2009) Wang and Gallivan (2009)
Knowledge Management	Policy manual Surfing web	Wiki	Sharing Rapid return Collective intelligence	Blinn et al. (2009) Eccleston and Griseri (2008) O'Reilly (2005)
Networking	Phone Face-to-face Email	Social networking Instant messaging Texting	Social capital	Blinn et al. (2009) Tan et al. (2009)
Marketing	TV ads	Viral videos RSS Social networking	Individual Personal Customizable Multiple channels	IEEE (2009)

continued on following page

Table 1. Continued

Use	Enterprise 1.0 Tools	Enterprise 2.0 Tools	Benefits	References
Scheduling	Assistants	Doodle Outlook	Time saving Cost saving Rapid return	
Scoring/Rating	Surveys	Social tagging Online survey tools	Rapid return Time saving Cost saving	Blinn et al. (2009)
Sharing	Resource sharing Collective librar-ies	Social tagging Podcast Wiki Blog	Social capital Multiple channels Increased productivity Collective knowledge Participation	Blinn et al. (2009) Anderson (2007)
Teamwork	Meeting Email Phone	Social networking	Time saving Cost saving Social capital	Tan et al. (2009)
Training	Face-to-face Low engagement Formal, central-ized	Online Social, peer-to-peer resources Webcasts 3D/Virtual worlds	Time saving Cost saving Just in time delivery	Eccleston and Griseri (2008) Woodruff (2009)

ENTERPRISE 2.0 MANAGEMENT FRAMEWORK

Since Enterprise 2.0 is really a myriad of services, applications, and technology tools, the authors developed a conceptual framework to explore the relationships of Enterprise 2.0 dimensions – technology, its use, and how the resulting user-generated content may lead to business value – with management implications affecting IT culture and policies within the enterprise. Miles and Huber-man (1994) explained that a conceptual framework helps to identify and explain the key dimensions of the studied topic including the main factors or variables and their relationships.

Figure 1 depicts the conceptual Enterprise 2.0 Management Framework. The first dimension, "technology," includes Web 2.0 tools such as blogs, wikis, tagging and social bookmarking, multi-media sharing, audio blogging and podcast-ing, RSS and syndication. Some include services and applications under technology tools, but the authors considered services and applications to

Figure 1. Enterprise 2.0 management framework

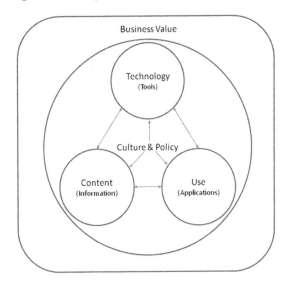

be a separate dimension, because the second di-mension, "use" of the Extranet 2.0 or Intranet 2.0 tools by employees, vendors, or customers, is a different management issue. CIOs must understand and consider the implications when employees or customers are using social networking services, data "mash-up" techniques, collaboration tools, or replicating office-style software in the browsers. The third key dimension is "content." Besides the typical business information generated and used within the enterprise from Enterprise 1.0 services, user-generated content and the benefits of social capital must be managed and in some cases encouraged, while in other cases controlled.

The Enterprise 2.0 Management Framework may be used to consider impacts on enterprise functions from new tools. For example, as shown in Figure 2, employees can increase their personal productivity by using new Web 2.0 tools such as WebEx,, or texting to hold mobile conferencing meetings or real-time texting to save time as well as money. These tools also improve collaborative sharing of information. Employee internal training and education applications also are being transformed by new Intranet 2.0 services. Instead of centralized formal training, enterprises are developing and delivering employee training and education by using social, peer-to-peer networking, and resources tools such as Podcasts, Second Life, AdobeConnect to improve training applications for customer service, and to

create virtual conferencing programs or real-time and recorded lectures for employees and customers (Figure 3).

A third example is determining how to use social networking services such as Facebook, blogs, and Twitter to produce social capital by building brand management, strengthening customer or business relationships, or developing new product features, as shown in Figure 4. The Enterprise 2.0 Management Framework can be used as a template to determine which Web 2.0 tools can enhance business applications to build value. The new services of social networking can lead to several new uses, such as learning management, content management, and knowledge management. Online coaching tools using Twitter and cell-phone connectivity will provide real-time training and feedback. Multi-channel communications including podcasts, webcasts, and videos will also be used to integrate training into an employee's daily life (Woodruff, 2009).

As with any technology, the culture of the organization and the policies within the organization moderate the potential business value of Enterprise 2.0. Denison (1996) defined organiza-

Figure 2. Enterprise 2.0 management framework use by employees

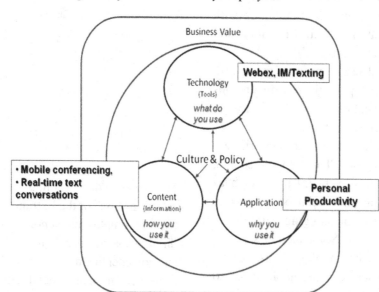

Figure 3. Enterprise 2.0 management framework use for training

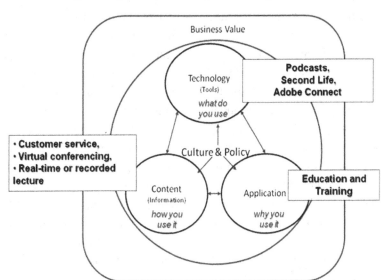

Figure 4. Enterprise 2.0 management framework use for marketing

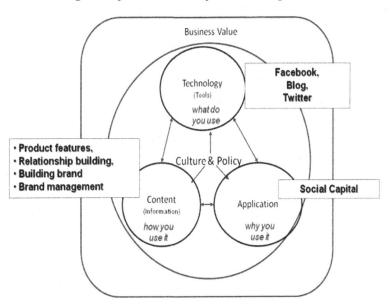

tional culture as the underlying structure of the organization, rooted in the values, beliefs, and assumptions held by organizational members. This is one of the challenges for CIOs dealing with social media within the enterprise. Who represents the company? For example, IBM has a social media culture where there is no single IBM "voice." All employees are encouraged to be the "voice" of IBM. IBM does have guidelines, but doesn't police their employees' use of social media within the enterprise. IBM's guidelines include involving IBMers in the social media planning and strategy, providing the necessary tools, and using crowd sourcing to develop innovative ideas (Hibbard, 2010.) The other extreme is the entertainment and venue industry where some marketing directors manage all enterprise social media to maintain a single "voice" for the venue. Alf Lamont, director of marketing and development for The Comedy Store in Los Angeles, is a pioneer in use of social networking tools to market business. In personal conversations with the author, he emphasized the importance of a single voice in his business. The friends of The Comedy Store develop an expectation of what and how they will learn about events and what is happening at The Comedy Store. Different slants on that expectation would send mixed messages to the friends about what was happening (Lamont, 2010).

Another question is how Enterprise 2.0 capabilities will affect values, beliefs, and assumptions of the employees who use the Intranet 2.0, as well as the vendors and the customers of the enterprise who use the Extranet 2.0. For one thing, to be successful, Enterprise 2.0 "must emerge bottom-up from the needs and activities of its users, rather than being driven top-down by developers" (Bicknell, 2008, p. 53). To determine appropriate policies and practices, the CIO must understand the potential threats (Bicknell, 2008). For example, information about an employee's organization, his or her work functions, etc., is usually viewable by all members of a particular social network. Does this matter? Is it important? Also, enterprise IP addresses can be tracked, which may lead to liability issues enterprises whose corporate messages or/ material is posted.

FUTURE RESEARCH

The first wave of Enterprise 2.0 applications has led social media specialists to identify a key lesson. Social media initiatives must establish a "culture of rapid response" that is supported by any employee who is qualified and passionate, not just the person with the proper title. Time is of the essence. Without passionate employees and customers, social media initiatives will not improve and become self-sustaining (Kim, 2008).

The authors are currently conducting a series of case studies to explore relationships among the three dimensions in the Enterprise 2.0 Management Framework. One goal of the study is to determine how these dimensions lead to increasing business value in three specific areas: knowledge management, the creation of social capital, and employee training and education. The enterprise case studies are divided into three categories. The first category extensively uses Enterprise 2.0 both within the business and as its primary customer relationship and communications system. These types of industries include entertainment, hospitality, and tourism industries. The second category only uses Enterprise 2.0 within certain functional units within the business such as marketing or public relations. Many companies fall into this second category. The third category currently blocks all or most Enterprise 2.0 applications within the workplace. Several of these lagging enterprises are beginning be test the social media waters by considering pilot implementations with several bleeding edge employees within their companies.

CONCLUSION

This series of case studies currently using or not using Enterprise 2.0 social media is expected to provide rich data that may lead to best practices for CIOs to better manage the enterprise social media IT of tomorrow. Little is known about the relationships and interactions of rapidly developing social networking technology tools and capabilities, employees and customer applications, the impact of user-generated content, and the social networking culture and policy as they impact business value. This research study should provide new understanding and potential practices for the next few years.

REFERENCES

Anderson, P. (2007). *What is Web 2.0? Ideas, technologies, and implications for education.* London, UK: JISC Technology & Standards Watch.

Bicknell, D. (2008). *Make Web 2.0 deliver business benefits.* Retrieved September 20, 2009, from http://www.computerweekly.com/Articles/2008/02/20/229486/make-web-2.0-deliver-business-benefits.htm

Blinn, N., Lindermann, N., Fäcks, K., & Nüttgens, M. (2009, August 6-9). Web 2.0 in SME networks – A design science approach considering multi-perspective requirements. In *Proceedings of the Fifteenth Americas Conference on Information Systems*, San Francisco, CA.

Daniel, D. (2007, June 22). *How CIOs can introduce Web 2.0 technologies into the enterprise.* Retrieved September 28, 2009, from http://www.cio.com/article/print/120850

Denison, D. R. (1996). What is the difference between organizational culture and organizational climate? A native's point of view on a decade of paradigm wars. *Academy of Management Review, 21*(3), 619–654.

Eccleston, D., & Griseri, L. (2008, March 18). *How does Web 2.0 stretch traditional influencing patterns.* Paper presented at the Market Research Society Annual Conference.

Hibbard, C. (2010). How IBM uses social media to spur employee innovation. *Social Media Examiner.* Retrieved November 5, 2010, from http://www.socialmediaexaminer.com/how-ibm-uses-social-media-to-spur-employee-innovation

IEEE. (2009). *IEEE and north Jersey section going Web 2.0, Facebook & LinkedIn.* Fort Lee, NJ: The IEEE Newsletter.

Kim, P. (2009). *Social media predictions.* Retrieved September 27, 2009, from http://www.beingpeterkim.com/2008/12/social-media-2009.html

Klemperer, P. (2006). Net effects and switching costs: Two short essays for the New Palgrave. *Social Science Research Network.* Retrieved September 25, 2009, from http://papers.ssrn.com/sol3/papers.cfm?abstract_id=907502

Kundisch, D., & Zorzi, R. (2009, August 6-9). Enhancing the quality of financial advice with Web 2.0 – An approach considering social capital in the private asset allocation. In *Proceedings of the Fifteenth Americas Conference on Information Systems*, San Francisco, CA.

Lamont, A. (2010). *Personal conversations with Alf Lamont, director of marketing and development.* Hollywood, CA: The Comedy Store.

Melville, N., Kraemer, K., & Gurbaxani, V. (2004). Review: Information technology and organizational performance: An integrative model of IT business value. *Management Information Systems Quarterly, 28*(2), 283–322.

Miles, M. B., & Huberman, A. M. (1994). *Qualitative data analysis: A sourcebook of new methods* (2nd ed., pp. 28–29). Newbury Park, CA: Sage.

Mrkwicka, K., Kiebling, M., & Kolbe, L. M. (2009, August 6-9). Potential of Web 2.0 applications for viewer retention: The case of viewer relationship management in German TV stations. In *Proceedings of the Fifteenth Americas Conference on Information Systems*, San Francisco, CA.

Nanacherla, A. (2009). Social networking's net worth. *Training & Development*, 18–19.

O'Reilly, T. (2005). *What is Web 2.0: Design patterns and business models for the next generation software.* Retrieved September 26, 2009, from http://oreilly.com/pub/a/oreilly/tim/news/2005/09/30/what-is-web-20.html

Preston, R. (2009, August 15). Down to business: Just what the IT industry needs – More regulation. *InformationWeek.* Retrieved September 26, 2009, from http://www.informationweek.com/story/showArticle/jhtml?articleID=219300149

Tan, W., Nguyen, T. T. D., Oo Tha, K. K., & Yu, X. (2009, August 6-9). Designing groupware that fosters social capital creation: Can Facebook support global virtual teams? In *Proceedings of the Fifteenth Americas Conference on Information Systems*, San Francisco, CA.

Teich, A. G. (2008). Using company blogs to win over decision-makers. *Publishing Research Quarterly*, *24*, 261–266. doi:10.1007/s12109-008-9090-y.

Vignette. (2009). *Extranet 2.0: Driving value and revenue through social media*. Retrieved from http://www.vignette.com/dafiles/docs/Downloads/WP-Extranet-2.0.pdf

Wang, J., & Gallivan, M. (2009, August 6-9). An empirical study on the adoption of instant messaging for work purposes. In *Proceedings of the Fifteenth Americas Conference on Information Systems*, San Francisco, CA.

Ward, T. (2009). *Intranet 2.0: Social media becomes mainstream on the corporate Intranet. Summary of the Intranet 2.0 Global Survey*. Toronto, ON, Canada: Prescient Digital Media.

Woodruff, S. (2009, February 19). A handful of training tools. *Impactiviti Blog*. Retrieved August 31, 2009, from http://impactiviti.wordpress.com/2009/02/19/a-handful-of-training

This work was previously published in the International Journal of Virtual Communities and Social Networking, Volume 3, Issue 1, edited by Subhasish Dasgupta, pp. 32-42, copyright 2011 by IGI Publishing (an imprint of IGI Global).

Chapter 5

Understanding Users' Continuance of Facebook:
An Integrated Model with the Unified Theory of Acceptance and Use of Technology, Expectation Disconfirmation Model, and Flow Theory

Chia-Lin Hsu
National Taiwan University of Science and Technology, Taiwan

Cou-Chen Wu
National Taiwan University of Science and Technology, Taiwan

ABSTRACT

The purpose of this study is to develop an integrated model designed to examine users' continuance of Facebook based on the unified theory of acceptance and use of technology (UTAUT), the expectation disconfirmation model (EDM), and flow theory. Empirical data collected from 482 users who have experience with Facebook are subjected to structural equation modeling based on the proposed research model. Results show that users' continuance intention of Facebook is determined by social influence, performance expectancy, effort expectancy, flow experience, and satisfaction. Satisfaction is significantly affected by flow experience and disconfirmation. Results also suggest that effort expectancy is positively related to flow experience. Based on the findings, managerial implications are discussed in this paper and directions for future research are also highlighted.

DOI: 10.4018/978-1-4666-4022-1.ch005

BACKGROUND

Social networking websites are a type of online application that has grown rapidly in prevalence and popularity over the last few years (Pempek, Yermolayeva, & Calvert, 2009). Social networking websites, such as Facebook, are a member-based Internet communities which allow participants to post profile information, such as usernames and photographs, and to interact with others in innovative ways, such as sending public or private online messages or sharing photos online (Pempek et al., 2009). Moreover, Facebook members may use the site to contact people they already know offline or to meet new people (Ellison, Steinfield, & Lampe, 2007). Facebook members can also join virtual groups based on common interests, learn each others' hobbies, interests, and musical preference, and check romantic relationship statuses through these profiles (Ellison et al., 2007). In addition, Facebook also offers many online games, such as Happy Farm, Restaurant City, Pet Society, Cafe World, and Mystical Fishbowl and so on. The rich entertainment functions provided by Facebook have resulted in heavy user immersion, and especially because its services are mostly free, it makes them affordable and attractive.

Facebook is estimated to have more than 500 million users (Facebook, 2011). As a convenient tool for Internet communication, Facebook has become an essential part of Internet users' lives. A number of previous studies have examined patterns of college students' use of Facebook. Such research has focused on different academic interests, including the characteristics of profile elements (Park, Kee, & Valenzuela, 2009; Raacke & Bonds-Raacke, 2008), identity presentation (Stutzman, 2006), surveillance and privacy concerns (Gross & Acquisti, 2005; Peluchette & Karl, 2008), social capital (Ellison et al., 2007) and social grooming (Tufekci, 2008), social well-being (Valkenburg, Peter, & Schouten, 2006), relationship marketing strategies for the Facebook generation (Meadows-Klue, 2008), and students' perceptions of instructor self-disclosure via Facebook (Mazer, Murphy, &

Simonds, 2007). While some studies (e.g., Gross & Acquisti, 2005) have indicated negative outcomes of Facebook use, such as stalking and identity theft, others (e.g., Donath & Boyd, 2004; Ellison et al., 2007; Wellman, Haase, Witte, & Hampton, 2001) have shown how Facebook can generate positive social outcomes, such as enhanced social capital and collaboration.

Much of the current researches on Facebook have primarily focused on connecting and reconnecting people, as well as addressing privacy and self-disclosure concerns. Relatively little attention has been paid to elucidating the factors that lead to users' motives for continuance of Facebook use. Accordingly, this study used an integrated model with the unified theory of acceptance and use of technology (UTAUT), the expectation disconfirmation model (EDM), and the flow theory, in an attempt to answer the question posed previously.

RESEARCH PURPOSE AND APPROACH

We combine three theoretical perspectives for the following reasons. Firstly, UTAUT has been proposed as an extension of technology acceptance model with many studies showing the validity of this framework in explaining acceptance of technology (Shin, 2009). In an empirical study, conducted by Venkatesh, Morris, Davis, and Davis (2003), the UTAUT has been found to explain 70% of variance in user's acceptance and use of information systems. The UTAUT holds that three key constructs (social influence, performance expectancy, and effort expectancy) are direct determinants of usage intention (Venkatesh et al., 2003). Accordingly, the three UTAUT constructs are used to explain users' continuance intention of Facebook. Secondly, the expectancy disconfirmation model (Oliver, 1977, 1980) theorized how deviation from expectation affects satisfaction (Tse, 2003). Consumers appraise a service or a product by comparing their service experience or product use with an expectation (Kucukarslan &

Nadkarni, 2008). This gap between expectation and real service or product experience determines consumer satisfaction, which in turn influences acceptance and usage behavior. Finally, the flow theory allows the measurement of the elements of pleasure and entertainment motivating users' continuance of Facebook (Koufaris, 2002). Flow theory has been used to describe a state in which "people are so involved in an activity that nothing else seems to matter" (Csikszentmihalyi, 1977). For instance, when users play online games, they are often in a state of flow. Other events occurring in users' surrounding environment lose significance and their sense of time becomes distorted (Novak, Hoffman, & Yung, 2000). Facebook users are also said to experience such a state when they satisfy their intrinsic motivations, such as enjoyment through immersion in Facebook. Convenient opportunities for interaction and rich entertainment have made many users, particularly the younger generation, immersed in the use of Facebook. Thus, flow theory was also incorporated to examine users' continuance intention of Facebook.

In summary, the purposes of this study are to prove that Facebook users are interested in both extrinsic and intrinsic motivation and better illustrate users' continuance intention of Facebook, in order to improve the development of social networking websites. Secondly, the empirical results of this study can be adopted by social networking service providers to identify directions for the improvement of their services by recognizing the important factors affecting users' continuance intention.

RESEACH MODEL AND HYPOTHESE

The current literature provides a rich basis with which to construct a research model. Figure 1 depicts the research model which will be used. The specific components of the model and related hypotheses are discussed in more detail.

Figure 1. Research model and hypotheses

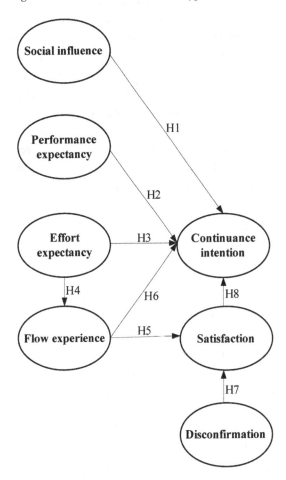

Hypotheses Regarding the UTAUT

Social influence is the degree to which online users perceive that importance of others believing that they should use Facebook (Venkatesh et al., 2003). Social influence represents a certain perceived pressure to perform a behavior, and reflects the extent to which individuals of a social network influence one another's intention of using Facebook (Venkatesh et al., 2003). The strength of social influence is positively associated with behavioral intention, since an individual's usage behavior is affected by their friends or relatives, through affiliating themselves with a similar networking system. Specifically, people are usually uncomfortable with uncertainty and will, consequently, tend to interact with a social network to consult on their adoption decisions by informational and normative social influences (Burkhardt & Brass, 1990; Katz & Tushman, 1979). Previous studies found that social influence can determine individuals' behaviors (Lin & Anol, 2008; Venkatesh & Morris, 2000; Wei, Marthandan, Chong, & Ooi, 2009). Lu, Yao, and Yu (2005) indicated that social influences may also help to form an individual's estimation of his or her confidence in, or ability to use, a system well, and that confirmed social influence has a direct positive impact on intention to adopt wireless Internet services via mobile technology. The hypothesis is thus derived as follows:

H1: Social influence is positively associated with the continuance intention of Facebook.

Performance expectancy is the expected degree to which an individual believes that using the system will help them gain something in real life (Venkatesh et al., 2003). The continuance intention of Facebook for an individual is likely to be driven by high levels of their performance expectancy, which provides substantial extrinsic motivation. Ajzen and Fishbein (1980), as well as Bhattacherjee (2001), indicated that a person who believes that performing a given behavior will lead to mostly positive outcomes will hold a favorable feeling towards performing the behavior. Specifically, an individual is more likely to form favorable feelings when website usage is perceived to be efficient. Moreover, Al-Gahtani, Hubona, and Wang (2007) confirmed that performance expectancy significantly affects the behavioral intention to use computers. Lin and Anol (2008) showed that performance expectancy is positively associated with users' intention to use network information technology. The hypothesis is thus proposed as follows:

H2: Performance expectancy is positively associated with the continuance intention of Facebook.

Effort expectancy is the expected degree of ease associated with using Facebook by individual users (Venkatesh et al., 2003). Intention of using Facebook may be promoted initially when they perceive that less effort is required. Research on effort expectancy has showed that it is positively associated with behavioral intention (Al-Gahtani et al., 2007; Lin & Anol, 2008). More specifically, having an easy to use interface for a website played a crucial role in improving behavioral intention. The hypothesis is thus proposed as follows:

H3: Effort expectancy is positively associated with the continuance intention of Facebook.

Hypotheses Regarding Flow

Flow has been described as a state of optimal psychological experience (Novak et al., 2000), resulting from engagement in a variety of activities, such as hobbies, writing, work and web use. Csikszentmihalyi (1977) suggested that flow experience is a state where the person's perceived skills matched the perceived challenges of an activity. Specifically, the occurrence of flow experience in a given situation requires a balance between a high level of challenge perceived by an individual and the high level of skill the individual brings to that situation. When flow experience occurs, an individual becomes entirely focused on their activity and experiences many positive characteristics, including great enjoyment (Jackson & Marsh, 1996). Accordingly, flow experience has been viewed as a crucial determinant of online customers' subjective enjoyment of website use (Koufaris, 2002; Lu, Zhou, & Wang, 2009; Wu & Chang, 2005). Trevino and Webster (1992) and Hsu and Lu (2004) have found that effortless usage towards information technology would contribute to and positively lead to flow experience. Therefore, the easy-to-use interface of a website plays an important role in forming flow experience. The hypothesis is thus derived as follows:

H4: Effort expectancy is positively associated with flow experience.

In an online context, researchers have theorized that such positive flow experiences can attract consumers, mitigate price sensitivity, and positively influence subsequent attitudes and behaviors (Novak et al., 2000). Specifically, researchers have shown that a compelling flow experience is positively related to consumer attitudes toward the focal website and the focal firm (Mathwick & Rigdon, 2004) and with the intention to revisit and spend more time at the website (Kabadayi & Gupta, 2005). Webster, Trevino, and Ryan (1993) found that flow experience is associated with exploratory behavior and positive subjective experience, while a positive correlation was also found between flow experience and satisfaction (Shin, 2006). O'Cass and Carlson (2010) confirmed that flow experience will increase positive consumer perceptions towards the website and lead directly to consumer satisfaction. In addition, Rettie (2001) indicated that flow experience appears to prolong Internet and website usage. Hsu and Lu (2004) showed that flow experience is positively related to the intention to play online games. Cyr, Bonanni, Bowes, and Ilsever (2005) found that customers who experience flow while shopping online will be likely to return to the site or purchase from it in the future. Consequently, based on the preceding discussion, the hypotheses are constructed as follows:

H5: Flow experience is positively associated with satisfaction.
H6: Flow experience is positively associated with the continuance intention of Facebook.

Hypotheses Regarding EDM

According to EDM (Oliver, 1980), satisfaction has been conceptualized as a performance and post-choice process. Satisfaction is the most direct motivator that determines an individual's continu-

ing intention to use information technology (Liao, Palvia, & Chen, 2009). Satisfaction is assumed to be a direct function of disconfirmation, defined as the difference between a user's perceived performance and pre-adoption expectations (Churchill & Suprenant, 1982; Oliver, 1980). The polarity of disconfirmation is positive when perceived performance is higher than pre-adoption expectations, namely, that the user is satisfied. In contrast, disconfirmation is negative when perceived performance falls short of expectations, namely, that the user is dissatisfied (Liao et al., 2009).

The relationship between disconfirmation and satisfaction has become a key point in the area of consumer research and has been examined in many empirical studies (Liao, Chen, & Yen, 2007; Liao et al., 2009; Oliver, 1997). Specifically, studies have found that disconfirmation has a strong and positive impact on satisfaction, which in turn affects continuance intention (Liao et al., 2007, 2009; Szymanski & Henard, 2001). The hypotheses are thus constructed as follows:

H7: Disconfirmation is positively associated with satisfaction.
H8: Satisfaction is positively associated with the continuance intention of Facebook.

METHODOLOGY

This study applied LISREL 8.54 to test the hypothesized relationships in the research model and used SPSS 12.0 to analyze the data, which includes generating descriptive statistics, and testing reliability and validity.

SAMPLE AND DATA COLLECTION

This study selected respondents with prior experience with Facebook in Taiwan as subjects to examine the hypothesized relationships in the proposed model. Statistics show in the Facebook's official website (Facebook, 2010), the global number of Facebook users exceeded 500 million. Among them, 1.39% (over 7 million) users have used Facebook in Taiwan, which accounts for more than 30% of the total population of Taiwan. The rapid growth of Taiwanese users provided further impetus for using them as the subjects in this study.

Although snowball sampling does not lead to representativeness, there are times when it may be the best method available. Using a snowball sampling technique, we distributed the survey questionnaires to friends, relatives, and colleagues who met the criteria of having at least one years experience with Facebook. Likewise, this group in turn distributed the questionnaires in the same manner to their friends, relatives, and colleagues, thus "snowballing" to obtain sufficient participants. In terms of data collection, all questionnaires were distributed to the respondents in person, via an interviewer. Before beginning the study, three postgraduate students were trained as interviewers, each able to thoroughly answer any questions from the respondents. Respondents who participated in the study and completed the questionnaire were offered a small gift (a ballpoint pen) as a token of gratitude. A total of 516 responses were received and after the removal of incomplete and duplicate responses, a total of 482 usable responses were included in the sample for analysis. A profile of the respondents is shown in Table 1.

Measurement Development

Measurement items in the questionnaire covered the constructs in the research model and were derived from existing literatures (Table 5 in the Appendix). Disconfirmation (3 questions), satisfaction (4 questions), and continuance intention items (3 questions) were adapted from Bhattacherjee (2001). Social influence, performance expectancy, and effort expectancy items (4 questions each) were adapted from Venkatesh et al. (2003). Flow experience was assessed us-

Table 1. Profile of the respondents

Gender	Frequency	Percentage (%)
Male	215	44.6
Female	267	55.4
Age		
<18	50	10.4
18–24	145	30.1
25–30	124	25.7
31–35	98	20.3
36–40	34	7.1
>40	31	6.4
Education Level		
High school or below	104	21.6
College	206	42.7
Graduate school or above	172	35.7
Occupation		
Public servant	95	19.7
Manufacturing	116	24.1
Business	102	21.2
Professional	17	3.5
Unemployed (e.g., student, retired, housewife)	152	31.5
Marital status		
Married	206	42.7
Single	276	57.3

ing scale items adapted from Novak, Hoffman, and Duhachek (2003). Each item was measured on a seven-point Likert scale (i.e., 1 = disagree strongly; 7 = agree strongly).

Before conducting the chief survey, we completed a pre-test to validate the instrument. The pre-test involved 30 respondents who have more than one year experience using Facebook. Respondents were asked to comment on the length of the instrument, the format, and the wording of the scales, as consistent with Lee (2009). Consequently, the instrument has substantiated content validity.

RESULTS AND DISCUSSION

Reliability and Validity Analysis

To analyze the internal consistency of the constructs, the Cronbach's α was calculated and tested its reliability. As shown in the Appendix, reliability coefficients exceeded the 0.7 cut-off value as recommended by Nunnally (1978). Therefore, all constructs in this study demonstrated acceptable reliability. Furthermore, the convergent validity of the measurements were evaluated with three measures proposed by Fornell and Larcker (1981) being the item reliability of each measure, the composite reliability of each construct, and the average variance extracted for each construct (Table 2). The item reliability of a measure was evaluated through its factor loading with the underlying construct (Shih, 2004). The results reveal that the factor loadings for all measures exceeded 0.5 on their underlying constructs, providing evidence of item reliability (Hair, Anderson, Tatham, & Black, 1995). Furthermore, the results show that the composite reliabilities of all constructs were between 0.83 and 0.90, thus providing evidence for composite reliability (Fornell & Larcker, 1981). In addition, the average variance extracted from each of the constructs exceeded 0.5, demonstrating convergent validity (Fornell & Larcker, 1981). Overall, the test of convergent validity indicated that the proposed constructs in the extended model were adequate.

If all the items within a construct correlate more highly with each other than with items measuring other constructs, these measures are regarded as possessing discriminant validity. Table 3 displays the squared intercorrelations among the study variables, indicating that the shared variance among the variables does not surpass the average variance explained. Hence, there is evidence of discriminant validity in this study.

Table 2. Reliability and factor loadings

	Factor Loading	Composite Reliability	Average Variance Extracted (AVE)
Social Influence (SI)		.87	.62
SI1	.78		
SI2	.79		
SI3	.80		
SI4	.78		
Performance Expectancy (PE)		.86	.60
PE1	.68		
PE2	.84		
PE3	.83		
PE4	.74		
Effort Expectancy (EE)		.85	.57
EE1	.75		
EE2	.73		
EE3	.83		
EE4	.76		
Flow experience (FE)		.86	.67
FE1	.81		
FE2	.87		
FE3	.78		
Disconfirmation (DIS)		.90	.74
DIS1	.92		
DIS2	.73		
DIS3	.92		
Satisfaction (SAT)		.83	.55
SAT1	.75		
SAT2	.78		
SAT3	.69		
SAT4	.75		
Continuance intention (CI)		.88	.72
CI1	.82		
CI2	.86		
CI3	.86		

Table 3. Squared intercorrelation among the study constructs

		1	2	3	4	5	6	7
1	Social influence	.79						
2	Performance expectancy	.10	.77					
3	Effort expectancy	.04	.01	.75				
4	Flow experience	.01	.00	.01	.82			
5	Disconfirmation	.03	.01	.04	.06	.86		
6	Satisfaction	.04	.01	.09	.06	.11	.74	
7	Continuance intention	.16	.04	.06	.05	.04	.09	.85

Notes: All correlations are significant at the 0.05 level. The diagonals represent the square root of average variance extracted.

Structural Model

Using structural equation modeling, the hypothesized relationships in the proposed research model were tested and analyzed. As seen in Table 4, the results showed that the χ^2 value of 686.99 (d.f. = 261) with a p-value of .001 indicated a good model fit. In addition, fit indices such as the Normalized Fit Index (NFI = 0.91), Non-Normed Fit Index (NNFI = 0.93), Comparative Fit Index (CFI = 0.94) and Incremental Fit Index (IFI = 0.94) all exceeded the suggested level of 0.9, indicating a good model fit. Furthermore, Hair, Anderson, Tatham, & Black (1998) suggested that if the Root Mean Square Error of Approximation (RMSEA = 0.058) is less than 0.08, this represents a reasonable error of approximation. The Root Mean Square Residual (RMR) in this study was equal to 0.067, which is below 0.08;

hence, it is regarded as evidence of good fit (Hair, Black, Babin, Anderson, & Tatham, 2006). In summary, the overall results suggested that the research model offered an adequate fit to the data.

Hypotheses Testing

We next examined the estimated coefficients of the causal relationships between constructs that validated the hypothesized effects. Figure 2 illustrates the estimated coefficients and their significance in the structural model. As seen in Figure 2, all of the hypotheses proposed in the research model were fully supported. Specifically, social influence, performance expectancy, and effort expectancy positively predicted continuance intention of Facebook ($\beta = 0.35$, $p < 0.001$; $\beta = 0.13$, $p < 0.05$; $\beta = 0.12$, $p < 0.05$), supporting H1, H2, and H3. The effect of effort expectancy

Table 4. Fit indices for structural model

Fit indices	Recommended value	Results
Chi-square/degrees freedom (χ^2/df)	<5.00 (Hair et al., 1998)	2.63
Root Mean Square Error of Approximation (RMSEA)	<0.08 (Hair et al., 1998)	0.058
Root Mean Square Residual (RMR)	<0.08 (Hair et al., 2006)	0.067
Normed fit index (NFI)	>0.90 (Hu & Bentler, 1999)	0.91
Non-Normed Fit Index (NNFI)	>0.90(Hair et al., 1998)	0.93
Comparative Fit Index (CFI)	>0.90 (Hu & Bentler, 1999)	0.94
Incremental Fit Index (IFI)	>0.90 (Hu & Bentler, 1999)	0.94

Figure 2. Results of structural modeling analysis

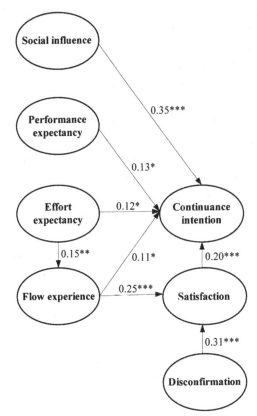

Notes: ***(*p*<0.001); **(*p*<0.01); *(*p*<0.05).
χ^2: 686.99; df: 261; GFI: 0.90; CFI: 0.94; NFI: 0.91;
NNFI: 0.93; IFI: 0.94; RMSEA: 0.058; RMR: 0.067.

on flow experience was significant ($\beta = 0.15$, $p < 0.01$), supporting H4. The hypothesized paths from flow experience were significant in predicting satisfaction and continuance intention of Facebook ($\beta = 0.25$, $p < 0.001$; $\beta = 0.11$, $p < 0.05$), supporting H5 and H6. Disconfirmation positively influenced satisfaction ($\beta = 0.31$, $p < 0.001$), supporting H7. The hypothesized paths from satisfaction were significant in predicting continuance intention of Facebook ($\beta = 0.20$, $p < 0.001$), supporting H8.

The tests of the structural model demonstrated that flow experience was a crucial factor influencing satisfaction and continuance intention of Facebook. Effort expectancy exhibited significant positive effects on flow experience. The

results also demonstrated that satisfaction and all three UTAUT constructs (social influence, performance expectancy, and effort expectancy) had significant impact on continuance intention of Facebook. Satisfaction is determined by flow experience and disconfirmation.

DISCUSSION

Facebook is one of the most popular social networking websites among Internet users as it enables people to connect and share with the people in their life. With the rapid growth in Facebook users in Taiwan, this raises interest in investigating what factors determine users' continuance intention of Facebook. Especially, the managers of social networking websites are eager to understand what factors determine users' continuance intention. In this research, we found that, apart from the three components of UTAUT (social influence, performance expectancy, and effort expectancy), flow experience and satisfaction were also important for Facebook users.

The results explain that Facebook users want to have flow experience and thus Facebook provider should endeavor to create compelling online experiences for users to induce their continuance intention. Consequently, Facebook provider has to pay close attention to how they design or 'engineer' controllable elements of the website for users to facilitate flow. That is, focus needs to be placed on improving attributes of the website (such as content, navigation, and responsiveness), which are considered important by users to cause flow experience. Thus, collecting such insights from the user provides information that helps managers in their allocation of resources and deployment of marketing capabilities over social networks to deliver flow experiences for users that facilitate favorable user behavior outcomes.

In addition, the factors that affect satisfaction are different and have to be focused by management in order to ensure information system success. Accordingly, system design and training programs need to highlight different components in order to improve satisfaction. Also, the relative importance of the central construct varies by user experience. Clearly, user experience is another factor in designing or redesigning information products. More specifically, understanding users' real needs and designing a featured system that fits the users' expectations are critical success factors in the initial stage of information system implementation. In order to make sure that the users do not have unrealistic expectations, executives and trainers need to devotedly communicate the system's actual capacities and limitations.

Social influence is another important predictor of intention to use Facebook. The result illustrates that users' continuance intention is determined by peers' opinions. Namely, when users find that people around them have adopted Facebook, they will be more eager to use it. In contrast, if influential peers have negative word of mouth (e.g., encountering criticism about security, accessibility, reliability, or party problems) to Facebook, then user perceived trust will be moderated through social influence, and found that social influence plays a facilitating role towards intention, by influencing the path from perceived security to intention. Without the prerequisite of social influence, users will have a low intention to use Facebook.

In addition to providing a platform that is efficient to fulfill user's performance expectation, the easy-to-use Facebook interface also played an important role in determining behavioral intention and in forming flow experience. If difficulties of use cannot be overcome, then the user may not experience flow; he or she may then abandon the Facebook use.

CONCLUSION AND IMPLICATION

As for the contributions of this research, we explored users' continuance intention of Facebook, where Internet usage is under fast development but where researchers have paid little attention to this phenomenon. Secondly, this study constructed a delicate research model for explaining users' continuance intention of Facebook by integrating UTAUT, EDM, and flow theory. Specifically, our results confirmed that users' continuance intention of Facebook is due not only to extrinsic motivation (social influence, performance expectancy, and effort expectancy), but also to intrinsic motivation (flow experience and user satisfaction). Moreover, effort expectancy showed significant positive effects on flow experience. Additionally, user satisfaction is mainly determined by flow experience and disconfirmation.

For researchers, this study proved that Facebook users are interested in both extrinsic and intrinsic motivation. Not only did they expect an efficient and easy-to-use Facebook platform, they also expected to have fun and enjoy a flow experience. Additionally, flow as a comprehensive concept deserves more research attention in the context of social networking websites and e-commerce.

For practitioners, the research offers several guidelines in improving services to draw and retain more users. Firstly, this study demonstrated that social influence, performance expectancy, and effort expectancy significantly affect users' continuance intention of Facebook. Specifically, when users actually perceive that important others believed that they should use Facebook, or perceive Facebook as a useful and effortless tool, this will encourage their continuance intention of Facebook. Thus, in addition to providing user sharing and communication effectiveness and efficiency, social networking service providers can improve their interface design and provide a clear and easy-to-use platform to users. Furthermore, in addition to using opinion leaders and even their own users to garner new users via their own networks, Lin and Anol (2008) indicated, word of mouth broadcasted through the social affiliation or influence may affect users' continuance intention of Facebook greatly.

Secondly, this study also showed that user satisfaction significantly influence continuance intention of Facebook. This implies that social networking service providers should endeavor to fulfill user satisfaction in facilitating continuance intention of Facebook. On the other hand, in order to get user satisfaction, social networking service providers should endeavor to satisfy users' expectations. Specifically, social networking service providers should make every effort to improve services and functions to satisfy user demands to the greatest extent possible. When users' real service or product experience is better than their expectations, they are positively disconfirmed and thus very satisfied.

Finally, notably, this study verified the effect of effort expectancy on flow experience. When users perceive using a system as effortless, flow experience will be encouraged. When users enter into a state of flow, both satisfaction and continuance intention will increase. Accordingly, the social networking service providers should endeavor to create an easy-to-use platform with which to facilitate flow experience. Furthermore, in addition to focusing on improving interactivity, content, navigation, and responsiveness of social network website, the social networking service providers could add rich entertainment functions to their sites, thus leading to more enjoyment by the user. This will also lead to flow experience by the users and in turn influence their satisfaction and continuance intention.

LIMITATIONS AND DIRECTIONS FOR FUTURE RESEARCH

While our findings offer meaningful implications for academic researchers and practitioners, this study has displayed some limitations. Firstly, this study focused on a particular social networking website–Facebook. Thus, future research should attempt to apply the findings to other contexts in order to broaden our scope. Secondly, this study takes Taiwanese users as the subjects, and thus the results of this study may not fully represent the results of other countries. Future research can look at whether the findings of this study hold in different countries. Finally, since this study was administered with a snapshot research approach, future research could collect data through a longitudinal study in order to track user continuance intention in terms of improvement in the factors influencing continuance intention of Facebook.

REFERENCES

Ajzen, I., & Fishbein, M. (1980). *Understanding Attitudes and Predicting Social Behavior*. Upper Saddle River, NJ: Prentice Hall.

Al-Gahtani, S. S., Hubona, G. S., & Wang, J. (2007). Information technology (IT) in Saudi Arabia: culture and the acceptance and use of IT. *Information & Management, 44*(8), 681–691. doi:10.1016/j.im.2007.09.002.

Bhattacherjee, A. (2001). Understanding information systems continuance: an expectation-confirmation model. *Management Information Systems Quarterly, 25*(3), 351–370. doi:10.2307/3250921.

Burkhardt, M. E., & Brass, D. J. (1990). Changing patterns or patterns of change: the effects of a change in technology on social network structure and power. *Administrative Science Quarterly, 35*(1), 104–127. doi:10.2307/2393552.

Churchill, G. A., & Suprenant, C. (1982). An investigation into the determinants of customer satisfaction. *JMR, Journal of Marketing Research, 19*(4), 491–504. doi:10.2307/3151722.

Csikszentmihalyi, M. (1977). *Beyond Boredom and Anxiety*. San Francisco, CA: Jossey-Bass.

Cyr, D., Bonanni, C., Bowes, J., & Ilsever, J. (2005). Beyond trust: web site design preferences across cultures. *Journal of Global Information Management, 13*(4), 25–54. doi:10.4018/jgim.2005100102.

Donath, J., & Boyd, D. (2004). Public displays of connection. *BT Technology Journal*, *22*(4), 71–82. doi:10.1023/B:BTTJ.0000047585.06264.cc.

Ellison, N. B., Steinfield, C., & Lampe, C. (2007). The benefits of Facebook "friends:" social capital and college students' use of online social network sites. *Journal of Computer-Mediated Communication*, *12*(4), 1143–1168. doi:10.1111/j.1083-6101.2007.00367.x.

Facebook. (2010). *Statistics*. Retrieved from http://www.facebook.com/press/info.php?statistics

Fornell, C., & Larcker, D. F. (1981). Evaluating structural equation models with unobservable variables and measurement error. *JMR, Journal of Marketing Research*, *18*(1), 39–50. doi:10.2307/3151312.

Gross, R., & Acquisti, A. (2005). Information revelation and privacy in online social networks. In *Proceedings of the ACM Twelfth Annual Workshop on Privacy* (pp. 71-80).

Hair, J. F., Anderson, R. E., Tatham, R. L., & Black, W. C. (1995). *Multivariate Data Analysis with Readings* (4th ed.). Upper Saddle River, NJ: Prentice Hall.

Hair, J. F., Anderson, R. E., Tatham, R. L., & Black, W. C. (1998). *Multivariate Data Analysis*. Upper Saddle River, NJ: Prentice Hall.

Hair, J. F., Black, W. C., Babin, B. J., Anderson, R. E., & Tatham, R. L. (2006). *Multivariate Data Analysis*. Upper Saddle River, NJ: Prentice Hall.

Hsu, C. L., & Lu, H. P. (2004). Why do people play on-line games? An extended TAM with social influences and flow experience. *Information & Management*, *41*(7), 853–868. doi:10.1016/j.im.2003.08.014.

Hu, L., & Bentler, P. M. (1999). Cutoff criteria for fit indexes in covariance structure analysis: conventional criteria versus new alternatives. *Structural Equation Modeling*, *6*(1), 1–55. doi:10.1080/10705519909540118.

Jackson, S. A., & Marsh, H. W. (1996). Development and validation of a scale to measure optimal experience: the flow state scale. *Journal of Sport & Exercise Psychology*, *18*(1), 17–35.

Kabadayi, S., & Gupta, R. (2005). Website loyalty: an empirical investigation of its antecedents. *International Journal of Internet Marketing and Advertising*, *2*(4), 321–345. doi:10.1504/IJIMA.2005.008105.

Katz, R., & Tushman, M. (1979). Communication patterns, project performance, and task characteristics: an empirical evaluation and integration in an R&D setting. *Organizational Behavior and Human Performance*, *23*(2), 139–162. doi:10.1016/0030-5073(79)90053-9.

Koufaris, M. (2002). Applying the technology acceptance model and flow theory to online consumer behavior. *Information Systems Research*, *13*(2), 205–223. doi:10.1287/isre.13.2.205.83.

Kucukarslan, S. N., & Nadkarni, A. (2008). Evaluating medication-related services in a hospital setting using the disconfirmation of expectations model of satisfaction. *Research in Social & Administrative Pharmacy*, *4*(1), 12–22. doi:10.1016/j.sapharm.2007.01.001 PMID:18342819.

Liao, C., Chen, J. L., & Yen, D. C. (2007). Theory of planning behavior (TPB) and customer satisfaction in the continued use of e-service: an integrated model. *Computers in Human Behavior*, *23*(6), 2804–2822. doi:10.1016/j.chb.2006.05.006.

Liao, C., Palvia, P., & Chen, J. L. (2009). Information technology adoption behavior life cycle: toward a technology continuance theory (TCT). *International Journal of Information Management*, *29*(4), 309–320. doi:10.1016/j.ijinfomgt.2009.03.004.

Lin, C. P., & Anol, B. (2008). Learning online social support: an investigation of network information technology based on UTAUT. *Cyberpsychology & Behavior*, *11*(3), 268–272. doi:10.1089/cpb.2007.0057 PMID:18537495.

Lu, J., Yao, J. E., & Yu, C. S. (2005). Personal innovativeness, social influences and adoption of wireless Internet services via mobile technology. *The Journal of Strategic Information Systems, 14*(3), 245–268. doi:10.1016/j.jsis.2005.07.003.

Lu, Y., Zhou, T., & Wang, B. (2009). Exploring Chinese users' acceptance of instant messaging using the theory of planned behavior, the technology acceptance model, and the flow theory. *Computers in Human Behavior, 25*(1), 29–39. doi:10.1016/j.chb.2008.06.002.

Mathwick, C., & Rigdon, E. (2004). Play, flow, and the online search experience. *The Journal of Consumer Research, 31*(2), 324–332. doi:10.1086/422111.

Mazer, J. P., Murphy, R. E., & Simonds, C. J. (2007). I'll see you on "Facebook": the effects of computer-mediated teacher self-disclosure on student motivation, affective learning, and classroom climate. *Communication Education, 56*(1), 1–17. doi:10.1080/03634520601009710.

Meadows-Klue, D. (2008). Falling in love 2.0: relationship marketing for the Facebook generation. *Journal of Direct Data and Digital Marketing Practice, 9*(3), 245–250. doi:10.1057/palgrave.dddmp.4350103.

Novak, T. P., Hoffman, D. L., & Duhachek, A. (2003). The influence of goal-directed and experiential activities in online flow experiences. *Journal of Consumer Psychology, 13*(1-2), 3–16. doi:10.1207/S15327663JCP13-1&2_01.

Novak, T. P., Hoffman, D. L., & Yung, Y. F. (2000). Measuring the customer experience in online environments: a structural modeling approach. *Marketing Science, 19*(1), 22–42. doi:10.1287/mksc.19.1.22.15184.

Nunnally, J. C. (1978). *Psychometric Theory.* New York, NY: McGraw-Hill.

O'Cass, A., & Carlson, J. (2010). Examining the effects of website-induced flow in professional sporting team websites. *Internet Research, 20*(2), 115–134. doi:10.1108/10662241011032209.

Oliver, R. L. (1977). Effects of expectation and disconfirmation on post-exposure product evaluation: an alternative interpretation. *The Journal of Applied Psychology, 62*(4), 480–486. doi:10.1037/0021-9010.62.4.480.

Oliver, R. L. (1980). A cognitive model of the antecedents and consequences of satisfaction decisions. *JMR, Journal of Marketing Research, 17*(4), 460–469. doi:10.2307/3150499.

Oliver, R. L. (1997). *Satisfaction: A Behavioral Perspective on the Consumer.* New York, NY: McGraw-Hill.

Park, N., Kee, K. F., & Valenzuela, S. (2009). Being immersed in social networking environment: Facebook groups, uses and gratifications, and social outcomes. *Cyberpsychology & Behavior, 12*(6), 729–733. doi:10.1089/cpb.2009.0003 PMID:19619037.

Peluchette, J., & Karl, K. (2008). Social networking profiles: an examination of student attitudes regarding use and appropriateness of content. *Cyberpsychology & Behavior, 11*(1), 95–97. doi:10.1089/cpb.2007.9927 PMID:18275320.

Pempek, T. A., Yermolayeva, Y. A., & Calvert, S. L. (2009). College students' social networking experiences on Facebook. *Journal of Applied Developmental Psychology, 30*(3), 227–238. doi:10.1016/j.appdev.2008.12.010.

Raacke, J., & Bonds-Raacke, J. (2008). MySpace and Facebook: applying the uses and gratifications theory to exploring friend networking sites. *Cyberpsychology & Behavior, 11*(2), 169–174. doi:10.1089/cpb.2007.0056 PMID:18422409.

Rettie, R. (2001). An exploration of flow during Internet use. *Internet Research*, *11*(2), 103–113. doi:10.1108/10662240110695070.

Shih, H. (2004). An empirical study on predicting user acceptance of e-shopping on the Web. *Information & Management*, *41*(3), 351–368. doi:10.1016/S0378-7206(03)00079-X.

Shin, D. H. (2009). Towards an understanding of the consumer acceptance of mobile wallet. *Computers in Human Behavior*, *25*(6), 1343–1354. doi:10.1016/j.chb.2009.06.001.

Shin, N. (2006). Online learner's 'flow' experience: an empirical study. *British Journal of Educational Technology*, *37*(5), 705–720. doi:10.1111/j.1467-8535.2006.00641.x.

Stutzman, F. (2006). An evaluation of identity-sharing behavior in social network communities. *Journal of the International Digital Media and Arts Association*, *3*(1), 10–18.

Szymanski, D. M., & Henard, D. H. (2001). Customer satisfaction: a meta-analysis of the empirical evidence. *Journal of the Academy of Marketing Science*, *29*(1), 16–35.

Trevino, L. K., & Webster, J. (1992). Flow in computer-mediated communication: electronic mail and voice mail evaluation and impacts. *Communication Research*, *19*(5), 539–573. doi:10.1177/009365092019005001.

Tse, A. C. (2003). Tipping behaviour: a disconfirmation of expectation perspective. *Hospital Management*, *22*(4), 461–467. doi:10.1016/j.ijhm.2003.07.002.

Tufekci, Z. (2008). Grooming, gossip, Facebook and Myspace. What can we learn about these sites from those who won't assimilate? *Information Communication and Society*, *11*(4), 544–564. doi:10.1080/13691180801999050.

Valkenburg, P. M., Peter, J., & Schouten, A. P. (2006). Friend networking sites and their relationship to adolescents' well-being and social self-esteem. *Cyberpsychology & Behavior*, *9*(5), 584–590. doi:10.1089/cpb.2006.9.584 PMID:17034326.

Venkatesh, V., & Morris, M. G. (2000). Why don't men ever stop to ask for directions? Gender, social influence, and their role in technology acceptance and usage behavior. *Management Information Systems Quarterly*, *24*(1), 115–139. doi:10.2307/3250981.

Venkatesh, V., Morris, M. G., Davis, G. B., & Davis, F. D. (2003). User acceptance of information technology: toward a unified view. *Management Information Systems Quarterly*, *27*(3), 425–478.

Webster, J., Trevino, L. K., & Ryan, L. (1993). The dimensionality and correlates of flow in human–computer interactions. *Computers in Human Behavior*, *9*(4), 411–426. doi:10.1016/0747-5632(93)90032-N.

Wei, T. T., Marthandan, G., Chong, A. Y. L., & Ooi, K. B. (2009). What drives Malaysian m-commerce adoption? An empirical analysis. *Industrial Management & Data Systems*, *109*(3), 370–388. doi:10.1108/02635570910939399.

Wellman, B., Haase, A. Q., Witte, J., & Hampton, K. (2001). Does the Internet increase, decrease, or supplement social capital? Social networks, participation, and community commitment. *The American Behavioral Scientist*, *45*(3), 436–455. doi:10.1177/00027640121957286.

Wu, J. J., & Chang, Y. S. (2005). Towards understanding members' interactivity, trust, and flow in online travel community. *Industrial Management & Data Systems*, *105*(7), 937–954. doi:10.1108/02635570510616120.

APPENDIX

Table 5. Measurement items

Social influence (SI) (adapted from Venkatesh et al., 2003) (reliability $\alpha = .84$) SI1. People who influence my behavior think that I should use Facebook. SI2. People who are important to me think that I should use Facebook. SI3. The senior management of this business has been helpful in the use of Facebook. SI4. In general, the organization has supported the use of Facebook.
Performance expectancy (PE) (adapted from Venkatesh et al., 2003) (reliability $\alpha = .78$) PE1. I would find Facebook useful in my life. PE2. Using Facebook enables me to more easily/quickly communicate with others. PE3. Using Facebook increases the efficiency of communication between others and myself. PE4. If I use Facebook, my ability to communicate conveniently with others will be increased.
Effort expectancy (EE) (adapted from Venkatesh et al., 2003) (reliability $\alpha = .79$) EE1. My interaction with Facebook would be understandable. EE2. It would be easy for me to become skillful at using Facebook. EE3. I would find Facebook easy to use. EE4. Learning to operate Facebook is easy for me.
Disconfirmation (DIS) (adapted from Bhattacherjee, 2001) (reliability $\alpha = .87$) DIS1. My experience with using Facebook was better than what I expected. DIS2. The service level provided by Facebook was better than what I expected. DIS3. Overall, most of my expectations from using Facebook were confirmed.
Satisfaction (SAT) (adapted from Bhattacherjee, 2001) (reliability $\alpha = .77$) SAT1. My overall experience of Facebook use was that I was very satisfied. SAT2. My overall experience of Facebook use was that I was very pleased. SAT3. My overall experience of Facebook use was that I was very contented. SAT4. My overall experience of Facebook use was that I was absolutely delighted.
Flow experience (FE) (adapted from Novak et al., 2003) (reliability $\alpha = .79$) FE1. When I was browsing this website (Facebook), I felt very captivated. FE2. When I was navigating this website (Facebook), time seemed to pass very quickly. FE3. When I was visiting this website (Facebook), nothing seemed to matter to me.
Continuance intention (CI) (adapted from Bhattacherjee, 2001) (reliability $\alpha = .86$) CI1. I intend to continue to use Facebook rather than discontinue its use. CI2. My intentions are to continue to use Facebook rather than other online social services. CI3. If I could, I would like to continue to use Facebook as much as possible.

Chapter 6
Evolution of Trust and Formation of Preference Clusters in Distributed Networked Structure

Purnendu Karmakar
Indian Institute of Technology Kharagpur, India

Rajarshi Roy
Indian Institute of Technology Kharagpur, India

ABSTRACT

Distributed network researchers are trying to address one important issue concerning networked structures and how the network came into existence, i.e., dynamics of network evolution. From the knowledge of social science it is observed that trust is one such metric that evolves with the network particularly where human interaction is involved. This work presents a "trust" model of the authors' studies and its various properties. In virtual (and "real") communities (chat rooms, blogs, etc.) behavioral segregation over time is observed. Differences in identities of interacting agents result in evolution of various degrees of "trust" (and "distrust") among them over a period of time. This process ultimately leads to emergence of self-segregation in behavioral kinetics and results in formation of preference clusters.

1. INTRODUCTION

Last decade has seen a tremendous growth in internet usage as well as emergence of numerous virtual communities and file sharing networks. These networks are generally distributed in nature. The distributed networked structures are human social network, P2P file sharing network, collaborative network, virtual community (http://www.orkut.com, http://www.paypal.com), and information source network in a search engine. An important characteristic of these systems is that nodes may

DOI: 10.4018/978-1-4666-4022-1.ch006

enter or leave the network anytime. The participation of large number of entities with conflicting interest in an open system requires a metric for faithful transaction. In real human social network under the same scenario one such metric is trust. Trust is a prevalent concept in human society that, in essence, concerns our reliance on the actions of other entities ("someone" or "something") within our environment. In human society, the fulfillment of even our most basic needs and desires depends on other people's actions. So, in human or human made network the notion of trust, reputation, co-operation will emerge particularly in the context of confrontation with strange and malicious behavior by the entities. In this work we use the words "entity", "node" and "agent" interchangeably.

2. MOTIVATIONS AND AIM

To study and to simulate behavioral kinetics of a virtual community we need a trust model. The trust model should be based on purely decentralized peer-to-peer architectures and algorithms. It should involve cooperative tasks or transactions, and model trust as a quantitative (e.g., monetary) unit, so as to combine trust estimates with transaction values. A similar design methodology was adopted by (Androutsellis-Theotokis et al., 2007). This allows design of algorithms for the estimation and propagation of trust estimates throughout the network and depicts the way trust is used in real life. Marsh in his thesis (Marsh, 1994) first formalized trust as a computational concept. In his dissertation he mentions that cooperation between individuals ultimately leads to the formation of groups (Marsh, 1994). In 2004 US Presidential election blogs played an important role. We intend to emulate that phenomenon in the form chat room dynamics and test a model that couples our trust model with a learning automata (Narendra & Thathachar, 1989; Thathachar & Sastry, 2004) type algorithm. The numerical computations show that the behavioral difference among agents of two different types ultimately leads to self-segregation of chat room preferences among agents. A similar notion is characterized and studied by Professor Lada Adamic (Adamic et al., 2005) using raw metadata about blog sphere. The focus of our work is the notion of evolution of trust i.e., allowing the bottom-up development of trust as a result of repeated transactions. In case of trust score calculation enabled cellular mobile phones it should be the case that in the address book of every subscriber there may be number of addresses but that particular subscriber will assign higher trust values to those with whom his previous conversation had some form of "positive" outcome and he will place a confidential special call to some "selected/trusted" person(s) only. We intend to investigate the fundamental reason behind the initiation and outcome of every communication, the role of trust in such scenarios and emerging properties of social networks over time. Please note that this sort of phenomena is well studied in the domain of conversation analysis (Pomerantz, 1984; Schegloff, 2007). This will help us better while designing secure routing protocols and secure QoS based services in ad-hoc networks and sensor networks. This also enhances security and confidentiality in web based social networks and help design trusted online transaction procedures in e-commerce applications like e-bay (http://www.ebay.com).

In what follows we discuss a mathematical representation of Trust in Section 3. Section 4 introduces proposed trust model. Section 5 is devoted for trust model validation under different social/logical mobility conditions and the robustness of our model is also discussed in the same. Section 6 studies group formation and emergence of trust based self-segregation in virtual communities. Section 7 presents the interpretation of our numerical calculations. We conclude in Section 8 and also present the scope of future work.

3. PROPOSED TRUST MODEL

Diego Gambetta (2000) offered a mathematical definition of trust in the article "Can We Trust Trust?" He defined trust as a probability, whose value is in the range 0 to 1. In his definition (Gambetta, 2000):

Trust (or, symmetrically, distrust) is a particular level of the subjective probability with which an agent assesses that another agent or group of agents will perform a particular action, both before he can monitor such action (or independently or his capacity ever to be able to monitor it) and in a context in which it affects his own action.

According to him trust can be viewed as something which can take a number of values ranging between complete distrust (0) and complete trust (1).

In this section we present the architecture for trust analysis to be used in assessing various scenarios. We use the functional definition previously described and assign values based on interactions between peers in such a way that at any iteration the trust of one peer with respect to some other peer can be expressed as a positive number between 0 and 1, a notion somewhat similar to Gambetta (2000). If in the concerned network behind every node there is a human participant then one of the factors that govern the network dynamics, i.e., growth pattern, we propose, is trust and with time the same also evolves. Trust is a relation between two entities for a specific action. The first entity is referred as subject and second entity as the agent. A notation {subject: agent, action} is used often to represent trust relationship. For each relationship one or multiple values can be assigned based on direct or indirect interaction, known as trust score, which determines the level of trust-worthiness. When the subject directly observes the agent's behavior, direct trust is calculated and when the subject receives information about the entity in question from other entities based on their past interactions, indirect trust is calculated. Total trust can be derived by combining these two trust scores. Now the combination can be plain addition, average or weighted sum of these two numbers or any other mathematical function of these two numbers appropriate for the situation concerned. We have pictorially represented our Trust calculation engine and its different modules (Figure 1). In the following sub sections we present in detail the internal functionalities of various modules. We can say direct trust stems out from current interaction behaviour while indirect trust emerges from past interaction behaviour.

Direct Trust Calculation

It is probabilistic whether an entity will interact with another entity or not. This decision is influenced by the trust record available about the trustee. The probability is calculated by the Direct Interaction Decision making model. The available literature on this topic indicates that it is determined by two factors: proximity (social, spatial or otherwise) and trust among the entities. In a network closeness or proximity can be the distance between the two nodes. For virtual communities "distance" can be virtual distance also. The smaller the distance, the more likely they will directly interact. From the network topology module we will know the distance between the entities. in case of direct interaction the interaction

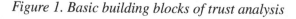

Figure 1. Basic building blocks of trust analysis

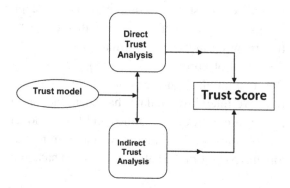

probability is given by $f\left(d_{AB}, T_{AB}\right)$ where d_{AB} is the distance between the nodes A and B and T_{AB} is the direct trust among them. From intuition and well established theory of social impact (Latane, 1981) the function should take the form:

$$f\left(d_{AB}, T_{AB}\right) = f_1(d_{AB}) \times f_2\left(T_{AB}\right) \qquad (1)$$

If the nodes (total number is N) are uniformly distributed in a geographical or virtual area then for some models the following is possible:

$$f_1(d_{AB}) = 1 / N \qquad (2)$$

$$f_2(T_{AB}) = T_{AB}{}^d = f_D(s, f) \qquad (3)$$

where, T_{AB}^d is the direct trust between A and B and $f_D(s, f)$ is the direct trust between the entities which is a function of "s" i.e., number of successful transactions and "f" i.e., number of unsuccessful/failed transactions among them.

Direct trust between two entities A and B is given by $T_{AB}{}^d = f_D(s, f)$ where s and f are the number of successful (satisfactory) and failed (unsatisfactory) interactions (transactions) respectively. One important issue is while computing trust how to calculate the indirect trust value based on recommendations. This is where Trust models play important roll. A Trust model usually contains two parts: *concatenation model* and *multi path model* as mentioned in Sun et al. (2007).

Indirect Trust Calculation

The concatenation model (based on Sun et al., 2007) is a function that calculates the indirect trust values between A and Y, denoted by T_{AY}^{ind} from the given T_{BY}^d (direct trust between B and Y) and T_{AB}^d (direct trust between A and B in the past) where

$$T_{AY}^{ind} = f_{ctp}\left(T_{AB}^d, T_{BY}^d\right) \qquad (4)$$

where, $f_{ctp}(.)$ is a function of the direct trust between (A, B) and (B, Y). The multipath model is a function that combines trust established through multiple paths. This function is denoted by $f_{mtp}(.)$

$$T_{AY}^{ind} = f_{mtp}\left(\left\{f_{ctp}\left(T_{AB_i}^d, T_{B_i Y}^d\right)\right\}_{i=1,2,3,..}\right) \qquad (5)$$

Let us describe a few total trust models of others in detail.

Simple Model: Used by many trust evaluation schemes (Sun et al., 2007). Here,

$$T_{AB}^d = f_D\left(s, f\right) \qquad (6)$$

$$f_D\left(s, f\right) = \frac{\left(s+1\right)}{s+f+2} \qquad (7)$$

$$f_{ctp}\left(x, y\right) = xy \qquad (8)$$

$$f_{mtp}(\{x_i\}_i) = avg(\{x_i\}_i) \qquad (9)$$

Probability Based Model: Here, the trust value T_{AB} is a scalar (Sun et al., 2007),

$$f_{ctp}\left(x, y\right) = xy + \left(1-x\right)\left(1-y\right) \qquad (10)$$

where, $f_{mtp}(.)$ is dependent on the data fusion model

Our Specific Model

In our model total trust between peers evolve along the following way:

Number of nodes is N. Each peer will interact with N-1 peers per round. The "distance" between the nodes is taken as closeness (which is usual in virtual community or community like structure) between them. Now, each peer engages in transaction with its neighbors. In every round for each peer there will be some satisfactory and unsatisfactory transactions. In our model we choose the simple model previously described with a few important modifications. Here, normalization is done through a different function. The success and failure is denoted by s and f respectively.

$$f_D(s, f) = (s - f) / (s + f)$$
(Our direct trust model) (11)

We go for this modified definition as we intend to incorporate both trust and mistrust in our model. This is the normalized trust and its value lies between (-1, 1).

$$c_{ij} = f_D(s, f) \tag{12}$$

$$f_{ctp}(i, k) = c_{ik} = c_{ij} \times c_{jk} \tag{13}$$

$$f_{mtp}(i, k) = t_{ik} = \left(\frac{1}{n}\right) \times \sum_j c_{ij} \times c_{jk} \tag{14}$$
$$\left(\text{Our indirect trust model}\right)$$

where, n is the number of paths with non-zero weights among all the indirect paths. Please note that we have only considered two hop paths while calculating indirect trust. Now trust between pairs is calculated as the sum of the direct and indirect trust. Again as direct and as well as the indirect trust is a number between (-1, 1), on addition they will produce a number between (-2, 2). To represent trust in (0, 1) we have to shift (map) the number in (0, 1). This is denoted as trust per round *trust_round*. We introduce an intermediate variable called *pre_trust* and the same is calculated as the following

$$pre\_trust = a \times direct\_trust$$
$$+(1 - a) \times indirect\_trust \tag{15}$$

where, $a=0.5$

The value of a is chosen to be 0.5 in order to offer equal weight to *direct_trust* and *indirect_trust* while calculating *pre_trust*. Where, *pre_trust* is related to *trust_round* by the following equation:

$$trust\_round = 0.5 \times (1 + pre\_trust) \tag{16}$$

Each variable in the previous few lines indicate the value of the corresponding quantity between i^{th} and j^{th} peer in k^{th} round. We introduce a variable $update(i, j, k)$ which is amount of change of total trust value between i^{th} and j^{th} peer in k^{th} round and the same can be calculated by the following equation:

$$i^{th}update(i, j, k) = update\_const$$
$$\times\left(trust\_round(i, j, k) - 0.5\right)$$

where

$$update\_const = 0.01; \tag{17}$$

Now, we define $trust(i, j, k)$ by the following equations

$$trust(i, j, k) = trust\_initial$$
$$+update(i, j, k), \text{ for } k = 1,$$

where

$$trust\_initial = 0.5 \tag{18}$$

$$trust(i, j, k) = trust\_round(i, j, k - 1)$$
$$+update(i, j, k), \text{ for } k \neq 1 \tag{19}$$

We normalize the trust because it is relatively easier to handle positive numbers between 0 and 1. Please note that at this stage we are working with the relatively simple trust model as described prior and the same has just one step memory. There is a rich literature on computational trust in various domains of computer science including semantic web. Most of those are enlisted in (Artz & Gil, 2007). In future we may include more complex models like those in our trust engine. Compared to Sun et al. (2007), our model does not include Direct Interaction Decision making, Recommendation Mechanism as well as Recommendation Trust block in the architecture. However, recommendation behavior is embedded in the indirect trust calculation process. Another major difference is the choice of direct trust calculation model. We modeled it as the ratio of difference between success and failure to total transactions held among the pair of agents. The intuition behind this is if we take in the numerator difference of successful and failed transaction number instead of successful transaction number only, the growth rate of direct trust will be slower. That will better capture the trust formation in a community.

4. TRUST MODEL VALIDATION

The simulation set up is designed to validate our trust model. Number of nodes (peers) is $N=10$. For initial experiments we consider two types of peers: one is "Democrat" (peer 1-5) and the other is "Republican" (peer 6-10). We assume that based on our knowledge on social behavior of human if there are two groups then individual activity is improvised by group activity. In order to study the robustness of our algorithm we introduce a third group of "peers". We assume, if two groups of people are involved in some kind of transaction or interaction and there is only two possible outcome of each interaction: success or failure, then it is more likely that interaction will be successful if it is between two agents of the

same group. Here "Democrats" are represented by blue colour; "Republicans" are represented by red colour and the third group, the malicious peers are represented by yellow colour. Traditionally in fields like mathematical sociology, computational physics, and socio-physics various models of interaction between agents in simulated artificial society or individuals in a real human community and resulting pattern of opinion formation or group formation is pretty well studied. Various mathematical models and computational experiments are proposed in this domain. One may look at the extensive literature that is available (Galam, 1996 b, 1997; Kohring, 1998; Latané, 1981, 1996, 2000; Lewenstein, 1992; Axelrod, 1997; Boudourides, 2003; Granovetter, 1973; Nowak, 1990; Sznajd-Weron, 2000; Deffuant, 2000; Kulakowski, 2009). Our basic model of agent identity does not change over time and serves as the basic "atom" of mutual interaction pattern. However, based on the same an attribute i.e., mutual trust /distrust evolve among agents over time and defines a higher level "molecule" in social kinetics model. Our computational emulation of bottom up self-segregation of the choice of "third place" (Oldenburg, 1989, 1991, 2000; Krassa, 2008) will show that this evolving "molecule" is the one that is driving the emergence of choice diversification pattern over time and a macro level manifestation is observed at the end. Although at this point we work on simple static identity model and with simple interaction and trust model. Given the richness of existing literature in each of these domains we plan to incorporate more complex models in our future analytical and computational studies. We also did not incorporate the idea of any underlying complex social network (Vega-Redondo, 2007), either static or temporarily varying, among the interacting agents. We may include the same in our future studies. However, we did incorporate the notion of social mobility, an indicator of frequency of social interaction, in our experimental model and did study the effect of the same in speed of convergence of the social kinetic process embedded inside the social chemistry among interacting agents through which the higher level molecule i.e., trust is evolving.

Uniform Social Mobility

Here based on recommendation range each peer chooses its partner for the round k. For each round it first decides with how many peers it is going to interact. Then, it further decides exactly with which peers it is going to interact. For, the first step each peer generates a uniformly distributed random number between 1 to (N-1), say "n". Now it randomly chooses "n" specific peers among N-1 peers. This is why this model is called the "uniform social mobility" model, where each peer is equally accessible to all other peers. By "mobility" we mean probability of choosing the number of peers for interaction per round by a specific peer. As for example in round 6, peer 2 may decide to interact with 3 peers and the peers are 1, 4, and 9. For each peer in each round $Max\_transaction\_no$, the total number of transactions in that round is generated which is a uniformly distributed random number between 50 and 100. Now, for round 1 it is divided equally among the n peers. For subsequent rounds,

$$
\begin{aligned}
&transactionnumber\left(i, j, k\right) \\
&= \frac{Trust\_norm\left(i, j, \left(k-1\right)\right)}{\sum_{j} Trust\_norm\left(i, j, \left(k-1\right)\right)} \\
&\times Max\_transaction\_no
\end{aligned}
\tag{20}
$$

where, $transactionnumber\left(i, j, k\right)$ is the number of transactions between i^{th} and j^{th} peer at k^{th} round. It has to be decided now whether the transaction is successful or not. As there are two groups, success or failure of a transaction depends on whether the peers belong to same group or different. In each round at a time only two peers are interacting. If both belong to the same group then with probability p_high each interaction/transac-

tion is going to be successful else, with probability p_low the same is going to be successful. For our model p_high is chosen to be 0.8 and p_low is chosen to be 0.2. Trust value of all the peers with respect to one "republican" peer is computed and plotted in the Y-axis vs. number of rounds which are plotted in the X-axis. The trust value of "republican" peers is plotted by lines with solid circles and "democrat" peers are plotted using lines with solid triangles. As expected the lines with solid circles come on top of the other bunch of plots (Figure 2).

Effect of Social Mobility

It has to be tested whether convergence rate of trust values of two different groups change with social mobility. The authors in Bruch et al. (2007) said that "neighborhoods change through the mobility of agents who are reacting to the composition of their own neighborhood and of other potential neighborhood destinations". As the agents move, they change the neighborhoods of other agents in the system, creating further moves by individuals who are trying to satisfy their preferences. We have to understand that this trust computation is a gossip based distributed computation problem where topology changes in every round. Therefore, neighborhood of a specific peer changes over time. There is a volume of work in distributed computation, ad hoc networks and emergence of patterns where gossip based distributed computation and effect of physical mobility on the same is being studied (Roychoudhury, 2005; Zelasity, 2005; Boyd et al., 2005) High physical mobility of specific type enables a peer to get other peers as neighbors more frequently and exchange information. In fact, it was recently shown that convergence speed of a distributed computation problem over a sensor network increases with certain type of mobility (Sarwate, 2009). It is also demonstrated in Singh (2008) that minimum critical probability of forwarding required for good percolation of in-

Figure 2. Trust plot with uniform social mobility

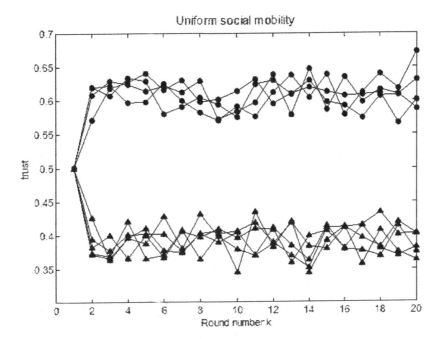

formation (Haas, 2006) over a grid network tends to fall when nodes exhibit mobility constrained by the underlying taxicab geometry (Krause, 1987). These results are consistent with the related results obtained in the domain of mobile wireless networks that mobility increases capacity of the ad hoc wireless networks (Grossglauser, 2002). Here, we have tested the effect of logical mobility of peers in social space on the convergence speed of this distributed gossip based trust computation model.

High Social Mobility

Here all the simulation parameters are same except the number of peers to be interacted with is non-uniformly distributed. Interaction probability with more people is on higher side. Here mobility is not exactly physical rather logical social mobility. High social mobility leads to high frequency of interaction with other peers. Similar phenomenon occurs in wireless ad-hoc networks with high physical mobility of certain

type. A candidate probability mass function for high social mobility is shown in Figure 3 as an example. The corresponding trust evolution is plotted in Figure 4.

Social Mobility Low

Here all the simulation parameters are same except that instead of number of peers to be interacted with is not uniformly distributed. Interaction probability with more people is on lower side. A candidate probability mass function for low social mobility is shown in Figure 5 as an example. The corresponding trust evolution is plotted in Figure 6.

With social mobility minimum and maximum the corresponding trust evolutions are plotted in Figure 7 and Figure 8 respectively.

If we compare the trust plots i.e., Figures 8, 7, 6, and 4 we can clearly see that increased social mobility i.e., greater frequency of social interaction causes a reduction in number of iterations required for convergence of the distributed trust computation problem under discussion.

Figure 3. High social mobility: pmf

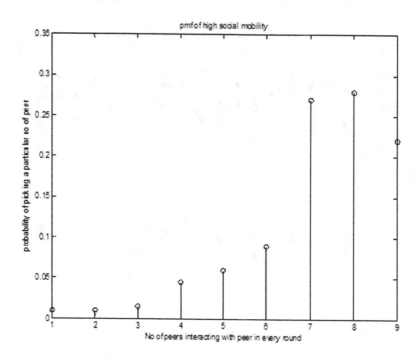

Figure 4. Trust plot with high social mobility

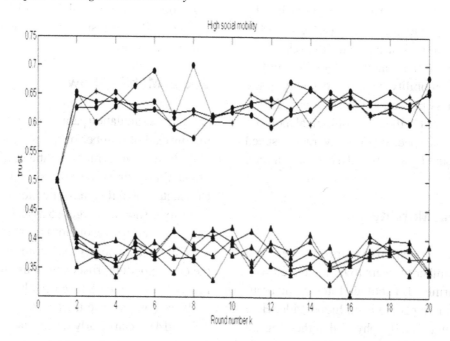

Figure 5. Low social mobility: pmf

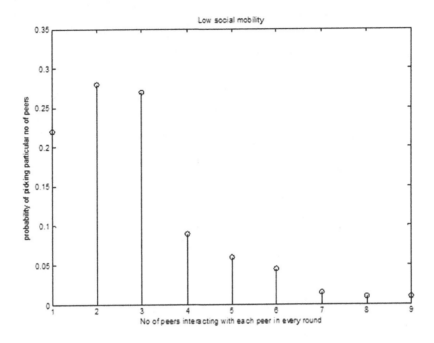

Figure 6. Trust plot for low social mobility

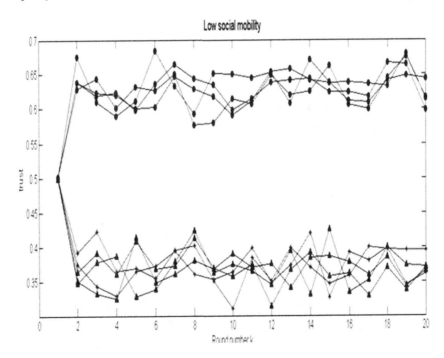

Figure 7. Trust plot for minimum social mobility

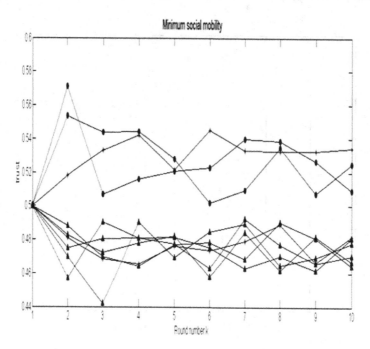

Figure 8. Trust plot for maximum social mobility

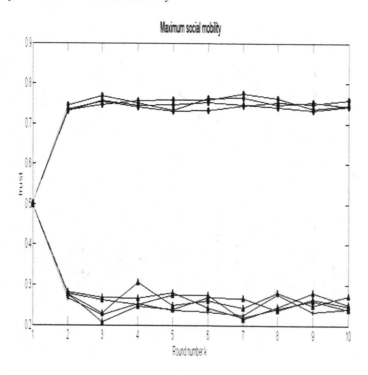

In another set of experiments other than democrat and republican another type of peer is considered which we call "the yellow peer". This is introduced to check the robustness of the algorithm. This type of peer is acting as malicious node. Plots are shown. Our experiments indicate that although existence of "yellow" peers creates some confusion among the other peers, by and large the qualitative nature of trust levels remain as expected (Figures 9 and 10).

5. SELF-SEGREGATION AND GROUP FORMATION

It was observed while studying the social kinetics of various human phenomenon that there are cases when a bottom up self segregation did appear at the end as a defining characteristics of the macroscopic pattern that is the central kernel of the issue under consideration. These observations and their simulation and model based validation does indicate that such segregation appears even without the existence of any central controlling agent prompting individual agents to pick their actions at any instant of time based on some centrally enforced law. Even self initiated actions taken by individual agents based on local spatial and temporal information can produce macroscopic group formation in a distributed fashion. Oldenburg (1989, 1991, 2000) did talk about the first place (residence), the second place (place of work), and the third place (the place to socialize) in the daily life of an individual. There is lot of work and empirical observations about bottom up self segregation in first, second, and third places.

Self Segregation in First Places

It is historically observed that certain regions within a city of any continent acquired certain stereotypical social or cultural image over a period of time. Notable examples are "the left bank or La Rive Gauche" (Portion of the city of Paris

Figure 9. Trust in presence of 5 yellow peers out of 50

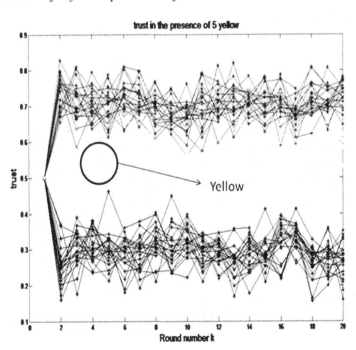

Figure 10. Trust in presence of 10 yellow peers out of 50

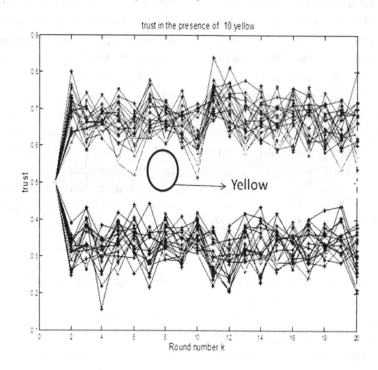

that is located at the left bank of river Seine), "the right bank or La Rive Droite" (Portion of the city of Paris that is located at the right bank of river Seine) and the "Latin Quarter" within the left bank. Apart from France in the neighboring country of Spain the Triana region within the city of Seville has got a somewhat different sense of identity because historically a large Spanish Roma population used to live there in *Corral* style community hall. There are considerable amount of study based on various models on the classic case of bottom up self segregation in first places (Bruch et al., 2007; Schelling, 1971, 1972). Recently, extensive computer simulations about this issue with an extended multidimensional identity model were performed and varieties of emergent segregation pattern were observed (Gilbert, 2002). In some of the simulation runs the hamming distance between the identity templates of two spatially close individual agents was considered as a measure of socio-cultural distance between them which triggers the individual choice of staying put or moving out from a particular geographical neighborhood. There are indeed a lot of real documentation about formation and existence of so called ethnic neighborhoods in some large metropolis of the world e.g., ethnic neighborhoods of New York City (Blake, 2002, http://www.walkingaround.com, and http://en.wikipedia.org/wiki/New_York_City_ethnic_enclaves). For example New York City's German neighborhood, "Little Germany" or "Kleindeutschland" was located in "Lower East Side" around Tompkins Square in what would later become known as "Alphabet city". Due to General Slocum disaster in 1904 a large part of this community moved to Yorkville in "Upper East Side". The Yorkville is bounded by 79th street to the south, 96th street and Spanish Harlem to the north, the East River to the East, and Third Avenue to the West. Similarly we find that people of Derawal ethnic group, originally native to the Derajat region (A cultural region of central Pakistan) live in Derawal Nagar, a small colony in New Delhi, which consists of two blocks:

A & B. It is reported in article titled "Upper West Side" in Wikipedia (the free encyclopedia) "While this distinction were never hard and fast rules, now mean little, it has the reputation of being home to New York City's affluent cultural and artistic workers, in contrast to the Upper East Side, which is perceived to be traditionally home to affluent, commercial and business type" (http://en.wikipedia.org/wiki/Upper_West_Side). In the Asian context such socio-cultural differentiation between different neighborhoods does appear in the urban geography of large metropolis like Delhi, as in the case between walled city area of " Old Delhi" and the "Lutyen's Delhi" area of New Delhi. Similar heterogeneity in the context of Kolkata is discussed in studying spatial history of Kolkata in the influential work of Chattopadhyay (2005). She concludes the resultant spatial built environment is not only an outcome of colonial legacy but a lot more complicated issues generate the complex topography. In some of these cases the resultant spatial pattern either of the built environment or that of socio-cultural tendencies or both might be caused due to top down enforcement of city planning and community planning by rulers of the land. However in many cases while not ignoring the influence of some underlying top down centralized process it can perhaps still be argued that bottom up self causation due to individual choice of agents based on local information at the micro level did play a huge role in generating the resultant macroscopic pattern in a distributed fashion.

Self Segregation in Second Places

In the paper Huberman et al. (2004), the e-mail network of a large multinational company, HP labs in Palo- Alto, was analyzed. As reported in that paper, from HP lab mail server in the period November 25, 2002 to February 18, 2003, 188773 emails were exchanged between 1485 HP Lab employee. A graph was constructed by placing edges between any two persons that has exchanged at least 30 e-mails of which at least 5 in both direction. The resultant graph made of 367 nodes and 1,110 edges had one giant connected component of 343 nodes and 6 smaller components. The modified Brandes Algorithm detected 60 additional distinct communities within the giant component. Studying these 66 communities along with the HP Corporate directory, it was found that 49 of those 66 communities consisted of individuals entirely within one organizational unit. The Figure 11 of that work maps e-mail communication within HP Lab onto the organizational hierarchy to demonstrate that e-mail communication tends to "cling" to the formal organizational chart. It is also shown that if the weak links in the e-mail communication graph are pruned by some threshold, then the resultant graph almost looks like the company hierarchy chart itself. They have also demonstrated in Figure 13 that an analysis of the e-mail data indicates the probability of linking between two individuals decays exponentially with their separation in the organizational hierarchy and the empirical data conforms to the model of Watts et al. (2002). Therefore, it is fare to conclude that in "second place" also a bottom up self segregation of individuals naturally arises.

Self Segregation in Physical Third Places

The third places according to Oldenburg are informal gathering places that work as a vital focal point of the social life of a community. Typically, "Beer Halls" in Germany, "Pizzerias" in Italy, "Cafes" in France and "Pubs" and "Taverns" in English culture served the role of third places in respective countries. In antiquity, Roman "Taverns" and in middle ages Saxon "Alehouses" served the same purpose. In Asia, "Chaikhanas" in Central Asian countries and "Tempura-ya" in Japan are the corresponding examples. In modern United States, many companies like Starbuck Chain define itself as the third place. Historically, the "ten eating clubs" of Princeton University on

Figure 11. Chat room visiting probabilities of peer 1 to 4 (1-5 are republicans 6-10 are Democrats)

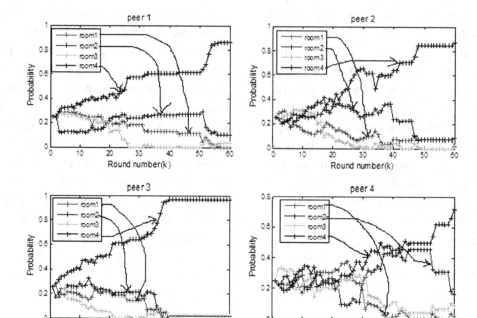

Figure 12. Chat room visiting probabilities of peer 5 to 8 (1-5 are Republicans 6-10 are Democrats)

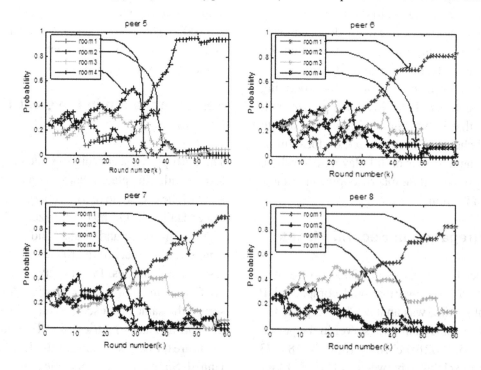

Figure 13. Chat room probabilities of peer 9 and 10 (1-5 are Republicans 6-10 are Democrats)

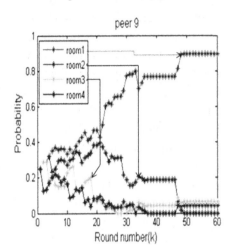
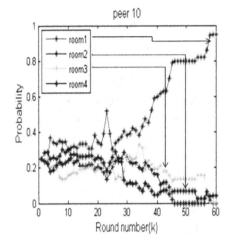

Prospect Avenue ("the street") served as informal gathering places for students. Five of which "Cap and Gown", "Tower", "Ivy", "Tiger Inn", and "Cottage" are biker clubs. The other five: "Cloister Inn", "Charter", "Colonial Club", "Quadrangle Club", and "Terrace" are non selective sign in clubs. As per the present regulation, unlike the fraternities and sororities (the so called "Greek Societies") these clubs are not gender specific and neither they are referral based like Harvard's "final clubs" or Yale's "secret societies" where new members are "punched" and "tapped", respectively. In early days, eating clubs were so different that then-university president Woodrow Wilson looked down on them as vehicles for social segregation and sought to mitigate their influence (Battey, 2006). However, in contemporary times such interpersonal barriers are not enforced rather prohibited by liberal laws of the land and as such there is no top down implementation of any form of segregation. However, typical stereotypes do exist about the prevailing cultural atmosphere of these clubs. The clubs have a particular stereotype and group of people associated with it. Ivy, the original club, is considered to be the home of "the northern elite". "Cottage", the second club, is supposedly populated by "the southern elite".

"Terrace" is known to be "artsy" and the "Charter" is for "the math and science people" (Battey, 2006). F.S. Fitzgerald, a Princeton alumnus, in his 1920 novel "This Side of Paradise" has described Ivy as " detached and breathlessly aristocratic" and Tiger Inn as " broad shouldered and athletic, vitalized by an honest elaboration of prep-school standards (Fitzgerald, 1920). On the other hand Cottage, of which he himself was a member, in his opinion, was "an impressive mélange of brilliant adventurers and well dressed philanderers". Winne Hu, an education reporter for New York Times comments in her July 2007 article titled "More Than a Meal Plan" that such description could apply even today. According to her these clubs have established identities that attract likeminded members (Hu, 2007). Cap and Gown is a favorite of athletes though "floaters and boaters" (swimmers and rowers) tend to go to Cloister Inn. Please note that in this context segregation is a personal choice as people are more comfortable around people they have the most in common with or as one may say whom they "trust" better. In fact, a strong correlation between "trust" and "interest similarity" is recently reported in Ziegler et al. (2007), though in a different context. It was noted by Fitzgerald and documented in recent publications (Guzzetta, 2006) that although eating clubs are independent organizations beyond the official jurisdiction of the administration of Princeton University they do play a huge dominant role in the undergraduate student life of Princeton as dining halls, libraries, and the center of social interaction: as a "third place". So this case study does illustrate that bottom up self segregation does take place there too. The Mermaid Tavern, a tavern on chip side in London, during the Elizabethan era, served as the site of the so called Friday Street Club allegedly founded by Sir Walter Raleigh and included towering literary figures like Ben Johnson, John Donny, John Fletcher, Francis Beaumont, and perhaps William Shakespeare as its patron. There are extended references on tavern and its witty conversation in *Master Francis Beaumont letters to the Ben Johnson*. Sometime in February, 1819 John Keats composed a poem on the legend of the tavern titled "Lines on the Mermaid Tavern". This too represents a case where people of certain profession and stature do converge at a certain "third place" to satisfy intellectual need (http://en.wikipedia.org/wiki/Mermaid_Tavern). Coffee Houses were first established in large numbers during Queen Anne's reign (1702-1714) and served as centers of social and political discussions. It is reported in Ashok (2011) that there were distinct coffee houses for different groups of people. Tories went to Cocoa Tree Chocolate House. The Whigs preferred St. James Coffee House. The poets met at Wills Coffee House and the scholars at Grecian Coffee House. Even there were coffee houses exclusively for Quakers. According to Brian Cowan, the Oxford Coffeehouses in England were a Place for likeminded scholars to congregate, to read as well as learn from and to debate each other. In 1739 there were 551 coffeehouses in London each attracted a particular type of crowd divided by occupation or attitude, such as Tories and Whigs, Wits and stockjobbers, Merchants and Lawyers, Booksellers and Authors, men of fashion or the "cits" of the old city center

(http://en.wikipedia.org/wiki/Cofeehouses). For example a coffeehouse called Lloyd's of London in Lombard Street, where underwriters of ship insurance met to get business done. Child's Coffeehouse, near Physicians Warwick lane and St. Paul's Church yard", was frequented by clergy and the doctors (http://en.wikipedia.org/wiki/English_cofeehouses_in_the_seventeenth_and_eighteenth_centuries). This trend continued in Hanoverian time. For several years Congreve presided over men of letters at Wills Coffee House. Café-Procope was the first coffee house in Paris established in 1686 by Francois Procope. Among the 400 hundred odd cafes that were operative in the city by 1720s, this one was a high class institution that served as center of enlightenment, frequented by people like Voltaire, Rousseau. On the other hand, there were places which according to Louis Sebastian Mercier represented an affiliation between cafes and immoral activities. Robert Darnton who studied Parisian café conversation in great detail did mention cafes earned their place in public sphere due to the type of conversation that took place within them. On the other hand most historians described the Parisian salons as an extension of the court society and not a place to be frequented by an average commoner. The College Street Coffeehouse of Indian coffee house chain located in Bankim Chatterjee Street, Kolkata, India is known to be a gathering place of poets, artists, actors, and intellectuals of the city and was a well known hang-out place of the "anti-establishment/non-conformist" types. Flurys in Park Street, Kolkata is on the other hand an upscale tea room visited by affluent artistic carefree Calcuttans. Therefore it is fare to conclude that public places of different countries of different era did carry an aura of type or identity with themselves depending on the type of people visited them and the content and the manners of the conversation that did take place there. Indeed one can clearly visualize the process of individual initiated bottom up self segregation in action.

Self Segregation in
Virtual Third Places

In modern times people have increasingly less spare time to visit a third place. Information technology revolution has unleashed the era of internet. So, we have these social networks which serve as the virtual third place. According to Fahey "We are experiencing the emergence of a new way for people to relate to each other and to meet new people using the so-called social web. What's more, this new model has a lot in common with the clubs of the 17th century, in UK and indeed with all the face-to-face clubs that exist today". He also argued that "every social network will, over time, attract people with similar cultural interests and affinities, and just like in the physical world these shared interests are far more important than the amenities of the club's meeting place" (Fahey, 2007).

Recently, there was a lot of discussion about the way learned bodies should conduct international academic and technical conferences in TCCC Mailing list. After a sufficient number of e-mail exchanges and projection of lot of opinions of heterogeneous nature, a few did ask for a moratorium on further discussions and some wanted to continue. As a consequence, it was proposed that in future such discussions on a specific topic can go to separate threads effectively creating a sub mailing list only for interested parties. It was also observed that the background software is so organized that this process does not require a central moderator rather participants can self organize themselves in specific threads while discussing a specific topic of limited interest. It is like people in a tavern can self segregate themselves in different tables or rooms based on the topic of their conversation (http://www.comsoc.org/~tccc/list.html).

Blog is a similar type of "virtual third place", where people write their opinions. Lada Adamic has reported in the paper (Adamic et al., 2005) that in US presidential election 2004 entire blog sphere was divided into two sub-spheres "con-servative" and "liberal". They found that "liberal and conservative blogs did indeed have different lists of favorite news sources, people, and topics to discuss, although they occasionally overlapped in their discussion of news articles and events". The division is more pronounced in the linking pattern between the blogs with more number of internal links than between the groups (Adamic et al., 2005). One can look at the blog-sphere data about linking patterns in Adamic et al. (2005).

In the article, "Investigating interactions of trust and interest similarity" (Ziegler et al., 2007), Zeigler and Golbeck presents a trust model that is more applicable in a rating or recommendation or product selling system. Their article does not shed light on a more general aspect of trust. The trust is not generated through continuing or multiple interactions or in any other way trust does not evolve here. Though context specificity is one important aspect of trust, but knowing the context beforehand might demotivate some of the agents to rate the context. Also in this way one can capture the direct trust or rating. The aspect of indirect trust is missing here. Another drawback is trust rating is Boolean: either 0 or 1 i.e., trustworthy or not. In real life there are levels of trust. In case of Film trust, though levels and indirect trust are considered, but the interaction time or number of interaction based on which the rating is given is not taken into consideration. Simply the model is stationary and cannot capture temporal evolution of trust. In contrast to this our model has some chat rooms and they are not labeled i.e., chat rooms are not identifiable at the beginning of the experiment however they will be identifiable over time. As an analogy, consider there are multiplexes where discussions and screening of movies take place. For ease of understanding let four types of movies are being screened there: Romantic, Sci-Fi, Horror, and Adventure. The multiplex plays movie in accordance with the audience inclination. If in that multiplex on the starting day there are a number of viewers who want to watch romantic movie then it will be screened. Over time the hall will earn reputation of playing a particular type of movie. Most important issue in their work is that it only shows a strong correlation between trust and interest similarity which is essentially a static snap-shot of the end result of a process. It shows the segregation but fails to demonstrate or arrive at a descriptive model that can chronicle the temporal evolution of self-segregation. For example, the temporal evolution of bottom up self segregation that was apparent in the recent discussions on TCCC mailing list which we mentioned cannot be modeled using something like the Zeigler approach. Similar assessment can be concluded about the data analysis work of Adamic as well and the data it reports. How the temporal evolution of the process took place that is not clear from Adamic's work (Adamic et al., 2005). On the contrary we can clearly show through our analytical model and related computation that an agent is characterized by her "identity" ("interest") which translates in varying degree of trust evolution among themselves once they start to interact. So we get from the basic "atom" the "identity" a higher level "molecule" that is "trust" which in turn drives the degree of future interactions and "quality of experience" that an agent enjoys while visiting a specific chat room. This "quality of experience" is the feedback from non-stationary random environment based on which the agent modifies her probability of selection of a chat room in next pass. Eventually this learning mechanism leads to some form of a "capture phenomena" so that agents with similar identity and resulting high trust level due to favorable interaction flocks together in same chat room irrespective of initial probability distribution of their choice vector. We speculate that the factor which influenced this kind of division is trust. It emerges as a consequence of the group of people's inclination towards a particular kind of belief system. So, their interactions with people belonging to a different group become emotionally less satisfactory and as a result less trust is generated through the same. This leads to less future interaction probability.

A Generalized Theory Based on Evolutionary Game Paradigm

Recently, Nowak et al. (2010) did present in Philosophical transactions of Royal society series B (Biological Sciences) an evolutionary game theory based description of repeated interaction in structured populations of finite size. By studying well mixed population, evolutionary graph theory, games in phenotype space, and evolutionary set theory and developing fundamental laws that determine how natural selection filters out winning candidates among competing strategies these researchers address the issue of evolution of cooperation. They conclude that cooperators prevail against defectors by clustering in physical and other spaces. This mechanism, called spatial selection, is the one that leads to the emergent pattern of evolution and sustenance of cooperation. In the conclusion of this article, the authors do note that human beings operate in social space within the frame work of direct or indirect reciprocity. According to them, direct reciprocity occurs when someone's behavior towards somebody else depends on what that person has done to this one in the past. On the other hand, indirect reciprocity means Mr. X's behavior towards Mr. Y also depends on what Mr. Y has done to others. They do note that direct and indirect reciprocity are yet to be combined with the framework presented in their article. On the contrary, in this work, rooted in the M.Tech thesis of first author (Karmakar, 2008), that predates their publication; we have taken care of the notion of both direct and indirect trust. Our formulation is based on learning automata paradigm which is different from but related to evolutionary game theory, the mathematical tool, they used. Moreover, we focus on trust driven spatial clustering, whereas, they describe spatial selection as a mechanism for evolution and sustenance of cooperation. The notion of trust based quality of experience that we introduced, plays an analogous role with what they call pay-off. Evolution of cooperation in the context of multi hop energy efficient wireless networks is studied in Lai et al. (2008) using non cooperative game theory but the formalism of trust is not incorporated in the same.

6. TRUST MODEL BASED COMPUTER EXPERIMENTATION TO EMULATE SELF SEGREGATION DYNAMICS IN VIRTUAL CHAT ROOMS

In order to emulate the phenomena mentioned in subsection D of previous section, we create a computer experiment. Our goal is to couple our trust model with a learning automata type algorithm so that at least qualitatively we can demonstrate similar emergent pattern. This will help in at least qualitative indirect validation of our trust model. We create four chat rooms which people will visit according to some probability and that act as virtual space for interaction. Once a few peers select a particular chat room they become "neighbours" for that round. For each peer we generate a random integer between 50 to 150 and this serves as the total number of interactions this peer is going to perform in this round with its neighbours. We divide the total number of interactions among its neighbours in the ratio of trust of neighbours with respect to this peer. If the peers are of same type then each interaction becomes successful with probability 0.8 and if they are of different type each interaction among them becomes successful with probability 0.2. They are calculating trust about other peers like the way they did in the experiments described in previous sections. However, here the neighbours and neighbourhood for a particular round gets defined by the way we just described. Apart from calculating trust each peer is also calculating the quality of experience they gather in the transactions. Initial probability of visiting each chat room is same, but based on experience they gain in the chat room with time the probability of visiting a particular chat room is modified. The chat room selection is based on

the quality of experience gained in a chat room in the previous round. Quality of experience is quantified by the following equation.

$$quality\ of\ experience = \frac{sum\ of\ satisfactory\ transaction\ number}{sum\ of\ all\ transaction\ number} \tag{21}$$

Simple algebraic manipulation yields a relationship between quality of experience and trust. Indeed let trust of agent j with respect to agent i ($i \neq j$) up to time epoch $(k-1)$ is denoted by $T_{ij}(k-1)$ and the probability of successful transaction between them is denoted by α_{ij}. Let us also denote Quality of experience of agent i at chat room u at time epoch k by $QOE_i^u(k)$ and let E denotes the expectation operation as in probability theory. One can easily show that expected value of quality of experience is sum of expected value of trust of interacting agents weighted by the probability of successful transaction between them. In particular, the following relationship exists.

$$E\left[QOE_i^u(k)\right] = \sum_{\substack{i \neq j, \forall j\ present\ in \\ chat\ room\ u\ at \\ time\ k}} \alpha_{ij} \times E\left(T_{ij}(k-1)\right) \tag{22}$$

Therefore, trust is like a molecule created due to interactions between agents characterized by identity that plays the role of basic atom in this process. Trust on its own gives rise to even higher level structure the quality of experience. We introduce a variable called "delta change" and the same is expressed as the following:

$$delta\ change = \alpha \times (quality\ of\ experience - 0.5),\ \alpha = 0.25 \tag{23}$$

Now probability of visiting a chat room is updated by the following rule. Let us assume the peer i went to the chat room u in the previous round and through the transactions it got an experience that results to delta change= *delta change (i, u, k)* where, *k* is the round index. Then the probability of visiting the same chat room by the same peer in the next round is modified by the following equation.

$$probability\left(i, u, k\right) = probability\left(i, u, \left(k - 1\right)\right)$$
$$+delta\ change(i, u, \left(k - 1\right))$$

$$(24)$$

If

$$probability\left(i, u, k\right) = probability\left(i, u, \left(k - 1\right)\right)$$
$$+delta\ change(i, u, \left(k - 1\right))$$

lies between 0 and 1. Otherwise if the same exceeds 1 left hand side of the Equation (24) is equated to

1. If the same falls below zero the left hand side of the equation is equated to zero.

The probability of visiting any other chat room *v* will be expressed as:

$$probability\left(i, v, k\right) = probability\left(i, v, \left(k - 1\right)\right)$$
$$+ \left(\frac{1}{M - 1}\right) \times \left(probability\left(i, u, k\right)\right)$$
$$-probability\left(i, u, \left(k - 1\right)\right)$$

$$(25)$$

Interestingly, as the time passes same group tend to get confined in same blog page(s) as shown by authors in Adamic et al. (2005). In Figures 11 through 24, the time evolution of fraction of democrats and republicans in chat rooms are shown. We varied the number of republicans in the pool of peers. We also plot the chat room

Figure 14. Chat room visiting probabilities of peer 1 to 4 (1-8 are republicans and 9-10 are democrats)

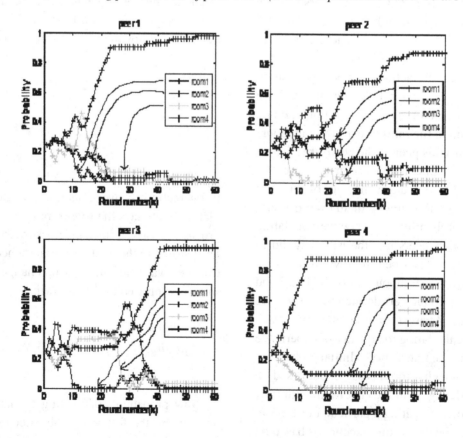

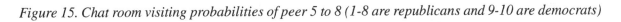

Figure 15. Chat room visiting probabilities of peer 5 to 8 (1-8 are republicans and 9-10 are democrats)

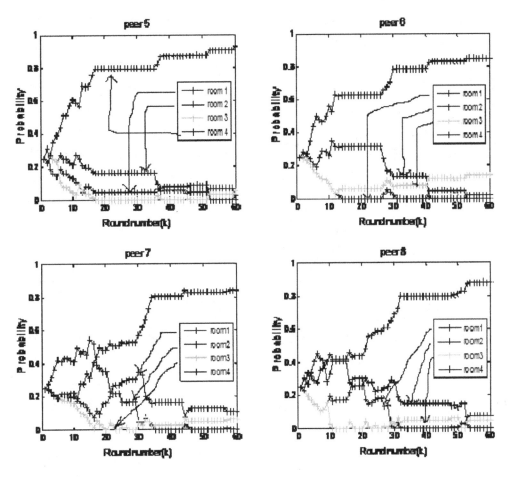

Figure 16. Chat room visiting probabilities of peer 9 and 10 (1-8 are republicans and 9-10 are democrats)

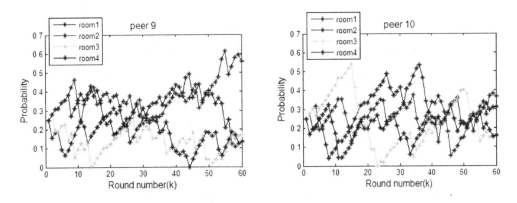

Figure 17. Chat room visiting probabilities of peer 1 to 4 (8 Republicans and 8 Democrats)

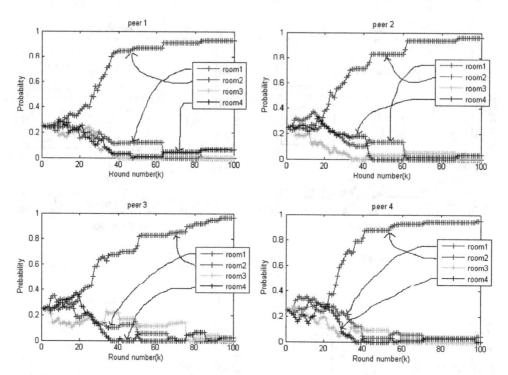

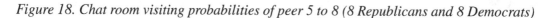

Figure 18. Chat room visiting probabilities of peer 5 to 8 (8 Republicans and 8 Democrats)

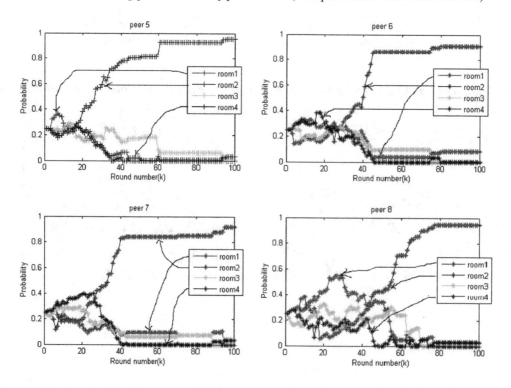

Figure 19. Chat room visiting probabilities of peer 9 to 12 (8 Republicans and 8 Democrats)

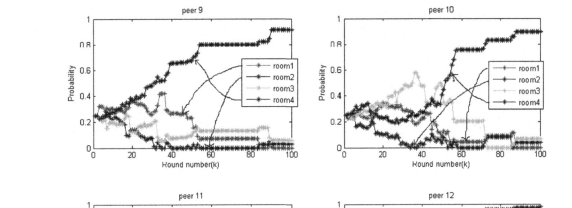

Figure 20. Chat room visiting probabilities of peer 13 to 16 (8 Republicans and 8 Democrats)

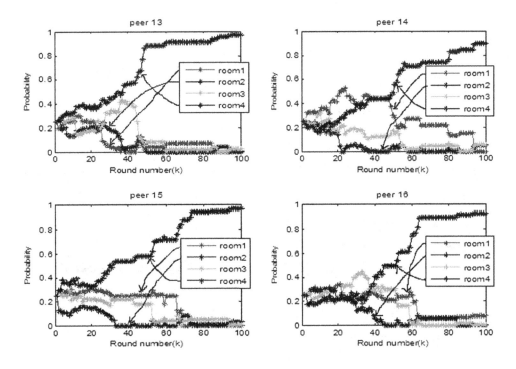

Figure 21. Chat room visiting probabilities of peer 1 to 4(5 Republicans and 5 Democrats)

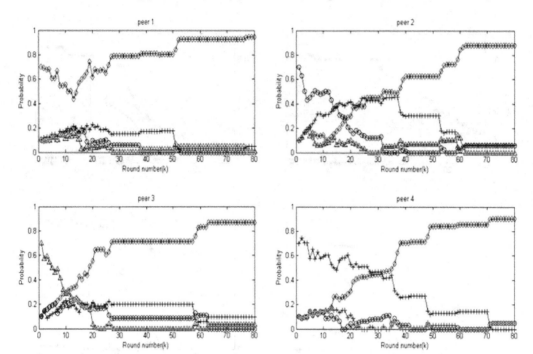

Figure 22. Chat room visiting probabilities of peer 5 to 8(5 Republicans and 5 Democrats)

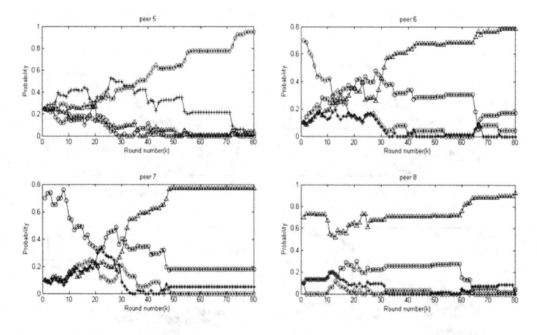

Figure 23. Chat room visiting probabilities of peer 9 &10(5 Republicans and 5 Democrats)

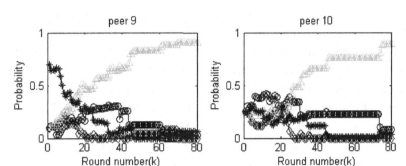

Figure 24. Cumulative moving average trust plots of peers with respect to peer 1

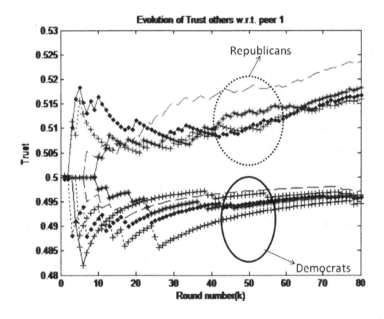

visiting probability of various peers vs. round number (time). Therefore, it is demonstrated in a descriptive manner in time domain that evolution of trust is the basic driving force that controls the quality of experience which in turn dictates and plays the role of a critic in a learning process through which birds of same feather eventually flocks together. For our first set of experiments the initial probability of visiting different chat rooms for every agent is uniformly distributed. However, later we change this initial distribution and use a skewed distribution as the initial one. Interestingly, in all possible cases the bottom up

self segregation does emerge and in fact, in case of skewed initial distribution prominent bifurcation appears even more quickly. Therefore, the details of this emergent macroscopic pattern of the end result are indeed dependent on initial conditions, but it nevertheless does appear under all possible initial settings.

We can say that friends (in this case peers from same group) are statistically similar. The chat rooms are not pre-labeled as a meeting place of a particular group neither chat rooms themselves selectively offer favorable service to some specific group. Also, the peers are not exchanging information about the chat rooms after each round. Still the sample path evolution of choice probabilities indicate that as if over a period of time similar peers are getting captured in specific chat room(s) which are distinctly different from the preferred chat room(s) of other peers. In other words, if the choice probability vector of similar (dissimilar) peers converges in distribution then in steady state their Bhattacharyya distance will be smaller(larger). Hence, it can be concluded that the segregation and the apparent capture phenomena observed is evolved over time in a bottom up fashion. As a result some place/chat room is more favorable to some group over time although it cannot be pre specified in which chat room their choice vector will be captured.

Plots for the set of experiments where initial chat room choice distribution of each agent is uniform (Figure 11 through 16).

Plots for the set of experiments where initial chat room choice distribution of each agent is uniform and total transactions are equally divided among neighbours in every round (Figure 17 through 20).

Plots for the set of experiments where initial chat room choice distribution of each agent is skewed (Figure 21 through 24).

7. INTERPRETATION

In first set of experiments the composition of the peers is divided equally i.e., 5 republicans and 5 democrats. The first set of plots show that the republicans are concentrated at chat room 2 and 4. That is the democrats are concentrated at chat room 1 and 3. Now if the composition of the peers is such that 8 republicans and 2 democrats then also this phenomenon i.e., self-segregation of chat room preference over time will be observed. Note that, initially for each peer every chat room is equally desirable. The same is indicated by the fact that each curve in visiting probability vs. round number plot starts with 0.25. In "Neighbor-

hood Choice and Neighborhood Change" Bruch and Mare argued that "high levels of segregation occur only when individuals' preferences follow a threshold function. If individuals' make finer-grained distinctions, among neighbourhoods that vary in racial composition, preferences alone do not lead to segregation" (BRUCH et al., 2007). Now the data taken in L. Adamic's work was prior to the US presidential election and as a result there is a polarization before election. In case of political preference the choice is strict in sense and it follows a threshold function. As a result it shows high degree of segregation. Similarly, in our case we adopted a strict threshold function. Hence, in our case also we have high level of separation. But in the set, where we have 2 democrats and 8 republicans as the number of democrats is only two, segregation is not so pronounced. So, this result indicates that formation of spatial preferences requires certain number of entities so that the minority can form a local majority in some "corner" and survive. Figures 17 through 20 demonstrates that if for every peer we have equal partition of transaction number or interactions with the neighbours in each round then appearance of segregation requires more number of iterations than the same in the trust based division of total number of interactions among all neighbours in every round. Therefore, it can be concluded that trust based partition of interactions enhances faster segregation of preferences and this causes a form of downward causation (Sawyer, 2005). Here although initially each chat room was equally desirable to each peer (each curve starts from 0.25 as mentioned before) gradually due to micro level local interaction among neighbours (occupants of a specific chat room in a specific round) a macro level segregation of chat room preference among peers is emerging over time. As a byproduct of this process peers develop different levels of trust among themselves and the same further influences the degree of future interaction among them and their chat room preferences. In subsection C we do plot the temporal evolution of probability of visiting various chat rooms for each peer when the initial distribution is kept skewed for most of them expect two. Here, we do observe self segregation of peers in different chat rooms and likeminded peers getting flocked together. In fact the process of segregation shows up much earlier, just after a few iterations and the degree of separation is even stronger in the end. We also do provide for the sake of completion the corresponding trust (cumulative moving average of trust) evolution with respect to peer 1 for all other peers in the Figure 24. It does demonstrate that people with similar identity eventually develops higher level of mutual trust among themselves due to continual relatively favourable mutual exchanges or interaction between themselves. That in turn creates good quality of experience which drives them to congregate at certain chat rooms at a selective manner.

8. CONCLUSION AND FUTURE WORK

Trust composition produces completely different intervention strategies. In case of social network trustee's mental state may change even though the situation remains same and while deriving trust, path sequence may become an important factor. In the social network "how co-operation evolved?" is a century old problem and yet not fully understood. But almost all the study figures it as an outcome of repeated game (Bayesian, PD or evolutionary). As co-operation is a decision based on trust (Deutsch, 1962) the evolution of trust can also be modeled by as an outcome of repeated PD in Multi Agent situation.

Schelling (1971, 1972) applied term "tipping" to explain the event that occurs "when some recognizable minority group in a neighborhood reaches a size that motivates the other residents to begin leaving. The term implies that subsequent entrants who take the place of those who leave are predominantly of the minority and that the process ultimately and irreversibly changes the composition of the neighborhood." The Schilling threshold applies to strict choice based situations. The authors in Bruch et al. (2007) show that changing the functional form of the utility function can dramatically alter the observed level of residential segregation. So, in a network if based on direct and indirect information about some node trust is assigned between each pair of nodes automatically we can expect a separation of trustworthy and malicious nodes.

As noted earlier, "We are experiencing the emergence of a new way for people to relate to each other and to meet new people using the so-called social web. What's more, this new model has a lot in common with the clubs of the 17th century, in UK and indeed with all the face-to-face clubs that exist today"(Fahey, 2007). We can argue that emergence and evolution of trust in distributed network will also follow this rule at least if human involvement is there. So, certain kind of training or learning phase should be there in this network. Page Rank algorithm (Brin et al., 1998) is very powerful and attack resistant. If the concept of trust is incorporated in the same search procedure will be enhanced definitely. In fact the same is incorporated in Trust rank algorithm. Here some good nodes are selected as trusted node. Now trust of other node is determined by calculating link matrix of the page to the trusted node using Eigen Trust algorithm (Kamvar et al., 2003). Intuitively, if the trust scores so obtained is categorized into some levels (Abdul-Rahman et al., 2000) by using some rule such as Dempster – Shafer theory (Shafer, 1976), or the computational model of trust and reputation as proposed by Lik Mui (2002), we may get improved search engine performance. In the presence of unfair rating in online market (eBay) by seller or buyer or both there is a need for online reputation system much like our society, which safeguards the interest of both the parties involved in transaction (Dellarocas, 2001, 2004; Manchala, 1998).In transaction based feedback system like E- commerce or P2P how level of trust is assigned to peers is an open area of research (Xiong et al., 2004).

Existing literature reports a lot of work on use of "trust" in internet applications (Grandison et al., 2000). There is still many questions to explore. Context specificity of trust is not tested in our model. We, have tested our simulation with very small (10-50) number of peer. We want to check it in a scenario of at least 10,000 nodes, and then we can verify the emerging patterns that may come out. In our model we assume complete information. Trust calculation in case of insufficient information will be an interesting research tropic.

In this work apart from coming up with our own computational trust model and performing various computer experiments to examine the correctness or robustness of the same we also, develop a model of trust driven bottom up self segregation in virtual third places. At the core, of this model where agents/ peers/ human beings behave like atoms (Galam, 1996a, 2004) lies a notion of human identity which in our simple model is just union of two points and that is the social space we consider. However, social space or identity space in political context can actually be much more complicated if we try to model different political positions using one or, more geometric axes representing independent political dimensions. An exact realistic model is debated over and over again by political scientists and there is no final agreement yet (Eysenck, 1956; Rokeach, 1973; Nolan, 1971; http://www.politicalcompass.org; Greenbarg, 2003; Inglehart, 2005). As we have reported before, Prof. Nigel Gilbert in his social simulations did use a multidimensional template to model identities of agents. Eminent, Nobel Laureate, Economist, Prof. Dr. Amartya Sen in his book, "Identity and Violence: The Illusion of Destiny", argues that violence is rooted in the tendency of the human being to identify with only one key trait of their identity– ethnicity or religion- to the exclusion of all others. He proposes that one can combat this tendency by rejecting this limited sense of identity and embracing a more complex understanding of her/his own human existence (Sen, 2006). Bib Latane and James H. Liu, in their article titled "Inter-subjective geometry of social space" tried to come up with a more detailed "description" of social space and did discuss the processes that differentiate the same from subjective psychological space and objective physical reality (Latane, 1996). Donald Black came up with a notion of social geometry, a theoretical strategy of sociological explanation, which proposes a multidimensional model to explain variations in the behavior of social laws. The model consists of five variables horizontal, vertical, corporate, cultural, and normative. This multidimensional amalgam called social space also allows interaction between this variables and correlation between them (Black, 1976, 1998). This model is based on an epistemological formalism called pure sociology which is free from psychology and teleology- and even people as such. In fact the social upward mobility of groups along the vertical economic axis is studied and discussed by various researchers as well as him and is called movement through social space. A similar notion called "Sanskritaisation" (Srinivas, 1952) explains a form of social change in caste based Indian Hindu Society. In this context latter horizontal movement through the social space of Indian society was also studied (Roy, 2009). The previous discussion illustrates that our identity model is indeed a very simple one and starting from socio-physicists like Galam to economist/ philosopher like Amatya Sen, a variety of academicians of various disciplines did come up with various complex qualitative and quantitative models. Black even manages to abstract out the dynamics of social space from the context of psychology and individual. Therefore, it will be interesting to investigate in future what sort of trust based macro pattern becomes emergent when more complex definitions of agent identity and embedding of the same in more complex description of social space is integrated in the simulation model.

We will also like to humbly note that in fact our interaction model which is somewhat motivated by the well established domain of conversation analysis in structured domain, is indeed simple. It somewhat resembles, the process of repeated arguments and counter-arguments in a court of law or board room negotiation or the same in Bard's duel ("kabir larai") of rural Bengal in "Anthony Phiringi-Bhola Moira" era (in this context it was known as "chapan-Utor") (Miah et al., 2003; Das, 2006; Sen, 1960, 1962). As noted before, there is an array of models describing human interaction dynamics and social impact of the same. Apart from older models of Abelson (1964), Axelord (1980, 1984), Schilling's (1971, 1972) basic model and well known Latane (1981) model, Sznajd (2000), Deffnaut (2000), Kohring (1998), Kulakowski (2009), and Plewczyn'ski (1998), each came up with their own specific model of interaction and social impact and discussed resultant emergent phenomena. The field is further enriched by works of various mathematical sociologist and socio-physicist like Galam, Stauffer and collaboration between socio-physicists like Galam with social scientists like Moscovici. It will be interesting to incorporate these complex interaction models in trust algorithm. Indeed literature survey indicates that there are not many works in this domain.

We have shown that trust developed as a consequence of interaction is dictating the degree of future interactions i.e., the temporarily varying weight of links of evolving underlying complex network and the quality of experience in visiting a chat room. Both leads to a learning process which we model by an actor critique type learning automata algorithm although our basic identity of agents remain unchanged. Now, as reported in Narendra and Thathachar (1989) and Thathachar and Sastry (2004) there are indeed various different types of learning automata type model. So, it can always be debated which specific model is most applicable in this context, given that we are talking trust driven learning, a process that has got something to do with emotional, social and interpersonal intelligence of agents (Thorndike, 1920; Gardner, 1983; Payne, 1983, 1986). Now, these issues too are studied under various models. Therefore, it is indeed an interesting open problem to find out which of computational learning algorithm should be used in such a context for precise emulation of reality.

REFERENCES

Abdul-Rahman, A., & Hailes, S. (2000, January). Supporting trust in virtual communities. In *Proceedings of the Hawaii International Conference on System Sciences*, Maui, HI.

Abelson, R. P. (1964). Mathematical models of the distribution of attributes under controversy. In Frederksen, N., & Gulliksen, H. (Eds.), *Contribution to mathematical psychology*. New York, NY: Holt, Reinehart, & Winston.

Adamic, L., & Glance, N. (2005). The political blogosphere and the 2004 US election: Divided they blog. In *Proceedings of the World Wide Web Conference 2nd Annual Workshop on the Web blogging Ecosystem: Aggregation, Analysis, and Dynamics.*

Androutsellis-Theotokis, S., Spinellis, D., & Vlachos, V. (2007). The MoR-Trust Distributed Trust Management System: Design and Simulation Results. *Electronic Notes in Theoretical Computer Science*, *179*, 3–15. doi:10.1016/j.entcs.2006.11.032.

Artz, D., & Gil, Y. (2007). A survey of trust in computer science and the semantic web. *Journal of Web Semantics: Science. Services and Agents on the World Wide Web*, *5*(2), 58–71. doi:10.1016/j.websem.2007.03.002.

Ashok, P. (2011). *The Social History of England*. Pradesh, India: Orient Blackswan.

Axelrod, R. (1980). More effective choice in prisoner's dilemma. *The Journal of Conflict Resolution, 24*(3), 379–403. doi:10.1177/002200278002400301.

Axelrod, R. (1984). *The evolution of co-operation.* New York, NY: Basic Books.

Axelrod, R. (1997). The dissemination of culture: A model with local convergence and global polarization. *The Journal of Conflict Resolution, 41,* 203–226. doi:10.1177/0022002797041002001.

Battey, A. (2006, April 4). Taking it to the street. *Yale Daily News.*

Blake, D. (1976). *Behaviour of Law.* New York, NY: Academic Press.

Blake, D. (1998). *The social structure of right or wrong* (Rev. ed.). San Diego, CA: Academic Press.

Blake, R. (2002). *Voices of New York (Spring MAP Class Project).* New York, NY: New York University.

Boudourides, M. (2003, February 12-16). A simulation of convergent-divergent public opinion formation on social networks. In *Proceedings of the 23rd Sunbelt International Social Network Conference,* Cancun, Mexico.

Boyd, S., Ghosh, A., Prabhakar, B., & Shah, D. (2005, March). Gossip algorithms: Design, analysis and applications. In *Proceedings of the IEEE Annual Joint Conference INFOCOM,* Miami, FL (Vol. 3, pp. 1653-1664).

Brin, S., & Page, L. (1998). The anatomy of a large-scale hyper textual Web search engine. *In* Proceedings of the Seventh International Conference on World Wide Web *(pp. 107-117).*

Bruch, E. E., & Mare, R. D. (2006). Neighborhood choice and neighborhood change. *American Journal of Sociology, 112*(3), 667–709. doi:10.1086/507856.

Chattopadhyay, S. (2005). *Representing Calcutta Modernity, Nationalism and the Colonial Uncanny.* London, UK: Routledge.

Das, K. (2006). Radha Birbhumer Kabiwala O Kabigan. *Paschim Banga, Birbhum,* 289-309.

Deffuant, G., Neau, D., Amblard, F., & Weisbuch, G. (2000). Mixing beliefs among interacting agents. *Advances in Complex Systems, 3,* 87. doi:10.1142/S0219525900000078.

Dellarocas, C. (2001, October). Analyzing the economic efficiency of eBay-like online reputation mechanisms. In *Proceedings of the 3rd ACM Conference on Electronic Commerce,* Tampa, FL.

Dellarocas, C. (2004). Building trust on-line: The design of robust reputation mechanisms for online trading communities. In Doukidis, G., Mylonopoulos, N., & Pouloudi, N. (Eds.), *Information society or information economy? A combined perspective on the digital era.* Hershey, PA: Idea Group.

Deutsch, M. (1962). Cooperation and trust: Some theoretical notes. In *Proceedings of the Nebraska Symposium on Motivation* (pp. 275-319).

Eysenck, H. J. (1956). *Sense and nonsense in psychology.* London, UK: Penguin Books.

Fahey, C. (2007). *The social web's coffeehouses, nightclubs, country clubs, and taverns.* Retrieved from http://www.graphpaper.com

Fitzgerald, F. S. (1920). *This side of paradise.* New York, NY: Scribner.

Galam, S. (1996a). When humans interact like atoms. In White, E., & Davis, J. H. (Eds.), *Understanding group behaviour (Vol. 1,* pp. 293–312). Mahwah, NJ: Lawrence Erlbaum.

Galam, S. (1996b). Fragmentation versus stability in bimodal coalitions. *Physica A, 230,* 174–188. doi:10.1016/0378-4371(96)00034-9.

Galam, S. (1997). Rational group decision making: A random field Ising model at t = 0. *Physica A*, *238*, 66–80. doi:10.1016/S0378-4371(96)00456-6.

Galam, S. (2004). Socio-physics: a personal Testimony. *Physica A. Statistical and Theoretical Physics*, *336*(1-2), 49–55. doi:10.1016/j.physa.2004.01.009.

Gambetta, D. (2000). Can we trust? In Gambetta, D. (Ed.), *Trust: Making and breaking cooperative relations* (pp. 213–237). Oxford, UK: University of Oxford.

Gardner, H. (1983). *Friends of mind*. New York, NY: Basic Book.

Gilbert, N. (2002, October 11-12). *Transformation of the welfare state: The silent surrender of public responsibility*. Paper presented at the Workshop on Agent Social Agents: Ecology, Exchange, and Evolution Conference.

Grandison, M. S. T., & Sloman, M. (2000). A survey of trust in internet applications. *IEEE Communications Surveys*, *3*(4), 2–16. doi:10.1109/COMST.2000.5340804.

Granovetter, M. (1973). The strength of weak ties. *American Journal of Sociology*, *78*, 1360–1380. doi:10.1086/225469.

Greenberg, J., & Jonas, E. (2003). Psychological motives and political orientation- the left, the right, and the rigid: Comment on Jost et al. (2003). *Psychological Bulletin*, *129*(3), 376–382. doi:10.1037/0033-2909.129.3.376 PMID:12784935.

Grossglauser, M., & Tse, D. (2002). Mobility increases the capacity of ad-hoc wireless networks. *IEEE/ACM Transactions on Networking*, *10*(4), 477–486. doi:10.1109/TNET.2002.801403.

Guzzetta, M. (2006, June 18). Independent arts editor. *The Nantucket Independent*.

Haas, Z. J., Halpern, J. Y., & Li, L. (2006). Gossip based ad-hoc routing. *IEEE/ACM Transactions on Networking*, *14*(3), 479–491. doi:10.1109/TNET.2006.876186.

Hu, W. (2007, July 29). More than a meal plan. *The New York Times*.

Huberman, B. A., & Adamic, L. A. (2004). Information dynamics in the networked world. Lecture Notes in Physics, 398(3), 371-398.

IEEE Communications Society. (n. d.). *TCCC mailing list*. Retrieved February 11, 2009, from http://www.comsoc.org/~tccc/list.html

Inglehart, R., & Welzel, C. (2005). *Modernization, cultural change and democracy (based on World Value Survey)* (p. 64). Cambridge, UK: Cambridge University Press.

Kamvar, S. D., Schlosser, M. T., & Garcia-Molina, H. (2003). The Eigen Trust algorithm for reputation management in p2p networks. In *Proceedings of the Twelfth International Conference on World Wide Web* (pp. 640-651).

Karmakar, P. (2008). *Evolution of trust in distributed structured network* (Unpublished master's thesis). Indian Institute of Technology, Kharagpur, India.

Kohring, G. A. (1998). Sing models of social impact: the role of cumulative advantage. *Journal de Physique. I*, *6*, 301. doi:10.1051/jp1:1996150.

Krassa, M. (2008). *Better together: Lively mains streets, vital neighborhood, and engaging public places*. Paper presented at the Cornelius O'Brien Conference.

Krause, E. F. (1987). *Taxicab geometry*. Mineola, NY: Dover.

Kulakowski, K. (2009). Opinion polarization in the Receipt-Accept-Sample model. *Physica A, 388*, 469. doi:10.1016/j.physa.2008.10.037.

Lai, L., & Gamal, H. E. (2008). On cooperation in energy efficient wireless networks: The role of altruistic nodes. *IEEE Transactions on Wireless Communications, 7*(5), 1868–1878. doi:10.1109/TWC.2008.060568.

Latané, B. (1981). The psychology of social impact. *The American Psychologist, 36*(4), 343–356. doi:10.1037/0003-066X.36.4.343.

Latané, B. (1996). Dynamic social impact: Robust predictions from simple theory. In Hegselmann, R., Mueller, U., & Troitzsch, K. (Eds.), *Modeling and simulation in the social sciences from a philosophy of science point of view*. Dordrecht, The Netherlands: Kluwer Academic. doi:10.1007/978-94-015-8686-3_15.

Latané, B. (2000). Pressures to uniformity and the evolution of cultural norms: Modeling dynamics of social impact. In Hulin, C., & Ilgen, D. (Eds.), *Computational modeling of behavior in organizations. The third scientific discipline* (pp. 189–215). Washington, DC: American Psychological Association. doi:10.1037/10375-009.

Latané, B., & Liu, J. H. (1996). Inter subjective geometry of social space. *The Journal of Communication, 46*(4), 26–34. doi:10.1111/j.1460-2466.1996.tb01502.x.

Lewenstein, M., Nowak, A., & Latane, B. (1992). The statistical mechanics of social impact. *Physical Review A., 45*, 703–716. doi:10.1103/PhysRevA.45.763 PMID:9907042.

Manchala, D. W. (1998). Trust metrics, models and protocols for electronic commerce transactions. In *Proceedings of the 18th International Conference on Distributed Computing Systems.*

Marsh, S. (1994). *Formalising trust as a computational concept* (Unpublished doctoral dissertation). University of Stirling, Stirling, UK.

Miah, S., & Islam, S. (2003). *Banglapedia: National Encyclopedia of Bangladesh* (*Vol. 4*, p. 119). Bangladesh: Asiatic Society of Bangladesh.

Mui, L. (2002). *Computational models of trust and reputation: Agents, evolutionary games, and social networks* (Unpublished doctoral dissertation). Massachusetts Institute of Technology, Cambridge, MA.

Narendra, K. S., & Thathachar, M. A. L. (1989). *Learning Automata: An introduction*. Upper Saddle River, NJ: Prentice Hall.

Nolan, D. (1971). *Classifying and analyzing politico-economic systems. The Individualist*. Society for Individual Liberty.

Nowak, A., Szamrej, J., & Latane, B. (1990). From private attitude to public opinion: A dynamic theory of social impact. *Psychological Review, 97*, 362. doi:10.1037/0033-295X.97.3.362.

Nowak, M. A., Tarmita, C. E., & Antal, T. (2010). Evolutionary dynamics in structured population. *Philosophical Transaction of the Royal Society B, 365*(1537), 19–30. doi:10.1098/rstb.2009.0215.

Oldenburg, R. (1989). *The great good place: Cafes, coffee shops, community centers, beauty parlors, general stores, bars, hang outs, and how they get you through the day*. New York, NY: Paragon House.

Oldenburg, R. (1991). *The great good place*. New York, NY: Marlow.

Oldenburg, R. (2000). *Celebrating the Third Place: Inspiring stories about the great good places at the heart of our communities*. New York, NY: Marlow.

Payne, W. (1983). A study of emotion: Developing emotional intelligence, self integration relating to fear, pain and desire. *Dissertation Abstracts International, 47*, 203A (AAC 8605928).

Plewczyn'ski, D. (1998). Landau theory of social clustering. *Physica A, 261*, 608–617. doi:10.1016/S0378-4371(98)00349-5.

Pomerantz, A. M. (1984). Agreeing and disagreeing with assessment: Some features of preferred/dis-preferred turn shapes. In Atkinson, J. M., & Heritage, J. (Eds.), *Structure of social action: Studies in conversation analysis*. Cambridge, UK: Cambridge University Press.

Rokeach, M. (1973). *The nature of human values*. New York, NY: Free Press.

Roy, M. (2009). *The Bharati and the Social Mobility in the Bengal*. Kolkata, India: Aruna Prakashani.

Roychoudhury, R. (2005). *Brownian Gossip: Exploiting node mobility for diffusing information in wireless networks*. Paper presented at the Workshop on Stochasticity in Distributed Systems.

Sarwate, A. D., & Dimakis, A. G. (2009). The impact of mobility on gossip algorithm. In *Proceedings of the 28th Annual International Conference on Computer Communication*, Rio de Janeiro, Brazil.

Sawyer, R. K. (2005). Social Emergence: *Societies as complex systems*. Cambridge, UK: Cambridge University Press.

Schegloff, E. A. (2007). *Sequence organization in interaction: a primer in Conversation Analysis (Vol. 1)*. Cambridge, UK: Cambridge University Press. doi:10.1017/CBO9780511791208.

Schelling, T. (1971). Dynamic models of segregation. *The Journal of Mathematical Sociology, 1*, 143–186. doi:10.1080/0022250X.1971.9989794.

Schelling, T. (1972). A process of residential segregation: Neighborhood tipping. In Pascal, A. (Ed.), *Racial discrimination in economic life* (pp. 157–184). Lexington, MA: D.C. Heath.

Sen, A. (2006). *Identity and violence: The illusion of destiny (issues of our time)*. New York, NY: W. W. Norton.

Sen, G. N. (1962). An English Kabiwala of Bengal. *Midwest Folklore, 12*(1), 27–30.

Sen, S. (1960). *History of Bengali Literature (Forwarded by Jawaharlal Nehru)*. New Delhi, India: Sahitya Academy.

Shafer, G. (1976). *A mathematical theory of evidence*. Princeton, NJ: Princeton University Press.

Singh, V. (2008). *Pattern formation using gossip* (Unpublished master's thesis). Indian Institute of Technology, Kharagpur, India.

Srinivas, M. N. (1952). *Religion and Society among the coorgs of South India*. Oxford, UK: Oxford University Press.

Sun, Y., & Yang, Y. (2007, June). Rust establishment in distributed networks: Analysis and modeling. In *Proceedings of the IEEE International Communications Conference*, Glasgow, UK (pp. 1266-1273).

Sznajd-Weron, K., & Sznajd, J. (2000). Opinion evolution in closed community. *International Journal of Modern Physics C, 11*, 1157–1166. doi:10.1142/S0129183100000936.

Thathachar, M. A. L., & Sastry, P. S. (2004). *Networks of Learning Automata: Techniques for Online Stochastic Optimization*. Boston, MA: Kluwar Academic. doi:10.1007/978-1-4419-9052-5.

Thorndike, R. K. (1920). Intelligent and its uses. *Harpers Magazine, 140*, 227–335.

Vega-Redondo, F. (2007). *Complex Social Networks (Econometric Society Monographs)*. Cambridge, UK: Cambridge University Press. doi:10.1017/CBO9780511804052.

Walking Around. (2004). *New York City's ethnic neighborhoods*. Retrieved April 22, 2009, from http://www.walkingaround.com

Watts, D. J., Doods, P. S., & Newman, M. E. J. (2002). Identity and search in social networks. *Science*, *296*, 1302–1305. doi:10.1126/science.1070120 PMID:12016312.

Wikipedia. (n. d.). *Ethnic enclave*. Retrieved March 18, 2009, from http://en.wikipedia.org/wiki/New_York_City_ethnic_enclaves

Xiong, L., & Liu, L. (2004). Peer trust: Supporting reputation-based trust for peer-to-peer electronic communities. *IEEE Transactions on Knowledge and Data Engineering*, *16*(16).

Zelasity, M. (2005). Engineering emergence through gossip. In Proceedings of the Joint Symposium on Socially Inspired Computing, AISB Convention, Hatfield, UK (pp. 123-126).

Ziegler, C. N., & Golbeck, J. (2007). Investigating interaction of trust and interest similarity. Decision Support Systems, 43(2), 460–475. doi:10.1016/j.dss.2006.11.003

This work was previously published in the International Journal of Virtual Communities and Social Networking, Volume 3, Issue 2, edited by Subhasish Dasgupta, pp. 17-50, copyright 2011 by IGI Publishing (an imprint of IGI Global).

Chapter 7
Social Shopping Development and Perspectives

Chingning Wang
National Sun Yat-Sen University, Taiwan

ABSTRACT

"Social shopping" (or social commerce), combining shopping and social networking, is an application of Web 2.0 in electronic commerce to benefit from users' social networks. This paper explores the development of the emergent "social shopping" and related perspectives. It incorporates comparisons between social shopping marketing and search engine marketing. For example, search engine marketing assumes shoppers are certain of their shopping goal; social shopping marketing assumes shoppers are uncertain of their shopping goals and gather shopping ideas from their peers. In this paper, the challenges in social shopping development are identified, including governing shopper communities and retrieving content from social networking sites. The author concludes that social shopping and e-commerce are not dichotomous concepts. Social shopping can be an evolutionary concept, meaning a singular EC site advancing with social networking functions, or a synergistic concept, meaning EC sites connecting with the other social networking sites to form strategic alliance.

INTRODUCTION

The interactive features of Web 2.0 and the pervasion of social media (also called social network media) like MySpace and Facebook have provided many commercial interests. Take MySpace as example. The number of profiles hosted on

MySpace was over 106 million (O'Malley, 2006). According to Jupiter Internet Shopping Model, US online population estimated to increase to 211 million by 2006, and the online retail sales estimated to reach $112.5 billion in 2006. At the end of August in 2006, MySpace accounted for 2.53% of all visits to e-commerce sites and 4.88%

DOI: 10.4018/978-1-4666-4022-1.ch007

of visits to all websites (O'Malley, 2006). It generates more traffic to shopping sites than MSN, and was ahead of eBay, Amazon, Gateway and Wal-Mart (O'Malley, 2006). Although social media's e-commerce efforts and business models are still immature, its potential is deemed promising and Wall Street recognizes its ability to transform market. Therefore, practitioners are eager to turn MySpace into a lucrative marketplace. Amazon and eBay, for example, have been in the vanguard to tap the commercial potential of MySpace and Facebook (Birchall, 2008).

Out of the commercial potential of social media, the term "social shopping" (also called "social commerce") is crafted to describe the combination of shopping and social networking activities through social media online. It is also viewed as a new category of e-commerce which is called 'social commerce' at the birth of a "referral economy" after 2005 (Harkin, 2007). The development and pervasion of social networks and social media continues. In 2010, we see 30 billion pieces of content shared on Facebook per month, 25 billion shared on Twitter, and 152 million blogs showing online in 2010 ("Internet 2010 in Numbers", 2010). Consequently, the commercial potential of social networks and social media (i.e., social shopping or social commerce) continues to attract attentions. Social commerce has paved it way through the hard time and begins to generate profits, however, it still faces several challenges and unsolved issues (Wang, 2009; Wang & Zhang, in press). Therefore, this emerging terrain provides many opportunities for both the researchers and the practitioners. As such, it is important to generate a holistic understanding to harness the potential of social media and social networking sites in the domain of social commerce.

Sorting into the trade literature, this paper attempts to explore the development of the emergent phenomenon of "social shopping" and identify perspectives on social shopping. Comparison of social shopping marketing and search engine marketing is incorporated in the discussion. To conclude on the accumulated trade literature, social

commerce and e-commerce are not dichotomous. Rather, social commerce is an evolution advanced from e-commerce.

SOCIAL SHOPPING IN THE PAST

A search through the literature found that the term "social shopping" is not novel. It is interesting to note that the concept of "social shopping" in the earlier literature is by no mean delineated in online setting as the newly literature after 2005 in the domain of e-commerce does. Rather, earlier literature bounded the concept of social shopping in an offline (or non-IT-mediated), face-to-face setting.

In an empirical study by Marshall and Heslop (1988), "social shopping orientation" along with "convenience shopping orientation" were used as predictors of consumers' use of self-service technology (i.e., automated teller machines). In their research, a predisposition to face-to-face personal interaction was viewed as the characteristic of social shopping orientation. Convenience shopping orientation, on the other hand, is characterized by technology-mediated feature. Their findings suggested that shoppers with a social shopping orientation do not perceive using self-service technology as advantageous while shoppers with a convenience orientation do. Their views and suggestions implied that users with social shopping orientation may be less favorable to the use of new technology that was viewed as lacking a personal interaction characteristic then.

Likewise, Tauber in an empirical study in 1995 differentiated "social shopping motives" from "personal shopping motives". According to Tauber (1995), social shopping motives include social experiences *outside the home,* communication with others, peer group attraction, status and authority, and pleasure of bargaining. These motives are different from personal shopping motives that emphasize more on self-gratification, role playing, diversion, learning about new trends, physical activity and sensory stimulation. Obviously, as a result of development of interactive information technology, many aspects of the classification used in the earlier literature appear to be collapsed and outdated. "Social shopping" in its present sense is not necessary to be social experience outside the home, nor a social interaction limited to face-to-face mode. As such, there is a need to revisit the concept of social shopping to capture the newer trends emerged with the application of interactive information technology in the domain of e-commerce.

SOCIAL SHOPPING REVISITED: SOCIAL SHOPPING PERSPECTIVES

Three perspectives to "social shopping" and their underlying assumptions identified from the trade literature are discussed in this section. Examples elicited from the practices are incorporated in the subsequent discussion. These three approaches serve as three perspectives in practice that address a fundamental question of what is social shopping: technical functional perspective, behavioral perspective and strategic perspective. Figure 1 presents the integrated framework of the three perspectives.

1. Interactive Technical Function Perspective

Two themes identified from the literature are and discussed next.

Figure 1. An integrated framework of social shopping

Theme 1: Network on Shopping Features Facilitated by Interactive Technical Applications (i.e., Web 3.0)

This view focuses on the technical evolution driven by peer-to-peer (p2p) recommendations to gather people into one place for shopping purposes. Peer-to-peer recommendations are facilitated through interactive technical functions such as user review systems, wish lists, blogging, shared videos and wiki sites. However, user generated recommendations is common and essential in e-commerce already. What social shopping advances from e-commerce is gathering the groups with specific shopping features and benefiting the groups with users' social networks (or social capitals). For example, ThisNext.com and iliketotallyloveit.com provide shopping features connecting shoppers with hard-to-find products through digital words of mouth, or networking with users. Osoyou. com, the first UK social shopping sites, operates like fashion-version Facebook connecting shoppers who like to know what celebrities do and the fashion trends. Its main purpose on social networking is to let users see what people whose taste they admire purchase and how these people think of them. User will further discover products they are not aware of before and further generate shopping intention (Harkin, 2008). Kaboodle. com or ShopStyle.com, for the other examples, let users generate wish lists, exchange viewpoints on items, post photos and make purchases (O'Malley, 2006; Tedeschi, 2006). These sites are designed for both browsing, blogging, and chatting with e-commerce related technology incorporated to facilitate specific shopping features (O'Malley, 2006; Tedeschi, 2006). But the underlying assumption of the practice of letting users see what other people purchase or include in their wish lists is to generate emotional purchase (i.e., follow the crowd). Furthermore, there are social shopping sites that provide team-buying feature through social networking. Nethaggler, for example, enables individual users group together for bargaining purpose. These diverse shopping features enabled by the interactive technical functions represent the distinctive cultures of interests inherent in the sites.

Theme 1 conceptualizes social shopping as a social group of users gathered for specific shopping purposes through interactive technical functions of a singular commercial site. According to the assumption of theme 1, e-commerce and social commerce (or online shopping and social shopping) are not dichotomous concepts with distinctive characteristics. Rather, social shopping is considered as an evolution from e-commerce to have a user community addressing specific shopping features.

Theme 2: Interactive Technical Functions Connecting Commercial Sites with Social Networking Sites

While theme 1 focuses on the social group enabled by the interactive technical functions of a singular commercial site, theme 2 focuses on a more synergistic, or symbiotic online business alliance connecting multiple sites through interactive technical functions. Namely, Commercial sites and social networking sites are connected through interactive technical functions. This synergistic evolution is reflected in the trend where existing e-tailer websites attempt to take advantage of the potentials of *social networking websites*.

Facebook and MySpace are well-known social networking websites. Not only these social networking sites aim to transfer the numbers of profiles into dollars, existing e-tailers also express interests to tap into the market potential presented by social networking sites. For instance, Ebay, partnered with Google, aims to expand their business to MySpace's giant social network (O'Malley, 2006). Amazon, for the other instance, has developed its own review and wish list systems, and further aims at integrating millions of Facebook users into its merchandizing opportunities by tying its own systems of shopping list and product

reviews into Facebooks' page; thereby Facebook users can see Amazon users' wish lists (Birchall, 2008). For another instance ThisNext' s social networking site letting their users transfer pictures or videos of their desired products from the site to users' personal blogs, plans to form partner with merchants who pay commissions on sales that come as a result of their products being featured on the sites (Tedeschi, 2006).

According to theme 2, social shopping is a connection between social networking sites and e-commerce sites though interactive technical functions. Still, it does not view e-commerce and social commerce (or online shopping and social shopping) as dichotomous concept. Rather social shopping is a synergistic concept driven by the commercial potential of social networking sites.

The previous discussion on interactive functional view is summarized in Table 1. This categorization helps us understand what types of social shopping sites, according to the interactive technical function view, are in practice. This categorization of social shopping sites, though not complete, reflects the distinctive cultures of interests inherent in the sites to the users, vendors, marketers and advertisers.

In spite of the potential opportunities mentioned before, social shopping in practice confronts the challenges to manage the technical hurdles effectively and efficiently. For example, how to get users download software required to perform the desired social shopping functions. Also, social shopping sites incorporating search engine applications need to tackle on how to retrieve content from social networking sites more effectively.

2. Social Shopping as Online Consumer Behavior

The view elicited from the trade literature perceives social shopping as a category of online consumer behavior. A recent study by technology research firm Gartern reported that online shoppers can be

Table 1. Features of social shopping sites based on interactive technical functions

Themes	Examples of Social Shopping Sites	Shopping Features	Assumptions
T1: Interactive Shopping features facilitated by interactive technical functions in a singular website	Kaboodle, ShopTyle.com, TheNext	***Exchanging shopping ideas:*** Users of the sites can see other users' wish lists, comments on items, purchased items and photo of products.	Users may not have concrete shopping idea but would generate it by seeing what other people purchase
	NetHaggler	***Team-buying:*** Website that lets individual buyer group together to bargain down the prices	Users are empowered with large scale economy
	ThisNext.Com	***Niche product searching:*** website connecting users with hard-to-find products	Users don't have to spend huge efforts into discovering niche products. Social network of the users reduce shopping efforts.
T2: Interactive technical functions connecting commercial sites with social shopping sites	Amazon, Ebay, vs. Facebook, MySpace	Users of social shopping sites can read products reviews provided by the e-tailers.	Turn social networking sites into business opportunities by forming alliance with commercial sites

differentiated into two types, goal-oriented *solo shoppers* and *social shoppers* (Voight, 2007). According to the study, solo online shoppers have specific needs and are certain on how and where to fulfill their needs. Social shoppers on the other hand may not have specific shopping needs and emphasize communication with other online shoppers to exchange shopping ideas via bulletin board, blog, wiki, shared videos etc. Although social shoppers may not have specific shopping needs, their communication, or collaboration with other shoppers may lead to purchase that had not planned to make (Voight, 2007). In this regard, social shopping behavior can be considered as collaborative behavior in social media among consumers.

As aforementioned, the concept of "social shopping" in the earlier literature is not delineated in online setting as the newly literature after 2005 in the domain of e-commerce does. Earlier literature positions the concept of social shopping in an offline (or non-IT-mediated), face-to-face setting.

The latest concept of "social shopper" identified in trade literature is similar to the concepts of "social shopping orientation" in Marshall and Heslop (1988) and "social shopping motives" in Tauber (1995) in terms of the predisposition to interacting, communicating with others. The major difference is that the latest view of social shopping in e-commerce refers primarily to online shopping behavior that is mediated by social networking technology, or social media. Moreover, the latest view of social shopping in e-commerce suggests that "social shopping orientation" is not confined to face-to-face interaction. As such, viewing the two concepts of "social shopping orientation" and "convenience shopping orientation" in the context of social commerce, they are no longer two dichotomous concepts. Obviously, as a result of the development of interactive information technology, many aspects of the classification used in the earlier academic literature appear to be collapsed and outdated (Table 2).

In sum, "social shopping" in its present sense which emphasizes the facilitator of social media is not necessary to be social experience outside the home, nor a social interaction limited to face-to-face mode. As such, there is a need to revisit the concept of social shopping as consumer behavior to capture the newer trends emerged with the application of interactive information technology in the domain of e-commerce.

Table 2. Evolutionary definitions of social shopping

Source	Terms	Characteristics	Notes
Marshall & Heslop (1988)	*Social shopping orientation*	A predisposition to face-to-face personal interaction	Off-line Setting
	Cf. Convenience shopping orientation	A predisposition to use self-service technology [operationalized as auto teller machine]	
Tauber (1995)	*Social shopping motives*	Emphasis on social experiences outside the home, communication with others, peer group attraction, status and authority, and pleasure of bargaining.	Off-line Setting (outside the home)
	Cf. Personal shopping motives	Emphasis on self-gratification, role playing, diversion, learning about new trends, physical activities and sensory stimulation.	
Garten Report (2007)	*Social shoppers*	Online shoppers emphasize communication with other shoppers to exchange shopping ideas.	Online Setting
	Cf. Solo Shoppers	Shoppers have specific needs and are certain on how to fulfill their needs.	

3. Social Shopping as Business Strategy

The third view considers social shopping as business strategies. Two themes are identified under this strategic perspective: business reengineering strategy and social media marketing strategy.

Theme 1: Business Reengineering Strategies

Theme 1 perceives social shopping as a business strategy aiming to reengineering aging concepts in e-commerce. E-commerce sites have largely focused on improving the purchasing process to make it as efficient and seamless as possible from a technical functional perspective. However, a recent trade study by a digital agency Blast Radius and California investigated into consumers' online shopping experiences and found that there is too much sameness among the online shopping experience provided by the retailers (Lazarus, 2006). The sameness reflected from the consumers' online shopping experience can no longer attract mercurial consumers (Lazarus, 2006). Indeed,

functional improvement is not the only advantage the shoppers want. No matter how efficient, easy, and seamless, online shopping does not provide a sense of social experience that people relate to physical shopping whereby people gather and share ideas with each other, as is shown in this trade study. As such, social shopping becomes a business reengineering strategy that enables commercial websites to take advantage of the Web 2.0 that is compatible with the social networking realities (Lazarus, 2006).

Here we can see the linkage between the perspective of business reengineering strategy and the perspective of interactive technical function we discussed in previous section. Indeed, interactive technical function is the core and is reframed by a strategic purpose. In this sense, interactive technical functions are reframed as social media (or social networking media) to reflect the strategic purpose it intends to achieve. The development of social media reengineers e-commerce strategy by incorporating social experiences into it. The underlying business reengineering assumption is to invigorate mercurial consumers' online shopping experiences with a sense of social atmosphere.

Theme 2: Social Media Marketing Strategy

Theme 2 perceives social shopping as marketing strategies emphasizing peer-to-peer recommendations through social media. The assumption underlying this theme is that people trust friends or whoever they consider as their peers, and is more likely to trust their recommendations. As such, peer-to-peer referral through social media is the key to this social media marketing strategy. While theme 1 of interactive technical function perspective emphasizes the technical aspect facilitating peer-to-peer recommendation, theme 2 of business strategy perspective conceived p2p as marketing strategy. The aim of social shopping marketing strategy is to create a community-like virtual space for like-minded people to share shopping ideas.

As aforementioned before that p2p recommendation is already basic in e-commerce, social shopping trade literature reframes it as marketing strategy aiming to reengineering predicaments of more conventional online marketing strategy. The predicaments serving as drivers of social shopping marketing strategies are elaborated later.

One of the drivers of social shopping behind this marketing strategy perspective is the predicament many small companies faced when competing with their larger counterparts in online marketing. Online marketing media such as banners, pop-up window and keyword advertising once was a useful vehicle for small companies with limited advertising budgets to reach consumers widely. However, intensified competition has driven up the prices, and further marginalized small companies (McCarthy, 2007). Small companies then seek alternative marketing opportunities through online word-of-mouth recommendations.

The other driver of social shopping as a new marketing strategy is brought about by the limitations of search engines marketing. One of the limitations of search engine marketing is the fraudulent clicks retrieved by search engines that endangers consumer's trust (McCarthy, 2007). The other limitation is that typical search engine cannot tell the shoppers what their peers think and recommend but retrieve the brand or product information provided by marketers (Tedeschi, 2006). As such, social shopping as alternative marketing strategy which intends to combine the existing power of and the emergent power of social networking came into being. It is worth of notice that social shopping is considered as ready to moves the current search engine marketing practices into the development of "Web 3.0" that can retrieve hyperlinks out of social networking sites (McCarthy, 2007).

Social shopping marketing strategy is considered as advancement from the typical search engine marketing strategies which can retrieve the names of the brands and retailers but cannot tell the users (or the shoppers) what their peers think or recommend. Online peer-to-peer recommendation is an important online marketing vehicle because people trust the most who they know or are familiar with. Comparisons between search engine marketing strategies and social shopping marketing strategies based on trade literature are outlined in Table 3 to visualize the aspects social shopping marketing strategy advances search engine marketing strategy.

This peer-referral marketing strategy of social shopping brings up new challenge to marketers on how to identify, target and manage relationships with those users who make the most influential recommendations. Since users are with different influence at different levels, a related assumption is that not every user is of equal value. Influential users are valued users. The discussion further shows that the business strategic view complements the consumer behavioral aspect in this regard. The other challenge for the marketers is to set up a rule to manage the community-like virtual space and to guide the line between user-generated content and marketer-generated content.

Table 3. Comparison of search engine and social shopping marketing strategies

	Search Engines Marketing	Social Shopping Marketing
Assumptions of Information Sources	Advertiser/vendor-generated content	(like minded) consumer-generated content;
Assumptions of Utilities	Data-crunching	Data-crunching + social networking
Assumptions of key to catch potential customers	Get to the top list	Word-of-mouth recommendation; peer referral
Assumptions of Consumers	Consumers are *certain of* what they want in advance; goal-oriented solo behavior	Consumers are *uncertain* about what they want and need to see what other people's doing; collaborative behavior
Challenges to marketers	Fraudulent clicks; increasing list price	Identify influential users

CONCLUSION

Three approaches to social shopping are reported in this paper. These three approaches represent three perspectives on what social shopping is in practice. These three approaches are rooted in the rationale of theories in use. The integrated framework and the underlying assumptions of the three approaches contribute to our field by developing potential theoretical foundations derived from the concepts of social shopping in practice.

The first perspective is interactive technical function view. Its first theme views social shopping as interactive technical functions provided by a singular commercial website to facilitate specific shopping features through users' social networks. The second theme under this perspective views social shopping as interactive function connecting commercial sites and social networking sites to enable the potential business power of social networking. The interactive technical functions drawing on the potential of Web 2.0 include user review systems, user wish lists, blogging and wiki. Having the interactive technical functions in a commercial site has been essential in e-commerce. Extending the interactive function of Web 2.0 to fully benefits from online users' social networks (or social capitals) to facilitate shopping purpose is considered the next generation of Web 3.0, which is the central thrust of social shopping.

The second perspective views social shopping as online consumer behavior. Social shopping behavior is considered as collaborative behavior among consumers facilitated by social media. The term "social shopping" has appeared in academic literature prior to 2005 to refer to shoppers who have the predisposition to face-to-face, non technology-mediated personal interaction (Marshall & Heslop, 1988; Tauber, 1995). However, with the pervasion of social media, the conception of social shopping in previous academic literature appears outdated. The third perspective views social shopping as business strategies. Theme 1 under this strategic perspective views social shopping as business reengineering strategy. The aim is to invigorate aging e-commerce strategies focusing on seamlessness and efficiency of online shopping experience by incorporating social atmosphere into online shopping experience. Theme 2 views social shopping as social media marketing strategy advanced from the limitations of more conventional online marketing strategy including search engine marketing strategy. In sum, these three perspectives are not competing with each other. Rather, they complement each other to provide a holistic view of what social shopping is in practice.

To conclude, social commerce and commerce are not dichotomous concepts. Social commerce is considered an evolution advanced from traditional e-commerce. The first perspective, the interactive technical function view, considers social shopping as traditional e-commerce sites providing social networking functions for shoppers, or traditional e-commerce sites forming alliance with social networking sites. The business strategy perspective also views social shopping as a reengineering of traditional e-commerce strategies aiming to invigorating online shopping with social atmosphere. The perspective of consumer behavior further considers social shopping as advancing from solitary online shopping to collaborative, or group shopping through social media. The common assumptions underlying e-commerce are that online shopping is largely an individual, solitary activity. Assumptions on online shoppers are that they know in advance what they want and search product information online rationally. Social shopping on the other hand assumes that shopping activities is not totally rational but has social and emotional aspects. Online shoppers would like to connect with people who they are familiar with, whose opinions they trust, or whose tastes they admire to exchange shopping ideas. Online shoppers may not always have clear shopping ideas but may generate spur-of-the-moment shopping intention after seeing what other people purchase or talk about.

This paper also identified several challenges to social shopping practitioners. These challenges include managing the technical hurdle of interactive functions of social media, governing the networked communities of online shoppers, and identified the influential users that are valued by other users. These challenges further highlight the directions worth of continuing attentions from the practitioners and researchers.

REFERENCES

Birchall, J. (2008, March 14). Amazon Taps Facebook Potential. *Financial Times,* p. 18.

Harkin, F. (2007). The Wisdom of Crowds. *Financial Times,* p. 6.

Harkin, F. (2008, February 19). The Luxury World After Web 2.0. *Financial Times,* p. 14.

Internet 2010 in Numbers. (2010). Retrieved from http://royal.pingdom.com/2011/01/12/internet-2010-in-numbers/

Lazarus, E. (2006). Social Shopping. *Marketing Magazine, 111*(38), 8.

Marshall, J., & Heslop, L. (1988). Technology Acceptance in Canadian Retail Banking: A Study of Consumer Motivations and Use of ATMS. *International Journal of Bank Marketing, 6*(4), 31–41. doi:10.1108/eb010836.

McCarthy, R. (2007, February). The Power of Suggestion: Social Shopping Sites Turn Online Shopping Into a Group Activity. *INC. Magazine, 29,* 48–49.

O'Malley, G. (2006). MySpace vs. eBay? Site Leaps into e-commerce. *Advertising Age, 77*(37), 6.

Tauber, E. (1995). Why Do People Shop? *Marketing Management, 4*(2), 58–60.

Tedeschi, B. (2006, September 11). Like Shopping? Social Networking? Try Social Shopping. *New York Times,* p. C6.

Voight, J. (2007). Study Says Web Shoppers Crave 'Social' Experience. *Adweek, 48,* 10.

Wang, C. (2009). Linking Shopping and Social Networking: Approaches to Social Shopping. In *Proceedings of the 15th Americas Conference on Information Systems (AMCIS).* Retrieved from http://aisel.aisnet.org/amcis2009/27

Wang, C., & Zhang, P. (in press). The Evolution of Social Commerce: People, Business, Technology and Information Aspects. *Communications of the Association for Information Systems.*

This work was previously published in the International Journal of Virtual Communities and Social Networking, Volume 3, Issue 2, edited by Subhasish Dasgupta, pp. 51-59, copyright 2011 by IGI Publishing (an imprint of IGI Global).

Chapter 8
Impact of Blogs on Sales Revenue:
Test of a Network Model

Guoying Zhang
Midwestern State University, USA

Alan J. Dubinsky
Midwestern State University, CALIMT Learning and Innovation Research Center, USA
& Purdue University, USA

Yong Tan
University of Washington, USA

ABSTRACT

In this study, blog data were collected and network parameters were captured to represent three common measurements of online Word-Of-Mouth: intensity, influence level, and dispersion. These parameters were then analyzed using a General Estimating Equation (GEE) model to test their effects on average weekly movie box office receipts. Findings indicated that all three parameters were significant in the model. The aggregated degree, representing WOM intensity, was positively significant, which was consistent with results from extant research. Further, diameter of a network, representing WOM dispersion, was observed to be positively significant, which validated the importance of spreading WOM as far as possible. Counter-intuitively, the aggregated size node, representing WOM influence level, was ascertained to be negatively significant, which might be explained by the possible negative stance from opinion leaders with high influence level. Applying network analysis methodology to blog entries, the present work differentiated itself from extant WOM literature that has focused chiefly on content analysis. The findings also provided managerial insights to companies interested in utilizing blogs as online WOM for marketing initiatives and implications for future research.

DOI: 10.4018/978-1-4666-4022-1.ch008

INTRODUCTION

Since their origin in 1995, blogs have played an indispensable role in information exchange over the internet. A blog (or weblog) is a website where one or more regular authors initiate discussion on topics of their interest. The web site allows comments to be added to the end of the blog author's entry, thus allowing a two-way conversation between author and reader as well as a many-to-many conversation among the readers (Dwyer, 2007). Blog entries are often posted on a regular basis and displayed in reverse chronological order.

The common web services hosting blogs include Blogspot by Google, Typepad, LiveJournal, MSN Space, and Facebook, among others. Further, in the past two years, Twitter, which is known as a micro-blogging service, has gained popularity among individual internet users as well as corporate bloggers (Riemer *et al.*, 2010). Based on the bloggers' interests, contents of blogs vary from political opinions, consumer experiences, and word-of-mouth recommendations to personal or business journal entries (Burns, 2005). Navigating through a blog site, people can easily identify the blogger's preferences for products, opinions on events, and past activities. This channel of capturing and propagating information has attracted prodigious attention from business organizations (e.g., Bampo *et al.*, 2008; Cohen, 2005; Kozinets *et al.*, 2010).

The user-generated contents provide a unique platform for companies to conduct customer segmentation and targeted advertising (Cohen, 2005). Further, business can easily leverage blogs to improve communications both within the organization and with customers. Internal company blogs can be a way of efficiently exchanging information as well as organizational knowledge to facilitate decision making. For example, Microsoft has many internal blog communities based on the product group; as such, developers can share their coding experiences (Yardi *et al.*, 2008). On the other hand, external blogs to the public can be tailored to perform tasks associated with public relations or customer services (Kelleher & Miller, 2006).

A major distinction between a blog and other online forums or message board communities is the palpability of the blog author. The blog's author is the sole creator who controls the flow of contents on the blog website. More than 133 million blogs have been indexed since 2002 by Technorati, which is one of the leading blog indexing sites (Technorati, 2009). Furthermore, 77 percent of internet users read blogs. Also, 56 percent of bloggers indicate that their blog has helped their company establish a positioning as a thought leader within the industry. In addition, 58 percent aver that their firm is better known in their industry because of their blog (Technorati, 2009).

Notwithstanding the potential importance of the foregoing *self-reported* positive effects of blogs, the present investigation was interested in the impact of blogs on an *objective* metric—revenue generated from a particular service (i.e., movie box office receipts). The impact of blogs was examined using solely selected *objective* (rather than subjective) measures. The study was undergirded utilizing extant word-of-mouth (WOM) research. WOM is a widely studied topic by marketing scholars (e.g., Elberse & Eliashberg, 2003; Eliashberg *et al.*, 2000; Mohr & Nevin, 1990). It traditionally refers to information that individuals obtain through interpersonal communication, such as face-to-face conversations. Bloggers often make reference links to and comment on other bloggers' posts. This observation offers a natural analogy between the linkage of blog posts and WOM communications in the offline community.

Admittedly, owing to the popularity of information exchange in online communities (Artz, 2009), much research (subsequently discussed) has employed WOM in the context of internet channels: social networks, user reviews and ratings posted on E-commerce websites, online discussion groups, blog websites, and so on. In the present study, however, online WOM was captured in the format of *blog* entries. Blog entries were chosen as the format because, among all online WOM designs, blogs have unique features (Domingos, 2005; Dwyer, 2007). First, bloggers often refer to and quote others' blog entries. Second, the linkage among the blog entries and blogs can be easily captured when one blogger is referring to other blog entries written by other bloggers. Third, if a social network is constructed using bloggers as the nodes in the network, then the quotation linkages among blog entries can be modeled as directed or undirected arcs in the network (Bampo *et al.*, 2008; Brown *et al.*, 2007; Jackson & Wolinsky, 1996). With a network structure established, conducting network analysis seemed appropriate.

Using network analysis, this investigation examined the impact of online WOM blog network characteristics on performance outcomes. Weekly movie box office receipts were used as a proxy for business performance owing to data availability and their objectivity. The design included selecting appropriate movie titles, extracting quotation links among blog posts with contents related to movie titles, constructing network structures for movie titles, and utilizing network analysis to assess blog WOM's impact on movie box office receipts (Nyblom *et al.*, 2003; Opsahl *et al.*, 2010). As such, the study partially answers a call by Sangwan *et al.* (2009) for conducting further research on virtual social networks.

Compatible with the work of Domingos (2005), three network characteristics were captured as having potential effects of WOM in a blog network: number of arcs from and to a node (degree), size of a node (in terms of the influence level of the node), and diameter of the network (the longest path from one node to another). These three were chosen for inclusion in the study using the logic.

- A highly connected network should be able to deliver WOM in an efficient way. Aggregated degree of nodes was thus measured for a movie network at each time period. *Degree* refers to the number of links

to and from a node (Borgatti *et al.*, 1998; Domingos, 2005). By aggregating the total degree of the network nodes, the connectivity of the network could be obtained. Conceivably, the greater the number of blog entries presented in the movie network, the higher the average weekly box office receipts.

- In order to have effective WOM, a blogger should be able to influence markedly his or her followers (Domingos, 2005). Essentially, such individuals serve as opinion leaders (e.g., celebrities). A network of homogenous nodes cannot capture differences among individual bloggers. Therefore, assigning the size for each node and the aggregated size of nodes in a movie network can capture the *influence level* of WOM. Presumably the aggregated influential level of bloggers in the movie network should have a positive effect on a movie's box office performance

- WOM travels from individual to individual, some who are farther remote than others. Distance is defined as the length of the shortest path between two nodes in the network. Further, *diameter of a network* is built as the largest distance between any pair of nodes (Wasserman & Faust, 1994). It quantifies how far apart the farthest two nodes in the network are. The farther WOM spreads—its diameter—the stronger the impact it conceivably will have on average box office receipts.

The rest of the paper proceeds as follows: Germane literature pertaining to WOM, blogs, and movie industry research is presented. Then, blog data of online WOM, as well as weekly movie box office receipts, are discussed in detail. Data analysis using General Estimating Equations (GEE) and concomitant findings are presented. Finally, managerial interpretation of the results and future research directions are proffered.

Literature Review

WOM has been widely studied and considered a recognized factor in driving consumer behavior, particularly in an offline venue. One such research stream has investigated how to measure WOM. In the traditional WOM format of private conversations, in general WOM is often measured through survey instruments. For instance, Elberse and Eliashberg (2003) used previous weekly box office receipts as an indicator of WOM. Eliashberg *et al.* (2000) modeled WOM in two dimensions—frequency and duration—both of which follow two independent exponential distributions. Mohr and Nevin (1990) proposed four types of communication measures: frequency, direction, modality, and content, among which face-to-face (WOM) is regarded as an informal means of conveying information.

Selected Online (Non-Blog) WOM Research

Owing to burgeoning use of, and interest in, online venues, scholars have recently expended much effort toward exploring WOM in the format of online conversations, messages, and user reviews. For example, Godes and Mayzlin (2004) collected data from message posts of a popular online user forum to measure the frequency and reach of online WOM. Liu (2006) collected WOM data from the Yahoo Movies message board to focus on the dynamic patterns of WOM. Utilizing cross-sectional and panel data over a two-year period, Chevalier and Mayzlin (2006) observed that online WOM in the format of user reviews influenced the sales of Amazon.com and BN.com. Gruen *et al.* (2005) investigated effects of online WOM in terms of customer knowledge exchange. Sen and Lerman (2007) examined existence of a negative effect in online WOM customer reviews. Awad and Ragowsky (2008) assessed whether the effect of online WOM in the format of customer reviews was moderated by gender. Goldenberg *et al.* (2001) proffered a simulation model to measure the effects of strong and weak ties conveying WOM over personal networks. Trusov *et al.* (2009) studied the impact of WOM marketing on member growth in a social networking site. Dwyer (2007) categorized online WOM into two distinct groups—social and informational—and introduced a metric to measure the value a community assigns to each WOM instance.

WOM Blog Research

As noted earlier, the present investigation used WOM as captured in the format of blog posts. Related work on WOM of blogs is also emerging in the marketing literature. Beyond providing a comprehensive review of online WOM using blogs, Kozinets *et al.* (2010) followed 83 blogs for six months to present a study of a marketing campaign. In their study, a network co-production model was also proposed as a sharp contrast to the traditional organic consumer-to-consumer model and the linear opinion leader-to-consumer model. The network co-production model is similar to the network model presented in this study; specifically, bloggers are acting as nodes in the movie network within the defined domain. In the computer science literature, some studies of blogs have also been undertaken. For example, Kumar *et al.* (2004) discovered that there exist time periods which have dense communication among inter-community blogs in terms of blog linkage creations. The authors proposed the concept of a time graph to capture topical and temporal features of online blog links. Gruhl *et al.* (2004) focused on information diffusion through blogs; they considered both blog contents (by categorizing topics into spike and chatter) and individual bloggers (by categorizing them into four types based their behavior during the life cycle of a certain topic).

Social Network Analysis Research

Another research stream related to the present study has utilized social network analysis (Tichy *et al.*, 1979). For instance, Jackson and Wolinsky

(1996) studied stability and efficiency of social and economic networks. Opsahl *et al.* (2010) advanced generalizations of network ties using both weights and intensity as metrics. Adopting social network analysis, Mayzlin (2002) discerned that adding more entries/openings into the network had decreasing marginal returns. Brown *et al.* (2007), employing social network analysis, provided evidence that individuals behaved as themselves in online social networks, and therefore, online communities could act as a social proxy for individual identification. Domingos (2005) built social network models in a larger network scale for purposes of data mining for viral marketing. Nyblom *et al.* (2003) developed a general methodology to deal with the association between a binary variable and network connections and applied it in the diffusion of organic farming in Finland. Borgatti *et al.* (1998) used existing network measures to formalize the notion of social capital. Liben-Nowell *et al.* (2005) introduced a model relating geography and social-network friendship. Skyes *et al.* (2009) offered a model of technology acceptance with constructs from social networks. Bampo *et al.* (2008) ascertained that social structure of digital networks is important in spreading viral messages.

Selected Movie Industry Research

Because this study examines blogs' WOM impact on movie box office receipts, a brief disquisition of germane literature in the movie industry is provided. Movies are different from durable goods, mainly because of the related high risk in marketing and production, relative short life span, and significant emphasis on the distribution channel (screens and theatres) (De Vany & Walls, 1999). Krider *et al.* (2005) used a state-space diagram to identify the "lead-lag puzzle" of demand and distribution relationship. Findings revealed that in the movie industry, demand leads distribution; therefore, marketing effort should be redirected to the post-launch period. Eliashberg

and Shugan (1997) examined the impact of film critics on box office performance; they ascertained that film critics should be viewed as a predictor of the film's total performance rather than as an opinion leader. Sawhney and Eliashberg (1996) proposed a "parsimonious" model to forecast gross box office receipts using early box office data (first three weeks after release). Eliashberg *et al.* (2000) further extended the previous model to a pre-release decision support system to forecast box office receipts. Swami *et al.* (1999) proffered a model to manage the allocation of movie screens using parallel machine scheduling formulation.

Method

Despite the abundance of extant research on both offline and online WOM, there is no published article examining the impact of online WOM using a network of blog entries. By applying social network analysis to blog entries, the relationship among user-generated contents can be explored. This relationship is similar to the widely studied relationship among users (Bampo *et al.*, 2008; Brown *et al.*, 2007; Skyes *et al.*, 2009), and it captures underlying linkages among relevant contents in blogs instead of purely analyzing the volume and valence of contents (Liu, 2006). Further, a time dimension was included in the analysis to control for the inherent time dynamics of weekly movie box office receipts (Sawhney & Eliashberg, 1996).

Data

Movie Data

Movie box office information was collected from IMDB (http://www.imdb.com), which has a comprehensive database of movie records. In order to gather sufficient information for each movie, the following search criteria, similar to Liu (2006), were used to generate the data set:

- A movie had to have been released within the past six months of the study. This criterion was enforced to ensure that no ongoing blog activities were involved when the data were collected.
- The worldwide box office receipts for the movie had to exceed $50 million. In order to collect a sufficient number of blog entries on the movies, popular titles were selected.
- A movie had to have corresponding blog data subsequent to its release. In order to construct the blog network for the movie, the blog data associated with the movie after its release was needed.

A total of 24 movies were identified that satisfied the foregoing criteria. Then, weekly box office information for each movie (using IMDB) was collected.

Word-of-Mouth Data

WOM data were collected by tracking linkages among blogs. Using a web service of API (Application Program Interface) provided by Technorati Inc., all blog entries directly linked to each movie title's URL in IMDB were identified. Blogs within the search domain included all those blogs indexed on Technorati. After the first layer of links was identified, further tracking was done to identify how these blog entries were linked by other blog entries. The tracking continued until a leaf node (i.e., a blog entry to which no one else had referred) was reached. By categorizing all this linkage information, a network with a blog as a node and a linkage as an arc captured how WOM spread via linkages among blogs.

The information collected for each blog entry included the following: *URL-to* (the destination blog address), *URL-from* (the originating blog address), *permalink* (the URL address of the exact post), and *creation* (the time stamp of the linkage creation). The aggregated number of all of these blog entries represented the WOM *intensity* of a

movie. Individuals often discuss movies in their blogs and thus generate buzz about a movie. As such, WOM intensity conceivably has an essential impact on weekly box office receipts. (The aggregated number of blog entries was assayed on a weekly basis. In this way, the blog data could be synchronized with the number of weeks a movie had been released.)

Not all WOM is equal in terms of its power in delivering information, expressing opinions, or convincing audiences (Domingos, 2005). Previous research on the *influence level* of WOM often has divided WOM sources into two categories: opinion leaders and ordinary followers (Buttle, 1998). In the present study, identifying the author of the blog entry was possible. Further, capturing the influence level of a blogger simply by the number of his or her audience bloggers appeared logical. In the API service provided by Technorati, such blog subscription data were presented as the number of in-bound blogs for a blog site. In fact, Technorati ranked all the blogs it indexed using this number of in-bound blogs. Conceivably, the more in-bound blogs, the greater the influence level of the blogger.

The last variable of interest was the *diameter of the network*. Diameter of a network is the largest distance between any pair of nodes (Wasserman & Faust, 1994). It quantifies how far apart the farthest two nodes are in the network. The farther WOM spreads, presumably the stronger the impact it has on weekly box office receipts. Diameter of a network was denoted as 0 if there were only *direct* blog links to the movie title's URL in IMDB. The largest diameter in the dataset was six, which indicated that there is at least one blog node which is *indirectly* linked to the movie title's URL by a path passing six other blog nodes.

In sum, the aggregated degree of a movie network was used to model WOM intensity; the aggregated size of the nodes (total number of in-bound blogs) of a movie network was employed to model WOM influence level; and the diameter of a movie network was utilized to model WOM dispersion. Liu (2006) averred that volume and valence are the two most commonly evaluation metrics. Here the intensity is similar to the volume metric. Other research has also studied the dispersion and influence level (Eliashberg *et al.*, 2000). Shown in Table 1 are the aggregated data for *one* of the movies in the data set.

The number of sites releasing the movie (the number of theaters that showed the movie) varied from week to week, and it varied across movies. Therefore, before final data analysis, data transformation was conducted for the dependent variable. The dependent variable in this study was *originally* to be weekly movie box office receipts. However, a movie's box office receipts are significantly determined by the *number of sites* releasing the movie (De Vany & Walls, 1999). Hence, in the final analysis, *average weekly box office per site* was adopted as the dependent variable to better capture WOM effects regardless of the number of sites.

Study Model

According to extant work (Eliashberg & Shugan, 1997; Krider *et al.*, 2005; Sawhney & Eliashberg, 1996), a movie's average weekly box office re-

ceipts, repeatedly measured on a weekly basis, might be correlated with one another along the time horizon. Therefore, in the study's model design, simply assuming that all the observations were independent was not deemed appropriate. This autocorrelation effect among the dependent variables was addressed using Generalized Estimating Equations—GEE (Hanley *et al.*, 2003; Liang & Zeger, 1986; Zeger *et al.*, 1988). The GEE method, an extension of the quasi-likelihood approach, is being increasingly used to analyze longitudinal and correlated response variables. It is an important method, especially when the repeated measures are binary or in the form of counts. Further, Pan (2001) proposed a modified Akaike Information Criterion (AIC), which is the model selection tool for maximum likelihood estimation. In his modification, the likelihood is replaced by the quasi-likelihood, and a proper adjustment is made for the penalty term. Therefore, evaluating GEE model fitness using the modified AIC was possible.

The dependent variable was the average box office receipts of movie i at week t per site, $AveBox_{it}$. GEE analysis was conducted using SPSS 16.0. It allowed for a variety of distributions of the

Table 1. Weekly data for movie 1

Week ID	Weely Box Office ($)	No. of Release Sites	No. Of Post Links	No. of InBound Blogs	Diameter of Network
1	21422815	2845	N/A	N/A	N/A
2	16275895	2869	64	623	1
3	16535700	2901	157	5081	1
4	7717530	2974	138	1497	1
5	5967005	3006	72	2222	1
6	4310270	2581	49	610	2
7	3120045	2153	55	850	1
8	1867805	1132	40	680	1
9	1025870	726	51	1164	2
10	623715	462	40	516	1
11	302680	322	35	223	0
12	303460	305	36	254	2
13	282150	285	31	275	1
14	200655	254	25	102	1
15	175070	254	11	395	0
16	119560	199	16	89	2
17	98410	160	35	253	1

dependent variables with link functions. Because the average weekly box office receipts were a non-negative count variable, negative binomial distribution was applied, and the estimation took its log transformation (White & Bennetts, 1996).

Several independent variables were used. First, the number of sites releasing the movie at week t ($Sites_{i,t}$) captured its potential impact on box office receipts. $Intensity_{i,t}$ represented WOM intensity on movie i at week t (the aggregated degree of nodes in the movie network i at week t). This variable was intended to capture WOM intensity in the format of blog entries specifically related to the movie. $Influence_{i,t}$ reflected WOM influence level for movie i at week t (the aggregated size of nodes in the movie network i at week t). This variable was included to measure how influential WOM in the format of blog entries would be (which is simply the total number of in-bound blogs subscribing to the focal blog). Interestingly, the correlation between $Intensity_{i,t}$ and $Influence_{i,t}$ was 0.2585. This low correlation seemingly indicated that there was no strong positive relationship between WOM intensity and influence level. Accordingly, the inclusion of both network characteristics in the model seemed reasonable. $Diameter_{i,t}$ was the diameter of the movie network i at week t (the longest path from the movie title's URL to a blog node). This variable was designed to measure WOM dispersion. Finally, movies are different from one another, and the week in which a movie is released likely affects box office receipts. Therefore, the *movieID* and the *weekID* were both incorporated into the model, thus capturing the unique characteristics of each week. Model information is portrayed in Table 2.

Results

The working correlation matrix in GEE represents the within-subject dependencies. Its size is determined by the number of measurements and thus the combination of values of within-subject

Table 2. Model information

Dependent Variable	AveBox
Probability Distribution	Negative binomial (1)
Link Function	Log
Subject Effect	movieID
Within-Subject Effect	weekID
Working Correlation Matrix Structure	Unstructured

variables (SPSS Inc., 2006). Because of possible correlation among the average weekly box office receipts measured each week, the working correlation matrix was identified as "unstructured" in the model estimation to avoid any assumption about independence among the repeated measurements of the dependent variable (Hanley *et al.*, 2003; Liang & Zeger, 1986; Zeger *et al.*, 1988).

$Diameter_{i,t}$, *movieID*, and *weekID* were all treated as *factors*, as they were *nominal* variables. $Diameter_{i,t}$ was treated as a nominal variable, mainly because the possible value of the variable had to be in the integer set of $\{0, 1, 2, 3, 5, 6\}$, which includes all the possible diameters in the dataset. Therefore, treating $Diameter_{i,t}$ as a continuous variable was not appropriate. $Sites_{i,t}$, $Intensity_{i,t}$, and $Influence_{i,t}$, however, were treated as *covariates* because they were *continuous variables*. Shown in Table 3 are the descriptive statistics of these covariates, as well as the $AveBox_{it}$.

Using GEE, certain configurations were specified. First, the model-based estimator was the negative of the generalized inverse of the Hessian matrix. The robust estimator (also called the Huber/White/sandwich estimator) was a "corrected" model-based estimator that provides a consistent estimate of the covariance (SPSS Inc.,

Table 3. Continuous variables

	N	Minimum	Maximum	Mean	Std. Deviation
AveBox	289	133	104284	2302.27	6699.88
Sites	289	4	3858	1075.67	1139.97
Intensity	289	0	792	59.47	88.62
Influence	289	0	32329	1565.37	3229.14

2006). In this study, the robust estimator was chosen for its superiority over the model-based estimator. Second, initial parameter estimation was conducted through the hybrid combination of Newton-Raphson and Fisher scoring. Iteration of estimations was stopped when parameter convergence reached the absolute change level at

10^{-6}. Shown in Table 4 is the model's goodness of fit. Both Quasi-likelihood under the independence model criterion (QIC) and QIC measure for choosing the best subset (QICC) were adopted for evaluation (SPSS Inc., 2006). The values of these criteria were 37.626 and 140.59, respectively.

Type III sums of squares were also calculated, as they have a major advantage in that they are invariant with respect to the cell frequencies as long as the general form of estimability remains constant (SPSS Inc., 2006). Thus, this type of sums of squares is often considered useful for an unbalanced model (Speed *et al.*, 1978). The data set employed was unbalanced in terms of the variable numbers of release weeks for various movies. Depicted in Table 5 are the tests of model effects. All factors and covariates were significant.

Table 4. Goodness of Fit[b]

Quasi Likelihood under Independence Model Criterion (QIC)[a]	37.626
Corrected Quasi Likelihood under Independence Model Criterion (QICC)[a]	140.59
Dependent Variable: AveBox	
Model: (Intercept), movieID, weekID, Diameter, Sites, Intensity, Influence	
a. Computed using the full log quasi-likelihood function.	
b. Information criteria are in small-is-better form.	

Parameter estimation is presented in Table 6. First, both movie and week factors were found to be significant, thus providing some validation for the choice of model with consideration of the fixed effects. The movies were different from one another, and the average box office receipts declined subsequent to the release week. Second, $Diameter_{i,t}$ was also a significant factor. Based on the significance level of the parameter for the different $Diameter_{i,t}$ levels, the network with diameter equaling 0, 1, 2, 3, or 5 had significantly lower average box office receipts than the network with a diameter of 6. In other words, the farther the WOM spread, the stronger the impact it had on average box office receipts. Third, $Intensity_{i,t}$ was a significant covariate. Essentially, the more blog entries joining the movie network, the higher the average box office receipts. This result provided some degree of confirmation that WOM over a movie network constructed by blogs has a significant positive effect on a movie's box office performance. Further, $Influence_{i,t}$ was a significant covariate. This covariate, however, had a *negative* parameter, which indicated that the greater the influence of WOM in the movie network, the lower the movie box office. A possible reason for this result might be owing to the lack of a content analysis of the blog post. For example, the opinion leader in the blog network might have offered more negative than positive critiques on movies than ordinary bloggers. Finally, the number of release sites, $Sites_{i,t}$, as a covariate, was also

Table 5. Tests of model effects

Source	Type III		
	Wald Chi-Square	df	Sig.
(Intercept)	18529.679	1	0.000
movieID	$2.050*10^7$	23	0.000
weekID	58386.523	22	0.000
Diameter	34.479	5	0.000
Sites	23.918	1	0.000
Intensity	15.584	1	0.000
Influence	4.391	1	0.036
Dependent Variable: AveBox			
Model: (Intercept), movieID, weekID, Diameter, Sites, Intensity, Influence			

Table 6. Parameter estimates

Parameter	B	Std. Error	95% Wald Confidence Interval		Wald Chi-Square	Hypothesis Test		Exp(B)	95% Wald Confidence Interval	
			Lower	Upper		df	Sig.		Lower	Upper
(Intercept)	5.701	0.2465	5.218	6.184	534.703	1	0.000	299.171	184.527	485.041
[MovieID=1]	0.366	0.0458	0.277	0.456	63.901	1	0.000	1.442	1.319	1.578
[MovieID=2]	-0.358	0.0451	-0.446	-0.269	63.059	1	0.000	0.699	0.64	0.764
[MovieID=5]	0.031	0.0251	-0.018	0.081	1.567	1	0.211	1.032	0.982	1.084
[MovieID=6]	-0.526	0.0423	-0.609	-0.443	154.487	1	0.000	0.591	0.544	0.642
[MovieID=7]	-0.718	0.0347	-0.786	-0.65	427.292	1	0.000	0.488	0.456	0.522
[MovieID=8]	0.439	0.0712	0.299	0.578	38.03	1	0.000	1.551	1.349	1.783
[MovieID=10]	-0.307	0.0418	-0.389	-0.225	54.134	1	0.000	0.735	0.678	0.798
[MovieID=11]	1.073	0.0732	0.93	1.217	215.24	1	0.000	2.926	2.535	3.377
[MovieID=12]	0.814	0.0609	0.695	0.933	178.674	1	0.000	2.257	2.003	2.543
[MovieID=13]	-0.642	0.0445	-0.73	-0.555	208.235	1	0.000	0.526	0.482	0.574
[MovieID=14]	1.048	0.078	0.895	1.201	180.247	1	0.000	2.851	2.447	3.322
[MovieID=15]	0.452	0.0642	0.326	0.577	49.539	1	0.000	1.571	1.385	1.781
[MovieID=16]	-0.228	0.042	-0.311	-0.146	29.606	1	0.000	0.796	0.733	0.864
[MovieID=17]	0.13	0.05	0.032	0.228	6.759	1	0.009	1.139	1.033	1.256
[MovieID=18]	-0.253	0.025	-0.302	-0.204	101.822	1	0.000	0.777	0.74	0.816
[MovieID=19]	0.234	0.0529	0.13	0.338	19.558	1	0.000	1.264	1.139	1.402
[MovieID=20]	-0.841	0.0395	-0.919	-0.764	452.369	1	0.000	0.431	0.399	0.466
[MovieID=21]	0.976	0.0299	0.918	1.035	1066.858	1	0.000	2.655	2.504	2.815
[MovieID=22]	0.251	0.0653	0.123	0.379	14.832	1	0.000	1.286	1.131	1.461
[MovieID=23]	0.667	0.0886	0.493	0.841	56.707	1	0.000	1.949	1.638	2.318
[MovieID=25]	0.363	0.0514	0.263	0.464	49.912	1	0.000	1.438	1.3	1.591
[MovieID=26]	0.195	0.0576	0.082	0.308	11.488	1	0.001	1.215	1.086	1.361
[MovieID=28]	0.032	0.0414	-0.049	0.113	0.595	1	0.441	1.032	0.952	1.12
[MovieID=29]	0[a]	.	.	.	.		.	1	.	.
[WeekID=2]	4.345	0.3626	3.634	5.056	143.578	1	0.000	77.097	37.877	156.927
[WeekID=3]	3.733	0.3229	3.1	4.366	133.657	1	0.000	41.821	22.208	78.755
[WeekID=4]	3.17	0.294	2.594	3.746	116.243	1	0.000	23.802	13.377	42.352
[WeekID=5]	2.651	0.2987	2.066	3.237	78.79	1	0.000	14.172	7.892	25.45
[WeekID=6]	2.297	0.2867	1.735	2.859	64.19	1	0.000	9.943	5.669	17.439
[WeekID=7]	1.87	0.2754	1.33	2.41	46.109	1	0.000	6.488	3.782	11.13
[WeekID=8]	1.718	0.2711	1.186	2.249	40.141	1	0.000	5.571	3.275	9.478
[WeekID=9]	1.553	0.2413	1.08	2.026	41.432	1	0.000	4.725	2.945	7.582
[WeekID=10]	1.351	0.23	0.9	1.801	34.47	1	0.000	3.86	2.459	6.058
[WeekID=11]	1.476	0.2055	1.073	1.879	51.606	1	0.000	4.377	2.926	6.547
[WeekID=12]	1.217	0.1993	0.826	1.607	37.269	1	0.000	3.376	2.284	4.989
[WeekID=13]	1.118	0.2211	0.685	1.551	25.57	1	0.000	3.058	1.983	4.717
[WeekID=14]	1.092	0.2153	0.67	1.514	25.707	1	0.000	2.979	1.954	4.544
[WeekID=15]	1.187	0.2478	0.701	1.672	22.936	1	0.000	3.277	2.016	5.325
[WeekID=16]	1.051	0.2559	0.55	1.553	16.878	1	0.000	2.862	1.733	4.725
[WeekID=17]	0.827	0.2522	0.333	1.321	10.755	1	0.001	2.287	1.395	3.748
[WeekID=18]	0.781	0.267	0.257	1.304	8.551	1	0.003	2.183	1.294	3.684
[WeekID=19]	0.686	0.3232	0.052	1.319	4.5	1	0.034	1.985	1.054	3.739
[WeekID=20]	0.673	0.2498	0.183	1.163	7.255	1	0.007	1.96	1.201	3.198
[WeekID=21]	0.181	0.3292	-0.464	0.826	0.302	1	0.582	1.198	0.629	2.285
[WeekID=22]	-0.213	0.1884	-0.582	0.156	1.279	1	0.258	0.808	0.559	1.169
[WeekID=23]	0.68	0.2711	0.149	1.212	6.297	1	0.012	1.974	1.161	3.359
[WeekID=24]	0[a]	.	.	.	.		.	1	.	.
[Diameter=0]	-0.319	0.0998	-0.514	-0.123	10.182	1	0.001	0.727	0.598	0.884
[Diameter=1]	-0.367	0.0924	-0.548	-0.186	15.768	1	0.000	0.693	0.578	0.831
[Diameter=2]	-0.231	0.0909	-0.409	-0.052	6.436	1	0.011	0.794	0.664	0.949
[Diameter=3]	-0.088	0.0738	-0.232	0.057	1.417	1	0.234	0.916	0.793	1.058
[Diameter=4]	-0.367	0.0761	-0.517	-0.218	23.326	1	0.000	0.693	0.597	0.804
[Diameter=6]	0[a]	.	.	.	.		.	1	.	.
Sites	0.000	6.66E-05	0.000	0.000	23.918	1	0.000	1.000	1.000	1.000
Intensity	0.001	0.0003	0.001	0.002	15.584	1	0.000	1.001	1.001	1.002
Influence	-2.04E-05	9.75E-06	-3.96E-05	-1.32E-06	4.391	1	0.036	1.000	1.000	1.000
(Scale)	1									
(Negative binomial)	1									
Dependent Variable: AveBox										
Model: (Intercept), movieID, weekID, Diameter, Sites, Intensity, Influence										
a. Set to zero because this parameter is redundant.										

positively significant in the model. Thus, the more sites that released the movie, the higher the average weekly box office receipts.

DISCUSSION

Using extant WOM research as the backdrop, the current investigation established a network using blogs pertaining to relatively recently released movies as the venue. In particular, interest focused on objective network parameters that influence objective performance (in this case, movie box office receipts). The movie network was constructed with nodes of blogs linking to the movie title's URL as well as linking to one another through blog entries. Specifically, WOM data were collected by tracking linkages among blogs. All blog entries directly linked to each movie title's URL were tracked. Study findings revealed the complexity of evaluating online WOM effects and provide managers with initial insight regarding how to promote WOM more effectively via blogs.

Findings and Contributions

Three crucial characteristics of online WOM in blogs were considered potential predictors of movie box office receipts—intensity, influence level, and dispersion (Domingos, 2005; Liu, 2006). These characteristics were captured in the movie network by measuring corresponding aggregated degree, aggregated node size, and diameter of the network, respectively.

The aggregated number of linkages among all blog entries represented the WOM *intensity* toward a movie. Study results indicated, essentially, that the greater the number of blog entries joining the movie network, the higher the average box office receipts. As such, a firm's sales of a particular product, product line, or brand (or even total sales) may well be influenced by the WOM generated from the blogosphere created by outsiders. The more that bloggers communicate about a particular enterprise's offerings, the greater the likelihood that the organization will experience enhanced financial outcomes.

As noted earlier, not all WOM is equal in terms of its *influence level* (power) in delivering information. In the current work, influence level referred to the size of a blogger's audience bloggers. This variable was included to measure how influential WOM in the format of blog entries would be. Conceivably, the more in-bound blogs, the greater the influence level of the blogger. Study results, though, revealed that influence level was negatively associated with movie box office receipts. The unanticipated outcome was likely a function of the absence of the valence of the blog post. (That is, the blogger may well have offered more negative than positive comments about the movie.) Nonetheless, this finding suggests that firms should attempt to cultivate potential opinion leaders (bloggers) so as to acquire auspicious support as new products or brands are launched.

Diameter was the third network variable of interest in the study. This variable was designed to measure WOM dispersion, as it represented the longest path from the movie title's URL to a blog node. The findings revealed that the farther WOM spread, the stronger (and more positive) the effect on average box office receipts. To the extent that companies can facilitate extended dissemination of information on blogs about their offerings, the greater is their performance of a given or multiple offerings.

Overall, the aggregated degree, representing WOM intensity, was positively significant, which was consistent with results from extant research (see similar results in Chevalier & Mayzlin, 2006; Trusov *et al.*, 2009). Further, diameter of a network, representing WOM dispersion, was observed to be positively significant, which validated the importance of spreading WOM as far as possible (see similar results in Godes & Mayzlin, 2004; Goldenberg *et al.*, 2001). Counter-intuitively, the aggregated size node, representing WOM influence level, was ascertained to be negatively significant, which might be explained by the possible negative stance from opinion leaders with high influence level. Regarding the opinion leader concept, Eliashberg and Shugan (1997) ascertained that film critics should be viewed as a predictor of the film's total performance rather than as an opinion leader. Kozinets *et al.* (2010) also pointed out that a network co-production model can generate results in sharp contrast to the traditional organic consumer-to-consumer model and the linear opinion leader-to-consumer model. Finally, compatible with movie industry empirical work, the study also followed captured time dynamics and found similar trends in movie box office receipts predicated on the number of weeks a movie had been released (see similar results in Sawhney & Eliashberg, 1996; Eliashberg *et al.*, 2000).

This investigation established a framework for analyzing online WOM in the format of blog entries. Applying network analysis methodology to blog entries, the present work differentiated itself from extant WOM literature that has focused chiefly on content analysis (Awad & Ragowsky, 2008; Gruen *et al.*, 2005; Sen & Lerman, 2007). The findings also provided managerial insights to companies interested in utilizing blogs as online WOM for marketing initiatives and implications for future research.

Future Research Directions

The present study has certain limitations that are suggestive of future research efforts. First, the investigation was conducted in the movie industry. Whether the findings are generalizable or pertinent solely to that industry is unknown. Perhaps network factors influencing firm performance vary across industries. Therefore, subsequent empirical work should consider other industries than that examined here. Indeed, exploring network effects in multiple sectors would be valuable. Reconnoitering this issue seems warranted given that certain products/services (e.g., restaurants, clothing pharmaceuticals) are more likely to generate

bloggers' interest than other products (i.e., less conspicuous products).

Only three network independent variables were included in the present study. Future endeavors should consider network factors excluded here. Although they do not appear to have natural corresponding indicators in the domain of WOM measurements, other measures such as betweenness, closeness, and structural equivalence, among others, could be considered (Wasserman & Faust, 1994). For instance, phenomena might entail importance of the position of a node in the network and possibility of clustering for blog sites. Ascertaining the influence of those and the current study's factors on firm financial metrics seem warranted.

This investigation considered only one kind of online forum—blogs. Multifarious alternatives exist. Accordingly, future research should consider alternate kinds of online venues such as online forums, user reviews, and social network activities, among others. Variables that influence firm performance in a blog venue may be different from those in other online milieu and thus merit attention.

REFERENCES

Artz, J. M. (2009). The current state and future potential of virtual worlds. *International Journal of Virtual Communities and Social Networking*, *1*(1), 14–22. doi:10.4018/jvcsn.2009010102.

Awad, F. N., & Ragowsky, A. (2008). Establishing trust in electronic commerce through online word of mouth: An examination across genders. *Journal of Management Information Systems*, *24*(4), 101–121. doi:10.2753/MIS0742-1222240404.

Bampo, M., Ewing, T. M., Mather, R. D., Stewart, D., & Wallace, M. (2008). The effects of the social structure of digital networks on viral marketing performance. *Information Systems Research*, *19*(3), 273–290. doi:10.1287/isre.1070.0152.

Borgatti, P. S., Jones, C., & Everett, G. M. (1998). Network measures of social capital. *Connections, 21,* 27–36.

Brown, J., Broderick, M. J., & Lee, N. (2007). Word of mouth communication within online communities: Conceptualizing the online social network. *Journal of Interactive Marketing, 21*(3), 2–20. doi:10.1002/dir.20082.

Burns, E. (2005). *Blogs continue to gain traction.* Retrieved October 19, 2011, from http://www. clickz.com/3502201

Buttle, F. A. (1998). Word of Mouth: Understanding and managing referral marketing. *Journal of Strategic Marketing, 6*(3), 241–254. doi:10.1080/096525498346658.

Chevalier, J. A., & Mayzlin, D. (2006). The effect of word of mouth on sales: Online book reviews. *JMR, Journal of Marketing Research, 43*(3), 345–354. doi:10.1509/jmkr.43.3.345.

Cohen, H. (2005). *Blog marketing strategies (and how to measure them).* Retrieved October 19, 2011, from http://www.clickz.com/3504241

De Vany, A., & Walls, D. (1999). Uncertainty in the Movie Industry: Does star power reduce the terror of the box office? *Journal of Cultural Economics, 23*(4), 285–318. doi:10.1023/A:1007608125988.

Domingos, P. (2005). Mining social networks for viral marketing. *IEEE Intelligent Systems, 20*(1), 80–82.

Dwyer, P. (2007). Measuring the value of electronic word-of-mouth and its impact in consumer communities. *Journal of Interactive Marketing, 21*(2), 63–79. doi:10.1002/dir.20078.

Elberse, A., & Eliashberg, J. (2003). Demand and supply dynamics for sequentially released products in international markets: The case of motion pictures. *Marketing Science, 22*(3), 329–354. doi:10.1287/mksc.22.3.329.17740.

Eliashberg, J., Jonker, J., Sawhney, M. S., & Wierenga, B. (2000). Moviemod: An implementable decision-support system for prerelease market evaluation of motion pictures. *Marketing Science, 19*(3), 226–243. doi:10.1287/mksc.19.3.226.11796.

Eliashberg, J., & Shugan, S. (1997). Film Critics: Influencers or Predictors? *Journal of Marketing, 61*(2), 68–78. doi:10.2307/1251831.

Godes, D., & Mayzlin, D. (2004). Using online conversations to study word-of-mouth communication. *Marketing Science, 23*(4), 545–560. doi:10.1287/mksc.1040.0071.

GoldenBerg, J., Libai, B., & Muller, E. (2001). Talk of the Network: A Complex systems look at the underlying process of word-of-mouth. *Marketing Letters, 12*(3), 211–223. doi:10.1023/A:1011122126881.

Granovetter, M. (1973). The strength of weak ties. *American Journal of Sociology, 78*(6), 1360–1380. doi:10.1086/225469.

Gruhl, D., Liben-Nowell, D., Guha, R., & Tomkins, A. (2004). Information Diffusion through Blogspace. In *Proceedings of the 13th International Conference on World Wide Web* (pp. 491-501).

Hanley, A. J., Negassa, A., & Edwardes, D. deB.M. (2003). Statistical analysis of correlated data using generalized estimating equations: An orientation. *American Journal of Epidemiology, 157*(4), 364–375. doi:10.1093/aje/kwf215 PMID:12578807.

Jackson, M. O., & Wolinsky, A. (1996). A strategic model of social and economic networks. *Journal of Economic Theory, 71*(1), 44–74. doi:10.1006/jeth.1996.0108.

Kelleher, T., & Miller, B. M. (2006). Organizational blogs and the human voice: Relational strategies and relational outcomes. *Journal of Computer-Mediated Communication, 11*(2), 1. Retrieved October 19, 2011, from http://jcmc.indiana.edu/vol11/issue2/kelleher.html

Kozinets, V. R., de Valck, K., Wojnicki, C. A., & Wilner, J. S. S. (2010). Networked Narratives: Understanding word-of-mouth marketing in online communities. *Journal of Marketing, 74*(2), 71–89. doi:10.1509/jmkg.74.2.71.

Krider, R. E., Li, T., Liu, Y., & Weinberg, C. B. (2005). The lead-lag puzzle of demand and distribution: A graphical method applied to movies. *Marketing Science, 24*(4), 635–645. doi:10.1287/mksc.1050.0149.

Kumar, R., Novak, J., Raghavan, P., & Tomkins, A. (2005). On the Bursty Evolution of Blogspace. *World Wide Web: Internet and Web Information Systems, 8*, 159–178.

Liang, K. Y., & Zeger, L. S. (1986). Longitudinal data analysis for discrete and continuous outcomes. *Biometrika, 73*(1), 13–22. doi:10.1093/biomet/73.1.13.

Liben-Nowell, D., Novak, J., Kumar, R., Raghavan, P., & Tomkins, A. (2005). Geographic routing in social networks. *Proceedings of the National Academy of Sciences of the United States of America, 102*(33), 11623–11628. doi:10.1073/pnas.0503018102 PMID:16081538.

Liu, Y. (2006). Word of mouth for movies: Its dynamics and impact on box office revenue. *Journal of Marketing, 70*(3), 74–89. doi:10.1509/jmkg.70.3.74.

Mayzlin, D. (2002). *The influence of social networks on the effectiveness of promotional strategies*. New Haven, CT: Yale School of Management.

Mohr, J., & Nevin, J. R. (1990). Communication Strategies in Marketing Channels: A theoretical perspective. *Journal of Marketing, 54*(4), 36–51. doi:10.2307/1251758.

Nyblom, J., Borgatti, S., Roslakka, J., & Salo, A. M. (2003). Statistical Analysis of Network Data—An Application to Diffusion of Innovation. *Social Networks, 25*, 175–195. doi:10.1016/S0378-8733(02)00050-3.

Opsahl, T., Agneessens, F., & Skvoretz, J. (2010). Node Centrality in Weighted Networks: Generalizing Degree and Shortest Paths. *Social Networks, 32*(3), 245–251. doi:10.1016/j.socnet.2010.03.006.

Pan, W. (2001). Akaike's information criterion in generalized estimating equations. *Biometrics, 57*(1), 120–125. doi:10.1111/j.0006-341X.2001.00120.x PMID:11252586.

Riemer, K., Richter, A., & Seltsikas, P. (2010). Enterprise Microblogging: Procrastination or productive use? In *Proceedings of the Americas Conference on Information Systems* (p. 50). Retrieved October 19, 2011, from http://aisel.aisnet.org/amcis2010/506

Sawhney, M. S., & Eliashberg, J. (1996). A parsimonious model for forecasting gross box-office revenues of motion pictures. *Marketing Science, 15*(2), 113–131. doi:10.1287/mksc.15.2.113.

Sen, S., & Lerman, D. (2007). Why are you telling me this? An examination into negative consumer reviews on the web. *Journal of Interactive Marketing, 21*(4), 76–94. doi:10.1002/dir.20090.

Speed, F. M., Hocking, R. R., & Hackney, O. P. (1978). Methods of Analysis of Linear Models with Unbalanced Data. *Journal of the American Statistical Association, 73*(361), 105–112. doi:10.2307/2286530.

SPSS Inc. (2006). *SPSS Advanced Models™ 15.0.* Chicago, IL: SPSS Inc..

Sunanda, S., Guan, C., & Siguaw, J. A. (2009). Virtual social networks: Toward a research agenda. *International Journal of Virtual Communities and Social Networking*, *1*(1), 1–13. doi:10.4018/jvcsn.2009010101.

Swami, S., Eliashberg, J., & Weinberg, C. B. (1999). SilverScreener: A modeling approach to movie screens management. *Marketing Science*, *18*(3), 352–272. doi:10.1287/mksc.18.3.352.

Sykes, A. T., Venkatesh, V., & Gosain, S. (2009). Model of acceptance with peer support: A social network perspective to understand employees' system use. *Management Information Systems Quarterly*, *33*(2), 371–393.

Technorati. (2009). *State of the Blogosphere 2009*. Retrieved October 19, 2011, from http://technorati.com/blogging/feature/state-of-the-blogosphere-2009

Tichy, M. N., Tushman, M. L., & Fombrun, C. (1979). Social network analysis for organizations. *Academy of Management Review*, *4*(4), 507–519.

Trusov, M., Bucklin, R., & Pauwels, K. (2009). Effects of Word-of-Mouth versus Traditional Marketing: Findings from an Internet Social Networking Site. *Journal of Marketing*, *73*, 90–102. doi:10.1509/jmkg.73.5.90.

Wasserman, S., & Faust, K. (1994). *Social network analysis: Methods and application*. Cambridge, UK: Cambridge University Press.

White, G. C., & Bennetts, R. E. (1996). Analysis of frequency count data using the negative binomial distribution. *Ecology*, *77*(8), 2549–2557. doi:10.2307/2265753.

Yardi, S., Golder, S., & Brzozowski, M. (2008). *The pulse of the corporate blogosphere*. Paper presented at the Conference Supplement of the Computer Supported Collaborative Works Poster Session.

Zeger, S. L., Liang, K. Y., & Albert, P. S. (1988). Models for longitudinal data: A generalized estimating equation approach. *Biometrics*, *44*, 1049–1060. doi:10.2307/2531734 PMID:3233245.

This work was previously published in the International Journal of Virtual Communities and Social Networking, Volume 3, Issue 2, edited by Subhasish Dasgupta, pp. 60-74, copyright 2011 by IGI Publishing (an imprint of IGI Global).

Chapter 9
A Comparative Study of Clustering Algorithms

Kanna Al Falahi
United Arab Emirates University-Al Ain, UAE

Saad Harous
United Arab Emirates University-Al Ain, UAE

Yacine Atif
United Arab Emirates University-Al Ain, UAE

ABSTRACT

Clustering is a major problem when dealing with organizing and dividing data. There are multiple algorithms proposed to handle this issue in many scientific areas such as classifications, community detection and collaborative filtering. The need for clustering arises in Social Networks where huge data generated daily and different relations are established between users. The ability to find groups of interest in a network can help in many aspects to provide different services such as targeted advertisements. The authors surveyed different clustering algorithms from three different clustering groups: Hierarchical, Partitional, and Density-based algorithms. They then discuss and compare these algorithms from social web point view and show their strength and weaknesses in handling social web data. They also use a case study to support our finding by applying two clustering algorithms on articles collected from Delicious. com and discussing the different groups generated by each algorithm.

INTRODUCTION

The web is a huge repository of information of all kinds and types. Through the years, the web has evolved dramatically. From the static Web 1.0, where webmasters create and upload web pages with limited interaction possibilities, to the more dynamic Web 2.0, where contents are collaboratively generated and communicated across blogs, feeds and social networks. The advent of Web 3.0 brought more intelligence to Web contents through the evolution of the Semantic Web

DOI: 10.4018/978-1-4666-4022-1.ch009

and more automation of services over the Web to further support machine-to-machine interactions (Wikipedia, 2010c).

The Semantic Web provides novel models for retrieving and analyzing Web information. Intelligent Web applications are emerging to analyze users' inputs, behaviors and respond accordingly to different contextual considerations. For example, what if you use a Web application to learn about Programming. The Web application would realize your experiential-learning style from your electronic profile and guides you along personalized instructional material that best meet your learning style. Semantic Web-based applications analyze interactions and profile users based on past history or pre-established records. Another possibility follows a case-based approach to match users with similar assets and aspirations to common Web experiences. The opportunity to analyze similarities within social context empowers Web experiences through identifying the commons to recommend preferential Web contents and services (Adomavicius & Tuzhilin, 2005).

Connectivity is a core feature of the above intelligent Web applications, where users share files, publish articles, comment on others' blogs or forums, view users' profiles and add new members to their connections. These are typical operations within today's social networks such as Facebook, MySpace and Twitter. To make useful inferences over social connections, intelligent Web applications need three typical knowledge-based modules (Marmanis & Babenko, 2009):

- **Content:** Represented by the hypermedia data of the considered domain and composed of inter-linked resources.
- **Reference:** Or the knowledge-base that tags and annotates domain content through rules, which categorize contents into meaningful folksonomies (Anfinnsen et al., 2010).
- **Algorithms:** Which run the inference engine modules on aggregated content.

People feed the Web with information every day. This continuous flow of information may result in some inconsistencies, as users will have myriad choices that need to be organized in an efficient manner. Data classification and clustering facilitate the process of analyzing and building meaningful inferences for example grouping similar Web pages could reveal serious problems such as mirrored Web pages or copyright violation (Haveliwala et al., 2000). In the intelligent Web, there are two algorithmic approaches to categorize data: Clustering and Classification (Marmanis & Babenko, 2009). These approaches are useful in performing targeted advertisements or personalizing Web experiences by allowing users to view posts that specifically interest them (Adomavicius & Tuzhilin, 2005) such as special content recommendation or page categorization (like Google News).

The objective of this paper is to provide means to identify individuals and data groups in the Web that are relevant to a given user. We focus on clustering algorithms in social Web context, particularly Hierarchical, Partitional and Density-based algorithms. We also discuss and compare six important algorithms used for this purpose namely: Link-based (Single-Link, Average-Link and MST Single-Link), K-means, ROCK and DBSCAN algorithms.

The rest of the paper is organized as follows: First, we define clustering and then, a section that discusses the different types of clustering techniques. We then introduce some terms and concepts related to clustering processes and provide an overview of different clustering algorithms. Following that we compare between the clustering algorithms presented in this paper. Next we illustrate a case study related to using clustering algorithms in social networks context and finally, we conclude the paper with a summary of work and suggestions for further future extensions.

CLUSTERING IN SOCIAL WEB

Creating associations among people in the form of groups is one of human natures. Previously, people used clustering in order to study phenomena and compare them to other phenomena based on a certain set of rules. Clustering refers to grouping similar things together. It is a classification of data or individuals into groups of similar instances. Each group is called a cluster. It consists of entities that embody some similarities and are dissimilar to entities belonging to other groups (Berkhin, 2002). We can find many definitions for clustering in the literature (Jain et al., 1999; Xu & Wunsch, 2005; Gower, 1971; Jain & Dubes, 1988; Mocian, 2009; Tan et al., 2005), but the most common definition is partitioning data or individuals sets into groups (called clusters), based on some criteria, that the instances within a cluster should share common similarities calculated using some distance measurements. We can define clustering in the context of social network by "cliques of individuals" with high affinity relationships internally and scattered affinity externally (Mishra et al., 2007). With clustering, we can find groups of interest that contain useful properties that can help to understand users' behaviours. Amazon for example provides users with recommendations based on their shopping experience and catalogue browsing behaviour. Twitter also started lately to recommend new "friends" (people to follow) to their users based on several factors, including the individuals these users follow, and the people these individuals follow as well (Twitter, 2010).

Clustering can be used for summarizing large inputs. So instead of applying algorithms on entire datasets, we can reduce a dataset based on specific clustering criteria (Marmanis & Babenko, 2009). Clustering analysis has been used in many research fields such as image analysis, data mining, pattern recognition, information retrieval and machine learning (Tan et al., 2005). In the Web, identifying groups of data or users would facilitate the availability of, and accessibility to information.

Using clusters in the Web is a prime objective of social networks, because of the inherent problem of identifying groups of individuals, which resulted from the huge number of Internet users, specially those present in social networks, and the tremendous amount of hyperlinked information. These huge sizes make it hard to analyze information over today's social Web.

CLUSTERING TYPES

There are many kinds of clustering algorithms available in the literatures (Jain et al., 1999; Xu & Wunsch, 2005; Mocian, 2009; Berkhin, 2002). They can be categorized based on the cluster structure (Hierarchical, Partitional), data types and structure (numerical, categorical) or data size (large datasets) (Marmanis & Babenko, 2009). In general, clustering approaches can be divided into four main types: hierarchical, partitional, density-based and meta-search controlled (Stein & Busch, 2005). In this research work, we discuss hierarchical, partitional, and density-based clustering, which we introduce next.

The Hierarchical and Partitional algorithms represent partitioning data into different non-overlapping subsets. A partition of a dataset $X = \{x_1, x_2, ..., x_N\}$, where $x_j = (x_{j1}, x_{j2}, ..., x_{jd}) \in \Re^d$ with each measure x_{ij} called a feature (attribute, dimension or variable) and d is the input space dimensionality (Xu & Wunsch, 2005), is a collection $C = \{C_1, C_2, ..., C_k\}$ of k non-overlapping data subsets. $C_i \neq \varnothing$ (non-null clusters) such that $C_1 \cup C_2 \cup ... \cup C_k = X$, where X is the super cluster and $C_i \cap C_j = \varnothing$ for $i \neq j$ (Hruschka et al., 2009). The data partition is overlapping if the condition ($C_i \cap C_j = \varnothing$ for $i \neq j$ is ignored and in that case the cluster will have sub-clusters of different enclosing levels (Hruschka et al., 2009).

Hierarchical Clustering

In hierarchical clustering, clusters are represented as a tree called dendrogram (Xu & Wunsch, 2008). They can be either top-down (divisive) or bottom-up (agglomerative). Most of these algorithms need a threshold parameter that tells the algorithm when to stop looking for subgroups. Figure 1 shows a graphical representation of divisive and agglomerative algorithms.

In divisive hierarchical clustering, the algorithm starts from the global cluster that contains all the elements, and then data is divided into sub-clusters. We need to find out which clusters to split and how to perform the splitting (Hammouda, 2001). In agglomerative hierarchical clustering, the algorithm starts from a single cluster and then each two clusters are merged together until the global cluster is reached. DH-SCAN is a hierarchical clustering algorithm (Naughton et al., 2006), used to group articles that refer to the same event and have similar common sentences.

The basic idea behind clustering is to find a distance/similarity measure between any two points, such as Euclidean distance, cosine distance etc. In particular, this is the shortest-path in linkage algorithms that are based on linkage metric to calculate the distance between two points. This category of algorithms includes single-link, average-link and MST link algorithms.

Hierarchical algorithms use a proximity matrix (or distance matrix) which is assumed to be symmetric, which means that it require a storage of $\frac{1}{2}n^2$ proximities, where n is the number of elements (Tan et al., 2005). The total space complexity is $O(n^2)$ and the time required for computing the proximity matrix is $O(n^2)$ (Xu & Wunsch, 2008). In general, agglomerative hierarchical clustering do not have difficulties in selecting initial points as the algorithm will starts from single clusters. But they are expensive algorithms, in terms of time and space, which limit their usage when applied to large-scale datasets (Xu & Wunsch, 2005). We focus on agglomerative hierarchical algorithms in this paper such as Single-Link, Average-Link and MST Single-Link algorithms.

Partitional Clustering

Partitional algorithms have fixed number of clusters, where data is divided into a number of subsets (Mocian, 2009). The most common example is the K-means algorithm that starts by selecting random means for K clusters and assign each element to its nearest mean. K-means algorithms are $O(tkn)$, where t is the number of iterations (Xu & Wunsch, 2008), K denotes the number of clusters and n the size of the data being clustered. These algorithms uses a number of relocation schemes that provide optimization to the clusters, which means the clusters can be refined at each revisiting step that gives an advantage over hierarchical clustering (Mocian, 2009).

Density-Based Clustering

In density-based algorithms the cluster is a dense region of data objects. The points density is higher inside the cluster than outside the cluster.

Figure 1. A dendrogram that represents Divisive against Agglomerative clustering. Two clusters are generated when cutting the dendrogram at a specific level.

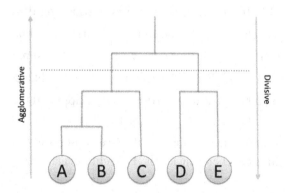

It is used the most when the shape of the clusters are irregular and contain noise and outliers (Ester et al., 1996). DBSCAN is an example of density-based algorithms. In the worst case, the time complexity for this algorithm is $O(n^2)$, but in low dimensional spaces the time would be reduced to $O(n \log n)$ (Tan et al., 2005).

Meta-Search Controlled Clustering

This category of clustering techniques treats clustering as an optimization problem where a global goal criterion is to be minimized or maximized (Ester et al., 1996). Even though these algorithms provide flexibility, their runtime is unacceptably high however. Cluster detection can be performed using genetic algorithms or a two-phase greedy strategy (Ester et al., 1996). In the research work presented in this paper, we focus on Hierarchical, Partitional and Density-based algorithms. In subsequent sections, we further discuss examples of these algorithms in details. But first, we introduce some related concepts and terms.

CONCEPTS AND TERMS

Distance and Similarity Measures

Any clustering algorithm has a similarity factor (proximity matrix) in order to organize similar objects together. It is important to understand the measures of similarity. What makes two clusters join? What makes two points similar? And how to calculate the distance (dissimilarity)?

Rui Xu and Donald Wunsch defined the function of distance or dissimilarity on a dataset X in their survey paper on clustering algorithms (Xu & Wunsch, 2005) by representing an $n \times n$ symmetric proximity matrix for a dataset of n elements, where the $(i, j)^{th}$ element represents the similarity or dissimilarity measure for the ith and the jth pattern (Xu & Wunsch, 2005).

The family of Minkowski distances is a very common class of distance functions (Hammouda, 2001) and can be represented as follows:

$$D(p_i, p_j) = \sqrt[w]{\sum (p_i - p_j)} \tag{1}$$

where w is a parameter with a value greater than or equal to 1. Based on the value of w, different distance functions can be represented such as Hamming distance ($w = 1$), Euclidean distance ($w = 2$), and Tschebyshev distance ($w = \infty$), Other similarity measures are *cosine correlation* measure and *Jaccard* measure (Hammouda, 2001). Further discussion about similarity measures can be found in (Xu & Wunsch, 2005).

Dendrogram Data Structure

One of the basic structures in the clustering environment is the dendrogram, which is a tree data structure that is used to form the hierarchical cluster. Figure 2 shows a sample dendrogram with four levels. The dendrogram can be represented as a set of triples $S = \{[d, k, \{...\}]\}$ where d represents the threshold, k is the number of clusters and $\{...\}$ is the set of clusters. Figure 2 shows a dendrogram of detecting a cluster in a group of

Figure 2. Dendrogram structure

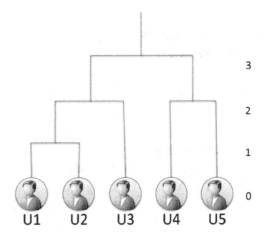

five users based on their distance similarities. The dendrogram could be represented by the following set $S = \{[0, 5, \{\{U1\}, \{U2\}, \{U3\}, \{U4\}, \{U5\}\}], [1, 4, \{\{U1,U2\}, \{U3\}, \{U4\}, \{U5\}\}], [2, 2, \{\{U1,U2,U3\}, \{U4,U5\}\}], [3, 1, \{U1,U2,U3,U4,U5\}]\}$ (Marmanis & Babenko, 2009). The dendrogram represents a set of clusters. Most of the algorithms considered in this paper are hierarchical algorithms.

Proximity Between Clusters

Proximity calculation is the most important step in identifying clusters. It is used to measure how close are the data object to each other or how far they are, differs according to the algorithm it is used with. For example agglomerative hierarchical clustering techniques such as single-link, complete link and group average each of them has its own way to determine the proximity threshold. The single-link defines the proximity as the closest distance between two elements in two different clusters or simply the shortest path between the two nodes in different clusters. Complete link calculates the largest distance between two points in two different clusters or the largest edge between the two nodes in different clusters. In the group average the proximity is defined to be the average length distance of all elements from the two different clusters (Tan et al., 2005). Figure 3 illustrates the three approaches.

AN OVERVIEW OF CLUSTERING ALGORITHMS

In this section we discuss and compare the following clustering algorithms:

1. Link-based Algorithms.
    a. The Single-Link Algorithm.
    b. The Average-Link Algorithm.
    c. The Minimum-Spanning-Tree Single-Link Algorithm.

Figure 3. Cluster proximity

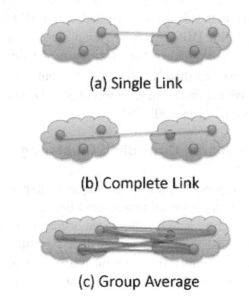

(a) Single Link

(b) Complete Link

(c) Group Average

2. The *K*-means Algorithm.
3. The Robust Clustering Using Links algorithm (ROCK).
4. The Density-Based Spatial Clustering of Applications with Noise algorithm (DBSCAN).

Link-Based Algorithms

The link-based algorithms are agglomerative hierarchical algorithms, where the dendrogram starts with individual objects and the proximity threshold is set to zero. Then the value of threshold is increased and based on that value the algorithm checks if two elements should be merged in one cluster or be kept disjoint. After a number of iterations all the elements will belong to a single super cluster.

The general algorithm for the hierarchical agglomerative algorithms can be described as shown in Algorithm 1.

The Single-link, Average-link and Minimum-Spanning-Tree algorithms, which are link-based algorithms of type agglomerative hierarchical, will be discussed next.

Algorithm 1. General hierarchical agglomerative algorithm

1. Set the proximity threshold and calculate the proximity matrix.
2. Start with individual clusters.
3. Based on the threshold merge the closest clusters.
4. Update the threshold according to the new clusters.
5. Repeat steps 3 and 4 until all the elements are in one super cluster.

The Single-Link

- **Single-Link Approach:** The single link algorithm is based on the distance between clusters that are connected by at least one edge. First it calculates the distance between the elements of the clusters. Then the proximity threshold is compared to the minimum distance to determine whether to merge the two clusters or not. The single–link distance between two clusters C_i and C_j could be represented by the following formula Hammouda (2001):

$$D(C_i, C_j) = \min_{x \in C_j, y \in C_i} (x - y) \qquad (2)$$

- **The Single-Link Algorithm:** The Single-link follows the general approach of the Linked-based algorithms described in Algorithm 1. The time and space complexity of the Single-Link algorithm is $O(n^2)$ (Xu & Wunsch, 2005). This complexity will be a problem when working with very large data, which is the case when clustering large real web datasets such as social networks.

The single link is sensitive to noise and outliers actually it has a problem of chain effect (Everitt et al., 2009) this occurs because single link algorithms merges two clusters just because there are two points in these two clusters that are close to each other, regardless the other points of the clusters that are far away. Single-link do not provide cure for this problem (Marmanis & Babenko, 2009), but algorithms such as ROCK could provide a solution.

The Average-Link

- **Average–Link Approach:** The average link algorithm is similar to the single-link algorithm but it uses different techniques to merge two clusters. It uses the average distance between any two points in the two different clusters and checks if it is less than the proximity threshold in order to merge the clusters.
- **The Average-Link Algorithm:** As with single-link algorithm we start with individual clusters and merge them until one cluster is formed, but unlike the single link the distance of all pairs of points between the two different clusters need to be calculated.

The average distance between two clusters C_i and C_j could be represented by the following formula:

$$D(C_i, C_j) = \frac{\sum_{x \in C_j, y \in C_i} (x - y)}{C_i \cdot C_j} \qquad (3)$$

The time and space complexity of the Average-Link algorithm is $O(n^2)$ (Xu & Wunsch, 2005). Which is similar to the single-link algorithms so it has the same problem.

The Minimum-Spanning-Tree Single-Link

- **The Minimum-Spanning-Tree Single-Link Approach:** Minimum Spanning Tree will connect all the elements of a given set in a way to minimize the sum of the adjacency values for the connected elements (Wu & Chao, 2004).

The MST single link alg orithm is a combination between the single link algorithms and the minimum spanning tree.

- **The Minimum-Spanning-Tree Single-Link Algorithm:** We will use the Prim-Jarnik algorithm (Wu & Chao, 2004) for minimum spanning tree with single link approach. This algorithm builds the minimum spanning tree starting from a single cluster (root) the algorithm could be expressed as shown in Algorithm 2.

The time and space complexity of the MST Single-Link algorithm is $O(n^2)$ (Marmanis & Babenko, 2009). This is similar to the single-link and average-link algorithms. The MST single link algorithms results in fewer clusters than the single link algorithm because the proximity circle do not expand as much as it did in single link.

The K-Means

- **K-Means Approach:** K-means is a Partitional algorithm. It uses the idea of centroid, which is the mean of a group of points. It has high performance characteristics and it is one of the oldest and most used clustering algorithms. Figure 4 illustrates the idea of centroid.
- **The K-Means Algorithm:** The K-means algorithm starts by choosing the K initial centroids. The simplest approach is to choose random centroids. Then the points

Figure 4. The Centroid approach

are assigned to their closest centroid to form K clusters (Kanungo et al., 2000). Depending on the points assigned to the cluster the centroid position is updated. We repeat the update until no more points to add or the centroids remain unchanged. The K-means algorithm can be represented as shown in Algorithm 3.

The K-means is fast compared to other clustering algorithms. Its computational time is $O(tkn)$ where t is the number of iterations, k represents the number of clusters and n is the number of data points we want to cluster. The space complexity for K-means is $O(n)$ which is much better than link based algorithms.

Different runs of the K-means will produce different results since we randomly initialize the centroids actually this will produce poor clustering results. So choosing the right initial centroids is very important in order to create a good quality clusters (Kotsiantis & Pintelas, 2004). It is better to choose centroids in regions with high concentration of data points as proposed by David Arthur and Sergei Vassilvitskii in their K-mean++ article (Arthur & Vassilvitskii, 2007).

Algorithm 2. MST single-link algorithm

1. Mark all elements of the graph as not visited.
2. Choose any element you like as the root and mark it visited (cluster C created).
3. The smallest-weight edge e= (v, u) that connects one vertex v inside the clustering C is chosen and added to the spanning tree T.
4. Repeat until all vertices are visited and the minimum spanning tree is formed.

Algorithm 3. K-means algorithm

1. Select K points as initial centroids.
2. Form K clusters by assigning each point to its closest centroid.
3. Re-compute the centroid of each cluster.
4. Repeat steps 2 and 3 until centroids are not changed.

The *K*-means is efficient for large datasets (Kotsiantis & Pintelas, 2004) and works well with numerical data. But the challenge occurs when it is used with categorical data such as strings since we need to find a good way to represent the non-numeric values in a numerical way.

The Robust Clustering using Links (ROCK)

- **ROCK Approach.** ROCK is an agglomerative hierarchical algorithm. It uses links as similarity measure rather than measures based on distance. It will cluster the points that have many common links. As an agglomerative hierarchical algorithm it starts from single clusters and merges these clusters until a super single cluster is formed. For the ROCK algorithm we need to define a minimum number of clusters that we want to form in order to stop the algorithm before all the elements are grouped in one single cluster.
- **Goodness Measure:** In the process of merging clusters in the ROCK algorithm we need to determine the best pair of clusters to merge together. Thus the goodness measure is used. Actually for ROCK algorithm the best clusters are those that maximize the goodness measure. The goodness measure for two clusters C_i and C_j is represented as follows (Rajeev et al., 1999):

$$g(C_i, C_j) = \frac{link[C_i, C_j]}{(n_i + n_j)^{1+2f(\theta)} - n_i^{1+2f(\theta)} - n_j^{1+2f(\theta)}}$$

(4)

where $link[C_i, C_j]$ represents the number of links between clusters C_i and C_j that is

$$\sum link(p_a, p_r)$$

(5)

Any pairs of clusters that will maximize the goodness measure will be the best pairs to merge. With algorithms that are based on similarity distance only, it will be difficult to determine if two clusters are separate because this kind of measurement may merge two clusters if there are two points close together even though these points do not have large number of common neighbours (Xu & Wunsch, 2008). Thus the ROCK algorithm uses links as its name implies. There is a link between two data points if a common neighbour exists between them. For the ROCK algorithm to merge two clusters the focus will be on the number of links n_i, n_j between all pairs points of the two clusters C_i, C_j. The large number of links should indicate a higher probability that the two points belong to the same cluster and should give the best cluster.

- **The ROCK Algorithm:** The ROCK algorithm needs the following arguments:

1. The set of points that we want to cluster.
2. The minimum number of clusters to have to stop the ROCK algorithm before all points are merged in one cluster.
3. Proximity that is required between two points in order to form a link between them.

The ROCK algorithm could be expressed as shown in Algorithm 4.

The space complexity of the ROCK algorithm is $O(n^2)$ (Marmanis & Babenko, 2009). While the time complexity is $O(n^2 \log n)$ (Rajeev et al., 1999).

Algorithm 4. ROCK algorithm

1. Create a cluster for each point.
2. Use goodness measure to evaluate if two clusters should be merged or not (the best are the one those maximize the value of goodness measure).
3. Repeat step 2 until the number of clusters formed is equal to the minimum number to stop or the number of cluster doesn't change between iterations.

ROCK algorithm is best used with categorical data such as keywords, Boolean attributes it uses the Jaccard coefficient to measure the similarity (Kotsiantis & Pintelas, 2004) and it works well on large data set. One of the advantages of using the ROCK algorithm is its ability to handle outliers effectively. Outliers are points that lie in a far distance from the other points. Which means these points can be easily discard, as they will never participate in the clustering process (Rajeev et al., 1999).

The Density-Based Spatial Clustering of Applications with Noise (DBSCAN)

- **DBSCAN Approach:** The DBSCAN algorithm is a density-based algorithm that uses density as a measurement other than links or distance between points.

Density-based algorithms are based on using density to identify the boundaries of objects. So clusters are identified based on points density within a specific region. Figure 5 explains this concept where we can identify three clusters. The points that don't belong to the clusters are identified as noise and DBSCAN is used to discover clusters and noise in a dataset.

The DBSCAN can be described as follows (Figure 6): any two core points should be put in the same cluster if they are close to each other within a distance *Eps* (Xu & Wunsch, 2008).

Figure 6. DBSCAN core points, border points and noise

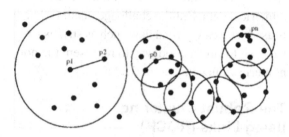

Where *Eps*, stands for epsilon, is a value that helps to define an epsilon neighbourhood for any given data point *p* (Ester et al., 1996).

To understand the concept of center points let us check Figure 6 that is similar to the Figure in Ester et al. (1996). The large circles are the epsilon neighbourhood for points *p* and *q* each of them is a center of one of the circles. The circle radius is *Eps* and *minPoints* represents the minimum number of points that must be inside the circle for a data point to be considered a core point. The points that are on the border of the cluster are called border points. A point p_1 is directly density-reachable from a data point p_2 with respect to *Eps* and *minPoints* if there is a list of points $p_1, ..., p_n, p_1 = q, p_n = p$ such that p_{i+1} is directly density-reachable from p_i (Ester et al., 1996). The following two conditions should be met:

1. p_1 inside the epsilon neighbour of p_2.

Figure 5. Density-based clustering

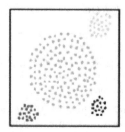  

2. There are more than *minPoints* data points inside the epsilon neighbourhood of p_2.

- **The DBSCAN Algorithm:** The DBSCAN algorithm is expressed in Algorithm 5.

The time complexity for DBSCAN algorithm is $O(n^2)$ (Wikipedia, 2010a), where n is the number of points. DBSCAN can handle noise and different shape clusters because it is based on density. It can discover many clusters that are not found by the *K*-means algorithm. But this algorithm will have problems with clusters of very different densities as the algorithm requires that the object neighbours have enough high density (Xu & Wunsch, 2005) and with high-dimensional data (Tan et al., 2005). The DBSCAN uses R*-tree in order to improve the queries of determining the points within the *Eps* distance (Kotsiantis & Pintelas, 2004). R*-tree will reduce the time complexity of the DBSCAN to $O(n \log n)$ (Ester et al., 1996).

CASE STUDY AND APPLICATION

In this section we will use a case study to further explain clustering algorithms. We will explain the scripting language we have used and how we setup the environment to run the algorithms and print the results. Also we will discuss the results obtained using each algorithm.

Algorithm 5. DBSCAN algorithm

1. Define the points as core, border, or noise points.
2. Eliminate noise points.
3. Put an edge between all core points that are within *Eps* of each other.
4. Make each group of connected core points into a separate cluster.
5. Assign each border point to one of the clusters of its associated core points.

The issue of identifying articles of similar topics is of great potential in the intelligent web environment, so in our case study we will use clustering algorithms to help in grouping similar articles. We collected the data from Delicious.com, which is a social bookmarking service that allows users to share, store and discover web bookmarks (Wikipedia, 2010b). Since we are dealing with categorical data and keywords, represented by the articles titles, we will use ROCK and DBSCAN algorithms to define the different clusters and group similar titles together.

Experiment Design

For our two experiments we have collected a list of 48 titles for different articles from Delicious.com and saved them in CSV file. For each title we assigned a unique ID and a username of the person who bookmarked that title. Two or more users can bookmark the same title. A sample of the dataset (11 out of 48 titles) is illustrated in Table 1.

The two algorithms are implemented in Java language provided by Marmanis and Babenko (2009). To execute and debug them we used BeanShell, which is a free Java interpreter. The latest Java JDK and Apache Ant should be installed in order for the BeanShell interpreter to work correctly. All of the code commands were executed through the command line in Windows OS environment.

ROCK Algorithm

First we used the ROCK Algorithm to cluster the dataset. The algorithm uses the Jaccard coefficient to measure the similarities between different titles. It compares the common terms or keywords in the titles and based on that similarity titles are grouped together.

To start the experiment we have loaded Delicious titles using the 15 most common terms only and stored them in an array. The ROCK algorithm invoked to cluster the dataset with a minimum

Table 1. Sample dataset collected from Delicious.com

ID	Name	Title
776	user01	Google sites to add social networking in "layers"
774	user01	40 Best And Highly Useful Websites For Adobe Photoshop Tutorials
740	user01	Nikon D7000: Camera Road Test With Chase Jarvis ǀ Chase Jarvis Blog
770	user01	Twitter is NOT a Social Network, Says Twitter Exec
722	user01	An open source collaborative network
744	user02	Google sites to add social networking in "layers"
710	user02	40 Best And Highly Useful Websites For Adobe Photoshop Tutorials
730	user03	Google sites to add social networking in "layers"
777	user03	40 Best And Highly Useful Websites For Adobe Photoshop Tutorials
756	user03	An open source collaborative network
733	user03	How To Discover Your Money Making Niche

number of clusters equal to 5. This parameter will allow the ROCK algorithm to stop before grouping all the data in one cluster. The threshold of 0.2 is used to represent the needed proximity between two points to be linked. Algorithm 6 represents the code used to execute the algorithm and print the result.

The results of our experiment for the ROCK algorithms at level 16 shows 8 clusters (Figure 7). We noticed that the algorithm clustered similar titles such as title ID 799 and title ID 688. Moreover there are clusters with similar titles but the algorithm did not merge them in one cluster such as cluster with title ID 520 and cluster with title ID 681. It also defined the non-obvious clusters such as titles with IDs 520, 566, 744, 730, 776 and 770 are grouped together as their titles contain terms that are related to "social network" topic. The ROCK algorithm will compare titles based on important keywords in these titles.

Algorithm 6. ROCK algorithm execution code

```
1. DeliciousDataset ds = DeliciousData.createDataset(15);

2. DataPoint[] dps = ds.getData();

3. ROCKAlgorithm rock = new ROCKAlgorithm(dps, 5, 0.2);

4. Dendrogram dnd = rock.cluster();

5. dnd.print(16);
```

DBSCAN Algorithm

We applied the DBSCAN algorithm to the same dataset. The algorithm used also the Jaccard coefficient to measure the similarities between different titles. To start the experiment we have loaded Delicious titles using the most 15 common terms only and stored them in an array. A Cosine distance is used as a distance metric. The DBSCAN algorithm invoked to cluster the dataset with a distance metric, *Eps (neighbour threshold)*, *minPoints* and the term frequency. Algorithm 7 represents the code used to execute the algorithm and print the result.

The results of our experiment for the DBSCAN algorithms are shown in Figure 8. The results were more accurate than the ROCK algorithm results. All similar titles are clustered together such as clusters 2 and 3 as you can notice the titles are exactly similar to each other. Non-similar titles in cluster 1 (title ID 776, title ID 556) and cluster 4 (title ID 722, title ID 711) also defined by the algorithm, where in cluster 1 it grouped the titles based on the keyword "social networks" and in cluster 4 it grouped all the titles related to "open source" topic. The algorithm also was able to recognize the noise elements where these points do not belong to any cluster.

Figure 7. ROCK algorithm results

```
bsh % dnd.print(16);
Clusters for: level=16, Goodness=1.973889261532508

<799:Nikon D7000: Camera Road Test With Chase Jarvis | Chase Jarvis Blog,
688:Nikon D7000: Camera Road Test With Chase Jarvis | Chase Jarvis Blog>

<708:40 Best And Highly Useful Websites For Adobe Photoshop Tutorials,
774:40 Best And Highly Useful Websites For Adobe Photoshop Tutorials,
710:40 Best And Highly Useful Websites For Adobe Photoshop Tutorials>

<722:An open source collaborative network,
715:An open source collaborative network>

<520:Twitter is NOT a Social Network, Says Twitter Exec ,
566:Twitter is NOT a Social Network, Says Twitter Exec ,
744:Google sites to add social networking in "layers",
730:Google sites to add social networking in "layers",
776:Google sites to add social networking in "layers",
770:Twitter is NOT a Social Network, Says Twitter Exec >

<740:Nikon D7000: Camera Road Test With Chase Jarvis | Chase Jarvis Blog,
720:Nikon D7000: Camera Road Test With Chase Jarvis | Chase Jarvis Blog>

<777:40 Best And Highly Useful Websites For Adobe Photoshop Tutorials,
795:40 Best And Highly Useful Websites For Adobe Photoshop Tutorials>

<681:Twitter is NOT a Social Network, Says Twitter Exec ,
500:Twitter is NOT a Social Network, Says Twitter Exec ,
790:Twitter is NOT a Social Network, Says Twitter Exec ,
780:Google sites to add social networking in "layers">

<735:40 Best And Highly Useful Websites For Adobe Photoshop Tutorials,
726:40 Best And Highly Useful Websites For Adobe Photoshop Tutorials>
```

Algorithm 7. DBSCAN algorithm execution code

```
1. DeliciousDataset ds = DeliciousData.createDataset(15);

2. DataPoint[] dps = ds.getData();

3. CosineDistance cosD = new CosineDistance();

4. DBSCANAlgorithm dbscan = new DBSCANAlgorithm(dps,cosD,0.7,2,true);

5. dbscan.cluster();
```

ANALYSIS AND DISCUSSION

In this section we discuss the complexity of clustering algorithms and other related issues. There are many criteria that decide the use of one algorithm over the others. The two main criteria are time complexity of these algorithms and do they handle data with high dimensionality.

Large Datasets

To deal with a large number of elements we need to think about the computational complexity of the algorithm under consideration, in other words how long does this algorithm take to construct the cluster. There is big difference between clustering group of people on Facebook with millions of registered users and clustering a local newsgroup of some hundred of users. To understand how crucial is the data size we need to understand how each algorithm deals with the memory size (space complexity) and the number of operations performed to cluster a set of data (time complexity). Table 2 shows both of these metrics for the algorithms discussed. Here k denotes the number of clusters, t the number of iterations, and n the size

Figure 8. DBSCAN Algorithm results

```
bsh % dbscan.cluster();
DBSCAN Clustering with NeighborThreshold=0.7 minPoints=2
Clusters:

1:
{776:Google sites to add social networking in "layers",
566:Twitter is NOT a Social Network, Says Twitter Exec ,
744:Google sites to add social networking in "layers",
780:Google sites to add social networking in "layers",
790:Twitter is NOT a Social Network, Says Twitter Exec ,
500:Twitter is NOT a Social Network, Says Twitter Exec ,
730:Google sites to add social networking in "layers",
770:Twitter is NOT a Social Network, Says Twitter Exec ,
681:Twitter is NOT a Social Network, Says Twitter Exec ,
520:Twitter is NOT a Social Network, Says Twitter Exec }


2:
{774:40 Best And Highly Useful Websites For Adobe Photoshop Tutorials,
708:40 Best And Highly Useful Websites For Adobe Photoshop Tutorials,
777:40 Best And Highly Useful Websites For Adobe Photoshop Tutorials,
726:40 Best And Highly Useful Websites For Adobe Photoshop Tutorials,
795:40 Best And Highly Useful Websites For Adobe Photoshop Tutorials,
735:40 Best And Highly Useful Websites For Adobe Photoshop Tutorials,
710:40 Best And Highly Useful Websites For Adobe Photoshop Tutorials}


3:
{740:Nikon D7000: Camera Road Test With Chase Jarvis | Chase Jarvis Blog,
530:Nikon D7000: Camera Road Test With Chase Jarvis | Chase Jarvis Blog,
688:Nikon D7000: Camera Road Test With Chase Jarvis | Chase Jarvis Blog,
685:Nikon D7000: Camera Road Test With Chase Jarvis | Chase Jarvis Blog,
799:Nikon D7000: Camera Road Test With Chase Jarvis | Chase Jarvis Blog,
720:Nikon D7000: Camera Road Test With Chase Jarvis | Chase Jarvis Blog}


4:
{722:An open source collaborative network,
590:An open source collaborative network,
711:XWiki - Open Source Wiki and Content-Oriented Application Platform,
600:An open source collaborative network,
715:An open source collaborative network,
756:An open source collaborative network}


5:
{690:Apple: Sorry, Steve Jobs Isn▯t a Ninja ,
736:Apple: Sorry, Steve Jobs Isn▯t a Ninja }


6:
{499:How To Discover Your Money Making Niche,
733:How To Discover Your Money Making Niche}


7:
{743:How To Create WordPress Themes From Scratch Part 1,
533:How To Create WordPress Themes From Scratch Part 3b,
694:How To Create WordPress Themes From Scratch Part 2,
510:How To Create WordPress Themes From Scratch Part 3a}

Noise Elements:
 {540:iPhone SDK 3.0 ▯ Playing with Map Kit - ObjectGraph Blog,
742:This Is The Second Time A Google Engineer Has Been Fired For Accessing User
Data,
577:Enhance your web forms with new HTML5 features,
545:Resize or Move a Complete Flash Animation in One Go,
746:10 Things You Didn't Know About the New #Twitter /via @gigaom #news #sm,
732:How To Handle Customers During Virtual Assistant Problems,
705:article on social media ad campaigns,
587:The Business Plan,
791:CSS Color Names,
601:Typography | Web Style Guide 3,
753:1 in 4 U.S. Adults Now Use Mobile Apps [STATS]}
```

of the data being clustered. It is obvious that the problem is with the $O(n^2)$ algorithms specially when n is large. Xu and Wunsch (2005) compared the time and space complexities of these algorithms and provided additional algorithms that can handle very large data sets such as CLARA, CLARANS and BIRCH.

It is obvious that hierarchical clustering algorithms are not suitable for large datasets because of their complexities. The K-means is the most efficient algorithm among them as the complexity is almost linear (Xu & Wunsch, 2005), but it cannot handle categorical data, which is very important when clustering the web. DBSCAN can be improved by using spatial indices on the

Table 2. Space and Time complexities for clustering algorithms

Algorithm name	Space complexity	Time complexity
Single-Link	$O(n^2)$	$O(kn^2)$
Avrage-Link	$O(n^2)$	$O(kn^2)$
MS Single-Link	$O(n^2)$	$O(n^2)$
K-eans	$O(n+k)$	$O(tkn)$
ROK	$O(n^2)$	$O(n^2 \log n)$
DBCAN	$O(n^2)$	$O(n^2)$ or $O(n \log n)$ with R*-tree

data points such as R*-tree that will reduce the time complexity for it from $O(n^2)$ to $O(n \log n)$ and generates more efficient queries (Xu & Wunsch, 2005). It is important to mention that indexing spatial data faces difficulties in high dimensions and this subject is an active area for research (Marmanis & Babenko, 2009).

High Dimensionality

The world that we deal with is of three-dimensionality and if we want to cluster worlds of higher dimensionalities we need to know that these worlds are governed by different rules and different proximities (Marmanis & Babenko, 2009). Actually higher dimensionality means larger computation, which will slow the algorithm down.

High dimensionality produces a problem in data separation as the distance between the point and its nearest neighbour has no difference than the distance from that point to other points when the dimensionality is high enough (Xu & Wunsch, 2008). The "curse of dimensionality" is a problem that is related to high dimensionality. The term was introduced by Bellman to indicate the exponential growth of complexity in a high dimensionality situation (Xu & Wunsch, 2005), which indicates that the distance between any set of points in high dimensions are the same. In such situation there

will be no effect for clustering algorithms that are based on distance measurements. Aggarwal (2002) provided a solution to this problem.

CONCLUSION

Clustering algorithms are an important approach to divide and analyze data. There are many different types of clustering each with its own technique. We can apply them on many phenomena in this world actually any dataset that consists of elements are qualified for applying clusters. We have discussed six clustering algorithms in this paper: single link, average link, MST single link, k-means, ROCK, and DBSCAN. The discussion was based on how accurate is to apply them on the social web.

The single-link, average-link, and MST single-link algorithms are agglomerative hierarchical algorithms. They do not perform efficiently (both with respect to time and space) on large data sets even though they are easily implemented algorithms. The k-means algorithm is a partitional algorithm, which is more efficient than Link-based algorithms. But it does not work with categorical data since it relies on the idea of centroid. Moreover it cannot handle outliers (the points that are far away from the main clusters) (Xu & Wunsch, 2005).

The ROCK algorithm is a hierarchical agglomerative algorithm that can handle categorical data since it relies on the links as measures more than the distance. But it has high time and space complexities.

The DBSCAN algorithm is a density-based algorithm that uses point density to identify clusters in a space. It can handle outliers even though its time and space complexity are high.

The algorithms discussed in this paper are used for the identification of groups of users and data on a website. We can combine algorithms such as the K-means with other algorithms. K-means is the preferred to use since it is simple and fast and can run on parallel computational platforms. Combining different algorithms together will maximize the benefits of these algorithms and guarantees the quality of resulted clusters (Kotsiantis & Pintelas, 2004). One example would be combining the efficient K-means algorithm with the powerful ROCK algorithm (if the data is Boolean or categorical) or DBSCAN algorithm (if the data is spatial). One scenario would be using K-means on the high-level clusters then process them with the ROCK or the DBSCAN algorithm.

REFERENCES

Adomavicius, G., & Tuzhilin, A. (2005). Toward the next generation of recommender systems: A survey of the state-of-the-art and possible extensions. *IEEE Transactions on Knowledge and Data Engineering, 17*(6), 734–749. doi:10.1109/TKDE.2005.99.

Aggarwal, C. C. (2002). Towards meaningful high-dimensional nearest neighbor search by human-computer interaction. In *Proceedings of the 18th International Conference on Data Engineering* (pp. 593-604).

Anfinnsen, S., Ghinea, G., & de Cesare, S. (2010). Web 2.0 and folksonomies in a library context. *International Journal of Information Management, 31*, 63–70. doi:10.1016/j.ijinfomgt.2010.05.006.

Arthur, D., & Vassilvitskii, S. (2007). k-means++: The advantages of careful seeding. In *Proceedings of the 18th Annual ACM-SIAM Symposium on Discrete Algorithms* (pp. 1027-1035).

Berkhin, P. (2002). *Survey of clustering data mining techniques (Tech. Rep.).* San Jose, CA: Accrue Software.

Ester, M., Kriegel, H.-P., J[UNKNOWN ENTITY &odie;]rg, S., & Xu, X. (1996). A density-based algorithm for discovering clusters in large spatial databases with noise. In *Proceedings of the 2nd International Conference on Knowledge Discovery and Data Mining* (pp. 226-231).

Everitt, B. S., Landau, S., & Leese, M. (2009). *Cluster analysis* (4th ed.). New York, NY: John Wiley & Sons.

Gower, J. C. (1971). A general coefficient of similarity and some of its properties. *Biometrics, 27*(4), 857–871. doi:10.2307/2528823.

Hammouda, K. M. (2001). *Web mining: Clustering web documents a preliminary review.* Waterloo, ON, Canada: Department of Systems Design Engineering, University of Waterloo.

Haveliwala, T. H., Gionis, A., & Indyk, P. (2000). Scalable techniques for clustering the Web. In *Proceedings of the Extended Abstracts of Webdb* (pp. 129-134).

Hruschka, E. R., Campello, R. J. G. B., Freitas, A. A., & Leon, P. (2009). A survey of evolutionary algorithms for clustering. *IEEE Transactions on Systems, Man and Cybernetics. Part C, Applications and Reviews, 39*(2), 133–155. doi:10.1109/TSMCC.2008.2007252.

Jain, A. K., & Dubes, R. C. (1988). *Algorithms for clustering data*. Upper Saddle River, NJ: Prentice Hall.

Jain, A. K., Murty, M. N., & Flynn, P. J. (1999). Data clustering: A review. *ACM Computing Surveys*, *31*, 264–323. doi:10.1145/331499.331504.

Kanungo, T., Mount, D. M., Netanyahu, N. S., Piatko, C., Silverman, R., & Wu, A. Y. (2000). An efficient k-means clustering algorithm: Analysis and implementation. *IEEE Transactions on Pattern Analysis and Machine Intelligence*, *2*(7), 881–892.

Kotsiantis, S. B., & Pintelas, P. E. (2004). Recent advances in clustering: A brief survey. *WSEAS Transactions on Information Science and Applications*, *1*, 73–81.

Marmanis, H., & Babenko, D. (2009). *Algorithms of the intelligent Web* (1st ed.). Greenwich, CT: Manning.

Mishra, N., Schreiber, R., Stanton, I., & Tarjan, R. (2007). Clustering social networks. In A. Bonato & F. R. K. Chung (Eds.), *Proceedings of the 5th International Conference on Algorithms and Models for the Web-Graphs* (LNCS 4863, pp. 56-67).

Mocian, H. (2009). *Survey of distributed clustering techniques (M.Sc. Internal Research Project)*. London, UK: Imperial College.

Naughton, M., Kushmerick, N., & Carthy, J. (2006). Clustering sentences for discovering events in news articles. In M. Lalmas, A. MacFarlane, S. Rüger, A. Tombros, T. Tsikrika, & A. Yavlinsky (Eds.), *Proceedings of the 28th European Conference on Advances in Information Retrieval* (LNCS 3936, pp. 535-538).

Rajeev, S. G., Rastogi, R., & Shim, K. (1999). Rock: A robust clustering algorithm for categorical attributes. In *Proceedings of the 15th International Conference on Data Engineering* (pp. 512-521).

Stein, B., & Busch, M. (2005). Density-based cluster algorithms in low dimensional and high-dimensional application. In *Proceedings of the Second International Workshop on Text-Based Information Retrieval* (pp. 45-56).

Tan, P.-N., Steinbach, M., & Kumar, V. (2005). Introduction to data mining (U.S. ed.). Reading, MA: Addison-Wesley.

Twitter. (2010, November). *Discovering who to follow* [Web log post]. Retrieved from http://blog.twitter.com/2010/07/discovering-who-to-follow.html

Wikipedia. (2010a). *DBSCAN*. Retrieved from http://en.wikipedia.org/wiki/DBSCAN

Wikipedia. (2010b). *Delicious.com*. Retrieved from http://en.wikipedia.org/wiki/Delicious.com

Wikipedia. (2010c). *Semantic Web*. Retrieved from http://en.wikipedia.org/wiki/Semantic_Web

Wu, B. Y., & Chao, K.-M. (2004). *Spanning trees and optimization problems*. Boca Raton, FL: Chapman and Hall/CRC Press.

Xu, R., & Wunsch, D. (2008). Clustering (IEEE Press Series on Computational Intelligence) (illustrated ed.). Piscataway, NJ: Wiley-IEEE Press.

Xu, R., & Wunsch, I. (2005). Survey of clustering algorithms. *IEEE Transactions on Neural Networks*, *16*(3), 645–678. doi:10.1109/TNN.2005.845141 PMID:15940994.

This work was previously published in the International Journal of Virtual Communities and Social Networking, Volume 3, Issue 3, edited by Subhasish Dasgupta, pp. 1-18, copyright 2011 by IGI Publishing (an imprint of IGI Global).

Chapter 10
Identifying Opinion Leaders for Marketing by Analyzing Online Social Networks

Niyoosha Jafari Momtaz
K. N. Toosi University of Technology, Iran

Abdollah Aghaie
K. N. Toosi University of Technology, Iran

Somayeh Alizadeh
K. N. Toosi University of Technology, Iran

ABSTRACT

Recently, the impact of social networks in customer buying decision is rapidly increasing due to effectiveness in shaping public opinion. This paper helps marketers analyze social network's members based on different characteristics and choose the best method for identifying influential people among them. Then, marketers can use these influential people as seeds to market products/services. Considering the importance of opinion leadership in social networks a comprehensive overview of existing literature has been done. Studies show, different titles (such as opinion leaders, influential people, market mavens and key players) are used to refer to the influential group in social networks whom we know as opinion leaders. The study shows all the properties presented for opinion leaders in the form of different titles are classified into three general categories including structural, relational and personal characteristics and based on studying opinion leader identification methods; appropriate parameters are extracted in a comprehensive chart to evaluate and compare these methods accurately.

DOI: 10.4018/978-1-4666-4022-1.ch010

INTRODUCTION

Marketing based on social networks refers to a collection of marketing activities that take advantage of social relationships between consumers to increase sales. There are different kinds of marketing using social networks like *word-of-mouth marketing, diffusion of innovation, buzz marketing* and *viral marketing* (Hill *et al.*, 2006). Between these instances of network-based marketing, word-of-mouth marketing has more creditability (Li & Du, 2011), because there is no direct link between the sender and the merchant. As a result, information is considered independent and subjective. In recent years, many researches in word-of-mouth marketing investigate discovering influential nodes in a social network. These influential people are called opinion leaders in the literature. Organizations interested in e-commerce need to identify opinion leaders among their customers, also the place (web site) which they are going online. This is the place they can market their products.

Social Network Analysis

Regarding the importance of interpersonal relationship, studies are looking for formal methods to measures *who talks to whom* in a community. These methods are known as social network analysis (Scott, 1991; Wasserman & Faust, 1994; Rogers & Kincaid, 1981; Valente & Davis, 1999). Social network analysis includes the study of the interpersonal relationships. It usually is more focused on the network itself, rather than on the attributes of the members (Li & Du, 2011). Valente and Rogers (1995) have described social network analysis from the point of view of interpersonal communication by "formal methods of measuring who talks to whom within a community." Social network analysis enables researchers to identify people who are more central in the network and so more influential. By using these central people or

opinion leaders as seeds diffusion of a new product or service can be accelerated (Katz & Lazarsfeld, 1955; Valente & Davis, 1999).

Importance of Social Networks for Marketing

The importance of social networks as a marketing tool is increasing, and it includes diverse areas (Even-Dar & Shapirab, 2011). Analysis of interdependencies between customers can improve targeted marketing as well as help organization in acquisition of new customers who are not detectable by traditional techniques. By recent technological developments social networks are not limited in face-to-face and physical relationships. Furthermore, online social networks have become a new medium for word-of-mouth marketing. Although the face-to-face word-of-mouth has a greater impact on consumer purchasing decisions over printed information because of its vividness and credibility, in recent years with the growth of the Internet and virtual communities the written word-of-mouth (word-of-mouse) has been created in the online channels (Mak, 2008). Consider a company that wants to launch a new product. This company can benefit from popular social networks like Facebook and Myspace rather than using classical advertising channels. Then, convincing several key persons in each network to adopt the new product, can help a company to exploit an effective diffusion in the network through word-of-mouth.

According to Nielsen's survey of more than 26,000 internet uses, 78% of respondents exhibited recommendations from others are the most trusted source when considering a product or service (Nielsen, 2007). Based on another study conducted by *Deloitte's Consumer Products group*, almost 62% of consumers who read consumer-written product reviews online declare their purchase decisions have been directly influenced by the user reviews (Delottie, 2007). Empirical studies have demonstrated that new ideas and practices spread through interpersonal communication (Valente & Rogers, 1995; Valente & Davis, 1999; Valente, 1995). Hawkins *et al.* (1995) suggest that companies can use four possible courses of action, including marketing research, product sampling, retailing/personal selling and advertising to use their knowledge of opinion leaders to their advantage.

The authors of this paper in a similar study have done a review of related literature using social networks for improving marketing response. They discuss the benefits and challenges of utilizing interpersonal relationships in a network as well as opinion leader identification; also, a three step process to show how firms can apply social networks for their marketing activities has been proposed (Jafari Momtaz *et al.*, 2011). While applications of opinion leadership in business and marketing have been widely studied, it generally deals with the development of measurement scale (e.g., Burt, 1999), its importance in the social sciences (e.g., Flynn *et al.*, 1994), and its application to various areas related to the marketing, such as the health care industry, political science (Burt, 1999) and public communications (e.g., Howard *et al.*, 2000; Locock *et al.*, 2001).

In this paper, a comprehensive review of studies in the field of opinion leadership and employing social networks to improve the marketing response is done. First, the concept of opinion leadership as well as different titles (opinion leaders, influential people, market mavens and key players) that has been introduced by different studies for referring to the influential group in social networks is discussed. Then, regarding the similarity of these titles on concept and common identification factors, by considering all definition and characteristics proposed for opinion leaders, influential people, market mavens and key players, three comprehensive classifications including structural, relational and personal characteristics are proposed. Next, the methods of opinion leader identification and

selection are reviewed and appropriate parameters for analyzing these methods are extracted and shown in a comprehensive diagram.

OPINION LEADERS

Nowadays, because of more availability of products via the internet consumers usually face a wide range of alternatives in their decision making process. Simon (1982) in the theory of bounded rationality declares that people do not have the enough ability to process and evaluate all that information. Instead of spending lots of time and money to analyze every option, people usually make their decision based on trust to others who are close to them and have common interests with.

In studies related to marketing and diffusion of information, there is a central idea that these trustworthy people play a vital role on the formation of public opinion (Watts & Dodds, 2007). These people are introduced with different names in the literature. They are called *opinion leaders* in the majority of the studies as well as *influential people*, *market mavens* or *key players* in other studies. However, the definition and usage of them are the same. Table 1 shows these titles in the opinion leadership theory presented in different studies.

The study of Lazarsfield and his colleagues is the starting point for opinion leadership theory in the 1940s and 1950s (Katz & Lazarsfeld, 1955; Lazarsfield *et al.*, 1948); they discovered that voting decisions were heavily influenced by relatives, friends and co-workers rather than media. Also, they suggested a *two-step flow* framework that shows the flow of information, which is formed under the influence of the mass media from an opinion leader to her followers or opinion seekers (Burt, 1999). Actually, a small portion of people that have a lot of influence on the others can act as filters or intermediaries and accelerate or stop the diffusion of information (Katz & Lazarsfeld, 1955; Watts & Dodds, 2007). In the

Table 1. Different titles in the opinion leadership theory

Opinion Leader	Influential people
Katz and Lazarsfeld 1955; Lazarsfeld *et al.,* 1948; Rogers and Cartano, 1962; Rogers, 1995-2003; King and Summers, 1970; Bandura, 1986; Engel *et al.,* 1987; Kelly *et al.,* 1991; Flynn *et al.,* 1994; Weimann, 1994; Hawkins *et al.,* 1995; Valente, 1996; Chau and Hui, 1998; Gilly *et al.,* 1998 ; Burt, 1999; Bansal and Voyer, 2000; Blackwell *et al.,* 2001; Kempe *et al.,* 2005; Lyons and Henderson, 2005; Feder and Savastano, 2006; Tsai *et al.,* 2006; Watts and Dodds, 2007; Yu, 2008; Ding and Liu, 2009; Merwe and Heerden, 2009; Li and Du, 2011;	Burson-Marsteller, 2001; Coleman *et al.,*1957; Ding & Liu, 2009; Merton, 1968; Strach, 2000; Keller & Berry, 2003.
	Market maven
	Fieck & Price, 1987; Merwe & Heerden, 2009; Williams & Slama, 1995; Walsh & Mitchell, 2001.
	Key player
	Bonacich, 1972; Freeman, 1979; Borgatti *et al.,* 1998; Borgatti, 2006.

decades after the introduction of two-step flow, the idea of opinion leaders or influential people and different ways of identifying these individuals has been widely studied in the diffusion of innovation (Coleman *et al.,* 1966; Rogers, 1995; Valente, 1995), social science (Burt, 1999) and marketing (Chan & Misra, 1990; Coulter *et al.,* 2002; Myers & Robertson, 1972; Van den Bulte & Joshi, 2007; Vernette, 2004). Rogers and Cartano (1962), define opinion leadership as "degree to which an individual is able informally to influence other individuals' attitudes or overt behaviors in a desired way with relative frequency." Opinion leaders are described by Katz and Lazarsfield (1955) as "individuals who lead in influencing others' options." Flynn *et al.* (1994) provide marketing perspective as follows: "as consumers frequently rely upon other people as sources of information, in addition to advertisements and

media, opinion leaders exert a disproportionate amount of influence on the decisions of other consumers."

Other studies are used *influential people* for describing this group of key people in the network (Burson-Marsteller, 2001; Coleman *et al.,* 1957; Ding & Liu, 2009; Merton, 1968). Burson-Marsteller defines influential people, as "they shape public opinion and share the uncanny ability to seamlessly spread information by word-of-mouth" (Burson-Marsteller, 2001). The Rober Strach Worldwide study (2000) declares that 8 percent of American online users are e-influential people (group who change the surfing habits of others).

Literature related to the diffusion of innovation and social networks also include another term in the form of so-called *market mavens*. Feick and Price (1987), define Market mavens as "individuals who have information about many kinds of products, places to shop, and other facets of markets, and initiate discussions with consumers and respond to requests from consumers for market information". In fact, they are opinion leaders on a wide range of subjects (Merwe & Heerden, 2009). Many studies declare that market mavens can influence the decision-making behavior of the majority of buyers (Fieck & Price, 1987; Williams & Slama, 1995; Walsh & Mitchell, 2001).

Some studies are concerned with identifying the set of *key players* in a social network (Bonacich, 1972; Freeman, 1979). Key players have the most number of direct links with community members or are along the shortest path between many pairs of nodes. They are placed in a structural optimal position and can accelerate the diffusion of every information, trend, behavior or product. The optimal selection of these people is dependent on for what they are needed. Borgatti (2006) has done a comprehensive study on key players' identification. Accordingly, he illustrates two main purposes for key player identification:

1. Optimally diffusing something through the network by using the key players as seeds.
2. Disrupting or fragmenting the network by removing the key nodes.

SPECIFICATIONS OF OPINION LEADERS: STRUCTURAL, RELATIONAL, AND PERSONAL CHARACTERISTICS

Since word-of-mouth has a wide impact on the opinions and purchase decisions of consumers, firm and marketers try to be more focused on the influential customers (Kiss & Bichler, 2008; Duan *et al.*, 2008), and identify people who are at the center of interactions (Keller & Berry, 2003). Properties expressed in different studies for opinion leaders are largely depending on the type of available data for the study and there is no comprehensive classification for the specification of opinion leaders. Kats and Lazarsfield (1955), specify three comprehensive criteria to identify opinion leaders: 1) personality and special characteristics, 2) capability and knowledge, and 3) strategic position in the network. This is the most complete classification in the opinion leadership studies because of considering both collective and personal factors. However, it does not consider the

type of relationship between people and social position in the network. In addition, regarding introducing similar concepts like opinion leader, influential people, market maven and key player as well as numerous studies that have been done after that of Katz and Lazarsfield (1955), there is no comprehensive classification for considering all of these concepts.

Since, in the majority of studies the concepts of opinion leaders and influential people are considered equal (Merwe & Heerden, 2009; Watts & Dodds, 2007), we propose three comprehensive categories including structural, behavioral and personal factors for identifying opinion leaders. This classification is based on all the specification proposed for opinion leaders, influential people, market mavens and key players discussed in the literature. Besides, considering the similarity between some of the specification described in various articles, a unique name has been put on the common features. Table 2 shows the features discussed in different studies related the three categories listed.

Structural Characteristics

Structural characteristics refer to the network topology and the position of a person in relation with other people. In addition, the personal

Table 2. Opinion leader identification factors

References	Specifications	Factors
Rogers, 2003; Rogers, 1995; Valente, 1996; Weimann, 1994.	Exposure of media or change agent	Structural
Merwe and Heerden, 2009; Katz, 1957; Rogers, 2003; Keller and Berry, 2003; Valente and Davis, 1999; Valente, 1995; Zhang *et al.*, 2010.	Prominence and central position	
Kempe *et al.*, 2005. Zhang *et al.*, 2010	Shorter distance with the most network members	

continued on following page

Table 2. Continued

References	Specifications	Factors
Li and Du, 2011; Weiman, 1994; Valente and Davis, 1999; Feder and Savastano, 2006; Zhang *et al.*, 2010.	Similarity between opinion leader and his follower	Relational ○➔○
Simmel and Frisby, 2004; Granovetter, 1973; Brown and Reinegen, 1987; Li and Du, 2011.	strength of relationships	
Simmel and Frisby, 2004; Munns, 1995; Li *et al.*, 2010; Morgan and Hunt, 1994; Jurvetson, 2008.	Trust	
Li and Du, 2011; Krackhardt and Stern, 1988; Nahapiet and Ghoshal, 1994; Nohria *et al.*, 1992.	Type of relationship	
Rogers, 2003; Lyons and Henderson, 2005; Li and Du, 2011.	Innovation	Personal ●
De Valck *et al.*, 2009; Rogers, 2003; Arndt, 1967.	High social involvement and more activity	
Li and Du, 2011; Freeman, 1979.	Prestige	
Rogers, 2003; Bandura, 1986.	Socioeconomic	
Li and Du, 2011.	Informative and knowledgeable	
1. Burson-Marsteller, 2001; Yu, 2008. 2. Saunders *et al.*,1974; Summers, 1970. Feder and Savastano, 2006; Xinyi, 2008. 3. Marshall & Gitosudarmo, 1995; Yu, 2008. 4. Levy, 1978 ; Polegato and Wall, 1980.	1. Age and gender 2. Education 3. Income 4. More attention to higher-quality information resources, such as newspapers and magazines	
De Valck *et al.* 2009; Li *et al.* 2010.	Regular visit	
Li *et al.*, 2010	Time of last visit	
Ho and Dempsey, 2010; Tong *et al.*, 2007.	Motivation and tendency	
Gilly *et al.*, 1998; Bansal and Voyer, 2000.	Reputation	

comments of network members about products are considered structural characteristics. Countless studies reveal that opinion leaders are more exposed to the external source of information such as media or change agents (Rogers, 1995, p. 92; Valente, 1996; Weimann, 1994, p. 217). Influential people are positioned at the center of interaction; they are well-connected and have relation with the majority of network members (Merwe & Heerden, 2009; Katz, 1957; Rogers, 2003; Keller & Berry, 2003; Zhang *et al.*, 2010; Valente & Davis, 1999; Valente, 1995). Another important point is that the impact of messages sent by opinion leaders is directly correlated with the number of users through which the information passes (Kempe *et al.*, 2005, Zhang *et al.*, 2010).

Relational Characteristics

Relational characteristics such as trust are related to interaction of people with each other. The relationship between an opinion leader and his follower is a perceptible indicator of the effectiveness of word-of-mouth marketing (Li & Du, 2011). Numerous studies indicate that diffusion is most efficiently when it occurs between individuals and their "near peers" whom they have chosen as their models (Valente & Davis, 1999; Weiman, 1994; Feder & Savastano, 2006; Zhang *et al.*, 2010). Other studies address the problem of information exchange from the higher social class groups to a lower social class group (Roling *et al.*, 1976; Van de Fliert, 1993). The effectiveness of word-of-mouth recommendations is also based on the tie strength (Granovetter, 1973; Brown & Reinegen, 1987). Stronger ties have more impact on customer behavior than weaker ties, as the opinion leader will be more persuasive. The strength level of relationships can be indicated by trust between people without performing a detailed investigation of intention (Simmel & Frisby, 2004). Relational factors also include the type of personal relations that people have developed with each other during their interaction (Nohria *et al.*, 1992). Nahapiet and

Ghoshal (1994) describe this as "two actors may occupy equivalent positions in similar network configurations, but if their personal and emotional attachments to other network members differ, their actions also are likely to differ in important respects". In some studies type of relationship between people has been used to opinion leader's identification process (Krackhardt & Stern, 1988). For example, Li and Du (2011) define four types of relationship: strangers, friends, good friends, and buddies to measure tie strength.

Personal Characteristics

Personal characteristics refer to individual profile features, and factors related to the personality. Rogers (2003) correlate Innovativeness, Cosmopoliteness, social participation and socioeconomic status with opinion leadership. Opinion leaders are more innovative (Lyons & Henderson, 2005; Rogers, 2003) and educated (Saunders *et al.*, 1974; Summers, 1970; Feder & Savastano, 2006; Xinyi, 2008), have higher income (Marshall & Gitosudarmo, 1995), and more attention to higher-quality information resources, such as newspapers and magazines (Levy, 1978; Polegato & Wall, 1980).

Burson-Marsteller's study conducted in 2001 to identify influential people in electronic platform reveals that gender plays an important role on opinion leadership; In general, men follow opinions and provide advice on technology, computers, whereas more women seek information about food, restaurants, health and fitness. Yu (2008) shows that opinion leaders are usually men at the medium or low income. According to other studies, opinion leaders are more educated, wealthy as well as have more income and cosmopolitan tendency (Rogers, 1995, p. 92; Valente, 1996; Weimann, 1994, p. 217). Li and Du (2011), introduced influential people as influential, knowledgeable, communicable, respective, and innovative. Some studies have shown that sociable people are more likely to participate in word-of-mouth because they enjoy being in relation with other people (Arndt, 1967; De Valck *et al.*, 2009). In addition to sociability, individual's base level of influence-ability, i.e., how a person accepts the opinions and experiences of others can have impact on his buying decision (McGuire, 1985). De Valck *et al.* (2009) declare that the frequency of visits and the amount of time spent during each visit are likely to affect the extent of community influence. Another important personal factor is reputation of a person that can make him an opinion leader (Gilly *et al.*, 1998; Bansal & Voyer, 2000). Also, motivation is a prominence factor for effectiveness of word-of-mouth marketing (Ho & Dempsey, 2010; Tong *et al.*, 2007).

EVALUATION PARAMETERS FOR OPINION LEADER IDENTIFICATION METHODS

As already discussed, many studies are concerned with identifying influential people in a social network. However, few studies have focused on opinion leader identification on an online platform (Ding & Liu, 2009; Tsai *et al.*, 2006). It is because of this that identification in the online environment needs to consider the semantic level of the message, the relationships among, the profiles of the platform participants, and the reliability of the message (Endo & Noto, 2003). Despite the various methods presented for identifying opinion leaders, no study takes into account the specification of appropriate parameters to evaluate these methods.

Understanding the evaluation parameters related to each method have a significant impact on the marketing decision marketing process, as it helps marketers choose the best method for identifying opinion leaders among their customers according to the available resources and output needed. By studying methods of identifying opinion leaders, we realize that these methods can be analyzed and compared base on factors like the type of input and output as well as the main technique of identification and selection. These parameters are shown in Figure 1.

Opinion leader identification methods vary based on the type of sources used. Sources used as input in the different methods could be divided into direct and indirect resources. Indirect sources mean the set of available information in an environment, such as structural and relational characteristics of network, as well as profile of customers. These sources contain information about the behavior and activities of customers in the network. On the contrary, direct sources indicate use of network members to collect information about leadership capabilities of other members through surveys. These sources need to access to the all or majority of members for conducting direct interviews and surveys to gain information about opinion leadership, different groups, communication channels and network topology (Feder & Savastano, 2006).

Output of opinion leader identification methods, independent of input resources can be either binary or a numerical value. Usually, output includes identifying some people as opinion leader

Figure 1. Appropriate parameters for evaluation and classification of opinion leader identification methods

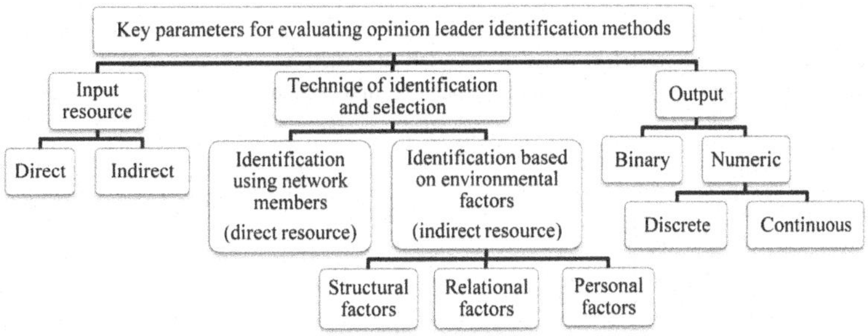

among other members of network. Hence, each node has a value of 0 or 1 that 1 indicates an opinion leader, and 0 indicates a non-leader member. In other cases, output includes a numerical value which indicates the degree of influence for a person. In this case, a discrete set of values or a numerical range could be used to refer to eligible values of influence for opinion leaders. Due to the importance of resources as an evaluation parameter, methods of opinion leader identification and selection are shown base on input resources in Table 3.

In some studies, the degree distribution is used to select the most influential people. Degree distribution as an indicator of networks shows the distribution of communication within the network. Many studies have considered top 10 percent of the degree distribution as the most influential people (Watts & Dodds, 2007; Keller & Berry, 2003; Ding & Liu, 2009). Some studies have

classified opinion leader identification methods into three general categories: 'self-reporting' (which is called also self-designating), 'sociometric' and 'key informant' methods (Engel *et al.*, 1987; Rogers & Cartano, 1962). In self-reporting method respondents are asked to evaluate their own capability to be an opinion leader. At first, King and Summers (1970) developed a seven-item, self-reporting scale for opinion leadership, and then other researchers like Childers (1986) and Flynn *et al.* (1994) adjusted a six-item scale from the original scale. In sociometric methods respondents are asked from whom they get advice and to whom they turn to seek advice on a particular topic (Engel *et al.*, 1987; Rogers & Cartano, 1962). In key informant methods, informed individuals, and not all members of the community can be asked to identify the people they think are opinion leaders (Engel *et al.*, 1987; Rogers & Cartano, 1962).

Table 3. Techniques of identification and selection based on resources used

References	Technique of identification and selection	Type of resource
Keller and Berry, 2003; Watts and Dodds, 2007; Coulter *et al.*, 2002.	Individuals in the top $q\%$ of the influence distribution $p(n)$	Direct resource
King and Summers, 1970; Childers, 1986; Flynn *et al.*, 1994.	Self-reporting or self-designating method	
Engel *et al.*, 1987; Rogers and Cartano, 1962.	Sociometric method	
Engel *et al.*, 1987; Rogers and Cartano, 1962.	Key-informant method	
Domingos and Richardson, 2001; Kempe *et al.*, 2005; Kempe *et al.*, 2003; Mossel and Roch, 2007; Estevez *et al.*, 2007; Surma and Furmanek, 2010; Zhang *et al.*, 2010; Even-Dar and Shapira, 2011.	Influence maximization problem and greedy algorithm	Indirect resource
Feder and Savastano, 2006; Li *et al.*, 2010; Li and Du, 2011; Merwe and Heerden, 2009; Ding and Liu, 2009; Hill *et al.*, 2006; Zhang *et al.*, 2010; Surma and Furmanek, 2010.	Selection based on structural, relational and personal factors	

All of these methods identify a ranking-based indicator of opinion leadership. However all of them need to access to the all community members as the main source of information to gather information about how many times a person is nominated as an opinion leader by the other members. In contrast, methods which use indirect resources utilize the information about the social network between people including structural and relational factors as well as members' personal specifications to evaluate the opinion leadership. We have classified other methods in the form of indirect methods into two general categories. The first class is the *influence maximization problem* which was defined by Domingos and Richardson (2001), and then some studies have investigated this problem with greedy algorithms. This problem can be formulated as finding the set K of influential individuals by introducing them with a new technology/product the spread/adoption of the technology/product will be maximized in a given social network. The study of Kempe *et al.* (2005) proves that in practice finding the optimal subset of size K is a NP-hard problem. The second class of studies employs the structural and relational of the network as well as profile characteristics of customer to identify opinion leaders. Table 4 summaries some important studies related to opinion leadership according to evaluating parameters.

As already mentioned, in a number of studies degree distribution are used to select influential people. Classical studies have suggested that influential people are those who have directly affected more than 3 or 4 of their neighbors (Coleman *et al.*, 1957; Merton, 1968). The number of affected neighbors is considered at least 14 in another study (Burson-Marsteller, 2001). Many studies have considered top 10% of degree distribution as the most influential people (Watts & Dodds, 2007; Keller & Berry, 2003; Ding & Liu, 2009).

Valente and Davis (1999) proposed a three step model to identify opinion leaders and use them as seeds for the marketing activities. In the first step, opinion leaders are selected using sociometric method or centrality (Borgatti *et al.*, 1998; Freeman, 1979). Second step includes generating optimal pairs by matching these leaders with their closest neighbors who have nominated them as an opinion leader. Then, the leaders can be given educational materials to educate or train those with whom they have been matched. This diffusion network support principles of learning theory (Bandura, 1986) and diffusion (Rogers, 1995; Valente & Rogers, 1995). The result of this study declares that learning occurs most efficiently when individuals are trained by their "near peers" whom they have chosen as their models.

The study of Merwe and Heerden (2009) shows that opinion leadership is non domain-specific and marketers do not to spend lots of time and money to identify opinion leaders in different domains. Accordingly, a framework for opinion leader identification is proposed in this study.

Xinyi (2008) investigates opinion leadership among the participants in the bulletin board systems. In this study self-reporting method is used to identify opinion leaders. Results of study dictate that bulletin board system participation history, frequently participation and time spent on bulletin board system every day has a significant positive relationship with opinion leadership.

Li *et al.* (2010) proposed a framework for finding potentially influential reviewers. In this framework, text-mining techniques as a modified PMI (Pointwise Mutual Information) measure are used to analyze and quantify the comments written by each reviewer. Meanwhile, the reviewing recency and frequency of the authors are quantified to measure the RFM scores of the reviewers. Then, the PMI- and RFM-based scores are combined using an ANN (artificial neural network) technique to determine whether a reviewer is valuable in word-of-mouth marketing. The output of the well-trained is a list of ranked influential reviewers.

As previously mentioned, some studies probe influence maximization problem in social networks. For example, in Estevez *et al.* (2007) a

Table 4. Evaluation parameters of important studies for identifying opinion leaders

References	Output	Method/Factor(S)	Input resources	Data set	Paper focus
Keller and Berry, 2003; Watts and Dodds, 2007; Ding and Liu, 2009	Binary	Select the top 10% of the influence distribution/degree distribution	Indirect	Simulated date	Challenging the assumption that using influential people will improve marketing efforts.
Valente and Davis, 1999	Binary	Sociometric method	Direct	Simulated date	Accelerating the diffusion of innovation via opinion leaders.
Merwe and Heerden, 2009	Numeric - discrete	Using Sociometric and Self-reporting methods as well as relational data for construct the social network, then use the Power measure to identify opinion leaders/ structural - relational	Both direct and indirect	Students of a college	Using social network theory in conjunction with opinion leadership concept to identify opinion leaders.
Xinyi, 2008	Binary	Self-reporting, six-item	Direct	Users of a Bulletin board system	Proposing a framework for identifying opinion leaders.
Li et al., 2010	Numeric-continuous	Personal-structural	Indirect	Epinions.com	Using a combination of RFM model and Text mining techniques to identify influential reviewer.
Estevez et al., 2007	Binary	Greedy algorithm	Indirect	We sites' hyperlinks	Examining influence maximization problem.
Feder and Savastano, 2006	Binary	Selection based on knowledge and education/ personal	Indirect	Data of some farmers in the Indonesia	Investigating the hypothesis of similarity between opinion leader and his follower.
Li and Du, 2011	Numeric-continuous	Proposing a framework named BARR for opinion leader identification/ structural, relational and personal	Indirect	Some weblogs	Identification of opinion leaders in online social blogs.
Hill et al., 2006	Binary	structural and personal	Indirect	Demographic and interpersonal data	Illustrating that analysis of interdependencies between consumers and customers' network will improve targeted marketing.
Surma and Furmanek, 2010	Binary	Structural	Indirect	Biznes.com	Employing data mining in social network to improve marketing response.
Zhang et al., 2010	Binary	Investigating hill climbing and general greedy algorithm against the centrality measure/ structural-relational	Indirect	Epinions.com	Proving that centrality can be as good as complex algorithms for opinion leader identification.

set covering greedy algorithm is presented for solving this problem and is verified by a data set of some websites' hyperlinks.

Feder and Savastano (2006) examine whether similarity between opinion leaders and their follower can cause a more effective word-of-mouth. They employ personal factor on a data set of Indonesian farmers to identify opinion leaders.

Li and Du (2011) propose a framework called BARR to identify opinion leaders in online social blogs. This framework first analyzes blogs based on blog content and comments of readers. Then, select opinion leaders based on specification of writers and readers and their relationship. This study shows that hot blog selection is a multi-attribute decision problem so TOPSIS which summarizes the Euclidean distance between measurements and the ideal solution is used to determine the popularity of a blog.

Hill *et al.* (2006) illustrate that analyzing the social network between customers can directly affect product/service adoption. The advantage of their study is using a real data set with regard to inadequate data in prior studies which cause fewer abilities to provide direct and statistical support for the hypothesis that network analysis will improve marketing activities. They show that consumers who have a link with prior customers adopt the service at a rate 3–5 times greater than baseline groups selected by the best practices of the firm's marketing team. In addition, firms and marketers can acquire new customers who would not have been identified based on traditional attributes.

The study of Surma and Furmanek (2010) dictate that even a rudimentary application of data mining techniques can improve marketing response. In this study, C&RT (classification and regression tree) approach is used to build a classification tree that enables firms to formulate some specific rules to select proper target group for marketing.

Zhang *et al.* (2010) compare a set of algorithms, including general greedy, hill-climbing and centrality-based algorithms to investigate which

of them can better identify key users with great influence. This study shows that out-degree can not reflect the influence of a node in the network, because a person can trust to whoever he likes. Indeed, in-degree would be a better measure to identify influence of members. Results of comparison between in-degree centrality, general greedy and hill-climbing algorithms show that a simple measure like centrality is as good as more complex algorithms.

CONCLUSION

The phenomenon of word-of-mouth in different social network of people has a wide impact on the opinion and decision of them. Hence, firms and marketers should try to focus on influential customers and identify people who are at the center of communications and interactions to market their product and services. These influential people are called opinion leaders in the majority of studies and can shape the public opinion. Studies show different titles are used to refer to this influential group of people in the social networks, as well as different methods are presented to identify and select these individuals. Identifying characteristics of opinion leaders and effective factors in each method can have a significant impact on marketer's decisions; they can select the best method for identifying opinion leaders with regard to their available resources and needed output. However, the characteristics of opinion leaders expressed in different studies, largely depend on their dataset and there is no comprehensive classification to identify opinion leaders. Also, appropriate parameter to analyze and compare opinion leader's identification methods is not specified.

Since in some papers, the definition and application of different titles for opinion leaders are considered equal, in this paper all the properties presented for the opinion leader, influential people, market maven and key players are classified into three comprehensive categories, including structural, relational and personal characteristics. Furthermore, effective parameters for analyzing opinion leader identification methods are extracted and displayed in a comprehensive chart. The main contribution of this article is a comprehensive study on opinion leadership theory as well as the type of analysis and classification that have been done on them. By identifying opinion leaders in social networks and use them for different purposes (such as introducing new products, diffusion of innovation, advertising), marketers are able to form a powerful word-of-mouth in the network, increase the product and brand awareness, and identify the needs of their customers properly.

REFERENCES

Arndt, J. (1967). *Word of mouth advertising: A review of the literature (Tech. Rep.).* New York, NY: Advertising Research Foundation.

Bandura, A. (1986). *Social foundations of thought and action: A social cognitive theory.* Upper Saddle River, NJ: Prentice Hall.

Bansal, H. S., & Voyer, P. A. (2000). Word of mouth processes within a services purchase decision context. *Journal of Service Research, 3*(2), 166–177. doi:10.1177/109467050032005.

Blackwell, R. D., Miniard, P. W., & Engel, J. F. (2001). *Consumer behavior.* Orlando, FL: Harcourt.

Bonacich, P. (1972). Factoring and weighting approaches to status scores and clique identification. *The Journal of Mathematical Sociology, 2*(1), 113–120. doi:10.1080/0022250X.1972.9989806.

Borgatti, S. P. (2006). Identifying sets of key players in a network. *Computational & Mathematical Organization Theory, 12*(1), 21–34. doi:10.1007/s10588-006-7084-x.

Borgatti, S. P., Everett, M., & Freeman, L. (1998). *UCINET 5 for Windows: Software for social network analysis.* Natick, MA: Analytic Technologies.

Brown, J., & Reinegen, P. (1987). Social ties and word-of-mouth referral behavior. *The Journal of Consumer Research, 14*(3), 350–362. doi:10.1086/209118.

Burson-Marsteller. (2001). *The power of online influencers.* Retrieved from http://www.burson-marsteller.com/Practices_And_Specialties/AssetFile/E-Fluentials%20Brochure.pdf

Burt, R. S. (1999). The social capital of opinion leaders. *The Annals of the American Academy of Political and Social Science, 566,* 1–22. doi:10.1177/0002716299566001004.

Chan, K. K., & Misra, S. (1990). Characteristics of the opinion leader: A new dimension. *Journal of Advertising, 19*(3), 53–60.

Chau, P. K., & Hui, K. L. (1998). Identifying early adopters of new IT products: A case for Windows 95. *Information & Management, 33*(5), 225–230. doi:10.1016/S0378-7206(98)00031-7.

Childers, T. L. (1966). *Medical innovation: A diffusion study.* Indianapolis, IN: Bobbs-Merrill.

Childers, T. L. (1986). Assessment of the psychometric properties of an opinion leadership scale. *Journal of Marketing Research, 23*(2), 184–188. doi:10.2307/3151666.

Coleman, J. S., Katz, E., & Herbert, M. (1957). The diffusion of an innovation among physicians. *Sociometry, 20*(4), 253–270. doi:10.2307/2785979.

Coulter, R. A., Feick, L. F., & Price, L. L. (2002). Changing faces: Cosmetics opinion leadership among women in the new Hungary. *European Journal of Marketing, 36*(11), 1287–1308. doi:10.1108/03090560210445182.

De Valck, K., van Bruggen, G. H., & Wierenga, B. (2009). Virtual communities: A marketing perspective. *Decision Support Systems, 47*(3), 185–203. doi:10.1016/j.dss.2009.02.008.

Deloitte. (2007). *New Deloitte study shows inflection point for consumer products industry: Companies must learn to compete in a more transparent age.* Retrieved from http://usstock.jrj.com.cn/2007-10-01/000002746415.shtml

Ding, F., & Liu, Y. (2009). A decision theoretical approach for diffusion promotion. *Physica, 388*(17), 3572–3580. doi:10.1016/j.physa.2009.05.016.

Domingos, P., & Richardson, M. (2001). Mining the network value of customers. In *Proceedings of the 7th International Conference on Knowledge Discovery and Data Mining* (pp. 57-66).

Duan, W., Gu, B., & Whinston, A. B. (2008). Do online reviews matter? – An empirical investigation of panel data. *Decision Support Systems, 45*(4), 1007–1016. doi:10.1016/j.dss.2008.04.001.

Endo, H., & Noto, M. (2003). A word-of-mouth information recommender system considering information reliability and user preferences. In *Proceedings of the IEEE International Conference on Systems, Man and Cybernetics* (pp. 2990-2995).

Engel, J. F., Blackwell, R. D., & Miniard, P. W. (1987). *Consumer behavior* (5th ed.). Chicago, IL: The Dryden Press.

Estevez, P. A., Wera, P., & Saito, K. (1968). Patterns of influence: Local and cosmopolitan influentials. In Merton, R. K. (Ed.), *Social theory and social structure* (pp. 441–474). New York, NY: Free Press.

Estevez, P. A., Wera, P., & Saito, K. (2007, August 12-17). Selecting the most influential nodes in social networks. In *Proceedings of the International Joint Conference on Neural Networks*, Orlando, FL (pp. 2397-2402).

Even-Dar, E., & Shapirab, A. (2011). A note on maximizing the spread of influence in social networks. *Information Processing Letters, 111*(4), 184–187. doi:10.1016/j.ipl.2010.11.015.

Feder, G., & Savastano, S. (2006). The role of opinion leaders in the diffusion of new knowledge: The case of integrated pest management. *World Development, 34*(7), 1287–1300. doi:10.1016/j.worlddev.2005.12.004.

Feick, L. F., & Price, L. L. (1987). The market maven: A diffuser of marketplace information. *Journal of Marketing, 51*(1), 83–97. doi:10.2307/1251146.

Flynn, L. R., Goldsmith, R. E., & Eastman, J. K. (1994). The King and Summers opinion leadership scale: Revision and refinement. *Journal of Business Research, 31*(1), 55–64. doi:10.1016/0148-2963(94)90046-9.

Freeman, L. C. (1979). Centrality in social networks: Conceptual clarification. *Social Networks, 1*(3), 215–239. doi:10.1016/0378-8733(78)90021-7.

Gilly, M. C., Graham, J. L., Wolfinbarger, M. F., & Yale, L. J. (1998). A dyadic study of interpersonal information search. *Journal of the Academy of Marketing Science, 26*(2), 83–100. doi:10.1177/0092070398262001.

Granovetter, M. (1973). The strength of weak ties. *American Journal of Sociology, 87*(6), 1360–1380. doi:10.1086/225469.

Hawkins, D. I., Best, R. J., Coney, K. A., & Carey, K. A. (1995). *Consumer behavior: Implications for marketing strategy* (6th ed.). Boston, MA: McGraw-Hill/Irwin.

Hill, S., Provost, F., & Volinsky, C. (2006). Network-based marketing: Identifying likely adopters via consumer networks. *Statistical Science, 21*(2), 256–276. doi:10.1214/088342306000000222.

Ho, J. Y. C., & Dempsey, M. (2010). Viral marketing: Motivations to forward online content. *Journal of Business Research, 63*(9-10), 1000–1006. doi:10.1016/j.jbusres.2008.08.010.

Howard, K. A., Rogers, T., Howard-Pitney, B., & Flora, J. A. (2000). Opinion leaders' support for tobacco control policies and participation in tobacco control activities. *American Journal of Public Health, 90*(8), 1282–1287. PMID:10937010.

Jafari Momtaz, N., Aghaie, A., & Alizadeh, A. (2011). *Social network for marketing: Benefits and challenges*. Paper presented at the 5th Symposium on Advances in Science and Technology. Mashad, Iran.

Jurvetson, S. (2008). *What exactly is viral marketing?* Retrieved February 18, 2009, from http://www.currypuffandtea.files.wordpress.com/2008/03/viral-marketing.pdf

Katz, E., & Lazarsfeld, P. F. (1955). *Personal influence: The part played by people in the flow of mass communications*. New York, NY: Free Press.

Katz, J. E. (1957). The two-step flow of communication: An up-to-date report on a hypothesis. *Public Opinion, 21*(1), 61–78. doi:10.1086/266687.

Keller, E., & Berry, J. (2003). *The influentials*. New York, NY: Free Press.

Kelly, J. A., St. Lawrence, J. S., Diaz, Y. E., Stevenson, L. Y., Hauth, A. C., & Brasfield, T. L. et al. (1991). HIV risk behavior reduction following intervention with key opinion leaders of population: An experimental analysis. *American Journal of Public Health, 81*(2), 168–171. doi:10.2105/AJPH.81.2.168 PMID:1990853.

Kempe, D., Kleinberg, J., & Tardos, E. (2003). Maximizing the spread of influence through a social network. In *Proceedings of the Ninth ACMSIGKDD International Conference on Knowledge Discovery and Data Mining* (pp. 137-146).

Kempe, D., Kleinberg, J. M., & Tardos, E. (2005). Influential nodes in a diffusion model for social networks. In *Proceedings of the 32nd International Colloquium on Automata, Languages and Programming* (pp. 1127-1138).

King, C. W., & Summers, J. O. (1970). Overlap of opinion leadership across consumer product categories. *Journal of Marketing Research, 7*(1), 43–50. doi:10.2307/3149505.

Kiss, C., & Bichler, M. (2008). Identification of influencers – measuring influence in customer networks. *Decision Support Systems, 46*(1), 233–253. doi:10.1016/j.dss.2008.06.007.

Krackhardt, D., & Stern, R. N. (1988). Informal networks and organizational crises: An experimental simulation. *Social Psychology Quarterly, 51*(2), 123–140. doi:10.2307/2786835.

Lazarsfeld, P. F., Berelson, B., & Gaudet, H. (1948). *The people's choice: How the voter makes up his mind in a presidential campaign*. New York, NY: Columbia University Press.

Levy, M. R. (1978). Opinion leadership and television news uses. *Public Opinion Quarterly, 42*(3), 402–406. doi:10.1086/268463.

Li, F., & Du, T. C. (2011). Who is talking? An ontology-based opinion leader identification framework for word-of-mouth marketing in online social blogs. *Decision Support Systems, 51*(1), 190–197. doi:10.1016/j.dss.2010.12.007.

Li, Y.-M., Lin, C.-H., & Lai, C.-Y. (2010). Identifying influential reviewers for word-of-mouth marketing. *Electronic Commerce Research and Applications, 9*(4), 294–304. doi:10.1016/j.elerap.2010.02.004.

Locock, L., Dopson, S., Chambers, D., & Gabbay, J. (2001). Understanding the role of opinion leaders in improving clinical effectiveness. *Social Science & Medicine, 5*(6), 745–757. doi:10.1016/S0277-9536(00)00387-7 PMID:11511050.

Lyons, B., & Henderson, K. (2005). Opinion leadership in a computer-mediated environment. *Journal of Consumer Behaviour*, *4*(5), 319–329. doi:10.1002/cb.22.

Mak, V. (2008). *The emergence of opinion leaders in social networks*. Retrieved from http://ssrn.com/abstract=1157285

Marshall, R., & Gitosudarmo, I. (1995). Variation in the characteristics of opinion leaders across cultural broad. *Journal of International Consumer Marketing*, *8*(1), 5–22. doi:10.1300/J046v08n01_02.

McGuire, W. J. (1985). Attitudes and attitude change. In Gilbert, D., Fiske, S. T., & Lindzey, G. (Eds.), *The handbook of social psychology* (*Vol. 2*). New York, NY: McGraw-Hill.

Merton, R. K. (1957). The role-set: Problems in sociological theory. *The British Journal of Sociology*, *8*(2), 106–120. doi:10.2307/587363.

Merwe, R. V. D., & Heerden, G. V. (2009). Finding and utilizing opinion leaders: Social networks and the power of relationships. *South African Journal of Business Management*, *40*(3), 65–76.

Morgan, R. M., & Hunt, S. D. (1994). The commitment-trust theory of relationship marketing. *Journal of Marketing*, *58*(3), 20–38. doi:10.2307/1252308.

Mossel, E., & Roch, S. (2007). On the submodularity of influence in social networks. In *Proceedings of the 39th Annual ACM Symposium on Theory of Computing* (pp. 128-134).

Munns, A. K. (1995). Potential influence of trust on the successful completion of a project. *International Journal of Project Management*, *13*(1), 19–24. doi:10.1016/0263-7863(95)95699-E.

Myers, J. H., & Robertson, T. S. (1972). Dimensions of opinion leadership. *JMR, Journal of Marketing Research*, *9*(1), 41–46. doi:10.2307/3149604.

Nahapiet, J., & Ghoshal, S. (1994). Social capital, intellectual capital, and the organizational advantage. *Academy of Management Review*, *23*(2), 242–267.

Nielsen. (2007). *Word-of-mouth the most powerful selling tool: Nielsen global survey*. Retrieved from http://www.nielsen.com/media/2007/pr_071001.html

Nohria, N., & Eccles, R. G. (Eds.). (1992). *Problems of explanation in economic sociology, networks and organizations: Structure, form, and action*. Boston, MA: Harvard Business School.

Polegato, R., & Wall, M. (1980). Information seeking by fashion opinion leaders and followers. *Family and Consumer Sciences Research Journal*, *8*(5), 327–338.

Rogers, E., & Kincaid, D. L. (1981). *Communication networks: A paradigm for new research*. New York, NY: Free Press.

Rogers, E. M. (1995). *Diffusion of innovations*. New York, NY: Free Press.

Rogers, E. M. (2003). *Diffusion of innovations* (5th ed.). New York, NY: Simon & Schuster.

Rogers, E. M., & Cartano, D. G. (1962). Methods of measuring opinion leadership. *Public Opinion*, *26*(3), 435–441. doi:10.1086/267118.

Roling, N., Ascroft, J., & Wa Chege, F. (1976). Diffusion of innovations and the issue of equity in rural development. *Communication Research*, *3*(2), 155–171. doi:10.1177/009365027600300204.

Saunders, J., Davis, J. M., & Monsees, D. M. (1974). Opinion leadership in family planning. *Journal of Health and Social Behavior, 15*(3), 217–227. doi:10.2307/2137022 PMID:4436526.

Scott, J. (1991). *Network analysis: A handbook.* Newbury Park, CA: Sage.

Simmel, G., & Frisby, D. (2004). *The philosophy of money.* London, UK: Routledge/Taylor & Francis Group.

Simon, H. A. (1982). *Models of bounded rationality (Vol. 2).* Cambridge, MA: MIT Press.

Starch, R. (2003). Online opinion leaders are highly influential. *Nua Internet Surveys.* Retrieved from http://www.nua.ie/surveys/?f=VS&art_id=905355852&rel=true

Summers, J. O. (1970). The identity of women's clothing fashion opinion leaders. *JMR, Journal of Marketing Research, 7*(2), 178–185. doi:10.2307/3150106.

Surma, J., & Furmanek, A. (2010). Improving marketing response by data mining in social network. In *Proceedings of the International Conference on Advance in Social Networks Analysis and Mining* (pp. 446-451).

Tong, Y., Wang, X., & Teo, H. H. (2007). Understanding the intention of information contribution to online feedback systems from social exchange and motivation crowding perspectives. In *Proceedings of the 40th Hawaii International Conference on System Sciences* (p. 28).

Tsai, T. M. Shih, C. C., & Chou, S. T. (2006). Personalized blog recommendation using the value, semantic, and social model. In *Proceedings of the 3rd International Conference on Innovations in Information Technology* (pp. 1-5).

Valente, T. W. (1995). *Network models of the diffusion of innovations.* Cresskill, NJ: Hampton.

Valente, T. W. (1996). Social network thresholds in the diffusion of innovations. *Social Networks, 18*(1), 69–89. doi:10.1016/0378-8733(95)00256-1.

Valente, T. W., & Davis, R. L. (1999). Accelerating the diffusion of innovations using opinion leaders. *The Annals of the American Academy of Political and Social Science, 566*(1), 55–67. doi:10.1177/0002716299566001005.

Valente, T. W., & Rogers, E. M. (1995). The origins and development of the diffusion of innovations paradigm as an example of scientific growth. *Science Communication: An Interdisciplinary Social Science Journal, 16*(3), 238–269.

Van de Fliert, E. (1993). *Integrated pest management: Farmer field schools generate sustainable practices. A case study in Central Java evaluating IPM training (Paper No. 93-3).* Wageningen, The Netherlands: PUDOC, Wageningen Agricultural University.

Van den Bulte, C., & Joshi, Y. V. (2007). New product diffusion with influentials and imitators. *Marketing Science, 26*(3), 400–421. doi:10.1287/mksc.1060.0224.

Vernette, E. (2004). Targeting women's clothing fashion opinion leaders in media planning: An application for magazines. *Journal of Advertising Research, 44*, 90–107. doi:10.1017/S0021849904040061.

Walsh, G., & Mitchell, V. W. (2001). German market mavens' decision making styles. *Journal of Euromarketing, 10*(4), 83–108. doi:10.1300/J037v10n04_05.

Wasserman, S., & Faust, K. (1994). *Social network analysis-methods and applications*. Cambridge, UK: Cambridge University Press.

Watts, D. J., & Dodds, P. S. (2007). Influentials, networks, and public opinion formation. *The Journal of Consumer Research*, *34*(4), 441–458. doi:10.1086/518527.

Weimann, G. (1994). *The influentials*. Albany, NY: State University of New York Press.

Williams, T. G., & Slama, M. E. (1995). Market mavens' purchase decision evaluative criteria: Implications for brand and store promotion efforts. *Journal of Consumer Marketing*, *12*(3), 4–21. doi:10.1108/07363769510147218.

Xinyi, A. G. (2008). *Who are the influentials in virtual community? Opinion leaders among participants in bulletin board systems*. Hong Kong: School of Journalism and Communication, The Chinese University of Hong Kong.

Yu, H. (2008). The exploration on the BBS opinion leadership filtering model. *The Journal of Communication*, *15*, 66–75.

Zhang, Y., Zhaoqing, W., & Xia, C. (2010, April 20-23). Identifying key users for targeted marketing by mining online social network. In *Proceedings of the 24th Conference on Advanced Information Networking and Applications Workshops*, Perth, Australia (pp. 644-649).

This work was previously published in the International Journal of Virtual Communities and Social Networking, Volume 3, Issue 3, edited by Subhasish Dasgupta, pp. 19-34, copyright 2011 by IGI Publishing (an imprint of IGI Global).

Chapter 11
Blog Influence Index:
A Measure of Influential Weblog

Norshuhada Shiratuddin
Universiti Utara Malaysia, Malaysia

Nor Laily Hashim
Universiti Utara Malaysia, Malaysia

Shahizan Hassan
Universiti Utara Malaysia, Malaysia

Mohd Fo'ad Sakdan
Universiti Utara Malaysia, Malaysia

Mohd Samsu Sajat
Universiti Utara Malaysia, Malaysia

ABSTRACT

Although weblogs are a popular medium of communication, their influence on society is unclear. In particular, studies that investigate the impact and influence of blogosphere on the community and government have not been fully exploited. Such studies are important especially to the government in reshaping and realigning the policies related to new media. This article presents the outcomes of a study to identify measures on how to assess the influence of weblogs. At least four dimensions are critical for measuring weblog influence, which are recognition (number of in links and number of visitors), activity generation (number of comments and number of posts), novelty (number of out links), and credibility of a blog (number of information presentation type, number of factual errors, and number of hyperlink citations). It is hereby proposed that these dimensions make up a measure called the Blog Influence Index.

INTRODUCTION

A weblog allows users to post comments, images, video clips or links to other web pages (Herring et al., 2004; Trammel & Gasser, 2004; Bausch et al., 2002; Blood, 2002; Mortensen & Walker, 2002). Studies by scholars show that peoples participate in weblogging for many reasons (Akritidis, Katsaros,

& Bozanis, 2009). A study by Efimova (2009), for example, reveals that people use weblog as personal thinking space. Weblogging is seen in this case as an alternative means to generate ideas and getting feedback from others in the blogosphere community. Recuaero (2008) conducted a study on selected webloggers in Brazil to ascertain their perceptions on the information they

DOI: 10.4018/978-1-4666-4022-1.ch011

publish. It was found that webloggers perceived what they publish as either personal information (about themselves) or useful information (general information). In addition, the study also identified five motivations for weblogging which are creating a personal space, sharing interaction, sharing knowledge, authority, and popularity.

Recuaero's finding is supported by another interesting study from Michael and Irit (2008) who identified seven areas of motivations or reasons for blogging activities which include self expression, introspection and artistic activity (similar to creating personal space), social contacts and documentation of life (similar to sharing interaction), sharing of information, knowledge, and interest (similar to sharing of knowledge), and recognition (similar to authority and popularity).

There are also studies which indicate that weblogs are used by certain group of influential people such as public and political leaders to gain support on their agendas or to sway peoples' opinion on specific public issues. Research by Kavanaugh et al. (2007) in Blacksburg and Montgomery County, Virginia, for instance, signifies that weblog can indeed be a very effective tool for political or opinion leaders. Political activists all over the world have long been using weblogs for campaigning purposes (Adamic & Glance, 2005).

The influence of weblogging should not be under-estimated (Gillmore, 2006; Keller & Berry, 2003). However, studies that investigate the impact and influence of blogosphere on the community and government are yet to be fully exploited. Such studies are very important especially to the government as they can help to reshape and realign the policies related to new media. Although there are several tools that can be adopted to assess blog influence, these tools have some weaknesses due to the use of inadequate measuring criteria. Furthermore, most of these tools are being used to rank blogs rather than measuring influence. Therefore, the main aim of this study is to identify criteria that can be used to measure blogs influence. Consequently, a Blog Influence Index is formulated.

The rest of the paper is organized as follows. The next section reviews existing studies related to the measurement of blog influence. Then, the phases involved in the development of the index are described. Next, a discussion on the formulation of the index is presented. The final part summarizes the outcomes and potential future work.

DIMENSIONS AND CRITERIA FOR BLOG INFLUENCE

Traditionally, a social media is considered a success through inbound links or the number of people subscribed to it. This criterion is however no longer credible and can be misleading. In fact, social media is a channel through which people connect, collaborate, participate, discuss, and make friends. As such, more criteria should be used to measure its success particularly in terms of influence.

Rank

In identifying the influence of blogs, several studies focus on the criteria in giving ranks to the blogs. The existing algorithms are used in giving ranks to web pages are not suitable to be applied on blogs due to sparseness and temporal aspects (Agarwal & Liu, 2008). This is because blogs in blogospheres are sparsely linked compared to web pages. Blog posts and bloggers influence eliminate over times faster than web pages. Some of the common algorithms applied on webpages are PageRank and HITS.

Several studies can be found which investigated the measures for blog success. Edelman, for instance, produces a social media index which proposes five criteria that can be used to measure any social media (Bentwood, 2007). The criteria are blog ranking (e.g., Google rank, Alexa rank, inbound links, number of subscribers), multi format (analysis of Facebook- number of friends), mini updates (analysis of Twitter - number of friends, followers, updates), Business cards

(LinkedIn - number of contact), visual (analysis of Flickr - number of uploaded photos), and favourites (analysis of Digg, del.icio.us). Another related study is by Rahaman, Srilakhsmi, and Yasin (2011) who developed a popularity ranking technique called BRank. Using real blog data, BRank is able analyse interconnections within blog communities to reveal blog popularities.

Blog Post

Another related study was by Seung et al. (2009) who studied the influence of Content Power Users (CPUs) on other blog users. CPUs refer to bloggers or users who can induce and convince other users to actively participate in blog services. It was found CPUs can play a key role in determining the success of a blog. In order to measure and determine the CPUs, a new method was proposed which is based on the analysis of blog posts or documents. The main criterion used is the exposure time of a blog post, which refers to how long it has been published in the blog. Although Seung's study focuses only on determining influential bloggers or power users, it has revealed the importance of blog posts as one of the determinants in measuring blog influence.

Activity Generation, Recognition, Novelty, and Eloquence

Agarwal (2008) proposed a preliminary model for identifying influential bloggers. He identified several dimensions to describe influential bloggers. These are activity generation, recognition, novelty and eloquence. Activity generation is measured based on how many comments a blog post receives. The property of recognition is described through in links to a post. Novelty can be indicated by the number of out links. Therefore, a novel idea will have smaller number of out links, as the idea of a post is of fresh issues which have never been discussed or raised by other blog-

gers and has very less links to other blog posts. Eloquence is measured based on the length of a blog post. The longer blog post indicates writing ability confidence of the blog owner to share idea with the others.

Authority, Pageviews per User, Bounce Rate, and Time on Site

From observation, there are two major blog assessment tools that are worth mentioning which are Technorati and Alexa. Technorati is initially an Internet search engine for searching blogs, competing with Google and Yahoo and ranks blogs based on authority. Technorati Authority is the number of blogs linking to a website in the last six months. This means that the higher the number of blogs linking to a particular blog, the more Technorati Authority the blog has. However, a blog can only be ranked using this technique, if it is registered with Technorati.

Alexa, on the other hand, is known for its toolbar and website. Once installed, the toolbar collects data on browsing behavior which is transmitted to the website where it is stored and analyzed. It offers a toolbar that gives Internet users suggestions on where to go next, based on the traffic patterns of its user community. Alexa also offers context for each site visited: to whom it was registered, how many pages it had, how many other sites pointed to it, and how frequently it was updated (Dawson, 1997). Alexa ranks sites based on tracking information of users of its Alexa Toolbar for Internet Explorer and from integrated sidebars in Mozilla and Netscape. At least three metrics to rank blog are used, which are Pageviews per User, Bounce Rate, and Time on Site. The major problem with the Alexa Rank is the fact that it is heavily skewed towards websites which have a large webmaster/tech audience. This is because webmasters or web savvy audiences are much more likely to have the Alexa toolbar installed than websites whose visitors are unaware of Alexa.

Credibility

Credibility of a blog is another dimension of great concern to not only the most technologically savvy (Finn & Gil de Zuniga, 2011). Measuring credibility objectively is difficult due to its subjectivity property (Ulicny & Baclawski, 2007). Although this is the case, researchers are working in this area by comparing blog topics against information from mainstream news, which are usually weighted as more credible. Another example is researchers are also looking at how to better determine whether the information is coming from a reliable source.

Telling the truth and presenting knowledge and sound arguments are often perceived as credible. Others that are perceived as credibility aspects are the content types, writing style, number of sentences, number of paragraphs, presentation forms, accuracy, believability, depth, fairness, full name inclusion, hyperlink citations, credentials of blogger, gender of blogger, aesthetic elements, interactive features, and affiliation (Armstrong & McAdams, 2009; Chung, Kim & Kim, 2010; Flanagin & Metzger, 2007; Fritch & Cromwell, 2001; Hilligoss & Rieh, 2008; Kelton, Fleischmann, & Wallace, 2008). However, excessive advertisements on a blog and a rarely updated blog often indicate lack of credibility.

A survey was conducted in this study to ascertain the factors that would affect weblog credibility in the Malaysian blogosphere. A total of 812 bloggers responded. It was found that the majority of the respondents (76.8%) were below 25 years old. Only 23.0% of the respondents were more than 26 years old. Female respondents (60.6%) took over their male counterpart (39.4%) in responding to the survey. About 21.7% of the respondents agreed that having weblogs enabled them to express themselves creatively; 21.7% stated that having weblogs allow them to network or meet new people; and 19.8% believed that weblog can be used to articulate idea. In addition, 13.1% stated that weblogs can channel creativity and 18.3% agreed that weblog could influence the way other people think. Other reasons for having weblogs were getting recognition, exploring one's own beliefs, and getting feedback on service and product.

Most of the respondents prefer visiting weblogs that are perceived credible and trustworthy. Respondents generally tended to agree that the use of more than one type of weblog presentation forms made them most likely to trust the information. The visual forms such as videos, photographs, and links to other web sites also made them more likely to trust the information. Using only text to present the information in weblogs tend to reduce the trust among the respondents.

Furthermore, weblogs containing spelling and grammar mistakes, having factual errors, exhibiting corrections of previous mistakes, using unnamed sources, showing one side of controversy, and having in-depth knowledge are factors which would affect trust toward the weblogs. Likewise, factors such as the presentation of information, accuracy of contents, language quality, hyperlink citations, and webloggers' ideological stands could affect users' trust on weblogs. However, number of sentences, number of paragraphs, full name inclusion, gender of blogger, aesthetic elements, interactive features, and affiliation were not perceived as affecting credibility. Some of these findings contradict previous studies by Armstrong and McAdams (2009), Chung, Kim, and Kim (2010), and Kelton, Fleischmann and Wallace (2008).

DEVELOPMENT PHASES OF BLOG INFLUENCE INDEX

Development of the index consists of seven sub phases, as depicted in Figure 1. First, blogs influence criteria were studied and analyzed. In identifying the influence of blogs, several studies which focus on the dimensions and criteria in giving ranks and credibility to the blogs were identified. A survey was also administered to select criteria for credibility.

Figure 1. Phases and outcomes

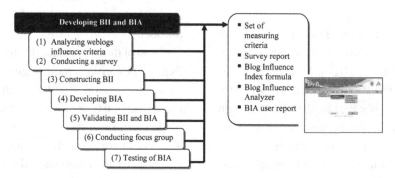

The next phase is the construction of the BII (which is explained in the formulation section). Once the BII is formulated, a Blog Influence Analyzer (BIA) was developed. BIA is a web tool, used to measure the influence of blogs. It executes three main processes, which are crawling blogs, inquiring yahoo search engine, and analyzing the raw data. BIA was developed using a number of technology mainly the Internet Information Service (IIS) 7.0, ASP.NET framework 3.5, Visual Basic.Net and SQL Server 2008.

Next, in validating the constructed BII, a focus group consisting of 25 randomly invited bloggers was conducted (Figure 2). The session was held in a-day workshop. They were asked to visit the top ten blogs, and then provide views on each one based on the selected criteria. This is then compared to the results produced by the BIA application. Validation of BII and BIA was also accomplished through competing in two innovation expositions, where awards were won for both competitions.

FORMULATION OF BLOG INFLUENCE INDEX

In this study, Agarwal's (2008) influential bloggers dimensions and also Alexa's ranking property, which is the number of average daily visitors over the past three months, are adopted. However, the property of eloquence as proposed by Agarwal is excluded as this property describes the characteristics of the blog authors in his or her ability in

Figure 2. Focus group session snapshot

writing lengthy piece of post, rather than describing the blogs. Some of the criteria identified are in links, number of comments received, number of out links, page rank and average daily visits. These criteria are then divided into influential dimensions called activity generation, recognition and novelty.

Activity generation as proposed by Agarwal (2008) is modified by including the number of blog posts, together with the number of comments. This is because in measuring for the activities in a blog, activities are generated from both the readers and blogger. Without comments from the readers, activity generation would not occur. Therefore, the number of blog posts is a measurement of activities from the blogger. In brief, higher values for both of these variables indicate higher degree of activity generation within a blog.

Additionally, the *recognition* as proposed by Agarwal (2008) is modified by considering the total number of visitors to a blog, as an additional variable that influences the degree of recognition. The definition of the number of total visitors is adopted from Pratt (2005). Visitor percentage value obtained from Alexa has a limitation due to the fact that its value is counted only based on the use of Alexa toolbar that are mainly utilized by webmasters and marketers (Pratt, 2005). The following is the formula used to obtain the number of total visitor:

Total visitor = visitor percentage * (0.036 * global Internet Users)

The value of visitor percentage is obtained from Alexa webpage based on a particular blog. The value 0.036 is referring to the population of blogs registered with Alexa. The value of global Internet Users is obtained from Internet World Stats. In brief, higher values for in links and number of visitor of a blog indicate that the blog is more recognized than the others.

Novelty is adopted without any modification as the researchers agree on this aspect. In brief, a higher value of out links indicates that the blog has lower level of novelty as the content discussed in the blog is heavily dependent on issues from other blogs.

In this study, *credibility* is taken as the number of information presentation type, number of factual errors, and number of hyperlink citations. The weblogger's ideological stand, number of sentences, number of paragraphs, full name inclusion, gender of blogger, aesthetic elements, interactive features, and affiliation are excluded as these are either a subjective measure or considered as not affecting credibility by the respondents.

In summary, it is proposed that the BII to consist of four dimensions, namely activity generation (A), recognition (R), novelty (N) and credibility (C), as depicted in Figure 3. Attached to each dimension are the proposed criteria for measuring blog influence, as summarized in Table 1.

Based on the criteria in Table 1, BII is calculated as follows:

BII = Activity generation (total no. of comments & total no. of blog post) + Recognition (total in links & total no. of visitors) + Novelty (total out links) + Credibility (total no. of info presentation type & total no. of factual errors & total no. of hyperlink citations)

Figure 3. Credibility of BII

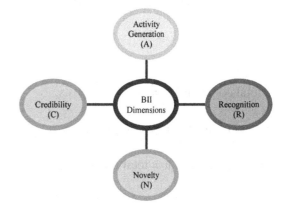

Table 1. Proposed criteria for measuring blog influence

Influential Dimensions	Criteria
Recognition (*R*)	Number of in links to a post and total visitor to the blog
Activity generation (*A*)	Number of comments received for blog posts and number of post
Novelty (*N*)	Number of out links
Credibility (*C*)	Number of information presentation type, number of factual errors, and number of hyperlink citations

$$BII = w_1 \sum_{i=1}^{n} A_i + w_2 \sum_{i=1}^{n} R_i -$$
$$w_3 \sum_{i=1}^{n} N_i + w_4 \sum_{i=1}^{n} C_i \qquad (1.0)$$

where:

w_i = weightage

Weighted values are given to these criteria in order to form the BII index. If for instance, the weighted value is taken as 1, it is suggested that the values for A and R should be equal, but higher than N or C. The weighted value for N should be less than C. The weighted values for these properties are shown in Equation (2.1).

$$BII = [w_1 (c + p) + w_2 (il + v)] - w_3 ol + w_4 (it + h - fe) \qquad (2.0)$$

$$= 0.35(c + p) + 0.35(il + v) - 0.1ol + 0.2 (it + h - fe) \qquad (2.1)$$

$$= 0.35(c + p + il + v) - 0.1ol + 0.2 (it + h - fe) \qquad (2.2)$$

where:

c = total comments, p = total blog posts,

il = total in links, v = total visitors,

ol = total out links, it = total info types,

fe = total factual errors, h = total hyperlink citations.

Since variables used in A and R are commonly used in other studies (e.g., Bentwood, 2007; Agarwal et al., 2008) related to measuring blog influence, this shows that these variables have been tested and recognized as indicators for measuring blog influences. Therefore, R and A are given equal weighted values which is higher than N and C. N is given the lowest weighted value since it describes the attractiveness of the blog content in gaining influence to one's blog. C is given a higher value than N since it is perceived as more essential. Also, the formulation considers the lower the number of factual errors, the higher the value of C. The detail computation for each property is elaborated in Equation (2.2).

The values for A, R and N are obtained through the following processes:

1. Crawling weblogs to compute the number of posts, comments, out links, info types and hyperlink citations.
2. Inquiring yahoo search engine to get the number of in links.
3. Analyzing all the raw data to compute weblog recognition, activity generation, and novelty.

However, the values for factual errors were manually analysed over the past three months. Determining factual errors was based on many topic-related materials such as mainstream news, magazines, reports, books, journals and online sources.

DISCUSSION

The significance of this study can be categorized into knowledge area, society and the government. Identifying the most influential weblogs in a country's blogosphere would provide essential information for the government in its monitoring plans and activities. Additionally, the influence index, dimensions and criteria used to determine these influential weblogs could further be applied to anticipate the influences of new upcoming weblogs in a country. The BIA tool also provides a platform for governments and new media regulators to identify the most influential blogs in respective to a country's blogosphere. The BII formulated and criteria identified also contribute to the knowledge area of this field, thus extending the work of Agarwal, Pratt, Seung, and Alexa from a slightly different perspective. Moreover, by ascertaining the social influences of these weblogs, would provide knowledge resources in terms of the influences of weblogs on attitudes, relationships and views between family, friends, employers and professional colleagues on topics such as education, business, politics and entertainment.

This study shows that social media such as weblog has gained tremendous popularity and is widely accepted as an alternative communication medium. In fact, weblogging has become part of many people's lives nowadays probably due its unique ability to present and share information. However, it was found that people tend to be selective in visiting and reading weblogs. Their involvements in weblogging heavily depend on and are correlated to their perceptions on weblogs' credibility and trustworthiness. This finding is supported by some previous studies such as those conducted by Richard and Cacioppo (1981), Roobina (1990), and Kamal and Chu (2008).

In validating the proposed BII formulation, it was applied to find the top 10 most influential blogs from 186 blogs in Malaysia. One interesting finding here is that 4 out of the 10 blogs belong to the entertainment category, followed by politics (2), lifestyle (2), sports (1), and technology (1). This indicates that entertainment weblogs are highly influential in the blogosphere community of Malaysia. Consequently, as a suggestion, perhaps the entertainment industry and all players involved should now turn to weblogs as an alternative marketing and promotional tool. Another implication of influential blogs is in the political scenario in Malaysia. The 12th Malaysian general election witnessed a drastic change and named as the "political tsunami" (The Star, 2008). The election results showed that the opposition pact of 37% in comparison to 9% in the election year 2004. If previously 91% Parliament seats were dominated by pro-government, it declined to 63%. This is said as a result of the emergence of alternative media. Constant effort by the opposition party through more high-tech modes of campaigning, especially through social media such as blogs, was fully maximised (Pandian, 2010).

Limitations

The scope of this study is limited to a number of issues. In particular, no distinction is made to the definition of "influential blog sites" and "influential bloggers." The issue of "influential bloggers vs. "active bloggers" and "influential posts vs. non-influential posts" were also not addressed. Moreover, how to differentiate "popular blog sites and popular bloggers" from "influential blog sites and bloggers" were not catered. Agarwal et al. (2008) further suggest that influential should also be looked at from the angles of long-term (maintain influence for a long time), average-term (maintain influence for 4-5 months), transient (influential for not more than 2 months) and burgeoning (recent and trendy issue).

Credibility also has a number of factors such as source, content and receiver (Danielson, 2006). All three are said to contribute to the concept of credibility. These however, were not included in this study. Ranking criteria as highly credible, having average credibility, or little credible was also not integrated.

Additional limitation is the BIA tool itself. There are rooms for improvement for this tool particularly on the criteria used to measure weblog influence. In future, effort should be made to add more relevant criteria. It is also proposed that such tool should be enhanced to include the ability to measure textual content of weblog. Although there are many weblogs in the cyberspace, this study focuses only on the popular weblogs in the blogosphere community of Malaysia which are listed in common weblog directory services and search engines. Both types of weblogs which are individual and community weblogs were included. In addition, this study is not limited to specific topics discussed in weblogs; instead all topics are taken into consideration except topics that are considered obscene and illegal.

CONCLUSION

The lack of credible criteria used in current weblog measuring tools has partly become the motivation of this study. This study indicates that blog influence can indeed be measured quantitatively. All the criteria for the four dimensions can be applied in the formulation of the BII formula and consequently the development of the BIA tool. The criteria used in the BII formulation are seen as reliable. However, further study ought to be conducted to test the robustness of the BII and the formula used for the BIA tool.

Despite many types of media which are readily available, this study shows that new media such as weblog has gained tremendous popularity and is widely accepted as an alternative communication medium. In fact, weblogging has become part of many people's lives nowadays probably due its unique ability to present and share information. However, it was found that people tend to be selective in visiting and reading weblogs and have certain perception towards media particularly pertaining to media credibility.

REFERENCES

Adamic, L., & Glance, N. (2005). The political blogosphere and the 2004 U.S. Election: Divided they blog. In *Proceedings of the 3rd International Workshop on Link Discovery*.

Agarwal, N. (2008). A study of communities and influence in blogosphere. In *Proceedings of the 2nd SIGMOD PhD Workshop on Innovative Database Research* (pp. 19-24).

Agarwal, N., & Liu, H. (2008). Blogosphere: Research issues, tools and applications. *SIGKDD Exploration Newsletter*, *10*(1), 18–31. doi:10.1145/1412734.1412737.

Agarwal, N., Liu, H., Tang, L., & Yu, P. S. (2008, February 11-12). Identifying influential bloggers in a community. In *Proceedings of the International Conference on Web Search and Web Data Mining* (pp.207-218).

Akritidis, L., Katsaros, D., & Bozanis, P. (2009). Identifying attractive research fields for new scientists. *Scientometrics*, *91*(3), 869–894. doi:10.1007/s11192-012-0646-4.

Armstrong, C. L., & McAdams, M. J. (2009). Blogs of information: How gender cues and individual motivations influence perceptions of credibility. *Journal of Computer-Mediated Communication*, *14*(3), 435–456. doi:10.1111/j.1083-6101.2009.01448.x.

Awis.blogspot. (2009). *Alexa features*. Retrieved February 12, 2009 from http://awis.blogspot.com/2009/04/more-new-alexa-features-demographics.html

Bentwood, J. (2007). *Distributed influence: Quantifying the impact of social media*. New York, NY: Edelman.

Chung, C. J., Kim, H., & Kim, J. H. (2010). An anatomy of the credibility of online newspapers. *Online Information Review*, *34*(5), 669–685. doi:10.1108/14684521011084564.

Danielson, D. R. (2006). Web credibility. In Ghaoui, C. (Ed.), *Encyclopedia of human-computer interaction*. Hershey, PA: Idea Group.

Dawson, K. (1997). *Alexa Internet opens the doors*. Retrieved July 28, 2008, from http://www.tbtf.com/archive/1997-07-28.html

Efimova, L. (2009, June). Weblog as a personal thinking space. In *Proceedings of the Twentieth ACM Conference on Hypertext and Hypermedia*.

Finn, J., & Gil de Zuniga, H. (2011). *Online credibility and community among blog users*. New Orleans, LA: American Society for Information Science and Technology. doi:10.1002/meet.2011.14504801110.

Flanagin, A. J., & Metzger, M. J. (2007). The role of site features, user attributes, and information verification behaviors on the perceived credibility of web-based information. *New Media & Society*, *9*(2), 319–342. doi:10.1177/1461444807075015.

Fritch, J. W., & Cromwell, R. L. (2001). Evaluating Internet resources: Identity, affiliation, and cognitive authority in a networked world. *Journal of the American Society for Information Science and Technology*, *52*(6), 499–507. doi:10.1002/asi.1081.

Gillmore, D. (2006). *We the media: Grassroots journalism by the people, for the people*. Sebastopol, CA: O'Reilly.

Herring, S. C., Scheidt, L. A., Bonus, S., & Wright, E. (2004). Bridging the gap: A genre analysis of weblogs. In *Proceedings of the 37th Annual Hawaii International Conference on System Sciences*.

Hilligoss, B., & Rieh, S. Y. (2008). Developing a unifying framework of credibility assessment: Construct, heuristics, and interaction in context. *Information Processing & Management*, *44*, 1467–1484. doi:10.1016/j.ipm.2007.10.001.

Interactive, S. X. S. W. (2006). *Web award winners*. Retrieved November 3, 2007, from http://2006.sxsw.com/interactive/web_awards/winner/

Kamal, S., & Chu, S. C. (2008). The effect of perceived blogger credibility and argument quality on message elaboration and brand attitudes: An exploratory study. *Journal of Interactive Advertising*, *8*(10), 26–37.

Kavanaugh, A., Zin, T. T., Rosson, M. B., Carroll, J. M., Schmitz, J., & Kim, B. J. (2007). Local groups online: Political learning and participation. *Computer Supported Cooperative Work*, *16*, 375–395. doi:10.1007/s10606-006-9029-9.

Keller, E., & Berry, J. (2003). *One American in ten tells the other nine how to vote, where to eat, what to buy. They are the influentials*. New York, NY: Free Press.

Kelton, K., Fleischmann, K. R., & Wallace, W. A. (2008). Trust in digital information. *Journal of the American Society for Information Science and Technology*, *59*(3), 363–374. doi:10.1002/asi.20722.

Kenix, J. L. (2009). Blogs as alternatives. *Journal of Computer-Mediated Communication*, *14*, 790–822. doi:10.1111/j.1083-6101.2009.01471.x.

Lievrouw, L. A., & Livingstone, S. M. (2002). *Handbook of new media: Social shaping and. consequences of ICTs*. London, UK: Sage.

Loc.gov. (1998). *ALEXA Internet donates archive of the World Wide Web to Library of Congress*. Retrieved October 13, 2008, from http://www.loc.gov/today/pr/1998/98-167.html

Michael, J., & Irit, A. (2008). Blogs – new source of data analysis. *Issues in Informing Science and Technology*, *5*(1), 433–445.

Mortensen, T., & Walker, J. (2002). Blogging thoughts: Personal publication as an online research tool. In Morrison, A. (Ed.), *Researching ICTs in context* (pp. 249–279). Oslo, Norway: InterMedia.

Pandian, S. (2010). Malaysia's 12th general election: An analysis. *European Journal of Soil Science*, *14*(4), 508–523.

Pratt, B. (2005). *The day the internet search engines stopped growing!* Retrieved November 11, 2009, from http://www.workoninternet.com/article_3691.html

Rahaman, S. F., Srilakhsmi, M., & Yasin, S. (2011). Quantification of social blog network using B-Rank technique and blog recommendation. *International Journal of Computer Science and Emerging Technologies, 2*(4), 455–462.

Recuero, R. D. C. (2008). Information flows and social capital in weblogs: A case study in the Brazilian blogosphere. In *Proceedings of the Nineteenth ACM Conference on Hypertext and Hypermedia* (pp. 97-106).

Richard, E. P., & Cacioppo, J. T. (1981). *Attitude and persuasion: Classic and contemporary approaches.* Dubuque, IA: William C. Brown.

Roobina, O. (1990). Construction and validation of a scale to measure celebrity endorsers' perceived expertise, trustworthiness, and attractiveness. *Journal of Advertising, 19*(3), 39–52.

Sekaran, U. (1992). *Research method for business* (2nd ed.). New York, NY: John Wiley & Sons.

Seung, H. L., Sang, W. K., Sunju, P., & Joon, H. L. (2009, June 28). Determining content power users in a blog network. In *Proceedings of the 3rd SNA-KDD Workshop*, Paris, France.

Surunhanjaya Komunikasi dan Multimedia Malaysia [SKMM]. (2008). Household use of the Internet survey. *Statistical Brief, 7*(1).

The Star. (2008). *Political tsunami.* Kuala Lumpur, Malaysia: The Star.

Trammell, K. D., & Gasser, U. (2004, May). *Deconstructing weblogs: An analytical framework for analyzing online journals.* Paper presented at the Communication and Technology Division, Internatimnal Communication Association, New Orleans, LA.

Ulicny, B., & Baclawski, K. (2007). New metrics for newsblog credibility. In *Proceedings of the International Conference on Weblogs and Social Media*, Boulder, CO.

This work was previously published in the International Journal of Virtual Communities and Social Networking, Volume 3, Issue 3, edited by Subhasish Dasgupta, pp. 35-45, copyright 2011 by IGI Publishing (an imprint of IGI Global).

Chapter 12
Analyzing Persian Social Networks:
An Empirical Study

Leila Esmaeili
University of Qom, Iran

Mahdi Nasiri
Iran University of Science and Technology, Iran

Behrouz Minaei-Bidgoli
Iran University of Science and Technology, Iran

ABSTRACT

Analysis of data in social networks is very important for researchers, sociologists, and academics. Given the size and diversity of web data in a Web 2.0 environment, analyzing this data has been a challenge. Since data act as inputs in such projects, the accuracy of the output is directly related to the input. Good data allows for extraction of valuable knowledge. In this article, the authors present their experiences with preparation and preprocessing of data in a Persian social network. The authors also report on the analysis of the data and findings.

INTRODUCTION

In recent years there has been a growing interest in web mining using scientific, social, political, and economic techniques. Organizations in different countries invest in social network analyses for different reasons. Analyses are mainly based on three methods: content analysis, structure analysis, and usage analysis. The type of analysis determines the manner in which researchers collect and prepare their data sets.

General web 2.0-based information systems, due to their free and interactive natures generate data that is not appropriate for web mining and

DOI: 10.4018/978-1-4666-4022-1.ch012

knowledge discovery. A large amount of data generated is textual in nature and needs to be pre-processed before knowledge discovery. Moreover, systems change over time, and the amount and type of data generate changes. Therefore, unstructured data, which is not in the right format has to be transformed into structured, usable data that can be used in web mining studies. This process of conversion is complex and time consuming. In general, preprocessing techniques, if performed before data mining, can significantly improve the mining process, and reduce processing time.

In most web mining, data mining, text mining, and social network analysis studies and projects, data preprocessing is considered an important stage. But many of these studies are conducted without preprocessing due to the difficulty in collecting large amounts of data. Sometimes studies are conducted using smaller data sets to make preprocessing faster.

In our analysis of Persian social networks we did not come across any study that included complete preprocessing of data. Most of the research was conducted using blogs. Studies were based on data that had been collected by other researchers or in some cases Persian data was translated into English and then preprocessed (Sheykh Esmaili, Jamali, Neshati, Abolhassani, & Soltan-Zadeh, 2006; Sahebi, Oroumchian, & Khosravi, 2008). Esmaeili et al. (2011) used data stored in Parsi-yar Persian social network database

to personalize recommended groups to users of the social network (Esmaeili, Nasiri, & Minaei-Bidgoli, 2011). The studied database consisted of content data and to some extent structured data. The data set was a raw one, which was analyzed for the first time. Complete preprocessing of a large volume of data in a Persian social network for the first time, classification of textual features are some of the study's strengths. In this study, we elaborate on some preprocessing experiments and provide details of statistical and network analysis of the data set.

The data set employed in our attempt included data from a Persian social network called Parsi-yar. Parsi-yar contained activities for 5 years and 6 months for 78467 users, 3359 groups within 19 categories, and 275 groups without a specified category (Table 1). Data could be classified into three categories: user information, group information, and other information. The category, other information, included user interactions in the network, their public and private messages, users' comments on messages, their friends, and their groups.

The organization of the rest of the paper is as follows. In the next section we explain the framework of data processing. This is followed by statistical analysis of research data and by network analysis of the data set. In the final section we provide a conclusion and areas of future research.

Table 1. Subjective classification of groups (active and inactive groups)

Category	Num. of groups	Category	Num. of groups	Category	Num. of groups
Revolution	100	Sport	167	History	37
Social	716	Entertainment	332	Literature	117
Sciences	191	Game	75	Morality and spirituality	129
Youth	72	Familial	28	News	71
Geography	41	Art	182	Hygiene	30
Buy and sell	31	Religion	335	Computer	352
Business	78				

DATA PREPROCESSING FRAMEWORK

Users usually register for membership of social networks without providing complete information about themselves. They either volunteer data for required items or give worthless or meaningless information, and only a few of them correct this in subsequent visits. This has been attributed to factors such as privacy concerns, or the rush to register quickly. Thus, there is always the problem of lack of data or worthless data in our social network databases. Since databases usually contain data in different fields with different data types, each of these data types demands different preprocessing techniques. Determining the best preprocessing techniques for each category of data type plays an important role in improving the quality and efficiency of data mining. In fact, 60 to 90% of the entire time needed in data mining should be spent in data preparation. Also, 75 to 90% of the success of data mining projects is associated with data preparation (Han & Kamber, 2006).

The result of low quality input is low quality data mining and as a result low quality decision-making (Pyle, 2004). According to Esmaeili et al.'s (2011) study, the main required information is the information of users and group members. For each group, the members should be specified and the required information for each user should include personal characteristics of users, his/her interests, relationship status and user interactions with other members, the membership status of the user in groups and user activities in groups (content and structure information).

The different data types in the Parsi-Yar database included: Textual (Farsi, English, informal Farsi, Fenglish, HTML tags), Numerical (for storing nominal, ordinal, interval and ratio characteristics), Date and Binary. Algorithms and data mining tools can be easily used for numerical and binary data but for non-numerical data, the data should be converted to a type of numerical data. Transforming data of date types, which are structured textual strings, to numerical data is not a big deal and can be performed easily. But it is different and more difficult for unstructured data with textual values. Each record contains 12 attributes without textual structure which includes user's job, expertise, and interests in various fields. It should be noted that the unique values of these attributes in the entire data set are in the interval of 1939 (for football attribute) to 5192 (for job attribute); these values should be classified with a specific method. Therefore in this study, the data preparation framework is divided into five sections: text data classification, data cleaning, data integration, data conversion and data reduction, while Han (Han & Kamber, 2000) has proposed this framework in 4 sections (data cleaning to data reduction). In fact, textual and unstructured data are prepared in a separate section so that there will be no concern regarding the textual values in the subsequent stages.

Textual Data Classification

One of the problems of textual data classification is the issue of multiple equivalents for each record in the Farsi language. Textual data was stored in various languages such as English, Farsi, and informal Farsi, and a mix of Farsi and English called Fenglish. Another problem in classification is caused by incorrect spelling. Due to these problems textual unstructured data should be handled differently so that it can be mapped into categories and classified. This type of textual classification methodology has number of problems:

- Data mining methods are needed for checking spellings. This requires a large amount of time and may change the research into a data mining study.
- Given that there is no reference library for the attributes of text, even text mining methods will be difficult. Available tools are not suitable for Persian texts.

Therefore, using an innovative method based on iterative and self-learning concepts ways of text mining, textual data, including Persian and non-Persian, were identified and classified. Unstructured data of user attributes were transformed to structured using a number of methods: by checking a few reference sites, collecting data using questionnaires, and conducting interviews. Based on the type of trait, two classification models were used for 12 attributes of users:

- Classification with three structures into 3 levels for job and expertise attributes. Individual's job and expertise cannot be classified in one level because this was based on the survey.

- One-level of classification for other attributes.

The general structure of value classification of 12 attributes of user profiles is shown in Figure 1. Besides using SQL queries, personal programs and algorithms were written in C#. In some stages manual control was performed (merging and semantic composition). Steps outlined in Figure 2 are as follows:

- Initial clearance of attribute values:
  - Remove signs and symbols, spaces longer than spaces between words and HTML tags.
  - Replace Arabic letters with their Persian equivalences.

Figure 1. Classification of unstructured values

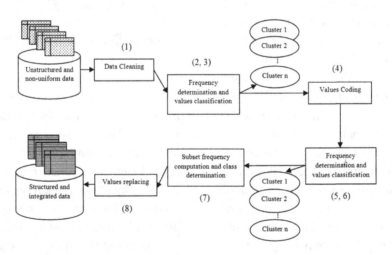

Figure 2. The overall structure of selecting target groups

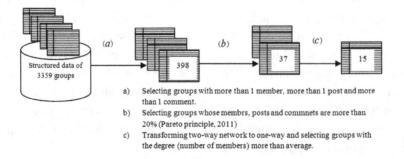

a) Selecting groups with more than 1 member, more than 1 post and more than 1 comment.
b) Selecting groups whose membrs, posts and commnets are more than 20% (Pareto principle, 2011)
c) Transforming two-way network to one-way and selecting groups with the degree (number of members) more than average.

○ Replace ASCII codes of Persian and Arabic characters with their corresponding Persian letters.

- Determine the frequency of database values based on unique values.
- Classify meaningful groups associated with the attribute type with regard to similar meanings. For instance values of teacher, instructor and lecturer were considered as a value for job attribute. Moreover, "undefined" category was allocated to null values or meaningless ones and "other" category to certain values with low frequency. In this study, these two categories were defined for each attribute in order to preserve and maintain the main data and not to assign value to attributes without value.
- Code the other non-classified and multi-valued attributes considered values of the main categories.
- Determine frequency of values coded in step 4.
- Classify values according to their frequency and mapping created categories onto categories of step 3 and recode the new categories.
- Map the remaining uncategorized codes from step 6 onto existing groups according to the highest possible frequency of subsets. For instance, assuming the frequency of A-B code is 190 and the frequency of A-D is 25, A-B-D code will be mapped to A-B group.
- Decrease the null and undefined values, after performing the categorization, null values were checked and if an attribute was associated with other attributes, the value of specified attribute was recorded for the null and undefined value. For example, for the user who has chosen football as his hobby and has not recorded his favorite sport, football was stored as his favorite sport.

These steps were performed several times on the 12-attribute value set to check that no value remained unclassified.

Data Cleansing

According to Ralph Kimball data cleansing is one of the three big issues in data storage. In fact, data storage is the quality control stage conducted before data analysis (Han & Kamber, 2000). Data cleansing in data repository, relational database and web based information systems is strongly required as these resources have redundant information due of various representations of similar values. Thus, to provide access to valid and compatible data, combining various representations and eliminating duplicate information is necessary. Depending on the number of data sources and the degree of their heterogeneity, it may be necessary to perform several steps of conversion and data cleansing (Rahm & Do, 2000).

Missing Values: The adopted policy and method in dealing with null and missed values in Esmaeili et al.'s (2011) study was to maintain and preserve the original data. Therefore, instead of using methods like average, mean or the value with the highest frequency, an "undefined" category was assigned for each attribute and null values were allocated to this category. Also, for some values, generalization of some attributes was used. For instance, a user has mentioned badminton as his hobby, but he has not mentioned his favorite sport, thus, we recorded badminton as his favorite sport.

In addition, for most attributes we did not consider data values which were recorded with "all," "none," "somewhat or slightly" or special items with low frequency as undefined values, rather we classified them into distinct categories according to the attribute. For values with low and specific frequency "other" class was defined and that class of values was assigned to "other" category. Moreover, for six main characteristics of members: age, date of birth, date of membership, weight, height, gender and education a different method was adopted.

Age: The two parameters that are associated with age were identified: Date of birth and date of membership. So, if date of birth and date of membership are known, age is calculated and vice versa.

Gender: According to the name that was registered in the user profile, gender of unknown individuals was specified. The gender of 63% of people who did not specify their gender was assigned. Thus, individuals' gender was assigned in three groups: male, female and unspecified. In determining individuals' gender based on their name, some books and esm.ir websites were used. Furthermore, semantic analysis of some names which were specified as Sir, Madam, and Mrs. Dr. helped us to identify some individuals' gender.

Height/Weight: According to gender and age, the average height or weight of people who were of the same age and gender of the one with unspecified height or weight was considered as the individual's height/weight.

Education: This characteristic was valued based on the work and expertise feature for some people such as engineers, students, technicians and others.

Noise Data: In webpages noise data mostly occur for user generated content. In this study, noise data were mainly for age, height and weight attributes. On the other hand, noise data among the members of the groups can be studied too, which was investigated in Esmaeili et al.'s (2011) study.

Age: To deal with the noise data, based on the valid global studies and reports such as Nilson (The Nielsen Company, 2009), the age range of social network users was chosen. According to the Iranian nation conditions and its values were chosen based on frequency. The assigned age range was (5, 80), therefore values outside this range were regarded as noise data and in value allocation; they were treated like null data.

Height: Identification of height noise data, they cannot be judged like other attributes. For instance, there is no relation between height and age, and we can only estimate one's height from the height of parents or that of children aged less than 2 years (Nwosu & Lee, 2008). Thus, certain noise data such as 25 cm, 3 m were identified and other cases were determined considering peers and people of the same gender.

Weight: In order to identify weight noise data, Body mass index (BMI) was used. Values lower than 14 and higher than 40 were taken as noise data (Wikipedia, 2011). Users' height and weight were modified based on their peers' height and weight average.

Conflict Reduction: Some of the features and attributes are incompatible and we can this conflict. As an example, the user's age at the time of registration added to his year of birth must be compatible with the year of his membership. Thus, incompatible data were identified and based on relevant attributes. Another example is the user's gender which was stored in two tables of the user information and in some cases they were not the same; thus, the user's gender was determined based on his/her name. Incompatibility in the number of group members, number of friends, was also investigated and resolved.

Redundancy Reduction: Some attributes like gender are stored in two tables of the initial database and in other cases both age and birth year are stored while one of them would suffice. In addition, due to server and website problems, some records are stored more than one time, like users' comments and messages. These were identified and deleted and information related to them was updated. In fact, this information is web structural information that specifies the relationship between users or users and groups.

Data Integration

In data mining process, data are gathered from various sources; therefore, there is a need to integrate these sources in a unique data set. Data integration is complex for three reasons: first, various sources include overlapping data which are dependent to each other. Second, data are stored in various models and schemas and finally, different data sources are capable of processing different types of requests (Levy, 2000). In Esmaeili et al.'s (2011) research, database set had been stored for duration of 5 years and 6 months and due to changes in giving different services to users, changes in website implementation and changes in database design, some of the information tables and some data had problems. These were identified and integrated based on expert judges and website designers. Since this step is related to the structure of Parsi-yar database, further information cannot be provided.

Data Conversion

Most important activities in data conversion step were normalization, feature extraction and generalization of data values.

Feature Extraction: For each user, attributes like number of members of the group, the number of user's friends, the total number of posts in groups, the total number of comments to posts in groups were identified based on the users' interactions with groups and other users. Some attributes were made based on the attributes relevance, which will be described in data generalization.

Data Generalization: Based on the relationship that existed between some attributes, new attributes were designed. For example, user's BMI was created based on his/her weight and height, the age range according to the user's age; year, month, season, day and date of user's membership in the social network were created based on membership date. In addition, for some textual attributes, value generalization was done, which has been mentioned before.

Normalization: In order to use data mining algorithms and increase computational speed, data values should be normalized. Values in the data set include nominal, ordinal, interval and ratio values, all of which are characterized by a different numerical range. The type of normalization method is based on type of values, and for categorical values

there is no special normalization method. These values must be converted into binary values and then the common normalization methods should be applied to make them normalized. Despite the increased accuracy of this method, due to the increase and expansion of the number of dimensions, it makes the calculations and running the algorithm difficult. For example, in this study we need 760 distinct values for categorical data in total! So, instead of creating a new feature for each value of each of the properties, stratified values were used and all attributes, both categorical and numerical ones, were normalized with Min-Max method. Since all values are normalized in the 0 to 1 interval and categorical value difference becomes low in this interval, concept and meaning change of these values did not lead to any difficulty in the analysis (Esmaeili et al., 2011; Baatarjav, Phithakkitnukoon, & Dantu, 2008).

Data Reduction: Data reduction is a very important issue in data mining and the aim of data reduction techniques is extracting a small subset of the massive amounts of data set while preserving the characteristics of the original data. This makes the difficult or impossible data mining operations to be performed efficiently and effectively (Li & Jacob, 2009). Two examples of these strategies include: Identifying and selecting a subset of irrelevant features or data with weak links and removing them; and sampling that includes selecting a subset of the data set which has the general characteristics of the data set (Han & Kamber, 2000; Kantardzic, 2002).

Due to the nature of the study and the social network under investigation, we are dealing with the structure of a two-mode network (Borgatti & Everett, 1997), that is, we have two data sets: group and the user. Considering the aim of Esmaeili et al.'s research (2011), the favorite group must be identified and according to that, users that are member of at least one of the groups are also selected. However, considering time and system constraints, it is not possible to select 3359 groups or 78467 users for processing. In addition, unlike global scales of social networks, 87.97% of the groups in Parsi-Yar have less than 10 members and although a long time elapsed since the formation of these groups, there was no activity for many groups.

In Parsi-Yar social network, 15 groups of those which were more active and popular were selected based on the structure of Figure 2, in three stages, as target groups. Ultimately, 1797 users who were members of at least one of these 15 groups were selected as users of the data set. Some users are members of multiple groups.

In order to reduce the data and to select valued characteristics and features in the analysis (the first strategy: the elimination of feature), supervised entropy (Claude, 1948) was used, which has been described with regard to its relationship with the recommender system by Esmaeili et al. (2011).

STATISTICAL ANALYSIS OF PARSI-YAR SOCIAL NETWORK

Apart from the linear graph and column charts which are used in most statistical software to show graphic data, there are several types of graphs for showing the summary data, including histogram, quantile plot (Q-P) and scatter plot. These graphs are useful for visual inspection of data (Han &

Kamber, 2000). In this section, using the histogram charts, we try to show the distribution of some characteristics in Parsi-Yar social network, its selected groups and their members.

Parsi-Yar Social Network

Statistical analysis conducted in this section is for Parsi-Yar social network, so there is a survey for 78467 users and 3359 groups. Most users of Parsi-Yar social network - except those who had not specified their location were from the provinces of Tehran, Isfahan and Khorasan. Therefore, Parsi-Yar social network can be classified as a national social network and is distinct from international social networks in structure and properties. For example, most users of Parsi-Yar social network are male (Figure 3), while according to the Pew Research Center, most users of international social networks are women (Hampton, Goulet, Rainie, & Purcell, 2011).

Considering the age range of users and also those whose education level is specified, most users are young and have a university degree or are university students. According to Figure 4, except for students, scholars and undergraduate students, most Parsi-Yar social network users are individuals who are self-employed and employees in education (teachers and professors).

Figure 3. Users' age and gender

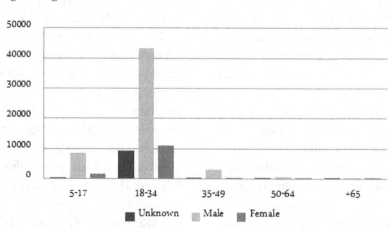

174

Figure 4. Job status of network users

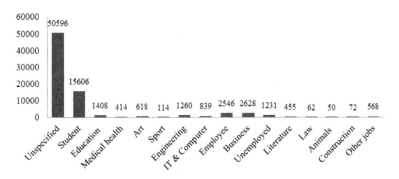

Considering the fact that most users are young, and most are single (Figure 5). It is interesting to find that the sum of divorce and separation among people with higher education, above high school diploma or more, is more than those individuals who are at a lower level of education. According to the studies conducted, most individuals in Parsi-Yar social network are single and do not communicate with others (Figure 6), in situations where male users are more than females, the number of women's relationships with other users is more than men's and even women's relation-ships with men is more than women's relationships with women, and even men's relationships with women (Figure 7).

Figure 8 specifies the position of users in the group. Horizontal axis shows the member groups and vertical axis is the number of users. Most users are not members of a group or are members of a single group. Figure 9 has plotted another position of groups. Horizontal axis shows the number of members and vertical axis is the number of groups. According to this chart, only 27 groups have more than 100 users and 87.97% of groups have fewer than 10 members.

Groups were ranked by the number of user posts and the replies and comments received for each subject is shown in Figure 10. Number of replies and posts could be considered as a criterion for the status of a group or user status in the group (active or inactive). Horizontal axis shows the number of posts and comments and the vertical axis shows the number of groups.

Figure 5. Marital status of network users

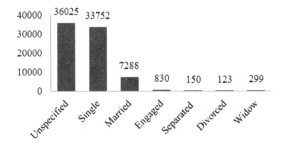

Figure 6. Number of users' friends in the network

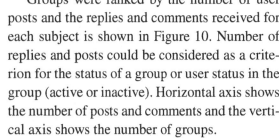

Figure 7. Users' connection average with regard to gender (Women's relations average: 7 persons, Men's relations average: 3 persons & People's relation average with unspecified gender: 3 persons)

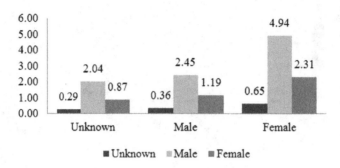

Figure 8. Users' ranking based on the number of member groups

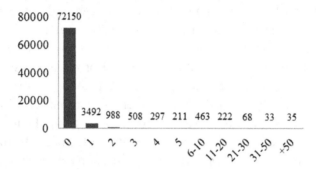

Figure 9. Group's ranking based on the number of members

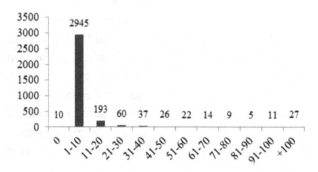

Figure 10. Group's ranking based on the number of posts and comments

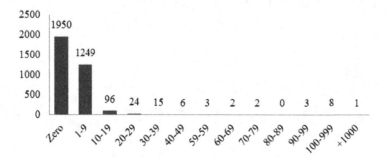

Selected Groups

Statistical analysis of this section is based on 15 groups and 1616 of their main members. Esmaeili et al. (2011) elaborated how they identified heterogeneous members of the groups. Members of target groups were mainly from the provinces of Tehran, Qom and are Khorasan, respectively. Moreover, the educational and occupational status of members of 15 groups and gender segregation based on age range is also proportional to the entire network. Overall, in the 15 target groups, the dominant gender was male and no group had a member who was older than 65 years. In addition, marital status of target groups with regard to the educational level is proportional to the total social network. Figure 11 shows the status of 15 groups with respect to the total number of posts and comments.

Based on statistical results, 20.42% of members of the selected groups did not communicate with others (Figure 12). The number of relationships of group members with other users was different from the whole network and men had more rela-

tionships (Figure 13). On average, women had relationships with 90 individuals and men were related to 94 individuals. Those who have specified their gender were associated with 63 cases.

PARSI-YAR NETWORK ANALYSIS

The studied network structure is a two-mode network which is undirected and un-weighted. Because one part of these networks consisted of users and the other part was groups, and each group was composed of several users. Thus, in this data set, three types of graphs can be investigated:

- Graph of social network users: in this case, nodes were users and edges were relations of friendship. There are 12661 nodes in this graph and due to hardware and processing limitations; it was not possible to perform the analysis on this graph.
- Two-mode graph of users and selected groups.

Figure 11. Ranking of 15 selected groups based on the number of posts and comments

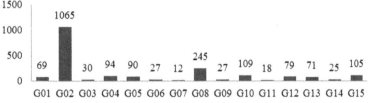

Figure 12. Number of friends of the 15 selected groups' members

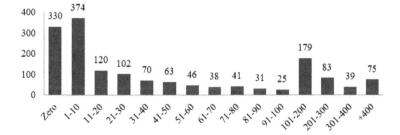

Figure 13. Communication average based on gender in 15 selected groups

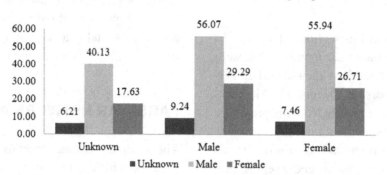

- Graph of user relationships of selected groups.

User-Group Graph

One method for modeling two-mode networks is to transform them into a common network which is the sum of the nodes of both sets, regardless of internal communication of each set (Hanneman & Riddle, 2005). Thus, in this graph, the number of nodes is the sum of the total number of users and 15 selected groups, instead of 1616 users. Edges

define the membership status of individuals in groups. Network structure with three different modeling forms is shown in Figures 14 and 15. The focused points of the edge are in fact 15 selected groups.

As can be seen, user-group graph is a sparse graph with low density, since almost two-thirds of users are related to only one group. We have specified main features and characteristics of this graph in Table 2. Also, in this graph considering the fact that the main focus is on groups, we have provided the characteristics of group nodes in

Figure 14. Illustration of user-group graph by Fruchterman-Reingo algorithm

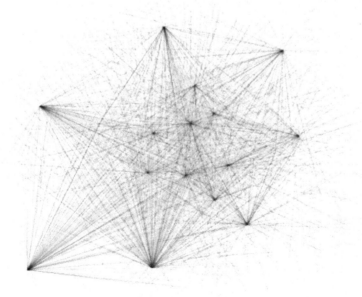

Figure 15. Illustration of user-group graph by Horel-Koren Fast Multi-scale algorithm

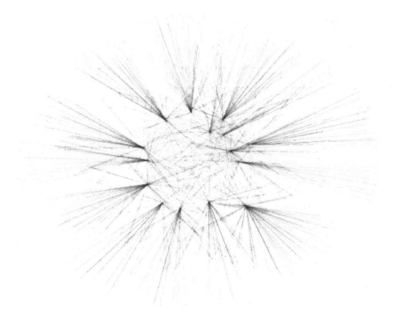

Table 2. Metrics of user-group graph

Graph Metric	Value
Graph Type	Undirected
Vertices	1631
unique edges	2651
Edges with duplicates	0
Total edges	2651
Self-loops	0
Connected components	1
Single-vertex connected components	0
Maximum vertices in a connected component	1631
Maximum edges in a connected component	2651
Maximum geodesic distance (diameter)	4
Average geodesic distance	3.617363
Graph density	0.0019943

Table 3. G01 and G11 groups are the two popular groups considering the degree levels and page rank. In addition, considering the closeness, more attention are given to them, and based on betweenness criterion, these two groups constitute a highway of other communications in user-group graph.

Graph of Members of Selected Groups

This graph consists of users that have friendly relations with other network members. So the number of people in the graph, regardless of the 373 individuals who have no contact with others, is 1243, and the individual nodes is not considered in the representation of the graph. Figures 16 and 17 show different representations of the communication graph of the target groups' members. Unlike the user-group graph which is sparse and has low density, the communication graph of group's members is dense and has high density.

Like user–group graph, the main features and criteria of graph of group's members are specified in Table 4. The density of this graph is 19 times more than the user-group graph. Table 5 has specified the situation of some criteria in the total graph.

Table 3. Main characteristics of groups in user-group graph

Group ID	Category	Degree	Page Rank	Closeness	Betweenness
G01	Social	355	105.284873	0.00024	369460
G02	Social	154	41.861456	0.000219	118160.2
G03	Social	208	54.737989	0.000224	169828.5
G04	Social	124	31.694116	0.000216	84411.26
G05	Sport	134	39.399754	0.000217	128911.5
G06	Morality and spirituality	207	58.684294	0.000224	192145
G07	Youth	198	57.934016	0.000223	195917
G08	Morality and spirituality	144	40.058748	0.000218	118325.2
G09	Revolution	125	37.410941	0.000216	113921.7
G10	Religion	145	41.652901	0.000218	131456.5
G11	Literature	259	76.669590	0.000229	264408.5
G12	Entertainment	124	34.708886	0.000216	107344.3
G13	Social	128	32.870014	0.000216	86467.75
G14	Social	199	54.459291	0.000223	175980.2
G15	Entertainment	147	43.167484	0.000218	136729.5

Figure 16. Graph of users in selected groups by Fruchterman-Reingo algorithm

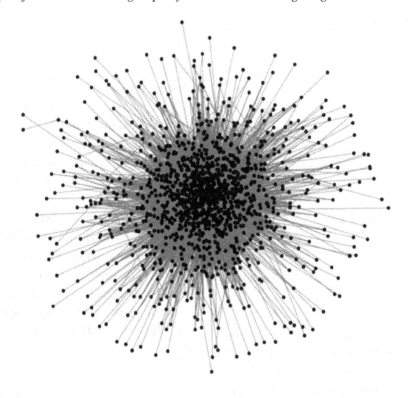

Figure 17. Graph of users in selected groups by Horel-Koren Fast Multiscale algorithm

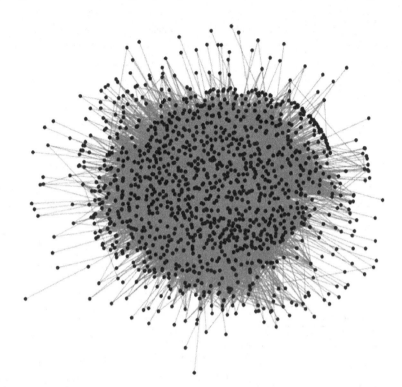

Table 4. User graph metrics in 15 selected groups

Graph Metric	value
Graph Type	Undirected
Vertices	1243
Unique edges	29354
Edges with duplicates	0
Total edges	29354
Self-loops	0
Connected components	1
Single-vertex connected components	373
Maximum vertices in a connected component	1243
Maximum edges in a connected component	29354
Maximum geodesic distance (diameter)	5
Average geodesic distance	2.292897
Graph density	0.0380281

Sub-Structures in the Network of Selected Group's Members

The graph of selected group's members is a connected component, which is composed of smaller groups and societies. To identify the underlying infrastructure and components of this network, Clause-Newman-Moore (CNM) (Clause, Newman & Moore, 2004) and Wakita-Tsurumi (WT) (Watika & Tsurumi, 2007) algorithms were used. Also, because the graph of group's members is more complex than the user-group graph, this graph was chosen to identify and assess subgroups and infrastructures.

CNM Algorithm: The result of CNM clustering for the detection of small communities of users graph is shown in Table 6. In this method, the

Table 5. Main metrics of users graph of selected groups

	Clustering Coefficient	Page Rank	Closeness	Betweenness	Degree
Minimum	0	0.165	0.000209	0	1
Maximum	1	19.463	0.000556	127418.575	694
Average	0.554	1	0.000357	804.035	47.231
Median	0.567	0.534	0.000362	15.333	21

Table 6. Clustering details of users graph with CNM method

Group	C1	C2	C3	C4	C5
Vertices	427	723	85	6	2
Unique edges	9534	11435	305	5	1
Total edges	9534	11435	305	5	1
Connected components	1	1	1	1	1
Maximum vertices in a connected component	427	723	85	6	2
Maximum edges in a connected component	9534	11435	305	5	1
Maximum geodesic distance (diameter)	5	4	4	3	1
Average geodesic distance	2.10686	2.222169	2.138408	1.611111	0.5
Graph density	0.10483	0.043812	0.085434	0.333333	1

graph is divided into 5 sections and according to the specifications of each community clusters 4 and 5 can be identified as noise components of the graph network. These people are those who are very distinct in terms of communication with others and due to their poor communication are identified as individual clusters. Thus, the three main and related sections in the users graph are clusters 1, 2, and 3. One representation of the clustered users graph based on the Fruchterman-Reingo method is presented in Figure 18. In this graph each group is marked with a distinct color. Each cluster represents a community of users. The examination performed on each cluster, which was based on the association analysis, revealed that groups that have members from every community are stronger than the whole network in terms of dependence and relationships and members are more similar to the groups that they are a member of. Eliminating noise relationships from the

users graph yielded a denser graph, in which the geometric distance mean between users is less (0.038485817 and 2.285836, respectively).

WT Algorithm: The number of clusters formed in WT method is 35; 30 of which were identified as noise clusters because of having a degree lower than the mean. Table 7 shows the details of the main five clusters of selected groups users network. Main clusters are denser in comparison to the CNM method and the total network are segmented more uniform than the CNM. But in this method the number of noise sections is more. The graph resulted from eliminating noise relations of users graph, in comparison to CNM method and the whole graph, has more density and distances with lower geometric mean (0.042236457 and 2.280328, respectively). The representation of graph segmentation with Fruchterman-Reingo drawing method is specified in Figure 19.

Figure 18. Users graph illustration by CNM clustering

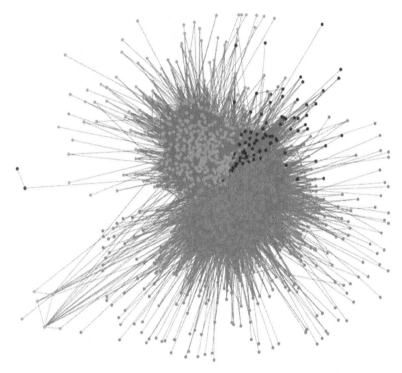

Table 7. Clustering details of users graph with WT method, eliminating the 30 noise clusters

Group	C1	C2	C3	C4	C5
Vertices	359	91	76	268	331
Unique edges	3891	584	183	3129	7439
Total edges	3891	584	183	3129	7439
Connected components	1	1	1	1	1
Maximum vertices in a connected component	359	91	76	268	331
Maximum edges in a connected component	3891	584	183	3129	7439
Maximum geodesic distance (diameter)	4	5	4	4	5
Average geodesic distance	2.129	2.11	2.324	2.114	2.055
Graph density	0.061	0.143	0.064	0.087	0.136

CONCLUSION

This study is the first attempt at preprocessing and preparing the data of a Persian social network "Parsi-Yar" and activities carried out in order to convert unstructured data into structured (clas-sifying attributes), cleansing, integration, conversion and data reduction were described. One of noteworthy points in this study is the scale of the problem which includes approximately 1 GB database size for about 5 years and 6 months of Parsi-Yar activity. Such investigation has not been

Figure 19. Users graph illustration by WT clustering

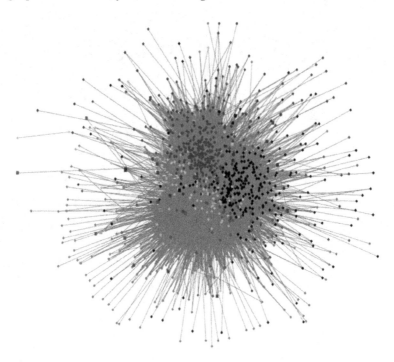

performed in Persian social networks and data used in this research are studied for the first time. Unlike most academic research, original data set of the study was created by researchers.

Parsi-Yar social network is a national social network and most of its users are young and are students and unlike most international social networks, the predominant gender is male. Users' profile was created with 49 distinct properties and according to investigations carried out, the selected data set has the main characteristics of the entire network and individuals who are in subgroups of users' graph clustering are more similar in terms of membership status in groups, in comparison to the entire network.

Given the importance and growth of social networks and transforming them into social media in a web environment and considering the different functions of this media, as well as national conditions, analyzing and identifying characteristics of social networks is useful both for growth and survival of a social network and for identifying functions and policies in national and international

level. Based on studies and analyses done on the basis of international social networks, it is clear that some features of national and international social networks are unique; thus, we cannot not make policy only on the basis of analysis of some international networks and generalize them to other countries. In these conditions, the best help of social network managers is giving the data and network information to researchers, maintaining the individuals' privacy policy. Due to the need for preprocessing process and considering the social network implementation, if appropriate filters are used for users' input data, which while prohibit users to insert meaningless information let them free to provide their content, preprocessing process will be carried out easier and faster and the recorded data are more valuable and meaningful. In future studies, we aim to transform multi-valued classes to double classes, so that we would have the minimum increase in dimension. In addition, we aim to change our network analysis to temporal network analysis and investigate and analyze network parameters in different time intervals.

REFERENCES

Baatarjav, E., Phithakkitnukoon, S., & Dantu, R. (2008). Group recommendation system for Facebook. In R. Meersman, Z. Tari, & P. Herrero (Eds.) *Proceedings of the Confederated International Workshop of On the Move to Meaningful Internet Systems* (LNCS 5333, pp. 211-219).

Borgatti, S. P., & Everett, M. G. (1997). Network analysis of 2-mode data. *Social Networks*, *19*(3), 243–269. doi:10.1016/S0378-8733(96)00301-2.

Claude, E. S. (1948). *A mathematical theory of communication.* Retrieved August 19, 2011, from http://www.en.wikipedia.org/wiki/Entropy_(information_theory)

Clause, A., Newman, M. E. J., & Moore, C. (2004). Finding community structure in very large networks. *Physical Review*, *70*(6), 2–3.

Esmaeili, L., Nasiri, M., & Minaei-Bidgoli, B. (2011). Personalizing group recommendation to social network users. In Z. Gong, X. Luo, J. Chen, J. Lei, & F. L. Wang (Eds.), *Proceedings of the International Conference on Web Information Systems and Mining* (LNCS 6987, pp. 124-133).

Hampton, K. N., Goulet, L. S., Rainie, L., & Purcell, K. (2011). *Social networking sites and our lives.* Washington, DC: Pew Research Center's Internet and American Life Project.

Han, J., & Kamber, M. (2000). *Data mining: Concepts and techniques.* San Francisco, CA: Morgan Kaufmann.

Han, J., & Kamber, M. (2006). *Data mining: Concepts and techniques* (2nd ed.). San Francisco, CA: Morgan Kaufmann.

Hanneman, A., & Riddle, M. (2005). Social network data. In A. Hanneman & M. Riddle (Eds.), *Introduction to social network methods* (Ch. 1). Riverside, CA: University of California, Riverside. Retrieved August 19, 2011, from www.faculty.ucr.edu/~hanneman/nettext/C1_Social_Network_Data.html

Kantardzic, M. (2002). *Data mining: Concepts, models, methods, and algorithms.* Piscataway, NJ: IEEE-Wiley. doi:10.1109/9780470544341.

Levy, A. Y. (2000). *Logic based artificial intelligence.* Boston, MA: Kluwer Academic.

Li, X., & Jacob, V. S. (2009). Adaptive data reduction for large-scale transaction data. *European Journal of Operational Research*, *188*(3), 910–924. doi:10.1016/j.ejor.2007.08.008.

Nwosu, B. U., & Lee, M. M. (2008). Evaluation of short and tall stature in children. *American Family Physician*, *78*(5), 597–604. PMID:18788236.

Pyle, D. (2004). *The handbook of data mining.* Boca Raton, FL: CRC Press.

Rahm, E., & Do, H. H. (2000). Data cleaning: Problems and current approaches. *IEEE Bulletin on Data Engineering*, *23*(4), 3–13.

Sahebi, S., Oroumchian, F., & Khosravi, R. (2008). An enhanced similarity measure for utilizing site structure in web personalization systems. In *Proceedings of the IEEE/WIC/ACM International Conference on Web Intelligence and Intelligent Agent Technology* (Vol. 3, pp. 82-85).

Sheykh Esmaili, K., Jamali, M., Neshati, M., Abolhassani, H., & Soltan-Zadeh, Y. (2006). *Experiments on Persian Weblogs.* Paper presented at the WWW Workshop on Web Intelligence.

The Nielsen Company. (2009). *Global faces and networked places: A Nielsen report on social networking's new global footprint*. Retrieved August 20, 2011, from www.blog.nielsen.com/nielsenwire/wp-content/uploads/2009/03/nielsen_globalfaces_mar09.pdf

Watika, K., & Tsurumi, T. (2007). Finding community structure in mega-scale social networks. In *Proceedings of the 16th International Conference on World Wide Web* (pp. 1275-1276).

Wikipedia. (2011a). *Human height*. Retrieved August 20, 2011, from http://www.en.wikipedia.org/wiki/Human_height

Wikipedia. (2011b). *Pareto principle*. Retrieved May 10, 2011, from http://www.en.wikipedia.org/wiki/Pareto_principle

This work was previously published in the International Journal of Virtual Communities and Social Networking, Volume 3, Issue 3, edited by Subhasish Dasgupta, pp. 46-65, copyright 2011 by IGI Publishing (an imprint of IGI Global).

Chapter 13
Action Research in Virtual Communities:
How Can this Complement Successful Social Networking?

Nana Adu-Pipim Boaduo

Walter Sisulu University, South Africa, & University of the Free State-Bloemfontein Campus, South Africa

ABSTRACT

Contextually, all tertiary institutions have four major responsibilities – teaching, research, publication, and community service. The adage "publish or perish" has become a thorn in the flesh of many university academic staff who rest on their laurels and do nothing about research, publication, and community engagement. Practising university academic staff are required by the nature of their profession to engage in regular research be it in their daily lecturing and supervision of students' research thesis or writing for publication. Currently, research has become the buzz-word in all tertiary institutions but not all of them take the pains to school academic staff in the practice of research in terms of the virtual communities where the institution is located. In the context of this paper, the author looks at action research through the eyes of teachers of all categories in virtual communities and how their involvement can complement successful social networking. The approaches used in this discussion are purely from empirical and exploratory perspectives and provide detailed discussion with emphasis on the application of action research for effective and efficient social networking considering the social, cultural, organizational and human cognitive perspectives.

DOI: 10.4018/978-1-4666-4022-1.ch013

INTRODUCTION

Boaduo (2011, p. 30) contends that "...nations cannot develop beyond the quality of their education systems." Lawal (2006) concurs with Boaduo's assertion that no nation develops beyond the quality of its education system, which is highly dependent on the quality of its research practitioners. To Lawal all researchers should be given the most appropriate tools during their training, including content knowledge and skills as well as applicable methodologies to be able to do their research work professionally. As already alluded to by Boaduo (2011) and supported by Lawal (2006) the quality of an education system depends on the quality of its teacher-researchers. Much of what teacher-researchers need to know to be successful is invisible to lay observers leading to the view that involvement in research requires little formal study. On the contrary, researchers of all categories seek answers to unanswered questions to enable them help their communities to learn and overcome their inherent community problems. All researchers learn about national development through literature and appropriate technology, curriculum, pedagogy, assessment, evaluation and measurement and how these could be applied in various virtual communities for their benefit. What the community of researchers offer to their virtual communities remain a secret and their key to success is a mystery (Shaeffer, 1990). This paper argues that the 21st century teacher-researchers in every level of their educational institutional set up require new initiatives in their preparation and further professional development to adequately meet the new challenges of the millennium virtual communities needs in terms of social networking for effective and efficient social cohesion.

NEED FOR CONTENT KNOWLEDGE AND SKILLS IN ACTION RESEARCH FOR VIRTUAL COMMUNITIES PRACTITIONERS (TEACHER-RESEARCHERS)

Action research must be a major priority foundation for research in teacher education and preparation in the 21st century (Boaduo, 2010). Professional teacher-researchers naturally seek answers to questions and solutions to problems that enable them to help their communities and students to learn. They are decision makers. They make thousands of choices on hourly basis regarding the choice of texts, literature, appropriate and relevant technology integration, curriculum, pedagogy, assessment and measurement. They are highly reflective and sensitive to the needs of their communities and students. In the process of articulation of their duties they encounter failures and successes. However, much of what teacher-researchers have to offer their communities and students remains a secret. Their key to success is a mystery. Teacher-researchers seek multiple means of looking at their world of teaching and learning and that of their communities and students by unlocking the secrets within their work environments. How they do all these remain a mystery which, they are the only people to understand. Action research has, however, become one of the major potential keys to help teacher-researchers unlock these secrets and help their communities and students towards effective and efficient social networking.

This section of the paper will provide detailed empirical evidence together with scholarly argument to address the issue of the need for teacher education and training institutions to provide teacher-researchers with in-depth action research content, practical knowledge and skills to enable them to meet the challenges of the twenty-first century virtual communities and students needs with confidence. The following perspectives will also be given elaborate attention:

- The need to provide teacher-researchers with action research tools.
- The application of action research paradigms.
- The necessity to make their findings substantive for the solution of day-to-day virtual communities and students problems that would arise in the 21st century virtual communities and institutions of learning environments.

Currently, most institutions of higher learning provide just rudimentary courses in general research methodology. These courses, in reality, do not prepare the teacher-researchers to become ardent researchers per se and apply their research training as well as their practical knowledge and skills acquired while in training to solve the daily problems they encounter in their virtual communities and students in the environments that they reside and interact. Action research courses provided to initial teacher-researchers in training do not actually equip them with the requisite content knowledge, skills and tools that they will need to conduct in depth action research in their communities in terms of appropriateness and applicability to enhance social networking.

Generally, the aim of educational research methodology courses in institutions of higher learning has been to help the teacher trainee produce a research document as partial fulfillment of the degree or diploma being sought after (Boaduo & Babitseng, 2006). What is provided to the students is highly limiting in content knowledge and skills to research because the time frame from the beginning to the end of compiling the research report is less than six months. To what extent can the student be taken in terms of content knowledge depth and practical application of the acquired skills in educational research methodology?

The 21st century teacher-researcher should be effective and efficient in research activities, especially with special attention to the application of action research methodology. They would need to become exceptional action researchers and should engage in regular action research to increase their experiences regarding content knowledge and skills in the virtual communities and institutional environments and improve the quality of education for their communities and students (Kincheloe, 1991). In addition, the 21st century teacher-researchers would have to engage in the debate about action research methodology in education by understanding meaningful action research themselves and should be engaged in complex critical action research to be able to make worthwhile contribution in the teaching-learning environment in terms of the benefits that will accrue to their communities and students. Generally, there is nowhere there is need to take prompt and immediate action about events and issues than in communities and institutional environments. The only people who qualify to do this are teacher-researchers and one efficient way to succeed in doing this is through the application of action research methodology.

The author, wholeheartedly, believes that 21st century teacher-researchers should be encouraged to explore their own voices and begin to renew the enthusiasm for the process of sharing their own work within a growing active action teacher-researcher movement that will help to expose them to a multiplicity of action research methodological activities professionally thereby making positive contribution towards the development of their communities and students they interact regularly.

THE CONCEPT ACTION RESEARCH AND ITS SIGNIFICANCE IN TEACHER EDUCATION AND TRAINING

There is need to look at the concept action research and how it applies to the teaching-learning environment, especially in the 21st century virtual communities and institutional environments. This will make the professional teacher-researcher to identify with the fact that action research is a major part of the professional practice and one sure way to provide direction to teacher-researchers to achieve success in their communities and institutional environments. For this reason, action research in this discussion will be taken to mean:

…immediate systematic study of a phenomenon with the aim of finding immediate and responsive explanations or solutions or understanding and finding patterns among what is studied so that action could be taken to arrest or improve the situation for the betterment of virtual communities and institutional environmental practice to be able to help virtual communities and students to learn effectively and efficiently. (Boaduo, 2001, p. 4)

From our virtual communities and institutional environments, problems of different kinds and magnitudes abound especially in the communities, classrooms, lecture halls, and during field work and these would quadruple in the 21st century various environments. Whenever such problems surface and pose threat to the survival and achievement of virtual communities and students and their progress, a critical study would have to be conducted to find solutions to resolve the threat and improve the situation. Action research can be applied in a practically applicable perspective for instant application leading to finding or suggesting a solution or solutions to the identified problems.

From ancient times to date, the main approach for finding solutions to problems has been research, research and nothing but research where scientists, social scientists, economists and all categories of professionals get to their fields, environments and laboratories to undertake studies to find solutions to the posing problems. These professionals are able to make meaningful contribution to resolve problems in their specific fields because they have the requisite knowledge, skills and the appropriate tools to use in this respect (Boaduo, 2010a).

It must be emphasised that from ancient times mankind has not given up hope when confronted with problems until a solution is found through protracted trial-and-error-research approach. The teaching profession has not made significant use of action research to improve practice especially in the 20th century and the only reason that could be advanced is that teachers in training institutions were not given in-depth requisite content knowledge and skills in action research and its practical application. Teaching is a unique profession and requires more study through progressive action research to be able to identify strategies, approaches, methods and plans to improve practice. The object of the teaching profession are virtual communities in which they reside and students who weird various characteristics which the practising teacher-researcher should be able to identify, isolate and classify into groups to be able to provide guidance required for the benefit of the students. Action research is a potential tool for professional teacher-researchers to use to achieve their professional aims. Here lies the significance of the need for teachers to be teacher-researchers at heart (Boaduo, 2005a, 2005b; Boaduo & Babitseng, 2000).

NEED TO PROVIDE 21ST CENTURY TEACHERS SOLID FOUNDATIONS IN ACTION RESEARCH METHODOLOGY

If 21st century teachers are to consider themselves as action researchers and use action research to improve their practice and help their communities and students, then the following conditions would have to be fulfilled in their entirety by teacher education and training institutions that train professional teachers (Boaduo & Babitseng, 2006).

- All categories of teachers – pre-school, primary, secondary, and tertiary – should have as part of their training a concise detailed course in action research and general research methods that would conceptualise and concentrate on the work that teachers do in their day to day practice and not just as a course to fulfill a condition for a degree or diploma certificate as has been the case at present in institutions that train teachers.

- When equipped with the required content and practical knowledge and skills in action research in particular and research methods in general, teacher-researchers must be the first people to initiate action research in their virtual communities and in the teaching-learning environments that have significant bearing on their professional practice because they have the requisite content knowledge, skills and experiences about the needs of their communities students and situations that confront them as well as the lives of the education institutions that they are located and operate daily.

- Decisions taken about action research in their operative environment which affect their condition and progress of their practice as professionals in the educative sphere must be theirs to make, implement and keep for use now and in the future.

- Educational researches that are related to teaching – be it in the communities, classrooms, lecture halls, during fieldwork or for the general improvement of the overall environment (physical infrastructure, institutional materials or methods, strategies and approaches) can be effective with the agreement of teacher-researchers (UNESCO, 1979). This can only be successfully accomplished if they are given in-depth training by the institutions which train them in action research methodology in particular and general research as a whole.

RESEARCH PARADIGMS AND THE ACTION RESEARCH TEACHER OF THE 21ST CENTURY

It is also pertinent to indicate that it would be necessary to introduce the 21st century teacher-researchers to the various research paradigms as well as approaches while in training with more emphasis on their application. The various approaches like qualitative and quantitative, participatory, empirical and historical as well as the situations in which teacher-researchers would be able to situate their research activities must be provided as tools to equip them. There should be regular virtual communities-based or school-based in-service training or development programmes to update them in new developments in the teacher-researcher environment as a result of the rapid flux of change in the scientific-technological world which is part of the 21st century global environment (Boaduo, 2010b).

Kinds of Action Research Tools Teacher-Researchers Should Know and Use

Generally, research has undergone massive metamorphosis over the years, and the changes, as expressed by Allen and Shockley (1996) are not as concise and neatly defined as it once was. The old formulae do not fit new questions, especially in the technologically advanced 21st century. For instance, quantitative experimental research renders images of controlled procedures resulting in statistical practices, but the virtual communities and classrooms or lecture halls as the play grounds where teachers regularly interact, are dynamic, complex and always evolving. This situation would even be more complex in the 21st century virtual communities and institutional environments. The rate of flux in the 21st century in communities, lecture halls and classrooms would place teacher-researchers on their toes to live up to the expectations of their students. Therefore, the 21st century research process should be dynamic and flexible enough to meet these contexts and the complexities of the teaching-learning environments. According to Atwell (1993, p. xiii), any research that the teacher engages in, in the 21st century physical environment should allow for inquiry must be:

...conducted in the full, messy context of the life of a classroom and communities providing rich descriptions of people in action.

This approach would help the 21st century teacher-researchers to unlock secrets within virtual communities, institutional environments, classrooms, lecture halls and in the field that often defy the rigour of traditional experimental conditions. The 21st century teacher-researchers, as action researchers, should be able to seek multiple means of looking at their world of teaching and learning and that of their communities and students. Their in-depth requisite content knowledge in action research can be the most instant panacea enabling them to find solutions confronting their communities and students.

Professionally, the 21st century teacher-researchers should be groomed in a variety of research approaches during and after their training (Boaduo, 2010b). There must be absolute diversity in the research activities that teacher-researchers would be engaged in. However, all researching teachers would need to share common process of reflecting on their practice, inquiring about it and taking action at the most appropriate time (Patterson & Shannon, 1993). Generally, the 21st century teacher-researchers would be required to seek to understand individuals, actions, policies and events that would make up their work and

working environment in order to make professional decisions. According to Patterson and Shannon (1993, p. 7):

...They (would need to) engage in moments of reflection and inquiry in order to take action that will help their communities and students learn better.

What is excellent about this description is that it recognizes all good teachers as participants in teacher action research fraternity. In this process, the key elements are that teacher-researchers ask questions, reflect on their own and students' learning, use multiple data sources which include observation, analysis of artefacts, conferences and seminars and then taking action on the new information that they have identified in the process of their action (Newman, 2002). The new information discovered opens up new vistas for further action research for improvement of practice, especially in their communities, institutional environments like classroom, lecture halls and in the field during fieldwork (Boaduo, 2011a, 2011b).

Furthermore, the 21st century teacher-researchers must be forerunners of protracted action research in order to improve and advance practice for their communities and posterity. Critical analysis of the application of action research from the website http://www.ed.gov/databases/ERIC_Digests/ed355205.html explains that:

...and action research is deliberate, solution-oriented investigation that is group or personally owned and conducted. It is characterised by spiralling cycles of problem identification, systematic data collection, reflection, analysis, data-driven, action taken and finally problem redefinition.

This does not necessarily indicate that solution has been found for the problem being researched. It just helps to identify with the procedure to follow to be able to conduct and complete the study being undertaken to find solution. This is where the teacher-researcher is at liberty to apply the most appropriate action research paradigm that will help to address the research problem effectively and efficiently.

The following paragraphs discuss the various research paradigms that the 21st century teacher-researchers should be familiar with if they are to make valid contribution to knowledge and the practice of action research for successful virtual communities and institutional environmental practice.

Methodologies in Action Research Relevant to 21st Century Teacher-Researchers

The significance of methodological paradigms in a research study is the ability to understand and decide on the most appropriate research paradigm that will suit a particular assignment so that the teacher-researcher is able to conduct the study to a successful conclusion. Mouton (1996) is of the view that methodological paradigms – for instance those related to quantitative, qualitative, action and participatory – are not merely collections of research methods with their applicable techniques. According to Boaduo (2005a, 2005b), methodological paradigms should always include certain assumptions and values regarding their use under specific circumstances. From the perspectives previously indicated, the teacher-researcher should be able to make a choice concerning applicable methods, techniques and the underlying philosophy regarding their use in a particular study. In this respect, the philosophy should include the theory of when and why to apply either of the paradigms or approaches and the awareness of the limitations of equally applicable and relevant various methods that could have equally been chosen for the study. In respect of the research being conducted by the teacher-researcher the complete understanding and application of the following are required for introspection.

- Every research paradigm, method or technique is task specific and the task is often defined by the research goal.
- Different research studies use different research paradigms, methods or techniques because they have different objectives.
- In all research studies the research paradigm, method or technique must be appropriate and relevant for the task at hand.
- The research paradigm, method or technique should apply to all the aspects of the research study – sampling, questionnaire design, interview schedule, data treatment, analysis, interpretation, findings and recommendations.

Since the late 1980s, action research has gained the attention of researchers in many fields of study and would even gain greater attention in the 21st century (McKernan, 1991; McTaggart, 1992; Masters, 2001; Kemmis & McTaggart, 1988). The 21st century teaching professional will find solace in this paradigm. Generally, action research is a process in which groups of people (teacher-researchers in this discussion) attain critical understanding and improvement of their situation through participatory plans, practices, observations and reflections. This fundamental feature of action research is part of the well-known iterative spiral propagated by Kemmis and McTaggart (1988) and Boaduo (2005, 2006). This is illustrated in Figure 1.

It also becomes a collective reflection by participants on systematic objectifications of their efforts to change the way they work through discourse, organisation and power relations to be able to actively contribute to and improve the practice of their profession (McTaggart, 1992). According to Hughes (2004, p. 1):

...action research is a process for developing practical knowledge for worthwhile purposes leading to health and happiness for people and communities.

Figure 1. Qualitative analysis as iterative spiral (Boaduo, 2006, p. 45)

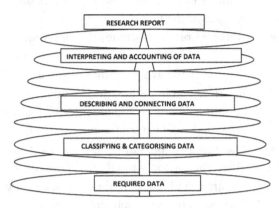

The 21ˢᵗ century teacher-researchers will love to make their communities healthy and happy through the application of practical knowledge. Reason and Bradbury, quoted by Boaduo and Babitseng (2007, p. 186) concur with the view and indicate further that:

...action research is about knowledge and practices that contribute to human well being and happiness.

Dick (2000) reiterates that action research is for practitioners, especially those of the 21ˢᵗ century, who want to improve several aspects of their professional practices or social processes while generating new knowledge. For these reasons, action research can serve different purposes, and provide different ways of understanding knowledge in its relationship to practice and different relationships to people and problems in their context (Bray, Lee, Smith, & Yorks, 2000). This reveals the fundamental differences in our understanding of the nature of inquiry, not simply methodological niceties as proposed by Reason and Bradbury sited by Boaduo and Babitseng (2007a, 2007b) but rather practical and applicable methodological niceties leading to effective and efficient social networking.

The 21ˢᵗ century teacher-researcher would be required to engage in a careful study of identified problems by devising improved ways to assist communities and students to master a specific subject and use the acquired knowledge and skills to find solutions to problems that confront them. As an addition to their successes, this can also be a beautiful case for introspection (Mouton, 1996). A project of this nature seeks to solve a practical problem for the benefit of virtual communities and students and at the same time add to the stock of knowledge if the findings are published and shared (Hughes, 2004).

Action research, therefore, refers to any process with the dual aim of changing a situation and producing knowledge for consumption (Masters, 2001). For this reason, action research has great potential for professional teacher-researcher practitioners; especially the 21ˢᵗ century teacher-teachers because it can make practitioners to combine research with everyday knowledge and experiences and improve their professional practice (Chandler & Torbert, 2003). They can also develop collaborative groups to observe their practices, collect and analyse data, reflect on what they have done and plan to improve both their own practices in the social, political and economic contexts in which they live and work (Hughes, 2004).

OTHER METHODOLOGICAL RESEARCH PARADIGMS FOR TEACHER-RESEARCHERS

Another research paradigm is participatory research which deserves mention to help advance the 21ˢᵗ century teacher-researchers capabilities to research. Boaduo (2005a, p. 8) is of the view that:

Participatory research paradigm is self reflective inquiry in social situations like the ones in which teacher-researchers always find themselves both inside and outside their communities and classroom or lecture hall situations. It helps to improve the rationality and justice of the social and educational practices, understanding them and the situations in which they are carried out.

Boaduo (2005a) further testifies that participatory research plays a liberating role of teacher-researchers in the learning process by providing them with the development of critical understanding of social problems, their structural causes and possibilities for overcoming them. It, therefore, calls for democratic interaction and intervention between the researcher and those among whom the research is conducted. Generally, the democratic interaction depends on the political participation of those involved in conducting research on the causes of the problem being investigated with the objective of finding a solution.

The 21st century teacher-researchers should know, understand and use the three main inter-related processes of participatory research during their training. These are:

- The collective investigation of problems and issues with the active participation of the constituency in the entire process.
- The collective analysis in which the constituency develops a better understanding of the structural causes of the identified problem (socio-economic, political, educational, cultural, or historical).
- The collective action by the constituency aimed at long-term, as well as short-term solutions of the identified problems.

The three processes previously listed are inseparable and the 21st century teacher-researchers must be well schooled in them. The integration of the three processes gives participatory research its fundamental strength and power over other research paradigms (Boaduo, 2010). The 21st century teacher-researcher should be able to know and understand that the processes are closely related to investigation, analysis and action. They can be identified separately in any participatory research study and each process incorporates aspects of the others. What 21st century teacher-researchers should know in participatory research is that the whole research process begins with people's concrete experiences (virtual communities) and situations and moves to include both theoretical analysis and critical action aimed at change that brings benefits to the constituency.

There are several reasons why 21st century teacher-researchers should be conversant with the principles of participatory research. Basically, it is an educational approach that equips teacher-researchers to help to bring about social change. It is not a recipe for change but a means to help bring about appreciable change especially in virtual communities. It is a democratic approach to investigation and learning which can be taken by individuals, groups and movements as a potential tool aimed at social change.

In any research study where the participatory research paradigm is applied, the following research questions must be considered in their entirety, especially during the planning and designing of the research proposal before the study is undertaken.

- What is the problem to be investigated?
- Who are the subjects?
- Who are the participants?
- How would they participate?
- Who has to learn in the process of investigating the identified problem?
- What has to be learned by the participants?
- Why should the participants learn what they have to learn?
- How would they participate in the whole learning process?
- What benefits would they derive from the whole process after completion?

The 21st century teacher-researchers should know the strengths of participatory research. The following authors Boaduo (2005a, 2005b), McNiff (1995), and Clark (1972) agree on the following:

- A critical analysis is encouraged throughout the research process and not just at the beginning or termination.

- The approach encourages active involvement on the part of all participants.
- It is positive in initiating and helping to bring about change and improvement.
- By using the classroom or lecture hall (for teachers) or the field as the study environment, the natural behaviour of participants is accommodated.
- As a research framework, it is flexible, relevant, adaptable and applicable.
- Finally, it describes relationships as they develop over time and accommodates changes in thinking which reflect mutations occurring in the context of the study being conducted.

Participatory research helps the teacher-researcher to address practical problems with theoretical and applicable practical relevance and transfers the knowledge from the research findings to the participants or the general public for rectification and application. The 21st century teacher-researchers need to be well schooled in it (Kodrzycki, 2002).

THE COMPLEMENTARITIES ISSUES

Teachers of all categories – pre-school, primary, secondary and tertiary - should be socialised into a scholarly research life style and be learned and exposed to the values of action and participatory research traditions especially during their training (Pease, 1967; Reskin, 1979), and the emphasis should be on various aspects of research that are relevant and applicable in the teaching-learning environment and would help the 21st century teacher-researchers to respond to the needs of their communities and students needs. Aspects like action and participatory research should be prominent and thoroughly taught during training (Blackburn & Havinghurst, 1979; Hunter & Kuh, 1987; Reskin, 1977, 1979, Boaduo, 2005a, 2005b, 2010a, 2010b). The training should equip 21st century teachers with both the knowledge and skills as well as the ability to identify problems, design and conduct a progressive study, write up the report, list findings and be able to undergo the refereeing process to get the results published (Hogan, 1981; Hunter & Kuh, 1987; Kuh & McCarthy, 1980; Zuckerman, 1977). The training should emphasise the need to conduct regular researches about impending problems that require the attention of the 21st century teacher-researcher for solution (Braxton, 1983; Cameron & Blackburn, 1981; Clark & Corcoran, 1986; Fulton & Trow, 1974; Hunter & Kuh, 1987).

NEED FOR THE 21ST CENTURY TEACHER-RESEARCHERS TO USE ACTION RESEARCH PARADIGM

From what have been discussed so far, there is no doubt about the necessity of the 21st century teachers to research regularly (Boaduo & Babitseng, 2007a, 2007b). In the teaching-learning environment, the 21st century teacher-researchers would encounter numerous problems every day. There are problems that may cross the success path of the students which the 21st century teacher would like to eliminate at all cost (Boaduo, 2005a, 2005b). To do this successfully requires strategies and approaches that would help to direct the 21st century teacher towards finding a lasting solution to those problems that may threaten the success of their communities and students. However, the 21st century teacher-researchers would be able to conduct regular researches if they have been given the required content knowledge and skills they need to be able to indulge in regular short or long term research projects.

Suggestions for 21st Century Teacher-Teachers to go about Their Action Research

This section provides a brief discussion about how the 21st century teacher-researchers should go about their research by touching on how to start and find time to gather data to be able to complete any chosen research study. Once the 21st century teacher-researchers have been schooled in in-depth research studies, the starting point is to identify the research problem and place it in a simple sentence that can be read and understood without questions. There should be statement of purpose (statement of the problem) and then research questions. Indicate why the study is being conducted (rationale). There is need for a brief literature review to place the study into open sesame. This indicates that the study has been looked at by someone from a different environment. That needs to be identified before one can put the study into proper perspective. It is necessary to identify the parameters within which the study will be confined (delimitations). State the possible problems that may hinder the completion of the study (limitations) and how these problems would be circumvented. Identify the subjects. Decide on the size of the sample population for the study. Identify a theory that will help to place the study into slot in the research fraternity (theoretical and conceptual frameworks). Most studies can be guided by a theory. State the significance and benefits. Provide the ethical considerations of the study and how valid and reliable collected data would be. List the data collection techniques and their reliability and validity with reference to the methodological paradigm that will be used. State the instruments that would be used to gather data and how the collected data would be treated, analysed and interpreted. Provide a time frame (from beginning to the end) for the study. If funds would be sought from providers, there is need to include budget statement. Give a brief description of how the final research report would be compiled (Boaduo, 2005a, 2005b). That is the basic format to help the 21st century teacher-researchers get started confidently.

The frequency at which the 21st century teacher-researchers should be engaged in research study should be left to individual judgment. It is a known fact that teacher-researchers will always engage in frequent research if they are confronted by problems on regular bases. For this reason, there can be no prescription concerning the frequency that research activities should be engaged in and as such are at liberty to make choices about the frequency to research.

Necessity to Make Action Research Reports Substantive to Educational Practice

Once the study has been conducted to a successful end, there will be complete write up report that will make the findings of the study available to the virtual community members or the teaching profession fraternity for consumption. Often times, such reports are published in professional journals or district or regional educational newsletters for dissemination. This concludes the essence of the 21st century teacher-researchers contribution to inform, improve and advance their professional practice and its social networking (Weiner, 2001; Glickman, 2001; McCall, 2001).

CONCLUSION

In sum, the author has made attempt to touch on the 21st century teacher-researchers as action researchers' in particular and general researchers' scenario by discussing the concept research and indicating the significance of research to the teaching-learning environment. It has been emphasised that there is need to provide in-depth training with solid foundation in research by institutions that provide education and training for teachers. Further to this, the author discussed the most important research tools that teacher-researchers need to be able to indulge in regular research with confidence and carry it to a conclusion. The need for teacher-researchers to research regularly has been briefly discussed. However, the frequency to research has been left to the professional teacher's discretion. It has been indicated that there is absolute need to make research findings available to the virtual communities and the teaching profession fraternity for dissemination to all practitioners to help improve practice by publishing research findings. That is the essence of action research in particular and research in general in professional practice.

REFERENCES

Allen, J., & Shockley, B. (1996). Conversations: Composing a research dialogue in University and school research communities encountering a cultural shift. *Reading Research Quarterly, 31*, 220–227. doi:10.1598/RRQ.31.2.6.

Atwell, N. (1993). Forward. In Patterson, L., Santa, C. M., Short, K. G., & Smith, K. (Eds.), *Teachers are researchers: Reflection and action* (pp. vii–x). Newark, DE: International Reading Association.

Boaduo, N. A. P. (2001). *Principles of practical research*. Unpublished manuscript, Dr. Boaduo Education Centre, Louis Trichardt, South Africa.

Boaduo, N. A. P. (2005a). Methodological choice and application in a research study: A framework for practitioners. *The African Symposium: Online Journal for the African Educational Research Network, 5*(3), 88-101.

Boaduo, N. A. P. (2005b). *Writing your first research proposal: A manual for first time and teacher researchers*. Unpublished manuscript, Dr. Boaduo Educational Consultants Pty Ltd, Gaborone, Botswana, South Africa.

Boaduo, N. A. P. (2006). Methodological choice and application in a research study: A framework for practitioner. *Bulletin of the Centre for Academic Development: Quality Assurance in Higher Education*, 38-50.

Boaduo, N. A. P. (2010a). Research methods for studying virtual communities. In Daniel, B. (Ed.), *A handbook of research on methods and techniques for studying virtual communities: Paradigms and phenomena*. Hershey, PA: IGI Global. doi:10.4018/978-1-60960-040-2.ch036.

Boaduo, N. A. P. (2010b). School-based continuing professional teacher development: A study of alternative teacher development initiative in the Eastern Cape Province of South Africa. *The African Symposium: An Online Journal of the African Educational Research Network, 10*(2), 75-83.

Boaduo, N. A. P. (2011a). *Practical educational research principles for practising teachers: Manual for teacher researchers*. Saarbrücken, Germany: LAP Lambert Academic.

Boaduo, N. A. P. (2011b). *Conceptual educational theories*. Saarbrücken, Germany: LAP Lambert Academic.

Boaduo, N. A. P., & Babitseng, S. M. (2006). *How do we prepare educators for a new role in the 21ˢᵗ century?* Paper presented at the ACEL and Microsoft iNet Online Conference.

Boaduo, N. A. P., & Babitseng, S. M. (2007a). The need for teachers to be researchers. *Journal of the African Educational Research Network, 7*(1), 183–191.

Boaduo, N. A. P., & Babitseng, S. M. (2007b, June 24-30). *New directions on teacher education*. Paper presented at the 27ᵗʰ Annual Conference International Society for Teacher Education (ITE) on The Future of Teacher Education for Professional Development, Stirling, Scotland.

Bray, J. N., Lee, J., Smith, L. L., & Yorks, L. (2000). *Collaborative inquiry in practice: Action, reflection and meaning making*. Thousand Oaks, CA: Sage.

Bryman, A. (2004). *Social research methods* (2nd ed.). Oxford, UK: Oxford University Press.

Chandler, D., & Torbert, B. (2003). Transforming inquiry and action: Interweaving 27 flavours of action research. *Action Research, 1*, 133–152. doi:10.1177/14767503030012002.

Clark, P. A. (1972). *Action research and organizational change*. London, UK: Harper & Row.

Dick, B. (2000). *A beginner's guide to action research*. Lismore, NSW, Australia: Southern Cross Institute of Action Research. Retrieved from http://www.scu.edu.au/schools/gcm/ar/arp/guide.html

Glickman, V. (2001, May 22-23). *Panel discussion*. Paper presented at the Pan-Canadian Education Research Agenda Symposium on From Theory into Practice: Teacher Education/Educator Training: Current Trends and Future Directions, Toronto, ON, Canada.

Hogan, T. D. (1981). Faculty research activity and the quality of graduate training. *The Journal of Human Resources, 16*, 420–415. doi:10.2307/145628.

Hughes, I. (2004). *Action & research: Action & research open web*. Retrieved from http://www2.fhs.usyd.edu.au/arrow/o/m01/rintro.htm

Hughes, I. (2004). Introduction. In I. Hughes (Ed.), *Action research electronic reader*. Sydney, Australia: The University of Sydney. Retrieved from http://www.fhs.usyd.edu.au/arrow/o/reader/rintro.htm

Hunter, D. E., & Kuh, G. D. (1987). The "write wing": Characteristics of prolific contributors to the higher education literature. *The Journal of Higher Education, 58*, 443–462. doi:10.2307/1981317.

Kemmis, S., & McTaggart, R. (1988). *The action research planner*. Geelong, VIC, Australia: Deakin University.

Kincheloe, J. L. (1991). *Teachers as researchers: Qualitative inquiry as a path to empowerment*. London, UK: Falmer.

Kodrzycki, Y. K. (2002). Education in the 21st century: Meeting the challenges of a changing world. Overview of the Federal Reserve Bank of Boston 47th Annual Conference themes. *Journal of Teacher Education, 57*(4).

Kuh, G. D., & McCarthy, M. M. (1980). Research orientation of doctoral students in educational administration. *Educational Administration Quarterly, 16*, 101–121. doi:10.1177/0013161X8001600209.

Lawal, H. (2006). Teacher education and the professional growth of the 21st century Nigerian teacher. *The African Symposium: Online Journal for the African Educational Research Network, 3*(2), 1-4.

Masters, J. (2001). *The history of action research* (Action Research e-Reports No. 3). Retrieved from http://www.fhs.usyd.edu.au/arrow/arer/003.htm

McCall, D. (2001, May 22-23). *Panel discussion*. Paper presented at the Pan-Canadian Education Research Agenda Symposium on From Theory into Practice: Teacher Education/Educator Training: Current Trends and Future Directions, Toronto, ON, Canada.

McKernan, J. (1991). *Curriculum action research: A handbook of methods and resources for the reflective practitioner*. London, UK: Kogan Page.

McNiff, J. (1995). *Action research: Principles and practice*. London, UK: Routledge.

McTaggart, R. (1992). *Action research: Issues in theory and practice*. Paper presented at the Methodological Issues in Qualitative Health Research Conference, Geelong, VIC, Australia.

Mouton, J. (1996). *Understanding social research*. Pretoria, South Africa: JL. Van Schaik.

Newman, J. (2002). *Participatory action research*. Retrieved September 24, 2007, from http://www. goshen.edu.soan96p.htm

Patterson, L., & Shannon, P. (1993). Reflection, inquiry, action. In Patterson, L., Santa, C. M., Short, K. G., & Smith, K. (Eds.), *Teachers are researchers: Reflection and action* (pp. 7–11). Newark, DE: International Reading Association.

Pease, J. (1967). Faculty influence and professional participation by doctorate students. *Sociological Inquiry*, *37*, 63–70. doi:10.1111/j.1475-682X.1967.tb00639.x.

Reskin, B. (1977). Scientific productivity and the reward structure of science. *American Sociological Review*, *16*, 420–504.

Reskin, B. (1979). Academic sponsorship and scientific careers. *Sociology of Education*, *52*, 126–146. doi:10.2307/2112319.

Shaeffer, S. (1990). Participatory approaches to teacher training. In Rust, V., & Dalin, P. (Eds.), *Teachers and teaching in the developing world. New York, NY*. Garland.

UNESCO. (1979). *Educational reform: Experiences and prospects (Education on the Move Series)*. Paris, France: UNESCO.

Weiner, H. (2001, May 22-23). *Panel discussion*. Paper presented at the Pan-Canadian Education Research Agenda Symposium on From Theory into Practice: Teacher Education/Educator Training: Current Trends and Future Directions, Toronto, ON, Canada.

Zukerman, H. (1977). *Scientific elite: Nobel laureates in the United States*. New York, NY: Free Press.

This work was previously published in the International Journal of Virtual Communities and Social Networking, Volume 3, Issue 4, edited by Subhasish Dasgupta, pp. 1-14, copyright 2011 by IGI Publishing (an imprint of IGI Global).

Chapter 14

Enhancing the Trust of Members in Online Social Networks:
An Integrative Technical and Marketing Perspective

Sandra A. Vannoy
Walker College of Business, Appalachian State University, USA

B. Dawn Medlin
Walker College of Business, Appalachian State University, USA

Charlie C. Chen
Walker College of Business, Appalachian State University, USA

ABSTRACT

The trust of members is essential to the sustainability of e-business. Unlike other business models, the success of online social networks is highly dependent upon the growth rate of social network size. In order to accelerate and continue the growth rate, online social networks need to be able to continuously roll out diversified services and use them to interest existing and new members. However, the nature of this business model can expose online social networks to ubiquitous security threats such as spam, viral marketing and viruses. In order to convince users to adopt social network services, cultivation of brand equity and trust in the online social networks is essential. This study integrates technical and marketing perspectives to examine the potential influence of website quality and brand equity on user satisfaction, thereby influencing users' formation of trust. A survey was conducted with 385 subjects to understand the causal relationships between the studied constructs. Regression analysis indicates that website quality, brand loyalty, brand association, and brand quality have a positive influence on user satisfaction, thereby increasing the trust of members in online social networks. Brand awareness shows no significant influence on user satisfaction. These findings lead us to derive theoretical and practical implications on the sustainable operation of online social networks.

DOI: 10.4018/978-1-4666-4022-1.ch014

INTRODUCTION

The proliferation of leading online social networks largely depends on the trust of users engaging the socialization process on their networks. A high degree of trust can accelerate the growth rate of network size, which sets leading social networks apart from mediocre networks. Social networks can show honesty and consideration of members' privacy by the way they operate. Those efforts can help develop trust from social network members and increase their intention to revisit.

The ability to increase users' trust is crucial for sustainable development of an e-business. Trust is an important psychological factor in the online environment, because buyers and sellers do not see each other. With the absence of rich face-to-face communication, this intrinsic cognition becomes the foundation for transactions in the virtual world. However, measuring and managing this psychological trait is difficult because it is invisible to users. As part of an effective e-business plan, fostering this trust can potentially increase consumer participation (Pénard & Poussing, 2010).

Trust formation is contingent upon the successful development of use and gratification. Use and gratification theory asserts that people choose different media based on whether they can satisfy a range of their needs (Blumler & Katz, 1974). On the Internet, human-to-machine relationships replace interpersonal relationships. The Internet mediates the formation of interpersonal relationships. The formation of smooth human-to-machine relationships depends on satisfying web experiences. The relationship building process evolves with how users choose to interact with websites and their satisfaction experience of each interaction.

User satisfaction can be improved via high website quality and positive user perceptions about vendors. The quality of a company's website can be enhanced by improving its technical design. Users' positive perceptions about the vendor can be supported through the incorporation of aspects such as personalization of service, third party as-surance and brand equity. This study examines how website quality and brand equity can contribute to a user's satisfying experience, thereby increasing a user's trust in socialization with others in online social networks.

LITREATURE REVIEW

Use and Gratification

Although social media are proliferating, they are not displacing traditional media. Users' decisions on media use depend on whether the media can satisfy their motives and needs (Kink & Hess, 2008). Social media need to compete with other media for users' attention. Creating the expectation that the chosen media will provide gratifying experiences to users could be an effective approach to get users' attention.

Use and Gratification theory asserts that gratifications sought (GS) and gratifications obtained (GO) can contribute to the intention of a user's continued use of products and services. GS focus on the expectancy value of media, whereas the focus of GO is on the actual value (Palmgreen & Rayburn, 1982). GS are the expectancy/belief that a medium possesses certain attributes that can satisfy user's motives and needs. GO are the evaluation of these attributes after using the chosen medium. The chance of using social media is higher if users have a higher GS. This study aims to investigate the building of user trust in social media via the improvement of GS.

The Effect of Website Quality on Use and Gratification

Website quality can increase user's intention of initial purchase and of continued purchase (Kuan, Bock, & Vathanophas, 2008). Website quality can be improved in many areas: accessibility, navigation, bandwidth control, security, user friendliness design, interactivity, and aesthetics. Absence of these features can cause the shopping process to be laborious and error-prone. Poor website quality will result in decreased customer satisfaction and willingness to stay with a particular e-vendor (Liang & Chen, 2009). Information systems quality has been an effective factor in gaining competitiveness for a company in today's dynamic environment (Aladwani, 2002). Website quality is an important IS aspect for attracting prospective users, and retaining existing customers. Website quality consists of four major categories from the perspective of users: (1) specific content, (2) content quality, (3) appearance, and (4) technical adequacy (Aladwani, 2002). Specific content refers to the usefulness and quality of content with regard to accomplishment of website goals (e.g., information dissemination, reputation building, and completing a transaction). Content quality refers to the attention to detail, clarity of diction, understandability of content and appropriate use of languages. Appearance of a website deals with website design, including aesthetics, visual design, user-friendliness, alignment, layout, and unified feel. Technical adequacy refers to the functionality of the website, including accessibility, optimization of bandwidth, and navigation ability.

Website quality is a crucial factor examined by users when deciding on adopting an unfamiliar web application. Enhancing website quality can increase customer trust (Euijin, 2003) and attract new users (McKnight, Choudury, & Kacmar, 2002) in e-business. A customer translates a website with faulty images, weak security controls, inaccurate information, broken links, and delayed response into poor corporate performance and reputation. Consequently, poor quality design can have disastrous results for online social sites. Gossip (e-word-of-mouth) is much more ubiquitous in online social networks than in the traditional community. Think about how quickly some breaking news story has been spread throughout the world via Web 2.0 technology (e.g., Twitter, Facebook). For the same reason, poor website quality can invite criticism and critique as Facebook receives complaints regarding its lax privacy policy. That is why Facebook simplified the privacy control feature in order to minimize the negative influence of poor website quality on user satisfaction due to complicated privacy control.

Given the afore described effect of website quality on use and gratification, we propose the following hypothesis:

H1: Website quality contributes to the use and gratification sought by users in online social networks.

The Effect of Brand Equity on Use and Gratification

Enhancing brand equity is an effective measure to combat against the increasing attrition rate of online users. Branding is a business process used to increase the brand equity or the value of brand, consisting of the combination of brand, brand name, and symbols (Aaker, 1992). Branding can enhance customers' perceptions of product values in and create market differentiation against competitors through the use of a recognized name, symbol, design or logo (Farquhar, Herr, & Fazio, 1990). Brand equity provides customers greater comfort online than offline in the e-commerce context (Bart, Shankar, Sultan, & Urban, 2005). In the face of the decline of traditional advertising media spending, many companies are turning to digital out-of-home media so that brands can continuously reach target audiences anywhere and anytime (Gambetti, 2010). Building brand equity is important to companies in both online and offline worlds.

Accounting and marketing professionals have different interpretations for brand equity (Barwise, 1993). From the accounting perspective, brand equity is an intangible asset. The total discounted value of the current and future cash profit equals the current value of brand equity (Brasco, 1988). Any additional cash flows that can be generated from the homogeneous product are brand equity

(Biel, 1992). Brand equity is the perceived value of customers from the marketing perspective (Keller, 1993). The perceived value has external effects on the actual value of products and services. The increase in customer awareness of and preference for the product are examples of the externalities caused by brand equity. Equipped with these externalities, a company has an upper hand in entering new markets, attracting customers, and increasing profits. Although the accounting and marketing fields have different interpretations, professionals in both fields agree that brand equity has the potential to help increase business profit (Kamakura & Gary, 1993).

Brand equity consists of four main elements, including brand loyalty, awareness, quality and association (Aaker, 1992). These four elements have contributed to customer-product loyalty, thereby increasing the bottom line profits of a company. Creating brand equity is a challenging task because it takes time to establish these four elements. The lack of brand equity could become an insurmountable barrier to the success of retaining existing users and increasing new users in the online social network.

The Brand Loyalty on the Use and Gratification

Social networks are collaborative platforms where users interact with each other. This social engagement attracts more users, as well as marketers, to participate in the collaboration process. Similarly, these free software-based communities grow by linking members through a shared brand loyalty (Casalo, Flavian, & Guinaliu, 2010). However, gaining and sustaining brand loyalty is a key challenge in highly competitive and fragmented social network markets. In the traditional environment, satisfying sales encounter experiences can increase brand loyalty (Brexendorf, Muhlmeier, Tomczak, & Eisend, 2010). However in the online social network, no sales encounters are present. Thus, the logic of enhancing brand loyalty via

sales encounter satisfaction is not applicable. With the sales encounter missing, brand loyalty among members becomes critical to the growth of social networks. For example, think about your friends defecting to other social networks. The network effect underlies the success of leading social networks. Brand loyalty of members is indispensible to the production of satisfying experiences in social networks.

The afore described effects of brand equity and loyalty on use and gratification leads to the following hypothesis:

H2: Brand loyalty can contribute to the use and gratification sought by users in online social networks.

The Effect of Brand Awareness on the Use and Gratification

Brand awareness is the extent by which a consumer possesses knowledge about or is familiar with a particular brand. Brand recall or brand recognition are two typical ways to measure the brand awareness level of users (Miladian & Nagendra, 2009). Brand recall is the ability of users to quickly retrieve their most familiar brand from memory when given the product category. Brand recognition is the ability of users to confirm their prior experiences with the brand. The proliferation of social media has created challenges for users to stay with a particular social medium and constantly update their profile in diversified social media. Among the vast array of social media choices, brand awareness plays an important role in helping users choose a social media. Every social network has its own pulse (e.g., content, user characteristics, and aesthetics). As part of a social network pulse, brand awareness and customer satisfaction are related to each other (Zuk, 2009). The effect of brand awareness on satisfaction evaluations and behavioral intentions is particularly obvious when services have experiential qualities (Tam, 2008). A survey of more than 20,000 online customers showed that retailer brand awareness would be the major reason these customers have the highest experience satisfaction and shop at their favorite vendors ("How to get, and keep," 2007). Social networks offer experiential services. Satisfaction evaluations of social network services heavily depend on the experiences of users and their friends. We conjecture that the more familiar users are with a particular social network, the higher the potential that they will have a satisfying experience. Therefore, the following hypothesis is posed:

H3: Brand awareness can contribute to the use and gratification sought by users in online social networks.

The Effect of Brand Quality on the Use and Gratification

Brand quality is a potent way to predict consumer preference, market share and profitability (Morton, 1992). In the face of intensified competition among populated social networks, a social network with high brand quality has a higher chance of attracting members and growing its network size. Brand quality judgment is subjective, because users perceive brand quality based on internal standards and information on competitive brands (Kirmani & Baumgartner, 1999). Therefore, a user's perceived brand quality is dynamic and is not totally dependent on the outcome of the service experience. Perceived brand quality has an indirect effect on brand equity via user satisfaction (Ha, Janda, & Muthaly, 2010). For each perceived quality improvement a brand can achieve, the experience satisfaction to users is likely to grow. For these reasons, we propose the following hypothesis:

H4: Brand quality can contribute to the use and gratification sought by users in online social networks.

The Effect of Brand Association on the Use and Gratification

Trustworthy brand associations can have a positive and lasting effect on customer's attitude toward e-business (Stoecklin-Serino & Paradice, 2009). Brand associations as part of brand equity can reinforce users' trust towards the use of social networks (Urban, Fareena, & William, 2000). When users cannot physically see and touch the products, brand associations can help users sense the presence of a trustworthy social network through brand associations (Dayal, Landesberg, & Zeisser, 1999).

Historically, businesses have used brand association as an integrated customer communication strategy to enhance and grow their brands (Spence & Essoussi, 2010). Initial brand associations shape components of consumer attitude, such as perceived satisfaction (Martinez & Pina, 2010). The employer brand association can help predict employee satisfaction (Davies, 2008). When deciding which social network to join, members are very likely to rely on brand association because of its reciprocal spill-over effect on consumer attitude.

Social media have been used as an Internet participatory marketing vehicle to increase brand association ("Outrider broadens search marketing," 2008). Nielsen mapped out the brand associations linked to a product before and after sharing certain information via Twitter (Quinton, 2009). Effective approaches to increasing users' association with other brands may include advertising about features in popular magazines and helping users quickly locate social network sites via search engines. Third party assurance, such as including the VeriSign security seal and recommendations from affiliated reputable websites, can also help increase the trust level of users. Small social network sites organizing their design in a similar fashion to other reputable social network sites can quickly gain additional trust from users. Many social networking websites in Asia use this strategy to quickly become leading Web 2.0

players. For instance, RenRen (http://www.renren.com) and YouKu are the leading counterparts of Facebook and YouTube, respectively, in China. Theoretical and practical practices imply that users are more likely to use online social networks by developing brand association, leading us to the following hypothesis:

H5: Brand association can contribute to the use and gratification sought by users in online social networks.

The Effect of Use and Gratification on Trust

Customer satisfaction is a process of evaluating products or services, and a response to the evaluation process (Fornell, 1992). A customer compares his perceptions of products and services with needs in the cognitive evaluative process (Westbrook & Reilly, 1983). Customers are satisfied with a product or service if it exceeds their expectation. Satisfying experiences can increase customer's trust in virtual community (Wu, Chen, & Chung, 2010). User satisfaction has been found to be an important factor for the increase of trust, thereby encouraging users to make repurchase decisions in e-businesses (Ha & John, 2010). Trust can drive service differentiation and user commitment to staying with the same service (Chenet, Dagger, & O'Sullivan, 2010). In the transaction-based online community, member satisfaction with the use of online social networks can increase the trust level of users, relationship commitment and loyalty (Wu, Chen, & Chung, 2010). Increased trust can increase usage intention of self-service technology, such as online social networks (Collier & Sherrell, 2010). Users satisfied with previous interactions are more likely to trust the online social network sites and will have higher intention of revisiting social websites. Thus, we propose the following hypothesis:

H6: Member satisfaction can contribute to user trust in social networks.

Figure 1 is the proposed theoretical framework that derives from the literature review. Six hypotheses were proposed to assess the relationships among the studied constructs.

RESEARCH METHODOLOGY

Trust in the e-business context is often measured with four types of trust: (1) calculation, (2) familiarity, (3) structural assurance, and (4) situational normality-based (Gefen, 2000). Calculative-based trust refers to trust that a user obtains through rational calculation of the costs and benefits of trusting another (Dasguta, 1988). Familiarity-based trust results from a user's past interactions with others (Williamson, 1993). An online user forms trust in a website when structural assurance conditions, such as contracts, regulations, accreditation, feedback, or security seals, are in place. Situational normality is the degree of consistency and reliability of websites where no abnormal conditions are present.

Calculative-based and familiarity-based trusts are interpersonal trust. In contrast, situational normality and structural assurance are institutional-based and impersonal trust (Pavlou & Lin, 2002). Since social networking involves both interpersonal and institutional-based trusts, these four factors are adopted to measure the trust construct. Geffen's (2000) survey instrument was modified to measure the trust of users in a social network. This revised survey instrument includes 13 questions.

Perceived website quality has a positive influence on online users' trusting beliefs. Users are more likely to form positive opinions about vendors if they have a higher perception of the quality of their websites (McKnight, Cummings, & Chervany, 1998). McKnight et al.'s (1998) original

Figure 1. Theoretical framework

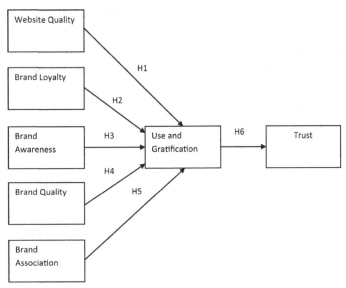

survey instrument was modified to measure the construct of perceived website quality. This revised instrument includes five questions.

The brand equity construct consists of five elements: brand loyalty, brand awareness, perceived quality, brand associations and market behavior (Aaker, 1991). Market behavior is a macro-factor, not suitable for measuring the brand equity from the perspective of users. Our survey instrument excludes this element.

Validity of Survey Instrument

The survey method has the potential error rate of 20-30%. These marginal errors can be reduced by using a survey instrument with high validity. All questions in the survey use the Likert scale of 1-5 with 1 "strongly disagree" and 5 "strongly agree." Thirty graduate students were invited to participate in a pilot test. The collected data from the pilot test was entered for the test of reliability of the survey instrument using Cronbach's α value. If the α value is greater than 0.7, the consistency of the questions used to measure a theoretical construct is robust enough (Cronbach, 1951).

Otherwise, any questions with an α value lower than 0.7 would be dropped from the questionnaire for the full-scale study.

A confirmatory factor analysis was administered to verify if the collected data confirm to the proposed theoretical model. The maximum likelihood estimation (MLE) value was used to assess the degree of confirmation of the proposed model. X-square values are used as parameters to estimate the suitability of the model. Goodness of fit index (GFI > 0.9), adjusted goodness of fit index (AGFI > 0.8), and root mean square residual (RMR < 0.05) are three indicators used to assess the reliability of the proposed framework.

Reliability and Validity Analysis

We assessed the reliability and validity of the adopted questionnaire via Cronbach's α coefficients. The higher the Cronbach's α coefficient, the higher reliability the questions used in the survey have. The overall Cronbach's α coefficient of the survey question is higher than 0.92, which is above the acceptable value of 0.7 (Nunnally, 1978). This finding indicates that the adopted survey has high intra-class correlations. However, Cronbach's α values of some items used to measure constructs of this study fall below 0.7. After removing items with low reliability, Cronbach's α coefficients were increased to 0.7820 for brand equity and 0.7311 for perceived website quality. Table 1 summarizes Cronbach's α coefficients of all questions used to measure each construct.

The validity test is to assess if the questionnaire can help accomplish the purpose of assessment. Since the questionnaire is constructed based on well-established theories and is applicable to the social networking study, the validity test of the questionnaire is acceptable.

Table 1. Reliability test

Category	Subcategory	Symbol	Inter-Item Correlations	Item Cronbach's α	Construct's Cronbach' α
Trust	Construct Assurance	SA1	0.4795	0.7392	0.7574
		SA2	0.6423	0.6514	
		SA3	0.6244	0.6609	
		SA4	0.4799	0.7417	
	Situation Normality	SN1	0.6123	0.7485	0.7954
		SN2	0.6650	0.6927	
		SN3	0.6383	0.7216	
U&G	Information Seeking	IS1	0.4621	0.7134	0.7141
		IS2	0.5654	0.5866	
		IS3	0.5768	0.5697	
	Convenience	CON1	0.5473	0.7207	0.7647
		CON2	0.5576	0.7167	
		CON3	0.5777	0.7040	
		CON4	0.6020	0.6946	
Website Quality	Website Quality	WQ1	0.6096	0.7849	0.8185
		WQ2	0.5912	0.7883	
		WQ3	0.6347	0.7762	
		WQ4	0.6341	0.7761	
		WQ5	0.5968	0.7889	
Brand Equity	Brand Loyalty	BL1	0.6657	0.6690	0.7993
		BL2	0.6702	0.6483	
		BL3	0.5434	0.7820	
	Brand Awareness	BA1	0.4810	0.7117	0.7414
		BA2	0.6489	0.6188	
		BA3	0.5275	0.6869	
		BA4	0.4965	0.7098	
	Perceived Quality	PQ1	0.4993	0.7072	0.7311
		PQ3	0.5995	0.5924	
		PQ4	0.5670	0.6293	
	Brand Association	BAS1	0.5515	0.7821	0.8018
		BAS2	0.6517	0.7362	
		BAS3	0.6425	0.7385	
		BAS4	0.6212	0.7500	

DATA ANALYSIS METHODS AND RESULTS

This study investigates the direct effect of technical (perceived website quality) and marketing factors (brand awareness, loyalty, quality and association) on users' satisfaction, and their indirect effect on the trust of users in social networks. A total of 398 students in a public United States-based university were invited to participate in the online survey. Out of 398 responses in the full-scale study, 381 valid responses were entered for further data analysis. The effective response rate is 95.7%. There are 238 males (60.9%) and 153 females (39.1%) in the population. All participants are students currently studying in a college of business at a public university in North Carolina. Table 2 shows the distribution of subjects with respect to their majors. Our survey shows that 35% of subjects in this study are management majors.

Table 3 shows the distribution of subjects with respect to their social networking experiences. Our survey shows that 58.1% of subjects in this study predominately have three-five years of social networking experiences. Table 4 shows the distribution of subjects with respect to their Facebook experiences. Our survey shows that 60.9% of subjects in this study predominately have two-four years of experience in Facebook.

Table 2. The profile of participants by majors

The Number of Years		Frequency	Percentage
Majors	Accounting	43	11.0%
	Computer Information Systems	54	13.8%
	Economics	9	2.3%
	Finance, Banking and Insurance	61	15.6%
	International Business	12	3.1%
	Management	137	35.0%
	Marketing	63	16.1%
	Other	53	13.6%

Table 3. Social networking experiences

The Number of Years		Frequency	Percentage
Social Networking Experiences	Less than 1	23	5.9%
	1 to 2	34	8.7%
	2 to 3	65	16.6%
	3 to 4	138	35.3%
	4 to 5	89	22.8%
	More than 5	42	10.7%

A majority of the participants (51.9%) spend no more than two hours on Facebook, followed by two-four hours (26.1%), and others (22%). The survey shows that 28.6% of subjects visit Facebook more than 14 times a week, followed by no more than six times (39.4%), and others (32%). This finding indicates that either the participants are heavy or light users of Facebook services. The participants primarily use the service of posting messages on the walls of members (85.6%), followed by photo sharing (72.2%), news feed (70.7%), and making friends (69.4%). Secondary services used by the participants include privacy control (47.8%), events promotion (32.1%), banding together with common interests or causes (26.5%), and free fun applications (26.2%).

Regression Analyses and Results

Technical and marketing factors are conducive to the increase of customer satisfaction, thereby

Table 4. Facebook experiences

The Number of Years		Frequency	Percentage
Social Networking Experiences	Less than 1	36	9.2%
	1 to 2	48	12.3%
	2 to 3	93	23.8%
	3 to 4	145	37.1%
	4 to 5	62	15.9%
	More than 5	7	1.8%

increasing user trust in social networks. Technical factors refer to website quality dimensions. Marketing factors include brand loyalty, awareness, quality and association. Table 5 provides the description of variables and their expected direction in the regression estimations. In order to understand the causal relationships between the studied constructs, two regression models are constructed as follows:

Model 1: Use and gratification as Dependent Variable

$$UG = \alpha_0 + b_1 T_1 + b_2 M_1 + b_3 M_2 + b_4 M_3 + b_5 M_4 + \epsilon$$

where;

UG = Use and gratifications; T_1 = Website Quality; M_1 = Brand Loyalty; M_2 = Brand Awareness; M_3 = Brand Quality; M_4 = Brand Association

Model 2: Trust as Dependent Variable

$$TRUST = \alpha_0 + b_1 UG_1 + \epsilon$$

where;

Table 5. Description of all variables

Variable	Variable Measurement	Predicted Sign
Dependent Variables		
Dependent Uses and Gratifications	I can learn new things from Facebook. Facebook is a good method to network with friends. Facebook is a good method to search information. I can receive useful information from Facebook. It is convenient to make friends on Facebook. It is convenient to network with friends on Facebook. I can get what I want with little effort and time from Facebook. I can use Facebook everywhere. Facebook is easy to use.	(n.a.)
Independent Variables		
Technical Variables Website Quality	The overall operations of Facebook are smooth. Facebook delivers services that I expect. Facebook's services are simple to use. I can easily network with friends on Facebook. Facebook clearly explains how my personal information can be transmitted to and shared among its affiliate companies.	(+)
Marketing Variables Brand Loyalty	I will still use Facebook even though I can choose to use other social network websites. Facebook is my first choice when doing online social networking activities. I will still use Facebook even though it has no advertisement. I will still be loyal to Facebook even though new social networking websites appear.	(+)
Brand Awareness	I am very familiar with Facebook. The first thing coming to my mind is Facebook when thinking about social networking websites. I had already heard of Facebook before first using the social networking website. Facebook is the most reputable social networking website.	(+)
Brand Quality	I like to use and buy Facebook's services very much. The service quality of Facebook influences me in using its services I am satisfied with the service quality of Facebook. Facebook's products and services are valuable to me.	(+)
Brand Association	If Facebook offers new products or services, I will adopt them. I like the image of Facebook very much. The advantages of using Facebook are clear to me. I think that Facebook is very different from other social network websites.	(+)

$TRUST_1$= Use and gratification

Five of the six hypotheses were supported, with the exception being Hypothesis 3. Table 6 shows a summary of linear regression results for both models. Model 1 shows that the explanatory power of the adjusted R^2 explained 38.95% (p=0.0001<0.01) of the variation of user satisfaction by technical and marketing factors. Model 2 shows that the explanatory power of the adjusted R^2 explained 17.1% (p=0.000<0.01) of the variation of trust by user satisfaction.

The estimated coefficients of factors were positive as expected, with the exception of the brand awareness factor. Additionally, the relationship between brand awareness and user satisfaction was not statistically significant. The other relationships were statistically significant, as expected. Website quality has the highest explanative power (β=32.585%; p<0.001) for user satisfaction, followed by brand loyalty (β=21.023%; p<0.001), brand association (β=15.978%; p<0.01), and brand quality (β=9.904%; p<0.01) (Table 7 and Table 8). Website quality, a technical factor, has the highest positive effect on the increase of customer satisfaction. Although these three marketing factors - brand loyalty, brand quality and brand association – also have influence on the increase of user satisfaction, their impact is not as strong as the technical factor. Finally, results indicate that user satisfaction has explanative power (β=43.1%; p<0.001) for trust. This indicates that users increase their trust in other users and online

Table 6. Analysis of variance

	DF	R Square	Adjusted R Square	Mean Square	F Value	P value
Model 1	5	153.33280	0.3895	30.66656	50.12	0.0001*
Model 2	1	0.173	0.171	22.322	80.605	0.000*

Note: * P < 0.01; Number of observations: 386

Table 7. Regression analysis of use and gratification as the dependent variable

Hypothesis	Variable	Coefficient	Standard Error	t Value
H1-Supported	Website Quality (b1)	0.32585	0.05631	5.79**
H2 - Supported	Brand Loyalty (b2)	0.21023	0.06538	3.22**
H3 – Not Supported	Brand Awareness (b3)	-0.05539	0.06166	-0.90
H4 – Weakly Supported	Brand Quality (b4)	0.09904	0.05985	1.65*
H5 - Supported	Brand Association (b5)	0.15978	0.06110	2.62**

** P < 0.01 ; * P < 0.1

Table 8. Regression analysis of trust as the dependent variable

Hypothesis	Variable	Coefficient	Standard Error	t Value
	Intercept	1.677	0.189	8.874
H6- Supported	Use and gratification	0.431	0.048	8.978**

** P < 0.01

social networks along with the increase of satisfying experience of using social services.

DISCUSSION

As indicated in the results of our analysis, a good deal of variation in user satisfaction with regard to social networking sites can be explained by technical and marketing factors, while in turn the user satisfaction has explanatory power in the variation of trust in social networking sites. These findings affirm that the hypothesized relationships between technical and marketing factors and user satisfaction, as well as between user satisfaction and trust, do exist. As provided in the results, website quality has the highest explanative power for user satisfaction, followed by brand loyalty, brand association, and brand quality. This finding indicates that user satisfaction can be increased along with the improvement in these four factors. Additionally, this study found that user satisfaction helps explain variation in trust. As the experience of participating in online social networks becomes more satisfying, users increase their trust in other users and online social networks.

The growth in the number of users is critical to the success of social networks. Trust is an indispensible engine for the continuing velocity of growth in social networks. In order to fuel the engine, the antecedents to building of trust in social networks need to be further examined. User satisfaction plays a central role in enhancing trust in members and social network services used to assist the socialization of members. The virtual social exchange process relies on the trade of personal, non-business information between users without explicit binding or legal contracts (Guo, Shim, & Otondo, 2010). User satisfaction can help minimize the uncertainty and perceived risk of the social exchange process. Minimization of uncertainty can increase user satisfaction and contribute to increased trust.

User satisfaction in social network websites is derived from both technical and marketing factors. A user's perceived website quality is an important contributor to the development of trust in e-commerce (Gefen, Karahanna, & Straub, 2003). The findings of this study corroborate with those of transaction-based e-business studies. Moreover, this study assesses the influence of brand equity on user satisfaction in relation to the effect of website quality. Four aspects of brand equity were examined with respect to their influence on user satisfaction. This study discovered that brand loyalty, brand quality and brand association were effective agents for creating user satisfaction. These three kinds of brand equity can enhance users' comfort in exchanging personal information with each other in the social network. Given limited resources, social networks should direct their attention to brand equity in the following order: brand loyalty, brand association and brand quality. Increasing brand loyalty via brand affiliation and the improvement of social network services can also substantially help improve user satisfaction. While current research in the retail context has found brand awareness a major reason customers have the highest experiential satisfaction ("How to get, and keep," 2007), this study did not affirm the finding. While social networks offer experiential services, satisfaction depends more upon on the experiences of users and their friends rather than branding.

IMPLICATIONS

User trust has significant influence on information and knowledge sharing behaviors in professional (Chen & Hung, 2010) and social virtual communities. This study asserts that user trust depends on positive user satisfaction, which can be improved via technical and marketing factors. Perceived website quality is an important technical factor. Brand loyalty, brand quality and brand association are three important brand equities for social networks to cultivate, because they can effectively increase user satisfaction with social network services. Brand awareness is less important relative to the other three brand equities. Website quality can be improved in a much shorter time than a brand can be built. Social network service providers interested in growing network size should take both the short-term and long-term approaches of increasing user satisfaction. Increases in user satisfaction will result in corresponding increases in user trust.

In the short term, website quality is critical to enhancing user satisfaction in social network services. The low exit and entry barriers to the adoption of social network websites make the website quality an even more important factor to consider. If users encounter poor bandwidth configuration, laborious navigation functionality, and ineffective search engine functions, they can easily switch from one social network to another. Conversely, users enjoy the social networking process and have trust in social network sites if their website quality is high. A study on the Name-Your-Own-Price (NYOP) auction model shows that effective information diffusion among prospective buyers about the seller's reserve price relies on the structure of the underlying social network (Hinz & Spann, 2010). Website quality can bring satisfaction to users by providing them with more accurate information to exchange, which in turn eases the socialization process. Many virtual community organizers find that website quality (e.g., usability, security, stability, loading times) is an enabler for user satisfaction (Williams, 1999). Website quality is an important facilitator for active user interaction in the social network, because it can reduce communication costs of dispersed actors (Schroder & Holzle, 2010). Managers of social network websites should recognize the importance of website quality and leverage it to improve user satisfaction.

In the long term, the success of building a brand depends on marketing activities such as positioning, credibility, well-blended communications and long-term cultivation of brand. All these activities aim to deliver the "core benefits" to customers. The core benefits of social network services are to help users socially network with each other and improve their social relationships with others. PepsiCo Foodservice has traditionally leveraged word-of-mouth as a marketing tool to increase customer's perception about the brand value of PepsiCo products (Smith, 2010). By taking the brand advocacy-driven approach, Dunkin' Donuts' fans are 35% more likely to recommend the brand than Starbuck's (Paynter, 2010). Fun games such as Dunkin's "Create the Next Doughnut Contest" drew fans together and increased customer loyalty and satisfaction. Brand building is part of a process toward creating user satisfaction. When users are excited about a brand, they are happy to voice to other members what they like about the brand and engage interactively (Reis, 2010). The more members spread the word about the brand, the happier these members. Similarly, the happier members are the more trust they have in each other and social networking sites.

CONCLUSION

Trust is fundamental to the continued growth of online social network sites. One of the key components to trust is one's willingness to put one's self in a vulnerable position. In relation to personal information which is shared in online social network sites, individuals are more likely to share this information with a site where the level of user satisfaction is high.

User satisfaction is indispensable to the trust-building process. As found in this study, relationships between trust and user satisfaction do exist. The higher the level of satisfaction that users have experienced, the more effort and time they will spend in the socialization process. User satisfaction arises from involvement in sustained interactions with social network sites. Noted in the findings, technical and marketing factors assist to increase customer satisfaction levels, thus encouraging more time spent within the social network. Additionally, users are encouraged to interact with social network sites if the website quality and brand equity are of a high level.

Website quality was found to ease the socialization process and create a high degree of interaction between members. Many social network sites profit from extensive utilization of services offered by third-party application developers, thus improving upon the users' satisfaction. Improving website quality is an effective technical solution to helping achieve short-term success for online social websites. There appears, that in order to achieve long-term success, online social websites need to focus on increasing brand equity. Effective measures should focus on building brand loyalty, brand quality and brand association. For hypothesis H3 (Brand awareness can contribute to the use and gratification sought by users in online social networks), the finding suggests that, increasing brand awareness is not as effective as the other three measures, because of the low entry and exit barriers to entering the new social networks. In order to accelerate the growth rate and stay competitive, online social network websites need to continuously address both technical and marketing challenges.

REFERENCES

Aaker, D. A. (1991). *Managing brand equity.* New York, NY: Free Press.

Aaker, D. A. (1992). The value of brand equity. *The Journal of Business Strategy, 13*(4), 27–32. doi:10.1108/eb039503.

Aladwani, A. M., & Palvia, P. C. (2002). Developing and validating an instrument for measuring user-perceived web quality. *Information & Management, 39,* 467–476. doi:10.1016/S0378-7206(01)00113-6.

Bart, Y., Shankar, V., Sultan, F., & Urban, G. L. (2005). Are the drivers and role of online trust the same for all Web sites and consumers? A large-scale exploratory empirical study. *Journal of Marketing, 69*(4), 133–152. doi:10.1509/jmkg.2005.69.4.133.

Barwise, P. (1993). Brand equity: Snark or boojum. *International Journal of Research in Marketing, 10*(1), 93–104. doi:10.1016/0167-8116(93)90036-X.

Biel, A. L. (1992). How brand image drives brand equity. *Journal of Advertising Research,* 6–12.

Blumler, J. G., & Katz, E. (1974). *The uses of mass communications: Current perspectives on gratifications research.* Thousand Oaks, CA: Sage.

Brasco, T. C. (Ed.). (1988). *How brand name are valued for acquisitions.* Cambridge, MA: Marketing Science Institute.

Brexendorf, T. O., Muhlmeier, S., Tomczak, T., & Eisend, M. (2010). The impact of sales encounters on brand loyalty. *Journal of Business Research, 63*(11), 1148–1155. doi:10.1016/j.jbusres.2009.10.011.

Casalo, L. V., Flavian, C., & Guinaliu, M. (2010). Relationship quality, community promotion and brand loyalty in virtual communities: Evidence from free software communities. *International Journal of Information Management, 30*(4), 357–367. doi:10.1016/j.ijinfomgt.2010.01.004.

Chen, C., & Hung, S. (2010). To give or to receive? Factors influencing members' knowledge sharing and community promotion in professional virtual communities. *Information & Management, 47*(4), 226. doi:10.1016/j.im.2010.03.001.

Chenet, P., Dagger, T. S., & O'Sullivan, D. (2010). Service quality, trust, commitment and service differentiation in business relationships. *Journal of Services Marketing*, *24*(5), 336. doi:10.1108/08876041011060440.

Collier, J. E., & Sherrell, D. L. (2010). Examining the influence of control and convenience in a self-service setting. *Academy of Marketing Science Journal*, *38*(4), 490. doi:10.1007/s11747-009-0179-4.

Cronbach, L. J. (1951). Coefficient alpha and the internal structure of tests. *Psychometrika*, *16*, 297–333. doi:10.1007/BF02310555.

Dasguta, P. (1988). *Making and breaking cooperative relations*. New York, NY: Basil Blackwell.

Davies, G. (2008). Employer branding and its influence on managers. *European Journal of Marketing*, *42*(5-6), 667. doi:10.1108/03090560810862570.

Dayal, S., Landesberg, H., & Zeisser, M. (1999). How to build trust online. *Marketing Management*, 64-69.

Euijin, K. (2003). *Factors impacting customers' trust in e-businesses: An empirical study of customers' initial trust in e-businesses*. Carbondale, IL: Southern Illinois University at Carbondale. doi:10.1109/HICSS.2005.272.

Farquhar, P. H., Herr, P. M., & Fazio, R. H. (1990). A relational model for category extensions of brands. *Advances in Consumer Research. Association for Consumer Research (U. S.)*, *17*, 856–860.

Fornell, C. (1992). A national customer satisfaction barometer: The Swedish experience. *Journal of Marketing*, *56*, 6–21. doi:10.2307/1252129.

Gambetti, R. C. (2010). Ambient communication: How to engage consumers in urban touch points. *California Management Review*, *52*(3), 34–52. doi:10.1525/cmr.2010.52.3.34.

Gefen, D. (2000). Customer loyalty in e-commerce. *Journal of the Association for Information Systems*, *3*, 27–51.

Gefen, D., Karahanna, E., & Straub, D. W. (2003). Trust and TAM in online shopping: An integration model. *Management Information Systems Quarterly*, *27*(1), 51–90.

Guo, C., Shim, J. P., & Otondo, R. (2010). Social network services in China: An integrated model of centrality, trust and technology acceptance. *Journal of Global Information Technology Management*, *13*(2), 76–99.

Ha, H., Janda, S., & Muthaly, S. (2010). Development of brand equity: Evaluation of four alternative models. *The Service Industries Journal*, *30*(6), 911. doi:10.1080/02642060802320253.

Ha, H., & John, J. (2010). Role of customer orientation in an integrative model of brand loyalty in services. *The Service Industries Journal*, *30*(7), 1025. doi:10.1080/02642060802311252.

Hinz, O., & Spann, M. (2010). Managing information diffusion in name-your-own-price auctions. *Decision Support Systems*, *49*(4), 474–485. doi:10.1016/j.dss.2010.05.008.

How to get, and keep, satisfied web customers. (2007). *Marketing News*, *41*(17), 31-32.

Kamakura, W. A., & Gary, J. R. (1993). Measuring brand value with scanner data. *International Journal of Research in Marketing*, *10*, 9–22. doi:10.1016/0167-8116(93)90030-3.

Keller, K. L. (1993). Conceptualizing, measuring, and managing customer-based brand equity. *Journal of Marketing*, *57*(1), 1–22. doi:10.2307/1252054.

Kink, N., & Hess, T. (2008). Search engines as substitutes for traditional information sources? An investigation of media choice. *The Information Society*, *24*, 18–29. doi:10.1080/01972240701771630.

Kirmani, A., & Baumgartner, H. (1999). Perceived quality and value, satisfaction and loyalty: New insights into processes underlying some familar constructs. *Advances in Consumer Research. Association for Consumer Research (U. S.), 26*(1), 598–598.

Kuan, H., Bock, G., & Vathanophas, V. (2008). Comparing the effects of website quality on customer initial purchase and continued purchase at e-commerce websites. *Behaviour & Information Technology, 27*(1), 3–16. doi:10.1080/01449290600801959.

Liang, C., & Chen, H. (2009). A study of the impacts of website quality on customer relationship performance. *Total Quality Management & Business Excellence, 20*(9), 971–988. doi:10.1080/14783360903181784.

Martinez, E., & Pina, J. M. (2010). Consumer responses to brand extensions: A comprehensive model. *European Journal of Marketing, 44*(7-8), 1182–1205. doi:10.1108/03090561011047580.

McKnight, D. H., Choudury, V., & Kacmar, C. (2002). Developing and validating trust measures for e-commerce: An integrative typology. *Information Systems Research, 13*, 334–359. doi:10.1287/isre.13.3.334.81.

McKnight, D. H., Cummings, L. L., & Chervany, N. L. (1998). Initial trust formation in new organizational relationships. *Academy of Management Review, 23*, 472–490.

Miladian, H., & Nagendra, B. K. (2009). Automobile scene: Brand-awareness, image and personality. *SCMS Journal of Indian Management*, 81-85.

Morton, J. (1992). Brand quality segments: Potent way to predict preference. *Marketing News, 26*(19), IR8.

Nunnally, J. C. (1978). *Psychometric theory*. New. York, NY: McGraw-Hill.

Outrider broadens search marketing offering with addition of social media marketing practice. (2008). *Marketing Business Weekly, 28*.

Palmgreen, P., & Rayburn, J. D. (1982). Gratifications sought and media exposure: An expectancy value model. *Communication Research, 9*(4), 561–580. doi:10.1177/009365082009004004.

Pavlou, P. A., & Lin, C. (2002). What drives electronic commerce across cultures? Acrosscultural empirical investigation of the theory of planned behavior. *Journal of Electronic Commerce Research, 3*(4), 240–253.

Paynter, B. (2010). Five steps to social currency. *Fast Company, 145*, 48.

Pénard, T., & Poussing, N. (2010). Internet use and social capital: The strength of virtual ties. *Journal of Economic Issues, 44*(3), 569–595. doi:10.2753/JEI0021-3624440301.

Quinton, B. (2009). *Social nets, video are sweet spots for online growth: Nielsen*. Retrieved from http://www.promotionalbuzz.com/2009/05/social-nets-video-are-sweet-spots-for-online-growth-nielsen/

Reis, D. (2010). *Quality vs. quantity: Sustainable social media strategy*. Retrieved from http://chiefmarketer.com/news/quality-vs-quantity-sustainable-social-media-strategy

Schroder, A., & Holzle, K. (2010). Virtual communities for innovation: Influence factors andn impact on company innovation. *Virtual Communities for innovation, 19*(3), 257-267.

Smith, S. (2010). Social media done right. *Restaurant Business, 109*, 20.

Spence, M., & Essoussi, L. H. (2010). SME brand building and management: An exploratory study. *European Journal of Marketing, 44*(7-8), 1037–1054. doi:10.1108/03090561011047517.

Stoecklin-Serino, C. M., & Paradice, D. B. (2009). An examination of the impacts of brand equity, security, and personalization on trust processes in an e-commerce environment. *Journal of Organizational and End User Computing, 21*(1), 36. doi:10.4018/joeuc.2009010101.

Tam, J. L. M. (2008). Brand familiarity: Its effects on satisfaction evaluations. *Journal of Services Marketing, 22*(1), 3–12. doi:10.1108/08876040810851914.

Urban, G. L., Fareena, S., & William, J. Q. (2000). Placing trust at the center of your Internet strategy. *Sloan Management Review, 42*, 39–48.

Westbrook, R. A., & Reilly, M. D. (1983). Value-percept disparity: An alternative to the disconfirmation of expectations theory of consumer satisfaction. *Advances in Consumer Research. Association for Consumer Research (U. S.), 10*, 256–261.

Williams, R. L. (1999). Managing an online community. *Journal for Quality and Participation, 22*, 54–55.

Williamson, O. E. (1993). Calculativeness, trust, and economic organization. *The Journal of Law & Economics, 36*(1), 453–486. doi:10.1086/467284.

Wu, J., Chen, Y., & Chung, Y. (2010). Trust factors influencing virtual community members: A study of transaction communities. *Journal of Business Research, 63*(9-10), 1025–1032. doi:10.1016/j.jbusres.2009.03.022.

Zuk, R. (2009). Pulse rate: Assess your social media channels regularly. *Public Relations: Tactics, 16*(11), 7.

Chapter 15
Virtual Research Conferences:
A Case Based Analysis

Kamna Malik
U21Global Graduate School, Singapore, Singapore

ABSTRACT

Research conferences provide an important platform for idea exchange and validation as well as for social networking and talent hunt. Online social networks and collaborative web tools can make conferences budget friendly for sponsors, flexible for attendees, and environment friendly for the society without loss of effectiveness. While many conferences have adopted such tools during pre and post conferencing stages, their use during actual meeting hours is very limited. This paper deliberates on the current and potential use of such technologies on various stages of a conference. It then presents the case of a pure virtual conference in comparison with a face to face conference with an aim to analyze the immediate benefits that virtual conferencing brings for organizers and participants. Perceived deterrents and potential benefits for various stakeholders are discussed. Suggestions are made for educational institutions to review their norms for conference sponsorships.

INTRODUCTION

The IEEE Engineering Management Conference (IEMC), 2001 was all set to go, when the devastating 9/11 happened and the conference got cancelled (Bellefeuille, 2010) as a follow up security measure. Not many minds may have actually registered this negligible fall out of the tragedy that disrupted many lives and large scale business operations. But think of it, if IEMC was

planned as a geographically dispersed or a truly space independent event, the conference might have still continued amidst the odds.

A space independent, albeit virtual, event may have been impractical a decade ago, but today it is feasible to organize a virtual conference in much lesser a time and at much lower a cost. In recent years, organizations have adopted virtual conferences, events and meetings to save time and cost and also to reach out to audience in different

DOI: 10.4018/978-1-4666-4022-1.ch015

geographies (King, 2008; Woolard, 2011). In research conferences also, now one can find online presentation option being offered as an alternate to onsite physical presentation. There has been some visible adoption of collaborative web tools (web based applications that allow two/multi way interaction among participants) for many more activities in research conferences. Use of social networks to handle conference queries and pre-conference publicity are also now practiced. However, the adoption of such tools during conference meeting hours is still in limited pockets and is not an integrated main stream manner of conducting conferences. Literature also does not adequately cover the current and potential application of such tools in the mega events of academic community i.e., research conferences.

This paper aims to emphasize the opportunities that collaborative web tools hold for research conferences. It begins with a brief about the purpose and organization of a typical research conference. It then explores the changing forms of conferences in the wake of recent technological advances and lists out suitable web tools that can be applied at various stages to improve the effectiveness of a conference. The case of a virtual conference is presented and compared with a physical conference having common environmental variables. The case analysis suggests immediate impact of collaborative web tools on the productivity of conference team as well as on time and cost savings. Opportunities as well as challenges involved in the tool adoption are discussed for various stakeholders, such as conference organizers, speakers, attendees, sponsors and technology solution providers of conference management systems.

RESEARCH CONFERENCES: PURPOSE AND ORGANIZATION

Research conferences are the life line of academic activity, a forum for new learning, incubator for idea generation, a testing ground for research proposals as well as a platform for visibility and social networking (Garcia, 2000; Hildreth & Woodrum, 2009; Kaser, 2008). Garcia (2000) views a conference as an opportunity to gain "valuable input and constructive criticism before submitting manuscripts to journals, book publishers, or grantors." He also equates a conference with a library and a place where "unexpected things can and do happen." Kaser (2008) describes conference as a place where you can actually get away from the constant distraction of electronic messaging and switch mental gears to take the time to think and reflect." The follow up of a conference paper is usually expected to be a journal publication. But, this does not always happen (Hildreth & Woodrum, 2009). One school of thought is to prefer conferences over journal publications owing to the speedy review process and faster dissemination often facilitated by a conference (Patterson, 2004; Vardi, 2009) but many scholars have also raised the concern about the quality of review of conference submissions (Al-Fedaghi, 2007; Patterson, 2004; Vardi, 2009).

Though most of the academic promotion committees still do not consider conference publications at par with journal publications (Truman, 2007; Vardi, 2009), fact of the matter remains that conferences are an integral part of scholarship and growth of the academic world as well as a necessary part of research budgets. Schroeder, O'Leary, Jones, and Poocharoen (2004), based on the findings of their study recommend that public administration scholars (including PhD students) participate and present research findings at professional conferences for scholarly success. McCormick and Pinderhughes (2009) suggest attending at least two conferences each year. Today, IEEE, the largest professional association for technological innovation, alone sponsors over 1,100 conferences and meetings a year, as claimed on their home page (http://www.ieee.org/conferences_events/index.html). As per the search results obtained from year-wise announcements made on an online portal, Academic Conferences Worldwide (http://www.conferencealerts.com), 52 conferences were announced for the year 2008, 74 for 2009, 104 for year 2010, and 102 for the year 2011 as in Dec 2011. Many of these conferences are recurring annual events with focused research goals, thus conference organizers strive to offer a quality forum for research as well as community building in addition to the goal of brand building in many cases. Most scholars plan conference visits as a necessary part of their annual planner.

Research conferences are usually hosted by academic institutions or research communities and executed on a project basis. The project starts with the identification of team, theme and venue. Functional experts are invited to serve various committees on an honorary basis. Though there are no fixed rules around the tasks, team roles and responsibilities, Potvin (1983) and Bajec (n.d.) provide good detailing around this to help the first time conference organizers. The commonly used roles and activities in a conference are for Conference Head (also called the General Chair), Program Head, Publicity Head, Finance Head, Logistics Head, and Technology Head. Accommodation and meal account for the largest part of conference expense (Bajec, n.d.). Registration fee, sponsorships and at times, sale of proceedings are the main streams of revenue for conferences. The gestation period for an international level of research conference is usually around a year. Many activities are carried out during this period, which can be broadly grouped into four stages.

Planning Stage: This stage involves defining a format for the conference. Thereafter, activities like team formation, publicity, paper submission and review, selection of speakers and registration of attendees is carried out by the conference organizing team.

Pre-Conferencing Stage: This stage starts after the entire program schedule is set and the main conference is just a few days away. This stage sets up the tone for conference days by sending initial fillers such as warm up mail, program schedule, brief about key notes and other planned activities as well as guidelines.

Conferencing Stage: This is the execution stage of the conference and includes actual meeting hours during which intellectual deliberations by way of tutorials, workshops, invited talks, paper presentations etc. take place glued together with breakout sessions for refreshments, entertainment and networking.

Post-Conferencing Stage: This stage includes follow up activities to close books of account for the conference, collect feedback from team and participants for performance analysis and improvement. Additional efforts are also undertaken to ensure better circulation of research outcomes of the conference such as proceedings or recorded sessions and also for community building. This stage is particularly important for conferences that continue on an ongoing basis.

Conferencing stage is the key stage that facilitates multi-point collaboration among participants. However, one cannot ignore the importance of pre and post conferencing stages in giving the necessary trigger and sustained impact, respectively, of the intensity of intellectual exchange and collaborations that might happen during the conferencing stage.

CHANGING FORMS OF CONFERENCES

Conventionally, conferences take place in a face to face mode where interaction among participants happens only during the conferencing stage. In other stages, one to one interaction between the organizer and the participant is carried out through emails or other asynchronous modes of communication. Participants' interaction is left to individuals where organizers are not involved and thus remain unaware of the extent of networking and academic discussion that their conference has generated. Use of Information Technology (IT) tools has been primarily limited to emails, conference website, list servers and conference management system as the commonly used tools for managing conferences during planning and pre-conferencing stages.

Recently, there has been a visible progress towards the use of collaborative web tools such as wiki, blogs, social networking sites (SNS), YouTube etc. to aide a conference during the pre and post conference stages. Some conferences have started adopting online conferencing tools during the conference stage also either as the sole meeting option or as an extended option for presenters who cannot make it to the physical venue. For ease of deliberations in the following part of this paper, we shall refer to three types of conferences based on their extent of tool adoption during conferencing stage, namely physical (face to face) conferences, blended conferences and virtual conferences.

A physical conference will be referred to as one wherein interaction between attendees is facilitated only on the physical venue. At best, contact information of all attendees is shared for individual follow up interactions after the conference. In contrast to this, a virtual conference will be referred to represent the conference format where the conferencing stage is facilitated purely online and without any physical meeting at all. Blended conferences can be understood as the ones that use a mix of physical and online modes to enable better interactions and/or flexibility during one or more stages of the conference. For example, pre/post conference activities in a physical conference may use technology to generate multi-point interactions among participants and organizers.

Similarly, a blended conference may offer online presentations as an option for presenters who are unable to travel to the conference location. Although, it is not uncommon today for conferences to offer online presentation option for presenters (at a lesser cost also), such an alternate largely allows only pre-set presentations to be played during the conference schedule, as poster presentations or simply uploaded on conference website. As a result, a virtual presenter misses the opportunity to directly interact with the audience and is likely to get less attention when there are enough onsite presenters to talk to.

Some examples of pure online conferences which have been running annually for the past two or more years are: international online language conference (IOLC, http://www.iolc2010.ioksp.com), International online medical conference (IOMC, http://www.iomcworld.com/2010), International online conference (IOC, 2011), Virtual Conference on Business and Management (VCOBAM, http://www.u21global.edu.sg/vcobam) and K12 online conference (K12, http://k12onlineconference.org). Many more conferences have started following a blended mode where one can see an increasing use of face book and other social networks for publicity as well as the increasing multi-point interaction through the use of a variety of collaborative web tools. F8 – the Facebook conference (F8, http://www.facebook.com/f8) organized by Facebook for its application developers is a good example of blending the social network as a strong medium for multi-point interaction before/during/after the conference. Javaone Conference (Javaone, http://www.facebook.com/javaone) and Big East conferences (Bigeast, http://www.facebook.com/bigeastconference) also maintain strong presence on Facebook enabling multi-point collaboration.

Another recent trend, though not IT-centered, has been that of "unconferencing" (Goliath, 2009) where the program schedule is kept agile. During the conference, participants can propose a new presentation topic; speakers can volunteer and participants can do a spot choice of which presentation to attend next. Though quality of speakers and content may not always be ensured in such a setting, unconferencing brings home the appropriateness of conferences as a place for mutually setup forum for interactions by participants, for participants. It may get physically tiring for participants as they hop between notice boards and presentation rooms to find their next session of interest, nevertheless, the agility and rigor of discussions that it brings can be unmatchable, if managed well. Social networks and web conferencing can be a good fit to help manage such a format of the conference and help extend it beyond the limits of physical participants only.

In practice, conferences mix various tools to suit their needs and preferences. Table 1 presents the possible web tools used/usable in various stages of a conference with a purpose to have multi-point interactions on an ongoing basis. While the usage of tools in the planning stage will largely affect the productivity of the conference organizing team and may have negligible effect on the monetary or quality aspects of a conference, their adoption during the conferencing stage can bring in immediate monetary benefits for organizers as well as attendees. Adoption during post conferencing stage can bring in qualitative impact for participants in terms of more closely-knit communities.

The following section takes the case of a virtual conference and compares it with a physical conference of a similar academic standing to explore the impact of using collaborative tools during planning and conferencing stages of the conference.

PHYSICAL VS. VIRTUAL CONFERENCE: COMPARISON OF TWO CASES

Literature supports appropriateness of case methodology in understanding a less understood phenomenon and where theory and research are in their formative stages (Benbasat, Goldstein, & Mead, 1987; Ellram, 1996; Cooper & Morgan, 2008). Benbasat, Goldstein, and Mead (1987, p. 370) define a case study as examining "a phenomenon in its natural setting, employing multiple methods of data collection to gather information from one or a few entities (people, groups, or organizations)." Ellram (1996, p. 100) explains case study as "a self-contained experiment, with unique context that is part of the experiment" rather than a single observation. She adds, "a more common application of a case study research is to build theory that can then be tested using further case studies, survey data, or another relevant method"

Table 1. Example tools used/usable across the stages of a conference

Stage of the conference	Examples of commonly used/usable collaborative web tools	Possible activities that can benefit from adoption of collaborative web tools
Planning Stage	Wiki, blog, discussion forum, Social Networks	Publicity, collaborative planning tasks such as theme identification, generating call for paper, publicity, reviewers' bidding, assignment, discussion and conflict resolution, team set up, program schedule, speaker identification etc.
Pre-Conferencing Stage	Blog, vodcast, discussion forum, virtual reality, web conferencing tools, social networks	Demo sessions, introduction to speakers/their topic; tutorial sessions, posters and workshops, initiating ice breaking and social networking
Conferencing Stage	Virtual world platforms, web conferencing tools, social networks, live webcast, blogs, discussion forums, live chats, virtual blackboard	Join the live conference anywhere as an interactive participant/ speaker; Share feedback about the conference over the social network or other mediums; Watch the recorded conference any time/any where; Have poster sessions online
Post Conferencing Stage	Media recordings, social networks, blogs, wiki, discussion forums, live chats	Gathering participant feedback or polls; Continuing discussions with other participants or speakers after the presentation is over; Building of social groups and relations; evolution of special interest groups or research communities

(Ellram, 1997, p. 97). Cooper and Morgan (2008, p. 159) emphasize the benefits of case studies "for understanding situations of uncertainty, instability, uniqueness, and value conflict."

As virtual research conferences are still in their formative years and literature does not contain any specific details about their adoption and impact, case based analysis can serve as a valid trigger to form a research framework for further research investigations. For ease of reference, the virtual conference case will here onwards be referred to as Case A and the physical conference case as Case B.

Case Background

Case A under discussion is about a virtual conference initiated in 2009. The conference was organized by an online institution for higher learning with staff and students located in different countries across oceans and time zones. Owing to its inherent competence in handling virtual interactions, World-wide-web as the venue for its first conference was a natural, undisputed choice for its faculty. Owing to the success of the first conference, its sequel was organized in 2010 as well and is now expected to become an annual event. The 2009 conference had only its own faculty as the organizing team. The team members though located across continents had access to institutional intranet and thus used the internal wiki for planning the format for conference including call for papers, choice of speakers, finalization of review results, etc. In 2010, the conference attracted volunteers from other universities also to serve on the organizing team. With this mixed team formation, institutional intranet could not be used as a common tool for interaction, thus Pbworks (http://www.pbworks.com), an online free ware, was used for team communication during conference planning stage. The conferencing stage during both the years was carried out using webex (http://www.webex.com) in a real time

audio mode. Video mode was excluded to avoid bandwidth issues that presenters in many parts of the world still face.

Organizing team of Case A was well experienced in handling online interactions as each member had good years of experience in hosting and attending webinars and internal meetings using Webex and other tools. In addition, the organizers made sure to keep the interaction hours limited with crisp and information packed sessions to hold the attention of participants. All presenters were given a practice time a week before the conference days to get them at ease with the conferencing tool and etiquette. Their guiding principles were quite in line with what have also been suggested by some recent works like Gichora et al. (2010) and Meetignet (2008), about handing virtual conferences.

Case B represents a physical conference first held in 2007 and held every year thereafter. This conference was hosted by a premier business school in India. The organizing team comprised of members of two institutions, one in India (the host institution) and another in USA (the partner institution). In all its events thus far, the team members have been using emails for document exchange and Voice over Internet Protocol (VOIP) applications for team communications with members abroad.

Case Comparison

Case A and Case B are comparable because both conferences had a common initiator, who was also the general chair in both the conferences. Both the conferences were initiated by institutions well-accepted for quality of education in the field of management and IT. Both the conferences were the first international conferences ever conducted by the host institution. A key purpose of both the conferences was to extend their respective institutions beyond higher education services and encourage a research oriented culture among students and faculty. Both the conferences had the common field of research, common review format (double blind) and publication opportunity and neither of the two conferences had any backing of a research institution or community. Incidentally, the acceptance rate in both the conferences was also similar i.e., around 30%.

Both the conferences had key organizing members in different countries. Both used some form of collaborative tools, though different, during planning stage and also used third party hosted online conference management systems. No dedicated social networking forums were set up for the participants in either case. However, FaceBook and LinkedIn were extensively used for publicity of case A through existing networks of team members and the host institution. None of two cases offered any online community for post-conference activities. Table 2 presents an overview of the scale of the two conferences.

The core processes viz. initial format and team planning, website and other online tools setup, publicity, submission and reviews, and program schedule and execution planning remained the same in both the conferences and took nearly the same time. However, there was a significant time saving observed in many support processes when executed online. Approximately 34 weeks of the elapsed time and related person effort was directly reduced in the overall effort required for organizing the virtual conference in comparison with the physical conference. This is because many of the support processes that apply to a physical conference are just not needed for a pure online conference. Table 3 presents a comparative snapshot of the support processes in the two cases, illustrating the fact that the use of online tools during planning and conferencing stage has definite benefits in the time and cost saving.

Table 2. Scale of the two conferences under discussion

Parameter	Case A	Case B
Location of the host institution (sponsor)	Singapore	India
Location of key organizing members	India, Germany, Canada, Singapore	India, USA
Publication opportunity	Online proceedings with ISSN and possible inclusion in select listed journals	Printed conference proceedings with ISBN and possible inclusion in select listed Journals
Registration fee	Nil	INR 3000/6000 for student/non-student in South Asian countries USD 150/300 for student/non-student in other countries
Total registrations	50 (free but restricted by the number of licenses organizers had in-house)	64
Total Conferencing Time spread over 2 days	8 hrs (single track)	23 hours (6 hrs x 3 parallel tracks + 5 hours of common time)
Total Selected Submissions for Presentation	11 papers + 3 invited talks	47 papers + 3 invited talks
Geographic distribution of the contributing authors (pre-selection)	Well distributed with no two submissions from the same country	70% from the country of the host institute 14% from the country of the partner institute
Absentia	Nil	12%
Direct Expenses	Nil	14,775 USD approx
Deficit	Nil	1,705 USD approx

Table 3. Comparison of the key support processes and elapsed time in Case A and Case B (NA implies Not Applicable)

	Case A	Case B
Approx. Elapsed Time (Approx. 34 weeks of elapsed time was saved in virtual conference)		
Budget planning and approval	Nil as no direct income/expense involved; indirect expense involved utilization of existing internal resources	1 week
Venue selection and arrangements	Nil as the venue was the Web	2 weeks
Document preparation, submission and follow-ups for permission from external ministry	NA	4 week
Selection of the printer for proceedings publication through formal purchase board	NA	4 weeks
Brochure/invitation formats (such as CFP) design and printing	1 week	5 weeks
Agreement of layout of proceedings	2 days (no printer was involved as the proceedings were online)	2 weeks (involves printer and editorial team)
Typesetting and draft generation for proceedings	3 days	4 weeks
Proof reading by editors and revision by the printer	2 days (as no external printer involved)	2 weeks
Printing and accession of printed copies of the proceedings	NA	3 weeks
Selection and procurement of the conference kit	NA	1 week
Buffer time for visa and travel of the participants	NA	8 weeks
Person effort required by support staff on the days of the conference (includes extra hours needed before/after actual meeting hours)	10 person hours (1 person x 5 hours x 2 days) - to manage the session start, recording and administrative support, if needed [approx. 1.25 person days]	80 person hours (4 persons x 10 hours x 2 days) - to manage reception/registration desk [=10 person days or 2 person weeks]

The virtual conference did not involve any direct costs owing to the total absence of the cost of venue and meals. Though a web conferencing tool also involves a cost, the host institution already had licenses for Webex and hence saved any direct expense on this account also. In addition, it used an open source conference management system (http://www.easychair.org). As a result, Case A did not have any direct expenditure. Indirect expenses involved the cost of resources such as website developer, technology support group, time and effort of organizing the team and reviewers These expenses were at par with those in case B. This cost advantage was directly passed on to the participants as a free conference.

Case B could save on the cost of venue by utilizing its own physical campus; however, it did not have adequate lodging facilities to offer international quality of residency to international delegates. It also had the location disadvantage of being away from the main city where the international participants were to be accommodated. Thus, it had to hire a conference hall in the center of the city, to make it convenient for delegates coming from other cities and countries. As decent conference halls in the city were limited, the conference organizers of Case B had to book the venue around a year in advance and this became the first step towards conference planning. The booked venue included an auditorium with a capacity of 100 to accommodate all delegates during opening and closing sessions and also during common keynote addresses. Two small meeting rooms with a capacity of 25 each were also blocked to run parallel tracks. As per the payment norms of the venue, the conference organizers thus paid for 150 heads but actually used it only for 64 registered delegates.

Case B, as typical of any physical conference, offered tea breaks, lunches and a conference dinner to all delegates. In addition, taxi services, greetings and escorting of the guests, technical support staff in meeting rooms etc. were some of the critical services and expenses on the days of the conference. None of these services were applicable to case A. Though the organizers could go creative in arranging virtual breakout sessions, they intentionally kept it without frills and fancies till they have enough confidence in their ability in engaging and entertaining virtual people without losing the seriousness of discussion topics.

Number of submissions in the case A was much below that in the case B, however, the absentia in case A was nil as against around 12% in case B. Case B had three parallel tracks. As a result, the presenters in any parallel session did not get more than 20-25 attendees. In contrast, case A had single track and at least 30-35 persons were attending the virtual session at any time and created a rich forum for interaction. Case A received submissions from a wide range of countries across Asia, Europe and US, with no two submissions coming from the same country. Demography of the contributing authors in case B was skewed with 70% of the contributing authors belonging to India, the country of the host institution and another 14% were from USA and Latin America, which were the region of the partner institution.

KEY OBSERVATIONS AND DISCUSSIONS

Perceived Deterrents of the Virtual Conference

Looking through the conventional lens, one may note two major deterrents to the success of the virtual conference under discussion (i.e., case A explained in previous section). One is the absence of face to face (physical or at least video based) interaction and second, low participation. How-ever, analyzing the context from contemporary viewpoint, actually these deterrents worked in favor of the conference.

The conference organizers in case A intentionally chose it to be a synchronous audio conference as against the standard expectation of an audio-video conference. This was more of a business decision to counterfeit the bandwidth constraint that participants in many countries face even today. The aim of the organizers was to keep the technology requirements minimal so that an individual with a PC, microphone, speakers and broadband Internet connection could also join. As a result, the otherwise seemingly conservative mode of interaction actually helped in smooth run of the conference deliberations devoid of any technical glitches such as lost connection, cramped visuals or unsynchronized audio and video.

The low number of submissions in case A may be attributed to two reasons – first, being a new conference without any backing of established physical institution or research association. However, this factor was common for both the conferences. Second, the mindset of the universally accepted supremacy of physical interactions over the virtual interactions may have been a deterrent. As evident from some of the queries received by the organizers, many potential authors were not clear about the meaning of a virtual conference, as they explicitly enquired about the location. A group of perspective attendees (non-authors) even requested for invitation letters to get their visa processed indicating the general lack of understanding around the conduct of a virtual conference.

Debate and to an extent, pessimism around the suitability of technology based interactions has been a frequent phenomenon in literature. Nevertheless, there has been an availability of optimistic literature as well. An exploratory study conducted in late nineties comparing the effectiveness of virtual teams with the face to face teams reported, "While face to face teams reported greater satisfaction with group interaction process, the exchange of information was no more effective than in virtual teams" (Warkentin, 1997, p. 987). The study quoted Zack (1993) suggesting that computer mediated communication "while being less interactive is more appropriate for communicating within an established context." These observations were well supported by case A as one witnessed the focused discussions and richness of content in the virtual conference no less than those in the physical conference. Warkentin (1997) also anticipated that the relevance of web based conferencing will grow as corporate intranets become more widespread for intra-organizational communications. More recent studies (Flowers & Gregson, 2011; Chauhan & Chauhan, 2011) indicate the already growing trend of virtual exhibitions and events being adopted by business organizations, thus providing evidence that the decade old optimism is becoming a reality.

Because technology acceptance needs cultural change as much as it needs maturity and sophistication of relevant tools and technology, online conduct of the conferencing stage is bound to take some time for mass acceptance at a level comparable with physical conferences. Nevertheless, the scenario is expected to only improve with time. As per a recent study, over 60% early adopters of virtual conferencing use it for recreational purposes, while around 50% of them use it at work for brainstorming and idea generation (Navo, Navo, & Carmel, 2011). According to Navo et al., "those who currently use virtual worlds for entertainment — and are satisfied with the experience — are more likely to use them for work" (Navo, Navo, & Carmel, 2011, p. 17).

More recent trend of the rising number and growing membership of online social networking sites is an indicator of the increasing acceptance of collaborative web tools as a way to communicate and bridge geographical distances. Acceptance of such tools has an individual and a social pattern as well suggesting that virtual conferencing may be able to address a new audience as evident from the demographic analysis of case A and B. Marshall et al. (2009) reported the cultural patterns in adoption of online social ties suggesting countries with collectivist cultures having far more likelihood of having online friends who never met before.

Therefore, low initial participation in a virtual conference should be seen rather optimistically. The adoption of interactivity tools, ranging from asynchronous emails to real-time, synchronous video conferences and now virtual worlds has been on the rise over the past two decades. Another study conducted by Brown (2011) reports that for young people, relationships made in virtual space can be just as powerful and meaningful as those formed in the real world. The study also reveals that as the elderly become more comfortable with the Internet, they will increasingly turn to alternative spaces, such as virtual worlds, to find company or meet people with similar interests (p. 30). Shen, Huang, Chu, and Liao (2011) suggest that "factors influencing interpersonal attraction in the real world would also similarly influence interpersonal relationships in the virtual community" (p. 52); and virtual communities provide both cognitive/utilitarian functions e.g., seeking information, solving problems and affective/emotional functions e.g., social interactions (p. 64).

Education sector has not been among the front runners in technology adoption, so adoption of virtual conferences for research may also be anticipated as a slow phenomenon, nevertheless this is a phenomenon that is expected to grow with time as virtual interactions become a part of the normal life. It is thus worthwhile to overcome the perceived inhibitions and look at the possible benefits that one can derive by organizing and/or attending virtual conferences.

Potential Benefits of Virtual Conferences

As explained in the previous section, a top level view of benefits of virtual conferences suggests cost cut, speed, agility and continuity of interactions beyond time and space as the fundamental advantages for organizers as well as participants.

Though a pure online or virtual conference can result in immediate saving of time and cost, exact benefits that one may derive from the use of virtual interactions are largely dependent on the tool-task mix that one creates. Pure online/blended conferences can attract participants from distant as well as remote locations, who may not be able to physically travel to another country due to financial constraints or for more stringent reasons such as border securities and visa regulations. In pre-conferencing stage, the organizers and participants can break the ice by joining the online conference community forum. Speakers can attract more participation by sharing a preview of their talk. Delegates can make informed choice of sessions that may interest them – much before the conference actually begins. Furthermore, participants may significantly save on time, cost and effort of travelling, if the conference meeting is held online. Even if they miss a presentation either due to their total absence or because of attending a parallel track, one can always catch up later with the missed presentations, provided the conference proceedings are recorded.

Baldwin (2011) notes that most conferences have not yet invested in social media because the payoff isn't obvious. He further suggests that presenters who cannot make it to the conference can use conference blog as a way to promote their existing work or even the current work that they were unable to present. Research communities can evolve as a result of the online post conferencing activities, resulting in continuity of interactions on relevant research issues.

Conference organizers can reengineer the entire process leading to improved efficiency and effectiveness of resources and outcomes. The focus of the organizers' attention can be shifted to enriching the quality of interaction than the quality of rooms and food. In case A under discussion, organizers saved approximately 15 weeks of elapsed time on account of the publishing process of the printed proceedings involving a vendor. Though many conferences have now shifted to a

media (CD or flash drive) based proceedings, this option also needs additional time depending on the third party involvement. One near possibility is to replace the formal book format of proceedings with a more interactive audio/video form of proceedings. Online conferences can help reduce the overall cycle time even further. As attendees do not need buffer time to work for visa/invitation letters, online conferencing stage can start soon after the review decisions are frozen.

Conferences adopting peer reviews can use online discussions and voting mechanisms for reviewers during planning stage to make the review process faster and more effective. In conferencing/post-conferencing stage, participants' feedback may be used as a parameter to identify quality index as well as satisfaction index. Use of social networks and collaborative tools can help bring in agility and much more of customization for any conference. In the long run, these tools can also help organizers achieve the much needed recognition for providing a continuous forum for the thinkers.

As paid registration is usually the norm for conferences, participants often seek sponsorship from their employer or other funding agencies. Thus, while academic institutions wish to have their academic staff participating in conferences, budgetary and time constraints often become a deterrent restricting the number of conferences one can be permitted to attend in a year. Conferences can enable less costly (or free) options by applying judicious mix of online tools, and achieving economies of scale. For participants making virtual presentations, they do not incur expense on venue, travel and food, thus the cost of registration for online participants can magically drop and the conference organization may pass the whole/part of this cost advantage to attendees. Such a slashed cost of registration may be seen as a boon particularly for students and for economically weaker institutions/nationalities. Institutions that maintain norms for the number of sponsored conferences allowed per person per year may start looking at allowing a higher number of conferences by mixing online and physical modes while retaining their expense limits and still getting higher research output. In fact, with proper blending of tools, one can arrive at flexible pricing with reduced cost of conferencing and add-on cost for added services during pre and post conferencing stage for providing extra mileage option to participants. Not to forget, pure online conferences are environment friendly and thus are in the interest of the society at large.

CONCLUSION

Conference is a key form of social networking and collaboration among academia and research community as well as a critical part of research budgets of higher educational institutions. While quality and quantity of participants, and continuity of a conference are the key to its success; time, cost and logistics handling are also the critical issues that confront conference organizers as well as attendees. A typical conference involves planning, pre-conferencing, conferencing and post-conferencing stages. Though, most of the conferences today use IT during planning and pre-conferencing stages, use of IT during the conferencing stage (i.e., the actual meeting hours) is still in limited pockets.

For the purpose of this paper, conferences are termed as physical, virtual or blended based on whether they conduct the conferencing stage i.e., conference meeting hours in a traditional face to face mode, through use of online tools such as audio-video conferencing; or through mixed mode adoption of face to face and online interactions. With the help of a comparative case study of a physical and a virtual conference, this paper suggests that the virtual research conferences enable a much leaner and agile process thus demanding lesser resources on the part of organizers as well as participants with no less effective interactivity. It illustrates significant time and cost savings, as

well as widely distributed global participation as the immediate direct benefits for virtual conference organizers and attendees.

Even though the virtual conference under discussion received lesser number of paper submissions than those in the physical conference under study, no difference has been observed in the quality of interactions. This phenomenon of slow adoption seems to draw from the perceived supremacy of face to face interactions and the technological constraints associated with online interactions; as has been already observed and documented for domains such as e-commerce and e-learning. Nevertheless, the increasing adoption pattern and promises that a virtual research conference brings to all stakeholders makes a good business case for hosting as well as attending virtual research conferences. Educational institutes that sponsor scholars to attend conferences may review their norms and encourage a mix of physical and virtual conferences to improve research output in the same or reduced cost. Conference organizers may aim towards hosting multiple conferences in a year blended with online publication opportunities and social networks to enhance their impact on research and community development. Software service providers may consider offering integrated conferencing services encompassing conferencing platforms, virtual worlds, conference management systems and social networks.

The data for this case analysis has been gathered through direct observation, review of emails and statistics as well as through interactions with the key members of the organizing teams thus satisfying the needs of triangulation and establishing confidence.

Limitations and Directions for Further Research

Being a case based analysis, the major limitation of this paper may be viewed in terms of statistical generalizability. In addition, the scope of the selected cases is limited to research conferences in the field of global management and IT, and may not be applicable to regional conferences, research conferences in other streams which may have audience that is not technology-ready; and more importantly to business conferences which are not woven around the call for paper and author submissions. This study does not include virtual world based research conferences. Such a study may be taken as another research agenda.

Further research investigations are recommended to empirically investigate the perceptions and experience of the key stake holders of a conference notably authors, organizers, sponsoring institutions, participants and research communities with respect to virtual conferences. Immediate and long term benefits as well as constraints reported in this paper also need to be empirically investigated. More context specific studies are suggested to help understand various patterns such as the type of audience, quality of interaction, progress of research agenda and continuity of relationship enabled through virtual conferences, particularly when the post-conferencing stage is also activated through social media or other relevant technologies. Comparisons may also be drawn on the effectiveness of audio-video based conferences with those based of virtual worlds.

REFERENCES

Al-Fedaghi, S. (2007). Conferences under scrutiny. *Communications of the ACM, 50*(7), 123–126. doi:10.1145/1272516.1272543.

Bajec, P. (n.d.). *How to organize a conference – Step by step manual*. Retrieved July 24, 2011, from http://www.iapss.org/downloads/publications/iapss_conference_manual.pdf

Baldwin, T. (2011, January 4). *Making your authors' social networks work for your conference* [Web log post].

Bellefeuille, J., & Salem, S. (2004). Reflecting on IEMC 2003. *EMS Newsletter, 54*(1). Retrieved November 26, 2010, from http://www.ewh.ieee.org/soc/ems/EMnewsletter/04Q1.pdf

Benbasat, I., Goldstein, D. K., & Mead, M. (1987). The case research strategy in studies of information systems. *Management Information Systems Quarterly, 11*(3), 369–386. doi:10.2307/248684.

Brown, A. (2011). Relationships, community, and identity in the new virtual society. *The Futurist, 45*(2), 29–43.

Chauhan, R., & Chauhan, R. (2011). Collaborative virtual business events- Opportunities and challenges. In Malik, K., & Choudhary, P. K. (Eds.), *Business organizations and collaborative Web: Practices, strategies and patterns* (pp. 243–259). Hershey, PA: IGI Global. doi:10.4018/978-1-60960-581-0.ch015.

Cooper, D. J., & Morgan, W. (2008). Case study research in accounting. *Accounting Horizons, 22*(2), 159–178. doi:10.2308/acch.2008.22.2.159.

Ellram, L. M. (1996). The use of the case study method in logistics research. *Journal of Business Logistics, 17*(2), 93–138.

Flowers, A. A., & Gregson, K. (2011). Virtual worlds for collaborative meetings. In Malik, K., & Choudhary, P. K. (Eds.), *Business organizations and collaborative Web: Practices, strategies and patterns* (pp. 220–242). Hershey, PA: IGI Global. doi:10.4018/978-1-60960-581-0.ch014.

Gichora, N. N., Fatumo, S. A., Ngara, M. V., Chelbat, N., Ramdayal, K., & Opap, K. B. et al. (2010). Ten simple rules for organizing a virtual conference—Anywhere. *PLoS Computational Biology, 6*(2), e1000650. doi:10.1371/journal.pcbi.1000650 PMID:20195548.

Goliath. (2009). *Sick of canned keynote speeches? Try an unconference*. Retrieved August 5, 2011, from http://goliath.ecnext.com/coms2/gi_0199-13627137/Sick-of-canned-keynote-speeches.html

Hildreth, W. B., & Woodrum, M. A. (2009). Mapping a field's development: 20 years of ABFM conferences. *Public Budgeting & Finance, 29*(3), 15–27. doi:10.1111/j.1540-5850.2009.00934.x.

International Online Conference (IOC). (2011). *Going mobile online.* Retrieved June 10, 2011, from http://www.internationalonlineconference. org

Kaser, D. (2008). Just go. *Information Today, 25*(6), 1.

King, R. (2008, June 5). Virtual conferences' home advantage. *Business Week Online*, p. 14.

Marshall, B., Choi, J., El-Shinnaway, M. M., North, M., Svensson, L., & Wang, S. et al. (2009). Online and offline social ties of social network website users: An exploratory study in eleven societies. *Journal of Computer Information Systems, 50*(1), 54–64.

McCormick, J. P., & Pinderhughes, D. (2009, February 7). Promotion and tenure process as an exercise in strategic thinking. In *Proceedings of the Workshop at the American Political Science Association Teaching and Learning Conference*, Baltimore, MD. Retrieved July 27, 2011, from http://www.equity.psu.edu/sfm/docs/promo_tenure_09.pdf

Meetingsnet. (2008). Pull off a productive web conference. *Association Meetings, 20*(6), 39. Retrieved August 4, 2011, from http://meetingsnet. com/association-meetings/pull-productive-web-conference

Navo, S., Navo, D., & Carmel, E. (2011). Unlocking the business potential of virtual worlds. *MIT Sloan Management Review, 52*(3), 13–17.

Patterson, D. A. (2004). The health of research conferences and the dearth of big idea papers. *Communications of the ACM, 47*(12), 23–24. doi:10.1145/1035134.1035153.

Potvin, J. H. (1983). Planning and organizing an annual conference. *IEEE Transactions on Personal Communication, 26*(3), 123-152.

Schroeder, L., O'Leary, R., Jones, D., & Poocharoen, O. (2004). Routes to scholarly success in public administration: Is there a right path? *Public Administration Review, 64*(1), 92–103. doi:10.1111/j.1540-6210.2004.00349.x.

Shen, Y. C., Huang, C. Y., Chu, C. H., & Liao, H. C. (2010). Virtual community loyalty: An interpersonal-interaction perspective. *International Journal of Electronic Commerce, 15*(1), 49–73. doi:10.2753/JEC1086-4415150102.

Vardi, M. Y. (2009). Conferences vs. journals in computing research. *Communications of the ACM, 52*(5). doi:10.1145/1506409.1506410 PMID:21218176.

Warkentin, M. E., Sayeed, L., & Hightower, R. (1997). Virtual teams versus face-to-face teams: An exploratory study of a web-based conference system. *Decision Sciences, 28*(4), 975–996. doi:10.1111/j.1540-5915.1997.tb01338.x.

Woolard, C. (2011). Virtual now part of show. *B to B, 96*(4).

Zack, M. H. (1993). Interactivity and communication mode choice in ongoing management groups. *Information Systems Research, 4*(3), 207–239. doi:10.1287/isre.4.3.207.

This work was previously published in the International Journal of Virtual Communities and Social Networking, Volume 3, Issue 4, edited by Subhasish Dasgupta, pp. 32-45, copyright 2011 by IGI Publishing (an imprint of IGI Global).

Chapter 16
Retaining and Exploring Digital Traces:
Towards an Excavation of Virtual Settlements

Demosthenes Akoumianakis
Department of Applied Information Technology
& Multimedia, Technological Education
Institution of Crete, Greece

George Vlachakis
Department of Applied Information Technology
& Multimedia, Technological Education
Institution of Crete, Greece

Giannis Milolidakis
Department of Applied Information Technology
& Multimedia, Technological Education
Institution of Crete, Greece

Nikolas Karadimitriou
Department of Applied Information Technology
& Multimedia, Technological Education
Institution of Crete, Greece

Giorgos Ktistakis
Department of Applied Information Technology & Multimedia, Technological Education Institution
of Crete, Greece

ABSTRACT

The present work rests and elaborates on the assumption that social technologies are increasingly turned into computer-mediated virtual settlements, thereby allowing the excavation of a variety of enacted cyber-phenomena such as ad hoc online ensembles, informal social networks and virtual communities, on the grounds of "digital" traces or remains. In this vein, the authors motivate and present a method for virtual excavations that is tightly coupled to a transformational technology such as knowledge visualization. The analytical and explanatory value of the method is assessed using two case studies addressing representative genres of social technologies, namely web sites augmented with social plug-ins and social networking services. Analysis reveals intrinsic aspects of "digital" traces and remains, the form they take in today's social web and the means through which they can be excavated and transformed to useful information. It turns out that such virtual excavations, when organized and conducted carefully,

DOI: 10.4018/978-1-4666-4022-1.ch016

can be of benefit to enterprises, service organizations and public sector institutions. In addition, their tight coupling with knowledge visualization eliminates extensive data analysis as much of this work can be done using the visualization. On the other hand, and depending on the size of digital trace data, the choice of visualizations and the underlying toolkit are of paramount importance.

1. INTRODUCTION

The emergence of Web 2.0, the rapid adoption of social computing and the supporting technologies such as blogging and micro-blogging platforms, social commenting plug-ins, etc., turn users from passive information consumers into active content producers. This is mainly achieved through a variety of opportunities for sharing users' own content, commenting on articles submitted by others or responding to peers' contributions (Kim, Jeong, & Lee, 2010). In many cases, users may not have pre-existent relationships, may not know each other and may never interact again (Gochenour, 2006). Yet, such recurrent co-engagements amongst ambient affiliates frequently materialize into social bonds and a kind of "knowing" through co-practicing. Recent scholarship, although acknowledging the possibilities offered by social technologies and platforms to facilitate a variety of cyber-formations (Blanchard & Markus, 2004; Jacovi et al., 2011; Kim et al., 2010; Zhao, Grasmuck, & Martin, 2008), does not provide sufficient details on core features embedded in technologies and driving their distributed (re-) organizing capacity. As a result, it is not clear how new capabilities such as increased information and social connectivity amongst users, are implicated by technology-inscribed affordances such as user profiling mechanisms, moderating functions or simulations. At the same time, it becomes increasingly evident that intrinsic aspects of profile management and moderation, not only implicate new patterns of use (for instance multiple identity management across virtual settings), but also manifest a wealth of cultural knowledge about users. Consequently, there is a need to study systematically what it is that enables or constrains configurations of people, artifacts and social relations under different regimes of sharing and what technology features form pre-requisites for an improved understanding of enacted social formations and their practices in virtual settings.

The present work seeks to shed light into these questions by advancing a method that allows "digging" into technology and assessing its cooperative and inter-cooperative capability through the analysis of digital trace data. In effect, our approach follows the footsteps of virtual excavation (Jones, 1997); a concept introduced to provide insights into enacted phenomena such as virtual communities by assessing "digital" remains of online human endeavors. Digital trace data can be defined as:

… records of activity (trace data) undertaken through an online information system (thus, digital); A trace is a mark left as a sign of passage; it is recorded evidence that something has occurred in the past. For trace data, the system acts as a data collection tool, providing both advantages and limitations. (Howison, Wiggins, & Crowston, 2011, p. 769)

The definition rests on the assumption that certain (if not all) activities in virtual settings create electronic traces. Then, by working with these traces researchers could re-construct or gain insights into an online setting and the context within which such activities are conducted (Akoumianakis, 2010), just as archaeologists reconstruct and/or gain insights into a past culture by retrieving, working with, indexing and interpreting remains in conventional archaeological settlements (Fahlander & Oestigaard, 2004). The value of such "virtual" excavation is that it creates a "gold mine" of social data, reflecting deeper insights into online discourse, trends in user communities (i.e., opinions, interests and beliefs), prevalent online behaviors, "hidden" knowledge as well as how these are socially constituted and emerging through time. A pre-requisite however is the technology's-embedded capability to extract, analyze and ascribe meaning to such data which otherwise remain bytes of code. For this purpose, recent work exploits a variety of methods including graph-based techniques and algorithms (Lin, Sundaram, Chi, Tatemura, & Tseng, 2006; Zhou & Davis, 2007), social network analysis (Daniel & Schwier, 2010) and advanced knowledge visualization (Akoumianakis, 2011) to account for digital traces and remains. Using this lens and concrete case studies that reveal not only commonalities across regimes of sharing user-generated content, but also key differences, we attempt to qualify virtual excavations in an effort to gain insight into cyber-formations enacted online and the features that distinguish their genre.

The paper is structured as follows. The next section provides a reflection on the state of the art by examining related works and establishing the theoretical background and baseline. Then, an approach to virtual excavation is detailed in terms of basic steps, preparatory activities and cursory actions. To illustrate the approach, two case studies are discussed concentrating on prominent issues and findings. The paper is concluded with a summary and a brief indication of on-going and future work.

2. BACKGROUND AND MOTIVATION

2.1. Related Works

Digital traces of computer-mediated human collaboration and online co-engagement represent a valuable resource of information, as they reveal emergent configurations of people, artifacts and social relations in virtual settings. Over the years, they have been used for a variety of purposes ranging from ethnographic analysis of computer-mediated communication (Paccagnella, 1997), business intelligence (Jourdan, Rainer, & Marshall, 2008) and social network analysis (Jacovi et al., 2011). In today's social web, digital traces manifest themselves as "digital" remains representing comments to articles, responses to another user's contribution, tagging of items, opinion statements or trajectories of online user exchanges. The capacity to locate and process these remains creates new insights, not only for individual users, but also for wider communities such as enterprises, industry sectors and government. This is due to the form of digital traces which increasingly stimulates thinking on what collaborators do online by relating the means of interacting and socializing online to certain enacted social accomplishments in the execution of a joined agenda. In this manner, it is made possible to disentangle the relationship between features embedded in technology (i.e., user profiles and search engines), the way in which they are recurrently appropriated by people (i.e., updates in user profiles, search terms used) and the resulting emergent cyber-phenomena (i.e., online ensembles, virtual communities, cliques, etc.).

Most of the research on digital trace data focuses either on computational techniques that ascribe certain capabilities to technologies, or the use of trace data for specific purposes such as business intelligence or the identification of online formations of various types (i.e., virtual communities, on-line ensembles and cliques). The first category includes techniques such as crawling, meta-search engines and public Application Programming Interfaces (APIs). Crawling is the process of compiling searchable domain-specific document collections by exploiting structural information embedded in the Web which allows identification of additional, potentially appropriate resources. For instance, (Efimova & Hendrick, 2005) use crawlers that take advantage of blogrolls, RSS, weblog conversations, indicators of events, etc. to identify traces. Web crawlers follow links found in one page to additional pages and additional links. Sometimes, these crawlers are guided by algorithms that assess the potential relevance of new links before fetching the pages. Examples of the use of structural information to evaluate resources include PageRank (Brin & Page, 1998), which uses in-link analysis to rank results, and the HITS algorithm (Kleinberg, 1999), which identifies hubs and authorities.

Meta-searching is intended to facilitate access to and merging of information from disparate sources. The basic concept is to combine results from multiple search engines into a unified collection. This is typically achieved by processing queries from users, formatting the requests and passing them on to other search engines (Meng, Yu, & Liu, 2002). Consequently, the primary challenge for meta-search tools amounts to integrating local systems that use different indexing techniques and query types, discovering knowledge about component search engines, developing effective merging methods, and deciding where to place the software components of a meta-search engine.

More recent developments and the increasing recognition of the importance of sharing, interoperability and openness to third parties or platforms (Bodle, 2011) have pushed service providers to provide dedicated Application Programming Interfaces (APIs), thereby offering standardized protocols for accessing event-based data occurring over a period of time in a designated virtual setting. This trend is increasingly evident across a range of social networking services including Facebook, the Twitter micro-blogging platform and video-sharing services such as YouTube. This time, the concept is to standardize (in a protocol) and make available for third parties a variety of data ranging from data logs and interaction patterns to statistical evidence of online user activities.

Regarding the use of digital trace data, the available scholarship reports on applications in business intelligence, analysis of user behavior,

the identification of social formations such as ad hoc online ensembles, virtual communities and cliques, but also (non-social) aggregations of densely connected web pages or documents (usually referred to as or web communities). For instance, Marshall et al. (2004) examine analysis of blogs for business intelligence purposes. Benevenuto et al. (2009) use digital traces to analyzing spamming and content polluting behavior in online sharing services such as YouTube. Efimova and Hendrick (2005) rely on blogrolls, RSS, weblog conversations, and event indicators to identify user communities in blogosphere. Gruzd, Wellman, and Takhteyev (2011) in their recent study of Twitter report how they used its API (http://apiwiki.twitter.com) to automatically retrieve a variety of data about inter-tweet connectivity, such as who is connected to whom, who replies to whom, etc., to assess individual communities. Harrison's (2009) analysis of SecondLife examines the cultural artifacts users leave behind as they become engaged in play.

It is worth noting that depending on the scope of the inquiry, the techniques used for analyzing digital traces may also vary. A popular sociological methodology used widely is Social Network Analysis (Wasserman & Faust, 1994). It can be used to reveal patterns in social data and discover the underlying social structure in online ensembles. The three major types of analyses in the Social Network Analysis tradition include topological analysis (Albert & Barabási, 2002), centrality analysis (Freeman, 1979; Xu & Chen, 2005) and community analysis (Bulters & de Rijke, 2007; Lakshmanan & Oberhofer, 2010; Lin et al., 2006; Liu, Wang, Li, & Shi, 2011). Other useful methods discussed in the literature include graph-based techniques and algorithms (Lin et al., 2006; Zhou & Davis, 2007), content analysis (Efimova & Hendrick, 2005) and knowledge visualization (Akoumianakis, 2011).

2.2. Consolidation

Although these works share commonalities, they do not treat digital traces uniformly or even consistently. Furthermore, the results are not comparable, while certain validity issues are seldom addressed (Howison et al., 2011). Consequently, there is a gap due to the lack of a systematic method for managing digital traces and the broad range of related issues such where these traces reside, how are they compiled and what sense can be made of them. In the past there have been attempts to systematize the study of cyber-phenomena enacted in virtual settings, but these efforts addressed only parts of the challenge. One early attempt was Jones's (1997) theory of virtual settlements where, by drawing parallels with contemporary archaeology, the author defines the space where digital remains are retained and the conditions under which virtual communities can flourish. Jones conceived virtual settlements as online computer-mediated spaces that support (1) a minimum level of interactivity; (2) a variety of communicators (3) a common-public-space that hosts the communicators' interaction; and (4) a minimum level of sustained membership. These four conditions are also treated as pre-requisites for virtual communities. Jones' theory was received favorably by researchers and recent works build on and extend the basic concept by considering settlements other than computer-mediated communication spaces (Blanchard & Markus, 2004; Chin & Chignell, 2006; Efimova & Hendrick, 2005; Gruzd et al., 2011; Hewitt & Forte, 2006; Zhao et al., 2008; Zhou & Davis, 2007).

Nevertheless, the theory of virtual settlements makes certain assumptions that need not hold in today's social web. Firstly, the theory was explicitly aimed at analyzing a particular type of cyber-formation, namely virtual communities of people engaging in computer-mediated communication. Thus, it may not be sufficient for other type online ensembles that emerge as a result of business- or practice-oriented engagements. Secondly, there is no conclusive evidence that the four conditions defined by Jones are sufficient to trace communities that span boundaries, either thematic or technical. In fact the theory offers no insights into how to define a settlement's boundaries (Liu, 1999). Finally, Jones theory did not provide a strong definition of digital trace data and how these are created within a virtual settlement. As a result, artifacts manipulated, created, or otherwise experienced by users may be dismissed or underserved (Harrison, 2009).

The present research seeks to fill this gap by advancing a proposal for working with digital traces in virtual settlements by passing shortcomings of earlier efforts. In this vein, our method is intended to provide a structured, systematic, reusable and extensible instrument for organizing virtual excavations of computer-mediated spaces for a variety of purposes. Phrased differently, the method is not limited to studying only certain outcomes, such as for instance the identification of virtual communities. Rather, it is conceived as a general-purpose instrument that would be equally valid for gathering business intelligence, studying trends in service industries such as health care as well as making sense of cyber-formations such as online ensembles, practice-oriented arrangements and other temporary and informal digital configurations of people, artifacts and social relations. As for expected benefits, such a method could facilitate comparative studies across domains but also in depth analysis of "hidden" practices based on a set of well-defined criteria.

3. METHODOLOGY

3.1. Problem Statement

Our analysis thus far is grounded on the belief that digital traces do not offer only records of what is actually done with the technology at hand, but also useful insights into the user's individual or collective knowledge (Gruzd et al., 2011; Jacovi et al., 2011). Then, a challenging problem is revealing such knowledge and making it intelligible for different purposes (i.e., business intelligence, identification of virtual communities, assessment of online social networks, etc.). Guided by the need to systematize the way in which digital traces are extracted, compiled and managed, we have engaged in a variety of efforts to investigate intrinsic properties of computer-mediated spaces and the provisions made for digital trace data analysis. By linking these efforts to social theories (Jones, 1997) and contrasting them to contemporary archaeological inquiries, we have conceived a protocol for managing digital trace data and transforming them from bytes of code to valuable information and knowledge. Such a protocol establishes a form of virtual excavation grounded on four basic steps:

1. Identifying the settlement or settlements by designating where the excavation will take place (CMC medium, social web site, blog, social networking service, etc.); in case of multiple settlements, analysts should make careful and informed choices to guarantee quality of the retrieved data,

2. Locating the settlements' thematic boundaries, thus designating which traces are relevant, and the tactics of boundary crossing (in case of multiple virtual settlements),

3. Making the necessary provisions for retrieving data from the virtual settlement by studying (possible) limitations of the public API (if exists) or alternative strategies to collect data,

4. Devising suitable representations for digital remains so as to allow informative insights, pattern discovery, exploratory reviews, querying, etc.

Figure 1 presents the architectural design of the system developed to excavate through the virtual settlements. The system consists of four parts. The connection layer implements the desirable data access strategy (e.g., the public API) in order to collect the data. Data from the connection layer are automatically pushed to the data layer which is responsible for removing any

Figure 1. System architecture

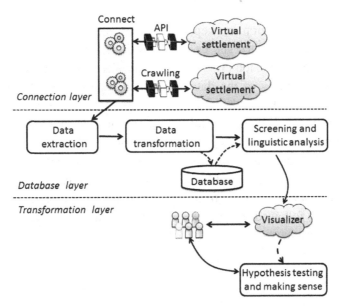

damaged or unwanted data elements and, in the case of multiple virtual settlements, for defining the boundary crossing tactics. Once the data layer's process is completed, the database layer stores the retained data in a relational database. Finally, the transformation layer compiles the appropriate visualizations and facilitates exploratory inquiries. Each system layer depends only in the previous layer.

3.2. Research Design

For the purposes of this study and in order to test the concept of virtual excavations and the system's architectural pattern, we selected two typical settings for detailed study. Each setting presents a different case in terms of technology genre. Both however, qualify as virtual settlements. The first case focuses on a web site in the news sector which is the online version (online magazine or webzine) of a widely known American printed weekly news magazine. The web site relies on an online commenting platform to facilitate user exchanges and social interaction. The second case examines a popular social networking service platform, namely Facebook. For both cases, we studied in detail their structure and embedded features as well as the provisions for extracting digital traces. To this end, the authors registered with the systems, but their contribution was kept minimum to avoid bias in data retained and extracted. For each case, certain inclusion criteria were devised to guarantee validity of the data set. In terms of boundaries, we selected thematic boundaries to constrain the valid sets of digital traces. Thus, for the online magazine we focused on pages in the thematic domain of health while for Facebook our search was constrained to online groups active in four types of cancer. Apart from these deviations, both cases followed strictly the four steps outlined in the previous section.

Regarding step (4) which is concerned with devising suitable representations, we aimed for a set of visualizations that would be case-neutral. Specifically, guided by relevant scholarship, we designed a standard set of layout managers on top of the Prefuse toolkit (Heer, Card, & Landay, 2005) to convey structural properties of online ensembles, member connectivity, narrative content analysis and animation for reconstructing elements of online engagements. The specific techniques recruited include: (1) a version of tree maps to provide a tentative classification of online remains (Johnson & Shneiderman, 1991); (2) a hybrid layout policy for classifying users' contribution in social zones (Perer & Shneiderman, 2006); (3) searchable word clouds for narrative analysis; and (4) animation-based reconstruction of the historical evolution of key phrases in user narrations (Cui et al., 2010; Rivadeneira, Gruen, Muller, & Millen, 2007). These were designed so as to be compatible with the relational database schema retaining digital traces irrespective of their host environment. Moreover, the visualizations were implemented using the same toolkit to ensure fairness in the performance and the results of the layout management policies.

It is important to note that with the design briefly reviewed above, the need for data analysis, coding or data validity checking were either minimized or eliminated. Instead, we relied on visualization properties, such as use of colors, node size and location, connection depth and social zones/clusters to bring to the surface aggregate formations and their relative structural properties. Animation was used with care and only for the purpose of reconstructing a past reality that extends across relatively large time intervals. Finally, dynamic querying was a feature implemented in most of the visualization to enable quick exploratory reviews and query refinement.

4. RESULTS

4.1. Setting 1: Online Magazine

This case presents experience with a popular online magazine. For purposes of anonymity we refer to the online magazine as NewsTime. Following the four steps described earlier the virtual excavation of online NewsTime is summarized as follows.

4.1.1. Virtual Settlement

NewsTime meets Jones's criteria, thus it can be considered as a virtual settlement, because it enables users to interact with other users and to contribute by commenting to an article. Users are able to create an account and use this account to submit their contribution (e.g., by posting a comment). By visiting the site, it is straightforward to establish not only records of multiple different users submitting their contribution, but also to confirm that there is recurrent engagement. Specifically, online activity is public and all users have access to it. Consequently, NewsTime web space acts as the meeting point for these users.

4.1.2. Settlement's Boundaries

For the purposes of the present analysis, the virtual excavation is limited to the health related articles of NewsTime which are hosted in a separate space on the magazine's website. These are divided into sub-categories such as addiction, cancer, drugs, etc. We relied on this classification to index articles as it makes the results more informative and potentially comparable to the second case study on online cancer groups. Another reason for selecting the specific domain is the increasing community interest on health-related aspects. We visited the health section of the online magazine on August 29, 2011 and we searched for all the articles that were published within the last 6 months (from March 1, 2011) and had 10 or more comments.

We found 87 different articles that met the above criteria. Those articles had 5,641 comments made by 3,546 different users.

4.1.3. Data Access Strategy

NewsTime offers no public API for accessing data. Instead, social encounters are facilitated by a social commenting widget named Disqus (http://disqus.com/). This widget allows users to connect by either creating a Disqus account or by using their login information from another platform such as Facebook, Google, Twitter, etc. Although Disqus offers an API, it is not public and is only available for the owners of the web page. Following detailed analysis of the way that Disqus works, an interface to this service was designed to allow retrieval of the publicly available user comments to articles. The data retrieved for each comment were the creation date; the content of the comment; the user and the web presence of the user; and the parent comment. Additionally, a crawler was implemented in order to retrieve information about each article, including the article topic, date of upload, the article title, the profile chosen by users, etc. In our database, we did not store sensitive user information such as names due to ethical issues.

4.1.4. Making Sense of Digital Remains

In order to understand users online activity in NewsTime, several established visualizations were recruited (with suitable extensions as discussed below) to provide meaningful insights to digital remains. Tree maps were used to identify the most popular domains where users post their comments. Figure 2 depicts the domains where most user activity is aggregated. Light blue lines contain the articles from the different domains of the NewsTime health web pages. Articles are represented as squares (yellow thick borders) making up a domain. Each article comprises smaller

Figure 2. Health domains in NewsTime

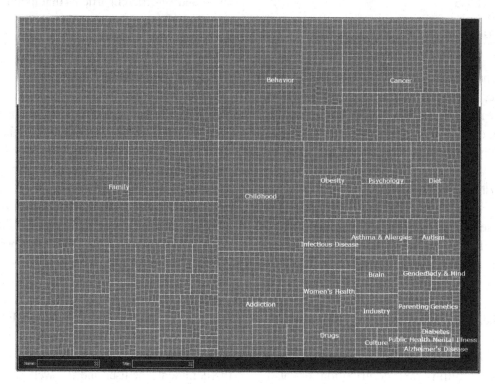

squares (yellow thin borders) representing user comments. A quick review of the visualization can provide insights to the relative online activity for different articles and/or domains. For instance, NewsTime users prefer to discuss about family related articles-issues rather than articles about drugs or psychology.

Using the tree map visualization in a slightly different way it is possible to shed light to other aspects of user activity. For instance, in Disqus a user can select to create an account on Disqus in order to submit her contribution or to select an identity from another service such as Facebook, Twitter, Google account, etc. Figure 3 presents the public profiles users select in order to submit their contributions. The light red squares represent the identity service used by a user. The yellow squares represent the article to which the user contribution took place and the smaller squares represent a user comment. In this visualization

an article may appear many times. At the lower part of the screen, the search mechanism can be used to identify the most common identity service employed in an article or within a domain.

For example, by typing the article's title at the search field, the dynamic display highlights (with pink color) all the comments of that article. In a similar manner, this can be done for each different domain (e.g., "family"). Here, as shown, the Disqus identity service comes first followed by Yahoo identity service. Further details on the user-created content can be obtained by placing the mouse over a comment which triggers a pop up window displaying details such as the user's id and the comment content, the title of the article which contains this comment, etc.

Another useful insight is obtained using the visualization in Figure 4 to make sense of the activity associated with a single article by accounting for interconnected nodes. This is useful as it

Figure 3. User identity services

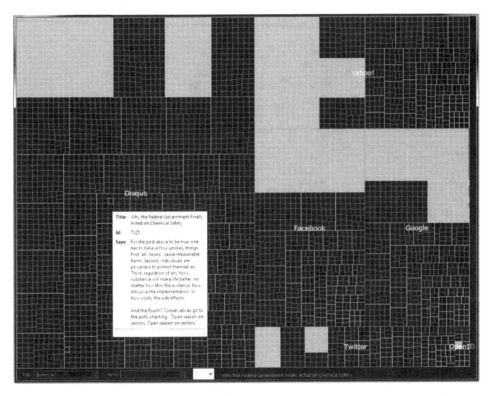

reveals the hierarchical structure of comments in NewsTime online articles and the way in which interconnections of potential interest (i.e., popular article and comments, online cliques or squads) are established. The specific graph uses nodes to represent the page, the comments and the sub-comments while edges are used to depict the relation of the nodes. The root node is the article and every connected node is a user comment. There is a different color tone of grey in each level of the graph. For instance, a comment that is not a response to another comment is coded in light gray color while a leaf is in darker gray. Each comment node contains a text (e.g., "lvl1", "lvl2") indicating its place in the hierarchy. Thus, "lvl1" is a response to the article, "lvl2" is a comment to another comment, and "lvl3" is a response to the response comment and so on and so forth. In the case that the mouse is over a node a pop up window will show up displaying user's id and the content of the comment.

In a similar fashion, Figure 5 displays the activity of all articles (or a collection of articles to be compared) within a graph. This allows us to classify and assess the articles by user responses to comments and thereby identify virtual spaces hosting meaningful social dialog between members. An obvious application of this form of visualization is in exploring topics of current interest (i.e., economic crisis, breast cancer) and the positions taken by members. Finally, it is worth mentioning that the visualizations presented above can be exploited synergistically to provide rich insights across a variety of topics.

4.2. Setting 2: Online Cancer Groups on Facebook

This case study examines social data and exchanges resident within Facebook. The specific scenario is concerned with Facebook groups related to breast cancer (See Acknowledgement). It is interesting

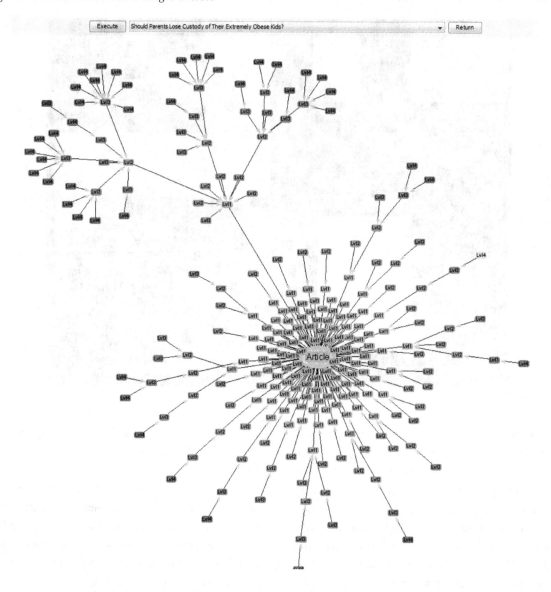

Figure 4. Contribution in a single article

not only because of its thematic focus but also because of the animation-based visualizations that have been developed to make sense of data spanning large periods of time (from 2007 until September 2011).

4.2.1. Virtual Settlement

Facebook meets Jones's criteria as it enables users to interact with other users and to contribute by sharing, posting wall posts, and commenting on

other users' wall posts. Users can create an account which is their web presence within Facebook. In a group, multiple different members can repeatedly submit their contribution, thus maintaining a recurrent record of collaboration. Group activity is public and every Facebook user has access to it. The group's web space is the meeting point of the users. Consequently, Facebook meets the four basic criteria for a virtual settlement.

Figure 5. Activity in multiple articles

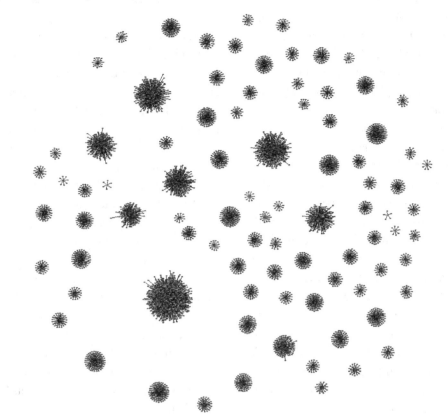

4.2.2. Settlement's Boundaries

Our excavation of Facebook entailed both thematic boundaries and technology-inscribed boundaries. The thematic boundaries were defined by selecting four types of cancer (prostate, breast, lung and colon) and using Facebook's built-in search facilities with the appropriate search terms (i.e., prostate cancer, breast cancer, lung cancer and colon cancer). The search was conducted on September 8, 2011 and returned 2,153 results for all four search terms (i.e., 526, 509, 590 and 528 respectively). 49 of these results represented duplicates in two or more searches. The total number of unique groups resulting from the initial search was 2104. From this set the following were excluded (1) 428 groups, as they were not public and their content was visible only for the group members; (2) 68 groups whose chosen language was not English; (3) 311 groups whose title did not include the search term (e.g., the group titled "support for cancer" was excluded); (4) 2 groups that were not related to cancer; (5) 2 groups addressing multiple types of cancer; and (6) 150 groups with less than 2 participants (<=2). It must be noted that groups with synonyms to the search terms were not excluded. For instance, the group titled "Colorectal Cancer Awareness" was included as a colon cancer group. Following the above inclusion process, the total number of groups constituting our sample was 1,143. For purposes of simplicity, the rest of this section discusses results for a single breast cancer Facebook group with 20,000 members.

4.2.3. Data Access Strategy

Facebook provides open APIs for accessing data retained by its servers. There have been various releases of APIs including Facebook Developer

(August 2006), Facebook Platform (May, 2007), Facebook Connect (May 2008), Open Stream (April 2009), and Open Graph with Instant Personalization (April 2010). Our study relied on data retained and accessed using the most recent release of Facebook Graph API (https://developers.facebook.com/). This API allows retrieval of data about group wall activity such as wall posts, comments, likes and information regarding the users that created that content such as gender. In order to download the wall activity of each eligible group a crawler was designed to store the data in a relational database. The crawler was designed to support the following functionality. For a given group id, it retrieves (using Facebook Graph API) and stores in a relational database the activity of the group. Active users are considered to be those who have had at least one interaction with the group's wall. A user interaction in the group's wall can be a wall post, a comment or a "like." For each activity, several data are captured such as the user who performed the activity, the type of the activity, and the activity's content. Due to ethical issues our database does not store private or otherwise user sensitive information such as names. In order to get all results in one day we had 12 computers running simultaneously our crawler.

4.2.4. Making Sense of Digital Remains

In order to understand user activity, a number of customized visual representations were designed to facilitate complementary views on remains residing in the groups' walls. It is important to note that in all visualizations the data set was subject to inclusion criteria (not presented in this paper) so as to ensure that groups considered satisfy basic conditions. In the course of the excavation, all relevant breast cancer groups were accessed to extract the retained group's wall posts. Wall posts might contain urls, videos, photos, or plain text. Figure 6 presents a tag cloud of what users post on the Facebook's group wall.

This was compiled after applying several filters to exclude meaningless posts from the data set so as to highlight the most popular words. As expected, words such as "cancer" and "breast" are very prominent in the users' commentary. However, the visualization reveals interesting side effects. One of them is the prominent state of the "http" and "www" words in the word cloud. Attempting to understand this state of affairs led us to dig further into the data set to encounter that much of the online traffic is by members advertising products, drugs, protocols, rather than patients.

Figure 6. Tag cloud of group's wall posts

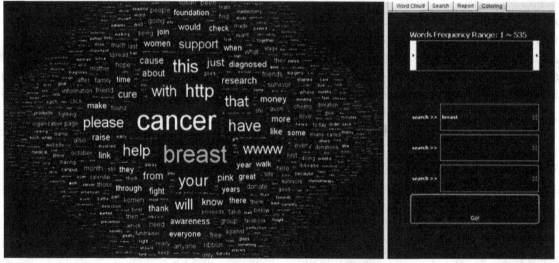

In a similar vein, Figure 7 presents users' contributions on the group's wall. The red node in the center of the graph represents the group. Dark blue nodes are the wall posts. Their size indicates the number of interactions on this post and is proportional to the total number of comments or likes users post under the specific post. The light blue nodes represent the type of contribution i.e., comments and likes of each wall post.

Using these conventions, the primary use of the visualization is in spotting the most popular or heavily responded wall posts.

Other useful findings come out when the analysis focuses on comparative assessments across groups or communities. For instance, Figure 8 provides insights to users' connectivity in relation to their contributions in four different cancer communities, namely breast, prostate, lung

Figure 7. Group's contribution

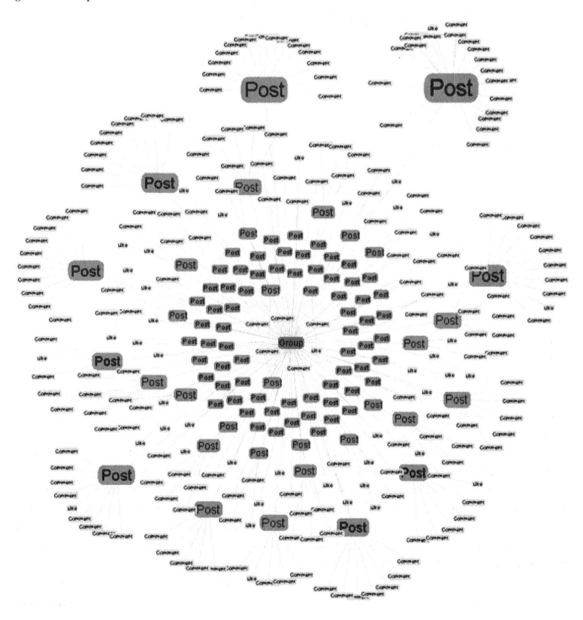

Figure 8. Classifying members' connectivity

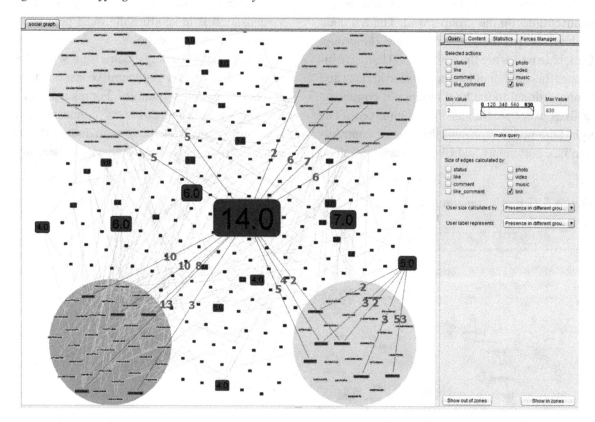

and colon cancer. By selecting specific users, the visualization highlights their total contributions and how they are spread across the four categories of cancer-related groups. It is also possible to further analyze a user's contribution by type of digital trace i.e., comment, posts, likes, etc.

Shifting the focus into what people do in each group, Figure 9 provides historical traces of social interaction in each cancer group across different points in time. This time the word cloud is re-calculated for each group to reveal the state of affairs in relation to selected words such as death, survivor rate, etc. Empirical research can indicate the specific words of interest with either positive or negative connotation, and through the use of size and color, analysts can assess the relative presence of these words within a group or across the four groups. Such analysis can reveal for instance, why breast cancer is reported to be more curable in relation to other types of cancer, why

certain type of activity such as posts with commercial announcements are more popular in certain types of groups where there is heavy load of user activities or the historical interval in which traffic in a certain community exceeds certain limits.

5. DISCUSSION AND CONCLUSION

In this paper, by drawing parallels with archaeological inquiries and re-working key concepts and themes, we have presented a method for virtual excavations of online settlements. At core, this effort is a step in the direction of gaining insights to the type, range and scope of cyber-structures emerging in virtual settlements by working with their "digital" remains. Such digital remains comprise online traces of (or data sets representing) user activities retained by virtual settlements.

Figure 9. Word cloud animation and cancer group activity

Using two case studies of a social web site and a social networking service, we have claimed that key features of such virtual excavations include (1) precise definition of the virtual settlement; (2) demarcation of thematic (or otherwise relevant) boundaries; (3) specification of what constitute digital traces of interest and the provisions necessary to extract them; and (4) techniques for making sense of digital traces. It turns out that the method raises several implications for researchers interested in the social study of computer-mediated spaces.

5.1. Implications

Cyber-archaeological treatments of virtual settlements rely on certain assumptions that distinguish them from contemporary archaeological inquiries.

Firstly, digital traces remain bytes of code until a point that specialized software brings them to light; thus interpretive capacity is bound by the type of tools used to extract, analyze and transform digital remains to a meaningful language. Secondly, online "tells" and their processing raises issues about privacy and security and the way these are inscribed into tools or platforms (Rosenblum, 2007). In the two cases examined in this paper, we relied on digital traces retained by the virtual settlements and exposed to researchers either through public APIs or dedicated interfaces. Nevertheless, there may be traces of interest which are not always released or made available for excavation in the public domain. Consequently, the explanatory value of any virtual excavation is bound by the limits and constraints imposed. Thirdly, virtual archaeological inquiries don't need to reflect a past and distant culture. They may be equally well tuned to disentangle the makings of recent, current or on-going cyber-phenomena. In fact, it is argued that this is precisely the area where virtual excavations of the type proposed in this paper may be mostly useful as a research inquiry in application domains such as business intelligence (Jourdan et al., 2008), e-health campaigns (Akoumianakis, Milolidakis, Akrivos, Panteris, & Ktistakis, 2010), ethnographic studies of Internet (Hine, 2000) and knowledge management (Schultze & Boland, 2000). It stands to argue therefore that virtual excavations need not be constrained by the absence of cultural participants as in the case of contemporary archaeology. Rather, virtual excavations can be designed so as to capitalize on qualitative techniques that bring to the surface currently prevalent views, end user opinion, perceptions, preferences and cultural perspectives.

The above suggest that virtual excavations necessitate considerations that lie beyond the scope of contemporary archaeological inquiry. This in turn surfaces the question of what it is that can be revealed through virtual excavations. Throughout this paper, we have consciously refrained from qualifying the potential outcomes of a virtual exca-

vation. In contrast to research efforts concentrating explicitly on the emergence of social formations in virtual settlements such as virtual communities (Efimova & Hendrick, 2005; Jones, 1997) or imagined communities (Gruzd et al., 2011), we believe that virtual excavations may shed light to additional cyber-phenomena such as virtual alliances, cliques and ad hoc online ensembles whose togetherness cannot be pre-determined. Consequently, we conceive virtual excavations as an effort to make sense of what it is that drives users' social connectivity in virtual settings; the new practices that stem out of such connectivity; and their implications for human and collective agencies. In this vein, the challenge amounts to devising methods for relating such connectivity to the users' manipulative actions on digital artifacts whose material conduct (i.e., button clicks, state changes, interim feedback, etc.) embodies cultural values (i.e., group membership, positive/negative thinking, etc.). Counting the number or frequency of such interactions to determine type, strength and direction of connections may be important, but not sufficient to explain the enacted phenomena. Instead, a focus on designated cultural artifacts is needed in order to establish the context for interpreting and ascribing meaning to online "tells". Thus, any virtual settlement needs to be examined in relation to the cultural artifacts it affords, the linguistic domain (i.e., specific objects, actions on objects and their consequences) through which these artifacts are appropriated, as well as the inscribed affordances that enable or constrain the type and range of digital traces retained.

5.2. Limitations and Future Research

The research presented has several limitations with some of them being pursued in on-going research and development activities. Firstly, we have addressed two different technology genres, namely a social web site augmented with an online commenting plug-in and a social networking platform. However, virtual excavations don't need to be confined to a single virtual settlement. In fact, cross-settlement inquiries may turn out to be both, more interesting and challenging. Secondly, our experiences indicate that there are cases where it may not be possible to extract the full range of the needed digital trace data. This is either due to the restricted design affordances of certain artefacts (e.g., a user can be tagged in a comment or a photo) or limitations of the APIs. For example, in our case studies, API constraints limited the range of digital traces made available for further processing. Moreover, it was not possible to access properties of user interactions with certain artifacts. For instance, the time of creating "like" button traces are not available. This is further complicated when cross-settlement analyses are planned as the various APIs available may pose challenges. Finally, regarding the techniques used to make sense of digital traces, the present work relies primarily on representing digital traces using visualizations. These however could be complemented by social network analysis and possibly interviewing strategies. Social network analysis could bring insights into patterns of relationships and interactions amongst users and lead to discovering the underlying social structure in user networks. On the other hand, interviewing could exploit the fact that, in contrast to contemporary archaeology where cultural participants have vanished, in virtual excavations participants are present and may be a source of valuable information.

5.3. Concluding Remarks

The present work discussed several scenarios to illustrate the notion of digital traces, how they are retained and the way in which they may obtain added value. It also pointed to methodological challenges that need to be addressed when designing and conducting virtual excavations. The main conclusion is that virtual excavations can bring about added value, but their design should take care to define the virtual settlement, its boundaries, the traceable "online" remains as well as the techniques through which such remains can be transformed to useful knowledge. On-going work concentrates on extending virtual excavations and the associated techniques to facilitate insights on boundary spanning in virtual settings. Specific challenges in this direction include the development of mechanisms for locating digital remains across virtual settlements and aggregating them in a manner that will lead to establishing richer insights on what collaborators do and the practices they become engaged across boundaries. Amongst other things, this is expected to test affordances that enable or constrain interoperability of virtual settlements and the mechanics through which it is attained.

ACKNOWLEDGMENT

Part of the present work was undertaken in the context of the EuroCancerComs project which is supported by FP 7 Science in Society Program of the EU.

REFERENCES

Akoumianakis, D. (2010). Tracing community life across virtual settlements. *International Journal of Virtual Communities and Social Networking*, *2*(4), 51–63. doi:10.4018/jvcsn.2010100104.

Akoumianakis, D. (2011). Learning as 'knowing': Towards retaining and visualizing use in virtual settings. *Journal of Educational Technology & Society*, *14*(3), 55–68.

Akoumianakis, D., Milolidakis, G., Akrivos, A., Panteris, Z., & Ktistakis, G. (2010). Clinical practice guideline management information systems: Cancer guidelines as boundary spanning tranformable objects of practice. In *Proceedings of the 2nd International Conference on Intelligent Networking and Collaborative Systems* (pp. 230-237). Retrieved from http://ieeexplore.ieee.org/xpls/abs_all.jsp?arnumber=5702100

Albert, R., & Barabási, A. L. (2002). Statistical mechanics of complex networks. *Reviews of Modern Physics, 74*(1), 47–97. doi:10.1103/RevModPhys.74.47.

Benevenuto, F., Rodrigues, T., Almeida, V., Almeida, J., & Goncalves, M. (2009). Detecting spammers and content promoters in online video social networks. In *Proceedings of the 32nd International ACM SIGIR Conference on Research and Development in Information Retrieval* (pp. 620-627).

Blanchard, A. L., & Markus, M. L. (2004). The experienced sense of a virtual community: Characteristics and processes. *ACM SIGMIS Database, 35*(1), 65–79.

Bodle, R. (2011). Regimes of sharing. *Information Communication and Society, 14*(3), 320–337. doi:10.1080/1369118X.2010.542825.

Brin, S., & Page, L. (1998). The anatomy of a large-scale hypertextual Web search engine. *Computer Networks and ISDN Systems, 30*(1-7), 107-117.

Bulters, J., & de Rijke, M. (2007). Discovering weblog communities. In *Proceedings of the International AAAI Conference on Weblogs and Social Media Boulder* (pp. 211-214). Retrieved from http://citeseerx.ist.psu.edu/viewdoc/download?doi=10.1.1.64.4037&rep=rep1&type=pdf

Chin, A., & Chignell, M. (2006). Finding evidence of community from blogging co-citations: a social network analytic approach. In *Proceedings of the IADIS International Conference on Web Based Communities*, San Sebastian, Spain (pp. 191-200). Retrieved from http://www.iadis.net/dl/final_uploads/200602L025.pdf

Cui, W., Wu, Y., Liu, S., Wei, F., Zhou, M. X., & Qu, H. (2010). Context preserving dynamic word cloud visualization. In *Proceedings of the IEEE Pacific Visualization Symposium* (pp. 121-128).

Daniel, B., & Schwier, R. A. (2010). Analysis of students' engagement and activities in a virtual learning community. *International Journal of Virtual Communities and Social Networking, 2*(4), 31–50. doi:10.4018/jvcsn.2010100103.

Efimova, L., & Hendrick, S. (2005). In search for a virtual settlement: An exploration of weblog community boundaries. *Communities & Technologies, 5*. Retrieved from https://doc.novay.nl/dscgi/ds.py/Get/File-46041/weblog-community-boundaries.pdf

Fahlander, F., & Oestigaard, T. (2004). The world as artefact. Archaeology as material culture studies. In Fahlander, F., & Oestigaard, T. (Eds.), *Material culture and other things: Post-disciplinary studies in the 21st century* (pp. 19–52). Gothenburg, Sweden: University of Gothenburg.

Freeman, L. C. (1979). Centrality in social networks conceptual clarification. *Social Networks, 1*(3), 215–239. doi:10.1016/0378-8733(78)90021-7.

Gochenour, P. H. (2006). Distributed communities and nodal subjects. *New Media & Society, 8*(1), 33–51. doi:10.1177/1461444806059867.

Gruzd, A., Wellman, B., & Takhteyev, Y. (2011). Imagining twitter as an imagined community. *The American Behavioral Scientist, 55*(10), 1294–1318. doi:10.1177/0002764211409378.

Harrison, R. (2009). Excavating Second Life. *Journal of Material Culture, 14*(1), 75–106. doi:10.1177/1359183508100009.

Heer, J., Card, S. K., & Landay, J. A. (2005). Prefuse: A toolkit for interactive information visualization. In *Proceedings of the SIGCHI Conference on Human Factors in Computing Systems* (pp. 421-430).

Hewitt, A., & Forte, A. (2006). *Crossing boundaries: Identity management and student/faculty relationships on the Facebook*. Poster presented at the CSCW, Banff, AB, Canada. Retrieved from http://citeseerx.ist.psu.edu/viewdoc/download?doi=10.1.1.94.8152&rep=rep1&type=pdf

Hine, C. (2000). *Virtual ethnography*. Thousand Oaks, CA: Sage. Retrieved from http://books.google.com/books?hl=en&lr=&id=X5w1P2_iMNYC&oi=fnd&pg=PP9&dq=Virtual+Ethnography&ots=ljRtHwWQny&sig=jo16ZHsOtCcnQdI0MZv1zZTL4Ss

Howison, J., Wiggins, A., & Crowston, K. (2011). Validity issues in the use of social network analysis for the study of online communities. *Journal of the Association for Information Systems, 12*(12), 767–797.

Jacovi, M., Guy, I., Ronen, I., Perer, A., Uziel, E., & Maslenko, M. (2011, September 24-28). Digital traces of interest: Deriving interest relationships from social media interactions. In *Proceedings of the 12th European Conference on Computer Supported Cooperative Work*, Aarhus, Denmark (pp. 21-40). Retrieved from http://www.springerlink.com/content/nk58m8jjm2847x33/abstract/

Johnson, B., & Shneiderman, B. (1991). Treemaps: A space-filling approach to the visualization of hierarchical information structures. In *Proceedings of the IEEE Conference on Visualization* (pp. 284-291). Retrieved from http://drum.lib.umd.edu/bitstream/1903/370/2/CS-TR-2657.pdf

Jones, Q. (1997). Virtual-communities, virtual settlements & cyber-archaeology: A theoretical outline. *Journal of Computer-Mediated Communication, 3*(3), 35–49.

Jourdan, Z., Rainer, R. K., & Marshall, T. E. (2008). Business intelligence: An analysis of the literature 1. *Information Systems Management, 25*(2), 121–131. doi:10.1080/10580530801941512.

Kim, W., Jeong, O. R., & Lee, S. W. (2010). On social Web sites. *Information Systems, 35*(2), 215–236. doi:10.1016/j.is.2009.08.003.

Kleinberg, J. M. (1999). Authoritative sources in a hyperlinked environment. *Journal of the ACM, 46*(5), 604–632. doi:10.1145/324133.324140.

Lakshmanan, G. T., & Oberhofer, M. A. (2010). Knowledge discovery in the blogosphere: Approaches and challenges. *IEEE Internet Computing, 14*(2), 24–32. doi:10.1109/MIC.2010.26.

Lin, Y., Sundaram, H., Chi, Y., Tatemura, J., & Tseng, B. (2006). Discovery of blog communities based on mutual awareness. In *Proceedings of the 3rd Annual Workshop on the Weblogging Ecosystem*, Edinburgh, UK.

Liu, G. Z. (1999). Virtual community presence in internet relay chatting. *Journal of Computer-Mediated Communication, 5*(1), 0.

Liu, X., Wang, Y., Li, Y., & Shi, B. (2011). Identifying topic experts and topic communities in the blogspace. In S. Lee, Z. Peng, X. Zhou, Y.-S. Moon, R. Unland, & J. Yoo (Eds.), *Proceedings of the 17th International Conference on Database Systems for Advanced Applications* (LNCS 7238, pp. 68-77). Retrieved from http://www.springerlink.com/index/H72Q8H3635160P27.pdf

Marshall, B., McDonald, D., Chen, H., & Chung, W. (2004). EBizPort: Collecting and analyzing business intelligence information. *Journal of the American Society for Information Science and Technology, 55*(10), 873–891. doi:10.1002/asi.20037.

Meng, W., Yu, C., & Liu, K.-L. (2002). Building efficient and effective metasearch engines. *ACM Computing Surveys, 34*(1), 48–89. doi:10.1145/505282.505284.

Paccagnella, L. (1997). Getting the seats of your pants dirty: Strategies for ethnographic research on virtual communities. *Journal of Computer-Mediated Communication, 3*(1).

Perer, A., & Shneiderman, B. (2006). Balancing systematic and flexible exploration of social networks. *IEEE Transactions on Visualization and Computer Graphics, 12*(5), 693–700. doi:10.1109/TVCG.2006.122 PMID:17080789.

Rivadeneira, A. W., Gruen, D. M., Muller, M. J., & Millen, D. R. (2007). Getting our head in the clouds: Toward evaluation studies of tagclouds. In *Proceedings of the SIGCHI Conference on Human Factors in Computing Systems* (pp. 995-998).

Rosenblum, D. (2007). What anyone can know: The privacy risks of social networking sites. *IEEE Security & Privacy, 5*(3), 40–49. doi:10.1109/MSP.2007.75.

Schultze, U., & Boland, R. (2000). Knowledge management technology and the reproduction of knowledge work practices. *The Journal of Strategic Information Systems, 9*(2-3), 193–212. doi:10.1016/S0963-8687(00)00043-3.

Wasserman, S., & Faust, K. (1994). *Social network analysis: Methods and applications.* Cambridge, UK: Cambridge University Press. doi:10.1017/CBO9780511815478.

Xu, J. J., & Chen, H. (2005). CrimeNet explorer: A framework for criminal network knowledge discovery. *ACM Transactions on Information Systems, 23*(2), 201–226. doi:10.1145/1059981.1059984.

Zhao, S., Grasmuck, S., & Martin, J. (2008). Identity construction on Facebook: Digital empowerment in anchored relationships. *Computers in Human Behavior, 24*(5), 1816–1836. doi:10.1016/j.chb.2008.02.012.

Zhou, Y., & Davis, J. (2007). Discovering web communities in the blogspace. In *Proceedings of the 40th Annual Hawaii International Conference on System Sciences* (pp. 85-85). Retrieved from http://ieeexplore.ieee.org/xpls/abs_all.jsp?arnumber=4076542

This work was previously published in the International Journal of Virtual Communities and Social Networking, Volume 3, Issue 4, edited by Subhasish Dasgupta, pp. 46-65, copyright 2011 by IGI Publishing (an imprint of IGI Global).

Compilation of References

Aaker, D. A. (1991). *Managing brand equity*. New York, NY: Free Press.

Aaker, D. A. (1992). The value of brand equity. *The Journal of Business Strategy, 13*(4), 27–32. doi:10.1108/eb039503.

Abdul-Rahman, A., & Hailes, S. (2000, January). Supporting trust in virtual communities. In *Proceedings of the Hawaii International Conference on System Sciences*, Maui, HI.

Abelson, R. P. (1964). Mathematical models of the distribution of attributes under controversy. In Frederksen, N., & Gulliksen, H. (Eds.), *Contribution to mathematical psychology*. New York, NY: Holt, Reinehart, & Winston.

Adamic, L., & Glance, N. (2005). The political blogosphere and the 2004 U.S. Election: Divided they blog. In *Proceedings of the 3rd International Workshop on Link Discovery*.

Adomavicius, G., & Tuzhilin, A. (2005). Toward the next generation of recommender systems: A survey of the state-of-the-art and possible extensions. *IEEE Transactions on Knowledge and Data Engineering, 17*(6), 734–749. doi:10.1109/TKDE.2005.99.

Agarwal, N. (2008). A study of communities and influence in blogosphere. In *Proceedings of the 2nd SIGMOD PhD Workshop on Innovative Database Research* (pp. 19-24).

Agarwal, N., Liu, H., Tang, L., & Yu, P. S. (2008, February 11-12). Identifying influential bloggers in a community. In *Proceedings of the International Conference on Web Search and Web Data Mining* (pp.207-218).

Agarwal, N., & Liu, H. (2008). Blogosphere: Research issues, tools and applications. *SIGKDD Exploration Newsletter, 10*(1), 18–31. doi:10.1145/1412734.1412737.

Aggarwal, C. C. (2002). Towards meaningful high-dimensional nearest neighbor search by human-computer interaction. In *Proceedings of the 18th International Conference on Data Engineering* (pp. 593-604).

Ahonen, M., & Lietsala, K. (2007). Managing service ideas and suggestions – Information systems in innovation brokering. In *Proceedings of the Tekes Haas Conference of Service Innovation*, Berkeley, CA.

Ajzen, I., & Fishbein, M. (1980). *Understanding Attitudes and Predicting Social Behavior*. Upper Saddle River, NJ: Prentice Hall.

Akoumianakis, D., Milolidakis, G., Akrivos, A., Panteris, Z., & Ktistakis, G. (2010). Clinical practice guideline management information systems: Cancer guidelines as boundary spanning tranformable objects of practice. In *Proceedings of the 2nd International Conference on Intelligent Networking and Collaborative Systems* (pp. 230-237). Retrieved from http://ieeexplore.ieee.org/xpls/abs_all.jsp?arnumber=5702100

Akoumianakis, D. (2010). Tracing community life across virtual settlements. *International Journal of Virtual Communities and Social Networking, 2*(4), 51–63. doi:10.4018/jvcsn.2010100104.

Akoumianakis, D. (2011). Learning as 'knowing': Towards retaining and visualizing use in virtual settings. *Journal of Educational Technology & Society, 14*(3), 55–68.

Akritidis, L., Katsaros, D., & Bozanis, P. (2009). Identifying attractive research fields for new scientists. *Scientometrics, 91*(3), 869–894. doi:10.1007/s11192-012-0646-4.

Aladwani, A. M., & Palvia, P. C. (2002). Developing and validating an instrument for measuring user-perceived web quality. *Information & Management, 39*, 467–476. doi:10.1016/S0378-7206(01)00113-6.

Albert, R., & Barabási, A. L. (2002). Statistical mechanics of complex networks. *Reviews of Modern Physics, 74*(1), 47–97. doi:10.1103/RevModPhys.74.47.

Al-Fedaghi, S. (2007). Conferences under scrutiny. *Communications of the ACM, 50*(7), 123–126. doi:10.1145/1272516.1272543.

Al-Gahtani, S. S., Hubona, G. S., & Wang, J. (2007). Information technology (IT) in Saudi Arabia: culture and the acceptance and use of IT. *Information & Management, 44*(8), 681–691. doi:10.1016/j.im.2007.09.002.

Allen, J., & Shockley, B. (1996). Conversations: Composing a research dialogue in University and school research communities encountering a cultural shift. *Reading Research Quarterly, 31*, 220–227. doi:10.1598/RRQ.31.2.6.

Anderson, P. (2007). *What is Web 2.0? Ideas, technologies, and implications for education.* London, UK: JISC Technology & Standards Watch.

Androutsellis-Theotokis, S., Spinellis, D., & Vlachos, V. (2007). The MoR-Trust Distributed Trust Management System: Design and Simulation Results. *Electronic Notes in Theoretical Computer Science, 179*, 3–15. doi:10.1016/j.entcs.2006.11.032.

Anfinnsen, S., Ghinea, G., & de Cesare, S. (2010). Web 2.0 and folksonomies in a library context. *International Journal of Information Management, 31*, 63–70. doi:10.1016/j.ijinfomgt.2010.05.006.

Armstrong, C. L., & McAdams, M. J. (2009). Blogs of information: How gender cues and individual motivations influence perceptions of credibility. *Journal of Computer-Mediated Communication, 14*(3), 435–456. doi:10.1111/j.1083-6101.2009.01448.x.

Arndt, J. (1967). *Word of mouth advertising: A review of the literature (Tech. Rep.).* New York, NY: Advertising Research Foundation.

Arthur, D., & Vassilvitskii, S. (2007). k-means++: The advantages of careful seeding. In *Proceedings of the 18th Annual ACM-SIAM Symposium on Discrete Algorithms* (pp. 1027-1035).

Artz, D., & Gil, Y. (2007). A survey of trust in computer science and the semantic web. *Journal of Web Semantics: Science. Services and Agents on the World Wide Web, 5*(2), 58–71. doi:10.1016/j.websem.2007.03.002.

Artz, J. M. (2009). The current state and future potential of virtual worlds. *International Journal of Virtual Communities and Social Networking, 1*(1), 14–22. doi:10.4018/jvcsn.2009010102.

Ashok, P. (2011). *The Social History of England.* Pradesh, India: Orient Blackswan.

Atwell, N. (1993). Forward. In Patterson, L., Santa, C. M., Short, K. G., & Smith, K. (Eds.), *Teachers are researchers: Reflection and action* (pp. vii–x). Newark, DE: International Reading Association.

Awad, F. N., & Ragowsky, A. (2008). Establishing trust in electronic commerce through online word of mouth: An examination across genders. *Journal of Management Information Systems, 24*(4), 101–121. doi:10.2753/MIS0742-1222240404.

Awis.blogspot. (2009). *Alexa features.* Retrieved February 12, 2009 from http://awis.blogspot.com/2009/04/more-new-alexa-features-demographics.html

Axelrod, R. (1980). More effective choice in prisoner's dilemma. *The Journal of Conflict Resolution, 24*(3), 379–403. doi:10.1177/002200278002400301.

Axelrod, R. (1984). *The evolution of co-operation.* New York, NY: Basic Books.

Axelrod, R. (1997). The dissemination of culture: A model with local convergence and global polarization. *The Journal of Conflict Resolution, 41*, 203–226. doi:10.1177/0022002797041002001.

Baatarjav, E., Phithakkitnukoon, S., & Dantu, R. (2008). Group recommendation system for Facebook. In R. Meersman, Z. Tari, & P. Herrero (Eds.) *Proceedings of the Confederated International Workshop of On the Move to Meaningful Internet Systems* (LNCS 5333, pp. 211-219).

Bajec, P. (n.d.). *How to organize a conference – Step by step manual*. Retrieved July 24, 2011, from http://www.iapss.org/downloads/publications/iapss_conference_manual.pdf

Baldwin, T. (2011, January 4). *Making your authors' social networks work for your conference* [Web log post].

Bampo, M., Ewing, T. M., Mather, R. D., Stewart, D., & Wallace, M. (2008). The effects of the social structure of digital networks on viral marketing performance. *Information Systems Research*, *19*(3), 273–290. doi:10.1287/isre.1070.0152.

Bandura, A. (1986). *Social foundations of thought and action: A social cognitive theory*. Upper Saddle River, NJ: Prentice Hall.

Bansal, H. S., & Voyer, P. A. (2000). Word of mouth processes within a services purchase decision context. *Journal of Service Research*, *3*(2), 166–177. doi:10.1177/109467050032005.

Bart, Y., Shankar, V., Sultan, F., & Urban, G. L. (2005). Are the drivers and role of online trust the same for all Web sites and consumers? A large-scale exploratory empirical study. *Journal of Marketing*, *69*(4), 133–152. doi:10.1509/jmkg.2005.69.4.133.

Barwise, P. (1993). Brand equity: Snark or boojum. *International Journal of Research in Marketing*, *10*(1), 93–104. doi:10.1016/0167-8116(93)90036-X.

Battey, A. (2006, April 4). Taking it to the street. *Yale Daily News*.

Bauer, H. H., Falk, T., & Hammerschmidt, M. (2006). eTransQual: A transaction process-based approach for capturing service quality in online shopping. *Journal of Business Research*, *59*(7), 866–875. doi:10.1016/j.jbusres.2006.01.021.

Baym, N. K. (1995). The performance of humor in computer-mediated communication. *Journal of Computer-Mediated Communication*, *1*(2). Retrieved from http://jcmc.indiana.edu/vol1/issue2/baym.html.

Bellefeuille, J., & Salem, S. (2004). Reflecting on IEMC 2003. *EMS Newsletter, 54*(1). Retrieved November 26, 2010, from http://www.ewh.ieee.org/soc/ems/EMnewsletter/04Q1.pdf

Benbasat, I., Goldstein, D. K., & Mead, M. (1987). The case research strategy in studies of information systems. *Management Information Systems Quarterly*, *11*(3), 369–386. doi:10.2307/248684.

Benevenuto, F., Rodrigues, T., Almeida, V., Almeida, J., & Goncalves, M. (2009). Detecting spammers and content promoters in online video social networks. In *Proceedings of the 32nd International ACM SIGIR Conference on Research and Development in Information Retrieval* (pp. 620-627).

Bentwood, J. (2007). *Distributed influence: Quantifying the impact of social media*. New York, NY: Edelman.

Berkhin, P. (2002). *Survey of clustering data mining techniques (Tech. Rep.)*. San Jose, CA: Accrue Software.

Bettencourt, L. A., Ostrom, A. L., Brown, S. W., & Roundtree, R. I. (2002). Client co-production in knowledge-intensive business services. *California Management Review*, *44*(4), 100–128.

Bhattacherjee, A. (2001). Understanding information systems continuance: an expectation-confirmation model. *Management Information Systems Quarterly*, *25*(3), 351–370. doi:10.2307/3250921.

Bicknell, D. (2008). *Make Web 2.0 deliver business benefits*. Retrieved September 20, 2009, from http://www.computerweekly.com/Articles/2008/02/20/229486/make-web-2.0-deliver-business-benefits.htm

Biel, A. L. (1992). How brand image drives brand equity. *Journal of Advertising Research*, 6–12.

Birchall, J. (2008, March 14). Amazon Taps Facebook Potential. *Financial Times,* p. 18.

Bjelland, O. M., & Wood, R. C. (2008). An inside view of IBM's 'Innovation Jam'. *MIT Sloan Management Review*, *50*(1), 31–40.

Blackwell, R. D., Miniard, P. W., & Engel, J. F. (2001). *Consumer behavior*. Orlando, FL: Harcourt.

Blake, D. (1976). *Behaviour of Law*. New York, NY: Academic Press.

Blake, D. (1998). *The social structure of right or wrong* (Rev. ed.). San Diego, CA: Academic Press.

Blake, R. (2002). *Voices of New York (Spring MAP Class Project)*. New York, NY: New York University.

Blanchard, A. L. (2007). Testing a model of sense of virtual community. *Computers in Human Behavior*.

Blanchard, A. L. (2007). Developing a sense of virtual community measure. *Cyberpsychology & Behavior, 10*(6), 827–830. doi:10.1089/cpb.2007.9946.

Blanchard, A. L., & Markus, M. L. (2004). The experienced sense of a virtual community: Characteristics and processes. *ACM SIGMIS Database, 35*(1), 65–79.

Blinn, N., Lindermann, N., Fäcks, K., & Nüttgens, M. (2009, August 6-9). Web 2.0 in SME networks – A design science approach considering multi-perspective requirements. In *Proceedings of the Fifteenth Americas Conference on Information Systems*, San Francisco, CA.

Blumler, J. G., & Katz, E. (1974). *The uses of mass communications: Current perspectives on gratifications research*. Thousand Oaks, CA: Sage.

Boaduo, N. A. P. (2001). *Principles of practical research*. Unpublished manuscript, Dr. Boaduo Education Centre, Louis Trichardt, South Africa.

Boaduo, N. A. P. (2005). *Writing your first research proposal: A manual for first time and teacher researchers*. Unpublished manuscript, Dr. Boaduo Educational Consultants Pty Ltd, Gaborone, Botswana, South Africa.

Boaduo, N. A. P. (2006). Methodological choice and application in a research study: A framework for practitioner. *Bulletin of the Centre for Academic Development: Quality Assurance in Higher Education*, 38-50.

Boaduo, N. A. P. (2010). School-based continuing professional teacher development: A study of alternative teacher development initiative in the Eastern Cape Province of South Africa. *The African Symposium: An Online Journal of the African Educational Research Network, 10*(2), 75-83.

Boaduo, N. A. P., & Babitseng, S. M. (2006). *How do we prepare educators for a new role in the 21st century?* Paper presented at the ACEL and Microsoft iNet Online Conference.

Boaduo, N. A. P., & Babitseng, S. M. (2007b, June 24-30). *New directions on teacher education*. Paper presented at the 27th Annual Conference International Society for Teacher Education (ITE) on The Future of Teacher Education for Professional Development, Stirling, Scotland.

Boaduo, N. A. P. (2010). Research methods for studying virtual communities. In Daniel, B. (Ed.), *A handbook of research on methods and techniques for studying virtual communities: Paradigms and phenomena*. Hershey, PA: IGI Global. doi:10.4018/978-1-60960-040-2.ch036.

Boaduo, N. A. P. (2011). *Practical educational research principles for practising teachers: Manual for teacher researchers*. Saarbrücken, Germany: LAP Lambert Academic.

Boaduo, N. A. P. (2011). *Conceptual educational theories*. Saarbrücken, Germany: LAP Lambert Academic.

Boaduo, N. A. P., & Babitseng, S. M. (2007). The need for teachers to be researchers. *Journal of the African Educational Research Network, 7*(1), 183–191.

Bodle, R. (2011). Regimes of sharing. *Information Communication and Society, 14*(3), 320–337. doi:10.1080/1369118X.2010.542825.

Bonacich, P. (1972). Factoring and weighting approaches to status scores and clique identification. *The Journal of Mathematical Sociology, 2*(1), 113–120. doi:10.1080/0022250X.1972.9989806.

Borgatti, P. S., Jones, C., & Everett, G. M. (1998). Network measures of social capital. *Connections, 21*, 27–36.

Borgatti, S. P. (2006). Identifying sets of key players in a network. *Computational & Mathematical Organization Theory, 12*(1), 21–34. doi:10.1007/s10588-006-7084-x.

Borgatti, S. P., & Everett, M. G. (1997). Network analysis of 2-mode data. *Social Networks, 19*(3), 243–269. doi:10.1016/S0378-8733(96)00301-2.

Borgatti, S. P., Everett, M., & Freeman, L. (1998). *UCINET 5 for Windows: Software for social network analysis*. Natick, MA: Analytic Technologies.

Boudourides, M. (2003, February 12-16). A simulation of convergent-divergent public opinion formation on social networks. In *Proceedings of the 23ʳᵈ Sunbelt International Social Network Conference*, Cancun, Mexico.

Boudreau, K. J., Lacetera, N., & Lakhani, K. R. (2008). Incentives versus diversity: Re-examing the link between competition and innovation. In *Proceedings of the Wharton Technology Conference*.

Bowen, D. E. (1986). Managing customers as human resources in service organizations. *Human Resource Management*, *25*(3), 371–383. doi:10.1002/hrm.3930250304.

Bowker, N., & Tuffin, K. (2002). Disability discourses for online identities. *Disability & Society*, *17*(3), 327–344. doi:10.1080/09687590220139883.

Boyd, S., Ghosh, A., Prabhakar, B., & Shah, D. (2005, March). Gossip algorithms: Design, analysis and applications. In *Proceedings of the IEEE Annual Joint Conference INFOCOM*, Miami, FL (Vol. 3, pp. 1653-1664).

Brabham, D. C. (2009). *Moving the crowd at Threadless: Motivations for participation in a crowdsourcing application*. Paper presented at the Annual Meeting of the Association for Education in Journalism & Mass Communication, Boston, MA.

Brasco, T. C. (Ed.). (1988). *How brand name are valued for acquisitions*. Cambridge, MA: Marketing Science Institute.

Bray, J. N., Lee, J., Smith, L. L., & Yorks, L. (2000). *Collaborative inquiry in practice: Action, reflection and meaning making*. Thousand Oaks, CA: Sage.

Bretschneider, U., Huber, M., Leimeister, J. M., & Krcmar, H. (2008). Community for innovations: Developing an integrated concept for open innovation. In León, J., Bernardos, A. M., Casar, J. R., Kautz, K., & DeGross, J. I. (Eds.), *Open IT-based innovation: Moving towards cooperative IT transfer and knowledge diffusion*. New York, NY: Springer. doi:10.1007/978-0-387-87503-3_28.

Brexendorf, T. O., Muhlmeier, S., Tomczak, T., & Eisend, M. (2010). The impact of sales encounters on brand loyalty. *Journal of Business Research*, *63*(11), 1148–1155. doi:10.1016/j.jbusres.2009.10.011.

Brin, S., & Page, L. (1998). The anatomy of a large-scale hypertextual Web search engine. *Computer Networks and ISDN Systems, 30*(1-7), 107-117.

Broom, A. (2005). The eMale: Prostate cancer, masculinity and online support as a challenge to medical expertise. *Journal of Sociology (Melbourne, Vic.)*, *41*(1), 87–104. doi:10.1177/1440783305050965.

Brown, A. (2011). Relationships, community, and identity in the new virtual society. *The Futurist*, *45*(2), 29–43.

Brown, J., Broderick, M. J., & Lee, N. (2007). Word of mouth communication within online communities: Conceptualizing the online social network. *Journal of Interactive Marketing*, *21*(3), 2–20. doi:10.1002/dir.20082.

Brown, J., & Reinegen, P. (1987). Social ties and word-of-mouth referral behavior. *The Journal of Consumer Research*, *14*(3), 350–362. doi:10.1086/209118.

Bruch, E. E., & Mare, R. D. (2006). Neighborhood choice and neighborhood change. *American Journal of Sociology*, *112*(3), 667–709. doi:10.1086/507856.

Bryman, A. (2004). *Social research methods* (2nd ed.). Oxford, UK: Oxford University Press.

Bullinger, A. C., & Moeslein, K. M. (2010). Online innovation contests – Where are we? In *Proceedings of the 16ᵗʰ Americas Conference on Information Systems*, Lima, Peru.

Bullinger, A. C., Haller, J., & Moeslein, K. (2009). Innovation mobs – Unlocking the innovation potential of virtual communities. In *Proceedings of the Fifteenth Americas Conference on Information Systems*, San Francisco, CA.

Bullinger, A. C., Neyer, A.-K., & Koelling, M. (2009). Is open innovation really open: A cross-cultural perspective. In *Proceedings of the 20th ISPIM Conference*, Vienna, Austria.

Bulters, J., & de Rijke, M. (2007). Discovering weblog communities. In *Proceedings of the International AAAI Conference on Weblogs and Social Media Boulder* (pp. 211-214). Retrieved from http://citeseerx.ist.psu.edu/viewdoc/download?doi=10.1.1.64.4037&rep=rep1&type=pdf

Burkhardt, M. E., & Brass, D. J. (1990). Changing patterns or patterns of change: the effects of a change in technology on social network structure and power. *Administrative Science Quarterly*, *35*(1), 104–127. doi:10.2307/2393552.

Burns, E. (2005). *Blogs continue to gain traction.* Retrieved October 19, 2011, from http://www.clickz.com/3502201

Burson-Marsteller. (2001). *The power of online influencers.* Retrieved from http://www.burson-marsteller.com/Practices_And_Specialties/AssetFile/E-Fluentials%20Brochure.pdf

Burt, R. S. (1999). The social capital of opinion leaders. *The Annals of the American Academy of Political and Social Science*, *566*, 1–22. doi:10.1177/0002716299956 6001004.

Buttle, F. A. (1998). Word of Mouth: Understanding and managing referral marketing. *Journal of Strategic Marketing*, *6*(3), 241–254. doi:10.1080/096525498346658.

Cai, S., & Jun, M. (2003). Internet users' perceptions of online service quality: A comparison of online buyers and information searchers. *Managing Service Quality*, *13*, 504–519. doi:10.1108/09604520310506568.

Carvalho, A. (2009). *In search of excellence - Innovation contests to foster innovation and entrepreneurship in Portugal.* Évora, Portugal: University of Évora.

Casalo, L. V., Flavian, C., & Guinaliu, M. (2010). Relationship quality, community promotion and brand loyalty in virtual communities: Evidence from free software communities. *International Journal of Information Management*, *30*(4), 357–367. doi:10.1016/j.ijinfomgt.2010.01.004.

Chandler, D., & Torbert, B. (2003). Transforming inquiry and action: Interweaving 27 flavours of action research. *Action Research*, *1*, 133–152. doi:10.1177/14767503030012002.

Chan, K. K., & Misra, S. (1990). Characteristics of the opinion leader: A new dimension. *Journal of Advertising*, *19*(3), 53–60.

Chase, R. B. (1978). Where does the customer fit in a service operation? *Harvard Business Review*, *56*(6), 137–142.

Chattopadhyay, S. (2005). *Representing Calcutta Modernity, Nationalism and the Colonial Uncanny.* London, UK: Routledge.

Chauhan, R., & Chauhan, R. (2011). Collaborative virtual business events- Opportunities and challenges. In Malik, K., & Choudhary, P. K. (Eds.), *Business organizations and collaborative Web: Practices, strategies and patterns* (pp. 243–259). Hershey, PA: IGI Global. doi:10.4018/978-1-60960-581-0.ch015.

Chau, P. K., & Hui, K. L. (1998). Identifying early adopters of new IT products: A case for Windows 95. *Information & Management*, *33*(5), 225–230. doi:10.1016/S0378-7206(98)00031-7.

Chen, C., & Hung, S. (2010). To give or to receive? Factors influencing members' knowledge sharing and community promotion in professional virtual communities. *Information & Management*, *47*(4), 226. doi:10.1016/j.im.2010.03.001.

Chenet, P., Dagger, T. S., & O'Sullivan, D. (2010). Service quality, trust, commitment and service differentiation in business relationships. *Journal of Services Marketing*, *24*(5), 336. doi:10.1108/08876041011060440.

Chen, I. Y. L. (2007). The factors influencing members' continuance intentions in professional virtual communities - A longitudinal study. *Journal of Information Science*, *33*(4), 451. doi:10.1177/0165551506075323.

Chesbrough, H. W. (2003). *Open innovation: The new imperative for creating and profiting from technology.* Boston, MA: Harvard Business School Press.

Chevalier, J. A., & Mayzlin, D. (2006). The effect of word of mouth on sales: Online book reviews. *JMR, Journal of Marketing Research*, *43*(3), 345–354. doi:10.1509/jmkr.43.3.345.

Childers, T. L. (1966). *Medical innovation: A diffusion study.* Indianapolis, IN: Bobbs-Merrill.

Childers, T. L. (1986). Assessment of the psychometric properties of an opinion leadership scale. *Journal of Marketing Research*, *23*(2), 184–188. doi:10.2307/3151666.

Chin, A., & Chignell, M. (2006). Finding evidence of community from blogging co-citations: a social network analytic approach. In *Proceedings of the IADIS International Conference on Web Based Communities*, San Sebastian, Spain (pp. 191-200). Retrieved from http://www.iadis.net/dl/final_uploads/200602L025.pdf

Chiu, C. M., Hsu, M. H., & Wang, E. T. G. (2006). Understanding knowledge sharing in virtual communities: An integration of social capital and social cognitive theories. *Decision Support Systems*, *42*(3), 1872–1888. doi:10.1016/j.dss.2006.04.001.

Christensen, C. M. (1997). *The innovator's dilemma: When new technologies cause great firms to fail*. Boston, MA: Harvard Business School Press.

Chung, C. J., Kim, H., & Kim, J. H. (2010). An anatomy of the credibility of online newspapers. *Online Information Review*, *34*(5), 669–685. doi:10.1108/14684521011084564.

Churchill, G. A., & Suprenant, C. (1982). An investigation into the determinants of customer satisfaction. *JMR, Journal of Marketing Research*, *19*(4), 491–504. doi:10.2307/3151722.

Clark, P. A. (1972). *Action research and organizational change*. London, UK: Harper & Row.

Claude, E. S. (1948). *A mathematical theory of communication*. Retrieved August 19, 2011, from http://www.en.wikipedia.org/wiki/Entropy_(information_theory)

Clause, A., Newman, M. E. J., & Moore, C. (2004). Finding community structure in very large networks. *Physical Review*, *70*(6), 2–3.

Cohen, H. (2005). *Blog marketing strategies (and how to measure them)*. Retrieved October 19, 2011, from http://www.clickz.com/3504241

Cohen, W. M., & Levinthal, D. A. (1990). Absorptive capacity: A new perspective on learning and innovation. *Administrative Science Quarterly*, *35*(1), 128–152. doi:10.2307/2393553.

Coleman, J. S., Katz, E., & Herbert, M. (1957). The diffusion of an innovation among physicians. *Sociometry*, *20*(4), 253–270. doi:10.2307/2785979.

Collier, J. E., & Sherrell, D. L. (2010). Examining the influence of control and convenience in a self-service setting. *Academy of Marketing Science Journal*, *38*(4), 490. doi:10.1007/s11747-009-0179-4.

Constant, D., Sproull, L., & Kiesler, S. (1996). The kindness of strangers: The usefulness of electronic weak ties for technical advice. *Organization Science*, *7*(2), 119–135. doi:10.1287/orsc.7.2.119.

Cooper, D. J., & Morgan, W. (2008). Case study research in accounting. *Accounting Horizons*, *22*(2), 159–178. doi:10.2308/acch.2008.22.2.159.

Correa, H., Ellram, L., Scavarda, A., & Cooper, M. (2007). An operations management view of the services and goods offering mix. *International Journal of Operations & Production Management*, *27*(5), 444–463. doi:10.1108/01443570710742357.

Correll, S. (1995). The ethnography of an electronic bar: The lesbian café. *Journal of Contemporary Ethnography*, *24*(3), 270–298. doi:10.1177/089124195024003002.

Coulter, R. A., Feick, L. F., & Price, L. L. (2002). Changing faces: Cosmetics opinion leadership among women in the new Hungary. *European Journal of Marketing*, *36*(11), 1287–1308. doi:10.1108/03090560210445182.

Creswell, J. W. (2002). *Research design: Qualitative, quantitative, and mixed methods approaches* (2nd ed.). Thousand Oaks, CA: Sage.

Cronbach, L. J. (1951). Coefficient alpha and the internal structure of tests. *Psychometrika*, *16*, 297–333. doi:10.1007/BF02310555.

Cronin, J. J., & Taylor, S. A. (1994). SERVPERF versus SERVQUAL: Reconciling performance-based and perceptions-minus-expectations measurement of service quality. *Journal of Marketing*, *58*(1), 125–131. doi:10.2307/1252256.

Csikszentmihalyi, M. (1977). *Beyond Boredom and Anxiety*. San Francisco, CA: Jossey-Bass.

Cui, W., Wu, Y., Liu, S., Wei, F., Zhou, M. X., & Qu, H. (2010). Context preserving dynamic word cloud visualization. In *Proceedings of the IEEE Pacific Visualization Symposium* (pp. 121-128).

Cyr, D., Bonanni, C., Bowes, J., & Ilsever, J. (2005). Beyond trust: web site design preferences across cultures. *Journal of Global Information Management*, *13*(4), 25–54. doi:10.4018/jgim.2005100102.

Da Cunha, J. V., & Orlikowski, W. J. (2008). Performing catharsis: The use of online discussion forums in organizational change. *Information and Organization*, *18*(2), 132–156. doi:10.1016/j.infoandorg.2008.02.001.

Daniel, D. (2007, June 22). *How CIOs can introduce Web 2.0 technologies into the enterprise*. Retrieved September 28, 2009, from http://www.cio.com/article/print/120850

Daniel, B., & Schwier, R. A. (2010). Analysis of students' engagement and activities in a virtual learning community. *International Journal of Virtual Communities and Social Networking*, 2(4), 31–50. doi:10.4018/jvcsn.2010100103.

Danielson, D. R. (2006). Web credibility. In Ghaoui, C. (Ed.), *Encyclopedia of human-computer interaction*. Hershey, PA: Idea Group.

Das, K. (2006). Radha Birbhumer Kabiwala O Kabigan. *Paschim Banga, Birbhum*, 289-309.

Dasguta, P. (1988). *Making and breaking cooperative relations*. New York, NY: Basil Blackwell.

Davies, G. (2008). Employer branding and its influence on managers. *European Journal of Marketing*, 42(5-6), 667. doi:10.1108/03090560810862570.

Dawson, K. (1997). *Alexa Internet opens the doors*. Retrieved July 28, 2008, from http://www.tbtf.com/archive/1997-07-28.html

Dayal, S., Landesberg, H., & Zeisser, M. (1999). How to build trust online. *Marketing Management*, 64-69.

De Valck, K., van Bruggen, G. H., & Wierenga, B. (2009). Virtual communities: A marketing perspective. *Decision Support Systems*, 47(3), 185–203. doi:10.1016/j.dss.2009.02.008.

De Vany, A., & Walls, D. (1999). Uncertainty in the Movie Industry: Does star power reduce the terror of the box office? *Journal of Cultural Economics*, 23(4), 285–318. doi:10.1023/A:1007608125988.

Deffuant, G., Neau, D., Amblard, F., & Weisbuch, G. (2000). Mixing beliefs among interacting agents. *Advances in Complex Systems*, 3, 87. doi:10.1142/S0219525900000078.

Dellarocas, C. (2001, October). Analyzing the economic efficiency of eBay-like online reputation mechanisms. In *Proceedings of the 3rd ACM Conference on Electronic Commerce*, Tampa, FL.

Dellarocas, C. (2004). Building trust on-line: The design of robust reputation mechanisms for online trading communities. In Doukidis, G., Mylonopoulos, N., & Pouloudi, N. (Eds.), *Information society or information economy? A combined perspective on the digital era*. Hershey, PA: Idea Group.

Deloitte. (2007). *New Deloitte study shows inflection point for consumer products industry: Companies must learn to compete in a more transparent age*. Retrieved from http://usstock.jrj.com.cn/2007-10-01/000002746415.shtml

Denison, D. R. (1996). What is the difference between organizational culture and organizational climate? A native's point of view on a decade of paradigm wars. *Academy of Management Review*, 21(3), 619–654.

Deutsch, M. (1962). Cooperation and trust: Some theoretical notes. In *Proceedings of the Nebraska Symposium on Motivation* (pp. 275-319).

Dick, B. (2000). *A beginner's guide to action research*. Lismore, NSW, Australia: Southern Cross Institute of Action Research. Retrieved from http://www.scu.edu.au/schools/gcm/ar/arp/guide.html

Ding, F., & Liu, Y. (2009). A decision theoretical approach for diffusion promotion. *Physica*, 388(17), 3572–3580. doi:10.1016/j.physa.2009.05.016.

Domingos, P., & Richardson, M. (2001). Mining the network value of customers. In *Proceedings of the 7th International Conference on Knowledge Discovery and Data Mining* (pp. 57-66).

Domingos, P. (2005). Mining social networks for viral marketing. *IEEE Intelligent Systems*, 20(1), 80–82.

Dominick, J. R. (1999). Who do you think you are? Personal home pages and self-presentation on the World Wide Web. *Journalism & Mass Communication Quarterly*, 76(4), 646–658.

Donath, J., & Boyd, D. (2004). Public displays of connection. *BT Technology Journal*, 22(4), 71–82. doi:10.1023/B:BTTJ.0000047585.06264.cc.

Duan, W., Gu, B., & Whinston, A. B. (2008). Do online reviews matter? – An empirical investigation of panel data. *Decision Support Systems, 45*(4), 1007–1016. doi:10.1016/j.dss.2008.04.001.

Dwyer, P. (2007). Measuring the value of electronic word-of-mouth and its impact in consumer communities. *Journal of Interactive Marketing, 21*(2), 63–79. doi:10.1002/dir.20078.

Ebner, W., Leimeister, J. M., & Krcmar, H. (2010). Community engineering for innovations: The ideas competition as a method to nurture a virtual community for innovations. *R&D Management Journal, 40*(4), 342–356.

Ebner, W., Leimeister, J.-M., Bretschneider, U., & Krcmar, H. (2010). Leveraging the wisdom of crowds: Designing an IT-supported ideas competition for an ERP software company. *Information Systems, 49*(89).

Eccleston, D., & Griseri, L. (2008, March 18). *How does Web 2.0 stretch traditional influencing patterns.* Paper presented at the Market Research Society Annual Conference.

Efimova, L. (2009, June). Weblog as a personal thinking space. In *Proceedings of the Twentieth ACM Conference on Hypertext and Hypermedia*.

Efimova, L., & Hendrick, S. (2005). In search for a virtual settlement: An exploration of weblog community boundaries. *Communities & Technologies, 5*. Retrieved from https://doc.novay.nl/dscgi/ds.py/Get/File-46041/weblog-community-boundaries.pdf

Elberse, A., & Eliashberg, J. (2003). Demand and supply dynamics for sequentially released products in international markets: The case of motion pictures. *Marketing Science, 22*(3), 329–354. doi:10.1287/mksc.22.3.329.17740.

Eliashberg, J., Jonker, J., Sawhney, M. S., & Wierenga, B. (2000). Moviemod: An implementable decision-support system for prerelease market evaluation of motion pictures. *Marketing Science, 19*(3), 226–243. doi:10.1287/mksc.19.3.226.11796.

Eliashberg, J., & Shugan, S. (1997). Film Critics: Influencers or Predictors? *Journal of Marketing, 61*(2), 68–78. doi:10.2307/1251831.

Ellison, N. B., Steinfield, C., & Lampe, C. (2007). The benefits of Facebook "friends:" social capital and college students' use of online social network sites. *Journal of Computer-Mediated Communication, 12*(4), 1143–1168. doi:10.1111/j.1083-6101.2007.00367.x.

Ellison, N., Heino, R., & Gibbs, J. (2006). Managing impressions online: Self-presentation processes in the online dating environment. *Journal of Computer-Mediated Communication, 11*(2), 415–441. doi:10.1111/j.1083-6101.2006.00020.x.

Ellram, L. M. (1996). The use of the case study method in logistics research. *Journal of Business Logistics, 17*(2), 93–138.

Endo, H., & Noto, M. (2003). A word-of-mouth information recommender system considering information reliability and user preferences. In *Proceedings of the IEEE International Conference on Systems, Man and Cybernetics* (pp. 2990-2995).

Engel, J. F., Blackwell, R. D., & Miniard, P. W. (1987). *Consumer behavior* (5th ed.). Chicago, IL: The Dryden Press.

Enkel, E., Perez-Freije, J., & Gassmann, O. (2005). Minimizing market risks through customer integration in new product development: Learning from bad practice. *Creativity and Innovation Management, 14*(4), 425–437. doi:10.1111/j.1467-8691.2005.00362.x.

Esmaeili, L., Nasiri, M., & Minaei-Bidgoli, B. (2011). Personalizing group recommendation to social network users. In Z. Gong, X. Luo, J. Chen, J. Lei, & F. L. Wang (Eds.), *Proceedings of the International Conference on Web Information Systems and Mining* (LNCS 6987, pp. 124-133).

Ester, M., Kriegel, H.-P., Jrg, S., & Xu, X. (1996). A density-based algorithm for discovering clusters in large spatial databases with noise. In *Proceedings of the 2nd International Conference on Knowledge Discovery and Data Mining* (pp. 226-231).

Estevez, P. A., Wera, P., & Saito, K. (2007, August 12-17). Selecting the most influential nodes in social networks. In *Proceedings of the International Joint Conference on Neural Networks*, Orlando, FL (pp. 2397-2402).

Estevez, P. A., Wera, P., & Saito, K. (1968). Patterns of influence: Local and cosmopolitan influentials. In Merton, R. K. (Ed.), *Social theory and social structure* (pp. 441–474). New York, NY: Free Press.

Euijin, K. (2003). *Factors impacting customers' trust in e-businesses: An empirical study of customers' initial trust in e-businesses*. Carbondale, IL: Southern Illinois University at Carbondale. doi:10.1109/HICSS.2005.272.

Even-Dar, E., & Shapirab, A. (2011). A note on maximizing the spread of influence in social networks. *Information Processing Letters*, *111*(4), 184–187. doi:10.1016/j.ipl.2010.11.015.

Everitt, B. S., Landau, S., & Leese, M. (2009). *Cluster analysis* (4th ed.). New York, NY: John Wiley & Sons.

Eysenck, H. J. (1956). *Sense and nonsense in psychology*. London, UK: Penguin Books.

Facebook. (2010). *Statistics*. Retrieved from http://www.facebook.com/press/info.php?statistics

Fahey, C. (2007). *The social web's coffeehouses, nightclubs, country clubs, and taverns*. Retrieved from http://www.graphpaper.com

Fahlander, F., & Oestigaard, T. (2004). The world as artefact. Archaeology as material culture studies. In Fahlander, F., & Oestigaard, T. (Eds.), *Material culture and other things: Post-disciplinary studies in the 21st century* (pp. 19–52). Gothenburg, Sweden: University of Gothenburg.

Farquhar, P. H., Herr, P. M., & Fazio, R. H. (1990). A relational model for category extensions of brands. *Advances in Consumer Research. Association for Consumer Research (U. S.)*, *17*, 856–860.

Fayard, A.-L. (2006). Interacting on a video-mediated stage: The collaborative construction of an interactional video setting. *Information Technology & People*, *19*(2), 152–169. doi:10.1108/09593840610673801.

Feder, G., & Savastano, S. (2006). The role of opinion leaders in the diffusion of new knowledge: The case of integrated pest management. *World Development*, *34*(7), 1287–1300. doi:10.1016/j.worlddev.2005.12.004.

Feick, L. F., & Price, L. L. (1987). The market maven: A diffuser of marketplace information. *Journal of Marketing*, *51*(1), 83–97. doi:10.2307/1251146.

Finn, J., & Gil de Zuniga, H. (2011). *Online credibility and community among blog users*. New Orleans, LA: American Society for Information Science and Technology. doi:10.1002/meet.2011.14504801110.

Fitzgerald, F. S. (1920). *This side of paradise*. New York, NY: Scribner.

Flanagin, A. J., & Metzger, M. J. (2007). The role of site features, user attributes, and information verification behaviors on the perceived credibility of web-based information. *New Media & Society*, *9*(2), 319–342. doi:10.1177/1461444807075015.

Fließ, S., & Kleinaltenkamp, M. (2004). Blueprinting the service company - Managing service processes efficiently. *Journal of Business Research*, *57*(4), 392–404. doi:10.1016/S0148-2963(02)00273-4.

Flowers, A. A., & Gregson, K. (2011). Virtual worlds for collaborative meetings. In Malik, K., & Choudhary, P. K. (Eds.), *Business organizations and collaborative Web: Practices, strategies and patterns* (pp. 220–242). Hershey, PA: IGI Global. doi:10.4018/978-1-60960-581-0.ch014.

Flynn, L. R., Goldsmith, R. E., & Eastman, J. K. (1994). The King and Summers opinion leadership scale: Revision and refinement. *Journal of Business Research*, *31*(1), 55–64. doi:10.1016/0148-2963(94)90046-9.

Fornell, C. (1992). A national customer satisfaction barometer: The Swedish experience. *Journal of Marketing*, *56*, 6–21. doi:10.2307/1252129.

Fornell, C., & Larcker, D. F. (1981). Evaluating structural equation models with unobservable variables and measurement error. *JMR, Journal of Marketing Research*, *18*(1), 39–50. doi:10.2307/3151312.

Freeman, L. C. (1979). Centrality in social networks conceptual clarification. *Social Networks*, *1*(3), 215–239. doi:10.1016/0378-8733(78)90021-7.

Fritch, J. W., & Cromwell, R. L. (2001). Evaluating Internet resources: Identity, affiliation, and cognitive authority in a networked world. *Journal of the American Society for Information Science and Technology*, *52*(6), 499–507. doi:10.1002/asi.1081.

Fueller, J. (2006). Why consumers engage in virtual new product developments initiated by producers. *Advances in Consumer Research. Association for Consumer Research (U. S.)*, *33*(1), 639–646.

Fueller, J., Bartl, M., Ernst, H., & Mühlbacher, H. (2006). Community based innovation: How to integrate members of virtual communities into new product development. *Electronic Commerce Research*, *6*(1), 57–73. doi:10.1007/s10660-006-5988-7.

Galam, S. (1996). When humans interact like atoms. In White, E., & Davis, J. H. (Eds.), *Understanding group behaviour* (*Vol. 1*, pp. 293–312). Mahwah, NJ: Lawrence Erlbaum.

Galam, S. (1996). Fragmentation versus stability in bimodal coalitions. *Physica A*, *230*, 174–188. doi:10.1016/0378-4371(96)00034-9.

Galam, S. (1997). Rational group decision making: A random field Ising model at t = 0. *Physica A*, *238*, 66–80. doi:10.1016/S0378-4371(96)00456-6.

Galam, S. (2004). Socio-physics: a personal Testimony. *Physica A. Statistical and Theoretical Physics*, *336*(1-2), 49–55. doi:10.1016/j.physa.2004.01.009.

Galbraith, C. S., DeNoble, S. B., Ehrlich, A. F., & Kline, D. M. (2008). Can experts really assess future technology success? A neural network and Bayesian analysis of early stage technology proposals. *The Journal of High Technology Management Research*, *17*(2), 125–138. doi:10.1016/j.hitech.2006.11.002.

Galegher, J., Sproull, L., & Kiesler, S. (1998). Legitimacy, authority, and community in electronic support groups. *Written Communication*, *15*(4), 493–530. doi:10.1177/0741088398015004003.

Gambetta, D. (2000). Can we trust? In Gambetta, D. (Ed.), *Trust: Making and breaking cooperative relations* (pp. 213–237). Oxford, UK: University of Oxford.

Gambetti, R. C. (2010). Ambient communication: How to engage consumers in urban touch points. *California Management Review*, *52*(3), 34–52. doi:10.1525/cmr.2010.52.3.34.

Gardner, H. (1983). *Friends of mind*. New York, NY: Basic Book.

Gefen, D. (2000). Customer loyalty in e-commerce. *Journal of the Association for Information Systems*, *3*, 27–51.

Gefen, D., Karahanna, E., & Straub, D. W. (2003). Trust and TAM in online shopping: An integration model. *Management Information Systems Quarterly*, *27*(1), 51–90.

Gichora, N. N., Fatumo, S. A., Ngara, M. V., Chelbat, N., Ramdayal, K., & Opap, K. B. et al. (2010). Ten simple rules for organizing a virtual conference—Anywhere. *PLoS Computational Biology*, *6*(2), e1000650. doi:10.1371/journal.pcbi.1000650 PMID:20195548.

Gilbert, N. (2002, October 11-12). *Transformation of the welfare state: The silent surrender of public responsibility*. Paper presented at the Workshop on Agent Social Agents: Ecology, Exchange, and Evolution Conference.

Gillmore, D. (2006). *We the media: Grassroots journalism by the people, for the people*. Sebastopol, CA: O'Reilly.

Gilly, M. C., Graham, J. L., Wolfinbarger, M. F., & Yale, L. J. (1998). A dyadic study of interpersonal information search. *Journal of the Academy of Marketing Science*, *26*(2), 83–100. doi:10.1177/0092070398262001.

Glaser, B. G., & Strauss, A. L. (1967). *The discovery of grounded theory: Strategies for qualitative research*. Chicago, IL: Aldine.

Glickman, V. (2001, May 22-23). *Panel discussion*. Paper presented at the Pan-Canadian Education Research Agenda Symposium on From Theory into Practice: Teacher Education/Educator Training: Current Trends and Future Directions, Toronto, ON, Canada.

Gochenour, P. H. (2006). Distributed communities and nodal subjects. *New Media & Society*, *8*(1), 33–51. doi:10.1177/1461444806059867.

Godes, D., & Mayzlin, D. (2004). Using online conversations to study word-of-mouth communication. *Marketing Science*, *23*(4), 545–560. doi:10.1287/mksc.1040.0071.

Goffman, E. (1959). *The presentation of self in everyday life*. New York, NY: Anchor Books.

GoldenBerg, J., Libai, B., & Muller, E. (2001). Talk of the Network: A Complex systems look at the underlying process of word-of-mouth. *Marketing Letters*, *12*(3), 211–223. doi:10.1023/A:1011122126881.

Goldstein, S. M., Johnston, R., Duffy, J. A., & Rao, J. (2002). The service concept: The missing link in service design research? *Journal of Operations Management, 20*(2), 121–134. doi:10.1016/S0272-6963(01)00090-0.

Goliath. (2009). *Sick of canned keynote speeches? Try an unconference*. Retrieved August 5, 2011, from http://goliath.ecnext.com/coms2/gi_0199-13627137/Sick-of-canned-keynote-speeches.html

Gower, J. C. (1971). A general coefficient of similarity and some of its properties. *Biometrics, 27*(4), 857–871. doi:10.2307/2528823.

Grandison, M. S. T., & Sloman, M. (2000). A survey of trust in internet applications. *IEEE Communications Surveys, 3*(4), 2–16. doi:10.1109/COMST.2000.5340804.

Granovetter, M. (1973). The strength of weak ties. *American Journal of Sociology, 78*(6), 1360–1380. doi:10.1086/225469.

Greenberg, J., & Jonas, E. (2003). Psychological motives and political orientation- the left, the right, and the rigid: Comment on Jost et al. (2003). *Psychological Bulletin, 129*(3), 376–382. doi:10.1037/0033-2909.129.3.376 PMID:12784935.

Gregson, P. H., & Little, T. A. (1998). Designing contests for teaching electrical engineering design. *International Journal of Engineering Education, 14*(5), 367–374.

Gross, R., & Acquisti, A. (2005). Information revelation and privacy in online social networks. In *Proceedings of the ACM Twelfth Annual Workshop on Privacy* (pp. 71-80).

Grossglauser, M., & Tse, D. (2002). Mobility increases the capacity of ad-hoc wireless networks. *IEEE/ACM Transactions on Networking, 10*(4), 477–486. doi:10.1109/TNET.2002.801403.

Gruhl, D., Liben-Nowell, D., Guha, R., & Tomkins, A. (2004). Information Diffusion through Blogspace. In *Proceedings of the 13th International Conference on World Wide Web* (pp. 491-501).

Gruzd, A., Wellman, B., & Takhteyev, Y. (2011). Imagining twitter as an imagined community. *The American Behavioral Scientist, 55*(10), 1294–1318. doi:10.1177/0002764211409378.

Guo, C., Shim, J. P., & Otondo, R. (2010). Social network services in China: An integrated model of centrality, trust and technology acceptance. *Journal of Global Information Technology Management, 13*(2), 76–99.

Guzzetta, M. (2006, June 18). Independent arts editor. *The Nantucket Independent*.

Haas, Z. J., Halpern, J. Y., & Li, L. (2006). Gossip based ad-hoc routing. *IEEE/ACM Transactions on Networking, 14*(3), 479–491. doi:10.1109/TNET.2006.876186.

Hackbert, P. H. (2009). Idea contests: A model for stimulating creativity and opportunity recognition. In *Proceedings of the 17th American Society of Business and Behavioral Sciences Annual Conference*, Las Vegas, NV.

Hagel, J. III, & Armstrong, A. (1997). *Net gain: Expanding markets through virtual communities*. Cambridge, MA: Harvard Business School Press.

Ha, H., Janda, S., & Muthaly, S. (2010). Development of brand equity: Evaluation of four alternative models. *The Service Industries Journal, 30*(6), 911. doi:10.1080/02642060802320253.

Ha, H., & John, J. (2010). Role of customer orientation in an integrative model of brand loyalty in services. *The Service Industries Journal, 30*(7), 1025. doi:10.1080/02642060802311252.

Hair, J. F., Anderson, R. E., Tatham, R. L., & Black, W. C. (1998). *Multivariate Data Analysis*. Upper Saddle River, NJ: Prentice Hall.

Hair, J. F., Black, W. C., Babin, B. J., Anderson, R. E., & Tatham, R. L. (2006). *Multivariate Data Analysis*. Upper Saddle River, NJ: Prentice Hall.

Hammouda, K. M. (2001). *Web mining: Clustering web documents a preliminary review*. Waterloo, ON, Canada: Department of Systems Design Engineering, University of Waterloo.

Hampton, K. N., Goulet, L. S., Rainie, L., & Purcell, K. (2011). *Social networking sites and our lives*. Washington, DC: Pew Research Center's Internet and American Life Project.

Han, J., & Kamber, M. (2000). *Data mining: Concepts and techniques*. San Francisco, CA: Morgan Kaufmann.

Hanley, A. J., Negassa, A., & Edwardes, D. deB. M. (2003). Statistical analysis of correlated data using generalized estimating equations: An orientation. *American Journal of Epidemiology*, *157*(4), 364–375. doi:10.1093/aje/kwf215 PMID:12578807.

Hanneman, A., & Riddle, M. (2005). Social network data. In A. Hanneman & M. Riddle (Eds.), *Introduction to social network methods* (Ch. 1). Riverside, CA: University of California, Riverside. Retrieved August 19, 2011, from www.faculty.ucr.edu/~hanneman/nettext/C1_Social_Network_Data.html

Harkin, F. (2007). The Wisdom of Crowds. *Financial Times*, p. 6.

Harkin, F. (2008, February 19). The Luxury World After Web 2.0. *Financial Times*, p. 14.

Harrison, R. (2009). Excavating Second Life. *Journal of Material Culture*, *14*(1), 75–106. doi:10.1177/1359183508100009.

Haveliwala, T. H., Gionis, A., & Indyk, P. (2000). Scalable techniques for clustering the Web. In *Proceedings of the Extended Abstracts of Webdb* (pp. 129-134).

Hawkins, D. I., Best, R. J., Coney, K. A., & Carey, K. A. (1995). *Consumer behavior: Implications for marketing strategy* (6th ed.). Boston, MA: McGraw-Hill/Irwin.

Heer, J., Card, S. K., & Landay, J. A. (2005). Prefuse: A toolkit for interactive information visualization. In *Proceedings of the SIGCHI Conference on Human Factors in Computing Systems* (pp. 421-430).

Helander, M., Lawrence, R., & Liu, Y. (2007). Looking for great ideas: Analyzing the innovation jam. In *Proceedings of the 9th WebKDD Workshop on Web Mining and Social Network Analysis* (pp. 66-73).

Herring, S. C., Scheidt, L. A., Bonus, S., & Wright, E. (2004). Bridging the gap: A genre analysis of weblogs. In *Proceedings of the 37th Annual Hawaii International Conference on System Sciences*.

Hewitt, A., & Forte, A. (2006). *Crossing boundaries: Identity management and student/faculty relationships on the Facebook*. Poster presented at the CSCW, Banff, AB, Canada. Retrieved from http://citeseerx.ist.psu.edu/viewdoc/download?doi=10.1.1.94.8152&rep=rep1&type=pdf

Hibbard, C. (2010). How IBM uses social media to spur employee innovation. *SocialMediaExaminer*. Retrieved November 5, 2010, from http://www.socialmediaexaminer.com/how-ibm-uses-social-media-to-spur-employee-innovation

Hildreth, W. B., & Woodrum, M. A. (2009). Mapping a field's development: 20 years of ABFM conferences. *Public Budgeting & Finance*, *29*(3), 15–27. doi:10.1111/j.1540-5850.2009.00934.x.

Hillery, G. A. (1955). Definitions of community: Areas of agreement. *Rural Sociology*, *20*(2), 111–123.

Hilligoss, B., & Rieh, S. Y. (2008). Developing a unifying framework of credibility assessment: Construct, heuristics, and interaction in context. *Information Processing & Management*, *44*, 1467–1484. doi:10.1016/j.ipm.2007.10.001.

Hill, S., Provost, F., & Volinsky, C. (2006). Network-based marketing: Identifying likely adopters via consumer networks. *Statistical Science*, *21*(2), 256–276. doi:10.1214/088342306000000222.

Hine, C. (2000). *Virtual ethnography*. Thousand Oaks, CA: Sage. Retrieved from http://books.google.com/books?hl=en&lr=&id=X5w1P2_iMNYC&oi=fnd&pg=PP9&dq=Virtual+Ethnography&ots=ljRtHwWQny&sig=jo16ZHsOtCcnQdI0MZv1zZTL4Ss

Hinz, O., & Spann, M. (2010). Managing information diffusion in name-your-own-price auctions. *Decision Support Systems*, *49*(4), 474–485. doi:10.1016/j.dss.2010.05.008.

Hofacker, C. F., Goldsmith, R. E., Bridges, E., & Swilley, E. (2006). E-services: A synthesis and research agenda. *Journal of Value Chain Management, 1*.

Hogan, T. D. (1981). Faculty research activity and the quality of graduate training. *The Journal of Human Resources*, *16*, 420–415. doi:10.2307/145628.

Ho, J. Y. C., & Dempsey, M. (2010). Viral marketing: Motivations to forward online content. *Journal of Business Research*, *63*(9-10), 1000–1006. doi:10.1016/j.jbusres.2008.08.010.

Hong, J., Lin, C., & Lin, Y. (2005). Operating a successful PowerTech creativity contest. *Journal of Technology Studies*, 25-31.

How to get, and keep, satisfied web customers. (2007). *Marketing News*, *41*(17), 31-32.

Howard, K. A., Rogers, T., Howard-Pitney, B., & Flora, J. A. (2000). Opinion leaders' support for tobacco control policies and participation in tobacco control activities. *American Journal of Public Health*, *90*(8), 1282–1287. PMID:10937010.

Howison, J., Wiggins, A., & Crowston, K. (2011). Validity issues in the use of social network analysis for the study of online communities. *Journal of the Association for Information Systems*, *12*(12), 767–797.

Hruschka, E. R., Campello, R. J. G. B., Freitas, A. A., & Leon, P. (2009). A survey of evolutionary algorithms for clustering. *IEEE Transactions on Systems, Man and Cybernetics. Part C, Applications and Reviews*, *39*(2), 133–155. doi:10.1109/TSMCC.2008.2007252.

Hsu, C. L., & Lu, H. P. (2004). Why do people play online games? An extended TAM with social influences and flow experience. *Information & Management*, *41*(7), 853–868. doi:10.1016/j.im.2003.08.014.

Hu, W. (2007, July 29). More than a meal plan. *The New York Times*.

Huberman, B. A., & Adamic, L. A. (2004). Information dynamics in the networked world. Lecture Notes in Physics, 398(3), 371-398.

Hughes, I. (2004). *Action & research: Action & research open web*. Retrieved from http://www2.fhs.usyd.edu.au/arrow/o/m01/rintro.htm

Hughes, I. (2004). Introduction. In I. Hughes (Ed.), *Action research electronic reader*. Sydney, Australia: The University of Sydney. Retrieved from http://www.fhs.usyd.edu.au/arrow/o/reader/rintro.htm

Hu, L., & Bentler, P. M. (1999). Cutoff criteria for fit indexes in covariance structure analysis: conventional criteria versus new alternatives. *Structural Equation Modeling*, *6*(1), 1–55. doi:10.1080/10705519909540118.

Hunter, D. E., & Kuh, G. D. (1987). The "write wing": Characteristics of prolific contributors to the higher education literature. *The Journal of Higher Education*, *58*, 443–462. doi:10.2307/1981317.

IEEE Communications Society. (n. d.). *TCCC mailing list*. Retrieved February 11, 2009, from http://www.comsoc.org/~tccc/list.html

IEEE. (2009). *IEEE and north Jersey section going Web 2.0, Facebook & LinkedIn*. Fort Lee, NJ: The IEEE Newsletter.

Inglehart, R., & Welzel, C. (2005). *Modernization, cultural change and democracy (based on World Value Survey)* (p. 64). Cambridge, UK: Cambridge University Press.

Interactive, S. X. S. W. (2006). *Web award winners*. Retrieved November 3, 2007, from http://2006.sxsw.com/interactive/web_awards/winner/

International Online Conference (IOC). (2011). *Going mobile online*. Retrieved June 10, 2011, from http://www.internationalonlineconference.org

Internet 2010 in Numbers. (2010). Retrieved from http://royal.pingdom.com/2011/01/12/internet-2010-in-numbers/

Jackson, M. O., & Wolinsky, A. (1996). A strategic model of social and economic networks. *Journal of Economic Theory*, *71*(1), 44–74. doi:10.1006/jeth.1996.0108.

Jackson, S. A., & Marsh, H. W. (1996). Development and validation of a scale to measure optimal experience: the flow state scale. *Journal of Sport & Exercise Psychology*, *18*(1), 17–35.

Jacovi, M., Guy, I., Ronen, I., Perer, A., Uziel, E., & Maslenko, M. (2011, September 24-28). Digital traces of interest: Deriving interest relationships from social media interactions. In *Proceedings of the 12th European Conference on Computer Supported Cooperative Work*, Aarhus, Denmark (pp. 21-40). Retrieved from http://www.springerlink.com/content/nk58m8jjm2847x33/abstract/

Jafari Momtaz, N., Aghaie, A., & Alizadeh, A. (2011). *Social network for marketing: Benefits and challenges*. Paper presented at the 5th Symposium on Advances in Science and Technology. Mashad, Iran.

Jain, A. K., & Dubes, R. C. (1988). *Algorithms for clustering data*. Upper Saddle River, NJ: Prentice Hall.

Jain, A. K., Murty, M. N., & Flynn, P. J. (1999). Data clustering: A review. *ACM Computing Surveys*, *31*, 264–323. doi:10.1145/331499.331504.

Johnson, B., & Shneiderman, B. (1991). Tree-maps: A space-filling approach to the visualization of hierarchical information structures. In *Proceedings of the IEEE Conference on Visualization* (pp. 284-291). Retrieved from http://drum.lib.umd.edu/bitstream/1903/370/2/CS-TR-2657.pdf

Johnston, R. (1999). Service operations management: Return to roots. *International Journal of Operations & Production Management, 19*(2), 104–124. doi:10.1108/01443579910247383.

Johnston, R., & Morris, B. (1985). Monitoring and control in service operations. *International Journal of Operations & Production Management, 5*(1), 32–38. doi:10.1108/eb054730.

Joinson, A. N. (2001). Self-disclosure in computer-mediated communication: The role of self-awareness and visual anonymity. *European Journal of Social Psychology, 31*(2), 177–192. doi:10.1002/ejsp.36.

Joinson, A. N., & Dietz-Uhler, B. (2002). Explanations for the perpetration of and reactions to deception in a virtual community. *Social Science Computer Review, 20*(3), 275–289.

Jones, Q. (1997). Virtual-communities, virtual settlements & cyber-archaeology: A theoretical outline. *Journal of Computer-Mediated Communication, 3*(3), 35–49.

Jøsang, A., Ismail, R., & Boyd, C. (2007). A survey of trust and reputation systems for online service provision. *Decision Support Systems, 43*(2), 618–644. doi:10.1016/j.dss.2005.05.019.

Jourdan, Z., Rainer, R. K., & Marshall, T. E. (2008). Business intelligence: An analysis of the literature 1. *Information Systems Management, 25*(2), 121–131. doi:10.1080/10580530801941512.

Jurvetson, S. (2008). *What exactly is viral marketing?* Retrieved February 18, 2009, from http://www.currypuffandtea.files.wordpress.com/2008/03/viral-marketing.pdf

Kabadayi, S., & Gupta, R. (2005). Website loyalty: an empirical investigation of its antecedents. *International Journal of Internet Marketing and Advertising, 2*(4), 321–345. doi:10.1504/IJIMA.2005.008105.

Kamakura, W. A., & Gary, J. R. (1993). Measuring brand value with scanner data. *International Journal of Research in Marketing, 10*, 9–22. doi:10.1016/0167-8116(93)90030-3.

Kamal, S., & Chu, S. C. (2008). The effect of perceived blogger credibility and argument quality on message elaboration and brand attitudes: An exploratory study. *Journal of Interactive Advertising, 8*(10), 26–37.

Kamvar, S. D., Schlosser, M. T., & Garcia-Molina, H. (2003). The Eigen Trust algorithm for reputation management in p2p networks. In *Proceedings of the Twelfth International Conference on World Wide Web* (pp. 640-651).

Kantardzic, M. (2002). *Data mining: Concepts, models, methods, and algorithms.* Piscataway, NJ: IEEE-Wiley. doi:10.1109/9780470544341.

Kanungo, T., Mount, D. M., Netanyahu, N. S., Piatko, C., Silverman, R., & Wu, A. Y. (2000). An efficient k-means clustering algorithm: Analysis and implementation. *IEEE Transactions on Pattern Analysis and Machine Intelligence, 2*(7), 881–892.

Karmakar, P. (2008). *Evolution of trust in distributed structured network* (Unpublished master's thesis). Indian Institute of Technology, Kharagpur, India.

Kaser, D. (2008). Just go. *Information Today, 25*(6), 1.

Katz, E., & Lazarsfeld, P. F. (1955). *Personal influence: The part played by people in the flow of mass communications.* New York, NY: Free Press.

Katz, J. E. (1957). The two-step flow of communication: An up-to-date report on a hypothesis. *Public Opinion, 21*(1), 61–78. doi:10.1086/266687.

Katz, R., & Tushman, M. (1979). Communication patterns, project performance, and task characteristics: an empirical evaluation and integration in an R&D setting. *Organizational Behavior and Human Performance, 23*(2), 139–162. doi:10.1016/0030-5073(79)90053-9.

Kavanaugh, A., Zin, T. T., Rosson, M. B., Carroll, J. M., Schmitz, J., & Kim, B. J. (2007). Local groups online: Political learning and participation. *Computer Supported Cooperative Work, 16*, 375–395. doi:10.1007/s10606-006-9029-9.

Kelleher, T., & Miller, B. M. (2006). Organizational blogs and the human voice: Relational strategies and relational outcomes. *Journal of Computer-Mediated Communication, 11*(2), 1. Retrieved October 19, 2011, from http://jcmc.indiana.edu/vol11/issue2/kelleher.html

Keller, E., & Berry, J. (2003). *One American in ten tells the other nine how to vote, where to eat, what to buy. They are the influentials.* New York, NY: Free Press.

Keller, E., & Berry, J. (2003). *The influentials.* New York, NY: Free Press.

Keller, K. L. (1993). Conceptualizing, measuring, and managing customer-based brand equity. *Journal of Marketing, 57*(1), 1–22. doi:10.2307/1252054.

Kelley, S. W., Donnelly, J. H. Jr, & Skinner, S. J. (1990). Customer participation in service production and delivery. *Journal of Retailing, 66*(3), 315–335.

Kellogg, D., & Nie, W. (1995). A framework for strategic service management. *Journal of Operations Management, 13*(4), 323–337. doi:10.1016/0272-6963(95)00036-4.

Kelly, J. A., St. Lawrence, J. S., Diaz, Y. E., Stevenson, L. Y., Hauth, A. C., & Brasfield, T. L. et al. (1991). HIV risk behavior reduction following intervention with key opinion leaders of population: An experimental analysis. *American Journal of Public Health, 81*(2), 168–171. doi:10.2105/AJPH.81.2.168 PMID:1990853.

Kelton, K., Fleischmann, K. R., & Wallace, W. A. (2008). Trust in digital information. *Journal of the American Society for Information Science and Technology, 59*(3), 363–374. doi:10.1002/asi.20722.

Kemmis, S., & McTaggart, R. (1988). *The action research planner.* Geelong, VIC, Australia: Deakin University.

Kempe, D., Kleinberg, J. M., & Tardos, E. (2005). Influential nodes in a diffusion model for social networks. In *Proceedings of the 32nd International Colloquium on Automata, Languages and Programming* (pp. 1127-1138).

Kempe, D., Kleinberg, J., & Tardos, E. (2003). Maximizing the spread of influence through a social network. In *Proceedings of the Ninth ACMSIGKDD International Conference on Knowledge Discovery and Data Mining* (pp. 137-146).

Kenix, J. L. (2009). Blogs as alternatives. *Journal of Computer-Mediated Communication, 14*, 790–822. doi:10.1111/j.1083-6101.2009.01471.x.

Kim, P. (2009). *Social media predictions.* Retrieved September 27, 2009, from http://www.beingpeterkim.com/2008/12/social-media-2009.html

Kim, W., Jeong, O. R., & Lee, S. W. (2010). On social Web sites. *Information Systems, 35*(2), 215–236. doi:10.1016/j.is.2009.08.003.

Kincheloe, J. L. (1991). *Teachers as researchers: Qualitative inquiry as a path to empowerment.* London, UK: Falmer.

King, R. (2008, June 5). Virtual conferences' home advantage. *BusinessWeek Online*, p. 14.

King, C. W., & Summers, J. O. (1970). Overlap of opinion leadership across consumer product categories. *Journal of Marketing Research, 7*(1), 43–50. doi:10.2307/3149505.

Kink, N., & Hess, T. (2008). Search engines as substitutes for traditional information sources? An investigation of media choice. *The Information Society, 24*, 18–29. doi:10.1080/01972240701771630.

Kirmani, A., & Baumgartner, H. (1999). Perceived quality and value, satisfaction and loyalty: New insights into processes underlying some familar constructs. *Advances in Consumer Research. Association for Consumer Research (U. S.), 26*(1), 598–598.

Kiss, C., & Bichler, M. (2008). Identification of influencers – measuring influence in customer networks. *Decision Support Systems, 46*(1), 233–253. doi:10.1016/j.dss.2008.06.007.

Klein, D., & Lechner, U. (2009). The ideas competition as tool of change management – Participatory behaviour and cultural perception. In *Proceedings of the 20th ISPIM Conference*, Vienna, Austria.

Kleinberg, J. M. (1999). Authoritative sources in a hyperlinked environment. *Journal of the ACM, 46*(5), 604–632. doi:10.1145/324133.324140.

Klein, H. K., & Myers, M. D. (1999). A set of principles for conducting and evaluating interpretive field studies in information systems. *Management Information Systems Quarterly, 23*(1), 67–93. doi:10.2307/249410.

Klemperer, P. (2006). Net effects and switching costs: Two short essays for the New Palgrave. *Social Science Research Network*. Retrieved September 25, 2009, from http://papers.ssrn.com/sol3/papers.cfm?abstract_id=907502

Kock, N. (1998). Can communication medium limitations foster better group discussion? An action research study. *Information & Management, 34*(5), 295–305. doi:10.1016/S0378-7206(98)00066-4.

Kodrzycki, Y. K. (2002). Education in the 21st century: Meeting the challenges of a changing world. Overview of the Federal Reserve Bank of Boston 47th Annual Conference themes. *Journal of Teacher Education, 57*(4).

Koh, J., & Kim, Y. G. (2003). Sense of virtual community: A conceptual framework and empirical validation. *International Journal of Electronic Commerce, 8*(2), 75–94.

Kohring, G. A. (1998). Sing models of social impact: the role of cumulative advantage. *Journal de Physique. I, 6,* 301. doi:10.1051/jp1:1996150.

Kotsiantis, S. B., & Pintelas, P. E. (2004). Recent advances in clustering: A brief survey. *WSEAS Transactions on Information Science and Applications, 1,* 73–81.

Koufaris, M. (2002). Applying the technology acceptance model and flow theory to online consumer behavior. *Information Systems Research, 13*(2), 205–223. doi:10.1287/isre.13.2.205.83.

Kozinets, V. R., de Valck, K., Wojnicki, C. A., & Wilner, J. S. S. (2010). Networked Narratives: Understanding word-of-mouth marketing in online communities. *Journal of Marketing, 74*(2), 71–89. doi:10.1509/jmkg.74.2.71.

Krackhardt, D., & Stern, R. N. (1988). Informal networks and organizational crises: An experimental simulation. *Social Psychology Quarterly, 51*(2), 123–140. doi:10.2307/2786835.

Krassa, M. (2008). *Better together: Lively mains streets, vital neighborhood, and engaging public places.* Paper presented at the Cornelius O'Brien Conference.

Krause, E. F. (1987). *Taxicab geometry.* Mineola, NY: Dover.

Krider, R. E., Li, T., Liu, Y., & Weinberg, C. B. (2005). The lead-lag puzzle of demand and distribution: A graphical method applied to movies. *Marketing Science, 24*(4), 635–645. doi:10.1287/mksc.1050.0149.

Kuan, H., Bock, G., & Vathanophas, V. (2008). Comparing the effects of website quality on customer initial purchase and continued purchase at e-commerce websites. *Behaviour & Information Technology, 27*(1), 3–16. doi:10.1080/01449290600801959.

Kucukarslan, S. N., & Nadkarni, A. (2008). Evaluating medication-related services in a hospital setting using the disconfirmation of expectations model of satisfaction. *Research in Social & Administrative Pharmacy, 4*(1), 12–22. doi:10.1016/j.sapharm.2007.01.001 PMID:18342819.

Kuh, G. D., & McCarthy, M. M. (1980). Research orientation of doctoral students in educational administration. *Educational Administration Quarterly, 16,* 101–121. doi:10.1177/0013161X8001600209.

Kulakowski, K. (2009). Opinion polarization in the Receipt-Accept-Sample model. *Physica A, 388,* 469. doi:10.1016/j.physa.2008.10.037.

Kumar, R., Novak, J., Raghavan, P., & Tomkins, A. (2005). On the Bursty Evolution of Blogspace. *World Wide Web: Internet and Web Information Systems, 8,* 159–178.

Kundisch, D., & Zorzi, R. (2009, August 6-9). Enhancing the quality of financial advice with Web 2.0 – An approach considering social capital in the private asset allocation. In *Proceedings of the Fifteenth Americas Conference on Information Systems*, San Francisco, CA.

Kuo, Y. F. (2003). A study on service quality of virtual community websites. *Total Quality Management and Business Excellence, 14,* 461–474. doi:10.1080/1478336032000047237a.

Kuo, Y. F. (2004). Integrating Kano's model into web-community service quality. *Total Quality Management & Business Excellence, 15*(7), 925–939. doi:10.1080/14783360410001681854.

Kwok, S. H., Lang, K. R., & Tam, K. Y. (2002). Peer-to-peer technology business and service models: Risks and opportunities. *Electronic Markets, 12*(3), 175–183. doi:10.1080/101967802320245947.

Lai, L., & Gamal, H. E. (2008). On cooperation in energy efficient wireless networks: The role of altruistic nodes. *IEEE Transactions on Wireless Communications, 7*(5), 1868–1878. doi:10.1109/TWC.2008.060568.

Laine, M. O. (2009). Bibliometric analysis and systematic review of management literature on virtual communities. In *Proceedings of the 9ᵗʰ European Academy of Management Conference*, Liverpool, UK.

Lakhani, K. R., & von Hippel, E. (2003). How open source software works: "free" user-to-user assistance. *Research Policy*, *32*, 923–943. doi:10.1016/S0048-7333(02)00095-1.

Lakshmanan, G. T., & Oberhofer, M. A. (2010). Knowledge discovery in the blogosphere: Approaches and challenges. *IEEE Internet Computing*, *14*(2), 24–32. doi:10.1109/MIC.2010.26.

Lamont, A. (2010). *Personal conversations with Alf Lamont, director of marketing and development*. Hollywood, CA: The Comedy Store.

Latané, B. (1981). The psychology of social impact. *The American Psychologist*, *36*(4), 343–356. doi:10.1037/0003-066X.36.4.343.

Latané, B. (1996). Dynamic social impact: Robust predictions from simple theory. In Hegselmann, R., Mueller, U., & Troitzsch, K. (Eds.), *Modeling and simulation in the social sciences from a philosophy of science point of view*. Dordrecht, The Netherlands: Kluwer Academic. doi:10.1007/978-94-015-8686-3_15.

Latané, B. (2000). Pressures to uniformity and the evolution of cultural norms: Modeling dynamics of social impact. In Hulin, C., & Ilgen, D. (Eds.), *Computational modeling of behavior in organizations. The third scientific discipline* (pp. 189–215). Washington, DC: American Psychological Association. doi:10.1037/10375-009.

Latané, B., & Liu, J. H. (1996). Inter subjective geometry of social space. *The Journal of Communication*, *46*(4), 26–34. doi:10.1111/j.1460-2466.1996.tb01502.x.

Lawal, H. (2006). Teacher education and the professional growth of the 21ˢᵗ century Nigerian teacher. *The African Symposium: Online Journal for the African Educational Research Network, 3*(2), 1-4.

Lawson, B., & Samson, D. (2001). Developing innovation capability in organisations: A dynamic capabilities approach. *International Journal of Innovation Management, 5*(3), 377–400. doi:10.1142/S1363919601000427.

Lazarsfeld, P. F., Berelson, B., & Gaudet, H. (1948). *The people's choice: How the voter makes up his mind in a presidential campaign*. New York, NY: Columbia University Press.

Lazarus, E. (2006). Social Shopping. *Marketing Magazine, 111*(38), 8.

Lechner, U., & Hummel, J. (2002). Business models and system architectures of virtual communities: From a sociological phenomenon to peer-to-peer architectures. *International Journal of Electronic Commerce, 6*(3), 41–53.

Leimeister, J. M., & Krcmar, H. (2004). Revisiting the virtual community business model. In *Proceedings of the 10ᵗʰ Americas Conference on Information Systems*, New York, NY (pp. 2716-2726).

Leimeister, J.-M., Huber, M., Bretschneider, U., & Krcmar, H. (2009). Leveraging crowdsourcing - Theory-driven design, implementation and evaluation of activation-supporting components for IT-based idea competitions. *Journal of Management Information Systems, 26*(1), 1–44.

Levy, A. Y. (2000). *Logic based artificial intelligence*. Boston, MA: Kluwer Academic.

Levy, M. R. (1978). Opinion leadership and television news uses. *Public Opinion Quarterly, 42*(3), 402–406. doi:10.1086/268463.

Lewenstein, M., Nowak, A., & Latane, B. (1992). The statistical mechanics of social impact. *Physical Review A., 45*, 703–716. doi:10.1103/PhysRevA.45.763 PMID:9907042.

Liang, C., & Chen, H. (2009). A study of the impacts of website quality on customer relationship performance. *Total Quality Management & Business Excellence, 20*(9), 971–988. doi:10.1080/14783360903181784.

Liang, K. Y., & Zeger, L. S. (1986). Longitudinal data analysis for discrete and continuous outcomes. *Biometrika, 73*(1), 13–22. doi:10.1093/biomet/73.1.13.

Liao, C., Chen, J. L., & Yen, D. C. (2007). Theory of planning behavior (TPB) and customer satisfaction in the continued use of e-service: an integrated model. *Computers in Human Behavior, 23*(6), 2804–2822. doi:10.1016/j.chb.2006.05.006.

Liao, C., Palvia, P., & Chen, J. L. (2009). Information technology adoption behavior life cycle: toward a technology continuance theory (TCT). *International Journal of Information Management, 29*(4), 309–320. doi:10.1016/j.ijinfomgt.2009.03.004.

Liben-Nowell, D., Novak, J., Kumar, R., Raghavan, P., & Tomkins, A. (2005). Geographic routing in social networks. *Proceedings of the National Academy of Sciences of the United States of America, 102*(33), 11623–11628. doi:10.1073/pnas.0503018102 PMID:16081538.

Lievrouw, L. A., & Livingstone, S. M. (2002). *Handbook of new media: Social shaping and. consequences of ICTs*. London, UK: Sage.

Li, F., & Du, T. C. (2011). Who is talking? An ontology-based opinion leader identification framework for word-of-mouth marketing in online social blogs. *Decision Support Systems, 51*(1), 190–197. doi:10.1016/j.dss.2010.12.007.

Limited, Q. E. (2008). Competing for defence ideas: Looking wider for innovation. *Strategic Direction, 24*(1), 35–37. doi:10.1108/02580540810839359.

Lin, Y., Sundaram, H., Chi, Y., Tatemura, J., & Tseng, B. (2006). Discovery of blog communities based on mutual awareness. In *Proceedings of the 3rd Annual Workshop on the Weblogging Ecosystem*, Edinburgh, UK.

Lin, C. F. (2008). The cyber-aspects of virtual communities: Free downloader ethics, cognition, and perceived service quality. *Cyberpsychology & Behavior, 11*(1), 69–73. doi:10.1089/cpb.2007.9932.

Lin, C. P., & Anol, B. (2008). Learning online social support: an investigation of network information technology based on UTAUT. *Cyberpsychology & Behavior, 11*(3), 268–272. doi:10.1089/cpb.2007.0057 PMID:18537495.

Lin, H. F. (2006). Understanding behavioral intention to participate in virtual communities. *Cyberpsychology & Behavior, 9*(5), 540–547. doi:10.1089/cpb.2006.9.540.

Lin, H. F. (2007). The role of online and offline features in sustaining virtual communities: An empirical study. *Internet Research, 17*(2), 119–138. doi:10.1108/10662240710736997.

Liu, G. Z. (1999). Virtual community presence in internet relay chatting. *Journal of Computer-Mediated Communication, 5*(1), 0.

Liu, X., Wang, Y., Li, Y., & Shi, B. (2011). Identifying topic experts and topic communities in the blogspace. In S. Lee, Z. Peng, X. Zhou, Y.-S. Moon, R. Unland, & J. Yoo (Eds.), *Proceedings of the 17th International Conference on Database Systems for Advanced Applications* (LNCS 7238, pp. 68-77). Retrieved from http://www.springerlink.com/index/H72Q8H3635160P27.pdf

Liu, Y. (2006). Word of mouth for movies: Its dynamics and impact on box office revenue. *Journal of Marketing, 70*(3), 74–89. doi:10.1509/jmkg.70.3.74.

Li, X., & Jacob, V. S. (2009). Adaptive data reduction for large-scale transaction data. *European Journal of Operational Research, 188*(3), 910–924. doi:10.1016/j.ejor.2007.08.008.

Li, Y.-M., Lin, C.-H., & Lai, C.-Y. (2010). Identifying influential reviewers for word-of-mouth marketing. *Electronic Commerce Research and Applications, 9*(4), 294–304. doi:10.1016/j.elerap.2010.02.004.

Loc.gov. (1998). *ALEXA Internet donates archive of the World Wide Web to Library of Congress*. Retrieved October 13, 2008, from http://www.loc.gov/today/pr/1998/98-167.html

Locock, L., Dopson, S., Chambers, D., & Gabbay, J. (2001). Understanding the role of opinion leaders in improving clinical effectiveness. *Social Science & Medicine, 5*(6), 745–757. doi:10.1016/S0277-9536(00)00387-7 PMID:11511050.

Lovelock, C. H., & Young, R. F. (1979). Look to consumers to increase productivity. *Harvard Business Review, 57*(3), 168–178.

Lui, S. M., Lang, K. R., & Kwok, S. H. (2002). Participation incentive mechanisms in peer-to-peer subscription systems. In *Proceedings of the 35th Annual Hawaii International Conference on System Sciences* (pp. 3925-3931).

Lu, J., Yao, J. E., & Yu, C. S. (2005). Personal innovativeness, social influences and adoption of wireless Internet services via mobile technology. *The Journal of Strategic Information Systems*, *14*(3), 245–268. doi:10.1016/j.jsis.2005.07.003.

Lu, Y., Zhou, T., & Wang, B. (2009). Exploring Chinese users' acceptance of instant messaging using the theory of planned behavior, the technology acceptance model, and the flow theory. *Computers in Human Behavior*, *25*(1), 29–39. doi:10.1016/j.chb.2008.06.002.

Lyons, B., & Henderson, K. (2005). Opinion leadership in a computer-mediated environment. *Journal of Consumer Behaviour*, *4*(5), 319–329. doi:10.1002/cb.22.

Madhavan, R., & Grover, R. (1998). From embedded knowledge to embodied knowledge: New product development as knowledge management. *Journal of Marketing*, *62*(4), 1–12. doi:10.2307/1252283.

Mak, V. (2008). *The emergence of opinion leaders in social networks*. Retrieved from http://ssrn.com/abstract=1157285

Malone, T. W., Laubacher, R., & Dellarocas, C. (2009). *Harnessing crowds: Mapping the genome of collective intelligence* (pp. 1–20). Cambridge, MA: MIT Press.

Manchala, D. W. (1998). Trust metrics, models and protocols for electronic commerce transactions. In *Proceedings of the 18th International Conference on Distributed Computing Systems*.

Marmanis, H., & Babenko, D. (2009). *Algorithms of the intelligent Web* (1st ed.). Greenwich, CT: Manning.

Marsh, S. (1994). *Formalising trust as a computational concept* (Unpublished doctoral dissertation). University of Stirling, Stirling, UK.

Marshall, B., Choi, J., El-Shinnaway, M. M., North, M., Svensson, L., & Wang, S. et al. (2009). Online and offline social ties of social network website users: An exploratory study in eleven societies. *Journal of Computer Information Systems*, *50*(1), 54–64.

Marshall, B., McDonald, D., Chen, H., & Chung, W. (2004). EBizPort: Collecting and analyzing business intelligence information. *Journal of the American Society for Information Science and Technology*, *55*(10), 873–891. doi:10.1002/asi.20037.

Marshall, J., & Heslop, L. (1988). Technology Acceptance in Canadian Retail Banking: A Study of Consumer Motivations and Use of ATMS. *International Journal of Bank Marketing*, *6*(4), 31–41. doi:10.1108/eb010836.

Marshall, R., & Gitosudarmo, I. (1995). Variation in the characteristics of opinion leaders across cultural broad. *Journal of International Consumer Marketing*, *8*(1), 5–22. doi:10.1300/J046v08n01_02.

Martinez, E., & Pina, J. M. (2010). Consumer responses to brand extensions: A comprehensive model. *European Journal of Marketing*, *44*(7-8), 1182–1205. doi:10.1108/03090561011047580.

Masters, J. (2001). *The history of action research* (Action Research e-Reports No. 3). Retrieved from http://www.fhs.usyd.edu.au/arrow/arer/003.htm

Mathwick, C., & Rigdon, E. (2004). Play, flow, and the online search experience. *The Journal of Consumer Research*, *31*(2), 324–332. doi:10.1086/422111.

Mayzlin, D. (2002). *The influence of social networks on the effectiveness of promotional strategies*. New Haven, CT: Yale School of Management.

Mazer, J. P., Murphy, R. E., & Simonds, C. J. (2007). I'll see you on "Facebook": the effects of computer-mediated teacher self-disclosure on student motivation, affective learning, and classroom climate. *Communication Education*, *56*(1), 1–17. doi:10.1080/03634520601009710.

McCall, D. (2001, May 22-23). *Panel discussion*. Paper presented at the Pan-Canadian Education Research Agenda Symposium on From Theory into Practice: Teacher Education/Educator Training: Current Trends and Future Directions, Toronto, ON, Canada.

McCarthy, R. (2007, February). The Power of Suggestion: Social Shopping Sites Turn Online Shopping Into a Group Activity. *INC. Magazine*, *29*, 48–49.

McCormick, J. P., & Pinderhughes, D. (2009, February 7). Promotion and tenure process as an exercise in strategic thinking. In *Proceedings of the Workshop at the American Political Science Association Teaching and Learning Conference*, Baltimore, MD. Retrieved July 27, 2011, from http://www.equity.psu.edu/sfm/docs/promo_tenure_09.pdf

McDermott, Ch. M., & O'Connor, G. C. (2002). Managing radical innovation: An overview of emergent strategy issues. *Journal of Product Innovation Management, 19*(6), 424–438. doi:10.1016/S0737-6782(02)00174-1.

McGuire, W. J. (1985). Attitudes and attitude change. In Gilbert, D., Fiske, S. T., & Lindzey, G. (Eds.), *The handbook of social psychology* (Vol. 2). New York, NY: McGraw-Hill.

McKernan, J. (1991). *Curriculum action research: A handbook of methods and resources for the reflective practitioner*. London, UK: Kogan Page.

McKnight, D. H., Choudury, V., & Kacmar, C. (2002). Developing and validating trust measures for e-commerce: An integrative typology. *Information Systems Research, 13*, 334–359. doi:10.1287/isre.13.3.334.81.

McKnight, D. H., Cummings, L. L., & Chervany, N. L. (1998). Initial trust formation in new organizational relationships. *Academy of Management Review, 23*, 472–490.

McNiff, J. (1995). *Action research: Principles and practice*. London, UK: Routledge.

McTaggart, R. (1992). *Action research: Issues in theory and practice*. Paper presented at the Methodological Issues in Qualitative Health Research Conference, Geelong, VIC, Australia.

Meadows-Klue, D. (2008). Falling in love 2.0: relationship marketing for the Facebook generation. *Journal of Direct Data and Digital Marketing Practice, 9*(3), 245–250. doi:10.1057/palgrave.dddmp.4350103.

Meetingsnet. (2008). Pull off a productive web conference. *Association Meetings, 20*(6), 39. Retrieved August 4, 2011, from http://meetingsnet.com/association-meetings/pull-productive-web-conference

Melville, N., Kraemer, K., & Gurbaxani, V. (2004). Review: Information technology and organizational performance: An integrative model of IT business value. *Management Information Systems Quarterly, 28*(2), 283–322.

Meng, W., Yu, C., & Liu, K.-L. (2002). Building efficient and effective metasearch engines. *ACM Computing Surveys, 34*(1), 48–89. doi:10.1145/505282.505284.

Merton, R. K. (1957). The role-set: Problems in sociological theory. *The British Journal of Sociology, 8*(2), 106–120. doi:10.2307/587363.

Merwe, R. V. D., & Heerden, G. V. (2009). Finding and utilizing opinion leaders: Social networks and the power of relationships. *South African Journal of Business Management, 40*(3), 65–76.

Messerschmitt, D. G., Peltonen, J., Laine, M. O. J., & Oza, N. (2008). *Community networked services: Learning from Web 2.0*. Retrieved from http://papers.ssrn.com/sol3/papers.cfm?abstract_id=1320947

Miah, S., & Islam, S. (2003). *Banglapedia: National Encyclopedia of Bangladesh* (Vol. 4, p. 119). Bangladesh: Asiatic Society of Bangladesh.

Michael, J., & Irit, A. (2008). Blogs – new source of data analysis. *Issues in Informing Science and Technology, 5*(1), 433–445.

Miladian, H., & Nagendra, B. K. (2009). Automobile scene: Brand-awareness, image and personality. *SCMS Journal of Indian Management*, 81-85.

Miles, M. B., & Huberman, A. M. (1994). *Qualitative data analysis: A sourcebook of new methods* (2nd ed., pp. 28–29). Newbury Park, CA: Sage.

Mills, P. K., Chase, R. B., & Marguiles, N. (1983). Motivating the client/employee system as a service production strategy. *Academy of Management Review, 8*(3), 475–485.

Mishra, N., Schreiber, R., Stanton, I., & Tarjan, R. (2007). Clustering social networks. In A. Bonato & F. R. K. Chung (Eds.), *Proceedings of the 5th International Conference on Algorithms and Models for the Web-Graphs* (LNCS 4863, pp. 56-67).

Mocian, H. (2009). *Survey of distributed clustering techniques (M.Sc. Internal Research Project)*. London, UK: Imperial College.

Mohr, J., & Nevin, J. R. (1990). Communication Strategies in Marketing Channels: A theoretical perspective. *Journal of Marketing, 54*(4), 36–51. doi:10.2307/1251758.

Moraga, A., Calero, C., & Piattini, M. (2006). Comparing different quality models for portals. *Online Information Review, 30*(5), 555–568. doi:10.1108/14684520610706424.

Morgan, R. M., & Hunt, S. D. (1994). The commitment-trust theory of relationship marketing. *Journal of Marketing, 58*(3), 20–38. doi:10.2307/1252308.

Mortensen, T., & Walker, J. (2002). Blogging thoughts: Personal publication as an online research tool. In Morrison, A. (Ed.), *Researching ICTs in context* (pp. 249–279). Oslo, Norway: InterMedia.

Morton, J. (1992). Brand quality segments: Potent way to predict preference. *Marketing News, 26*(19), IR8.

Mossel, E., & Roch, S. (2007). On the submodularity of influence in social networks. In *Proceedings of the 39th Annual ACM Symposium on Theory of Computing* (pp. 128-134).

Mouton, J. (1996). *Understanding social research*. Pretoria, South Africa: JL. Van Schaik.

Mrkwicka, K., Kiebling, M., & Kolbe, L. M. (2009, August 6-9). Potential of Web 2.0 applications for viewer retention: The case of viewer relationship management in German TV stations. In *Proceedings of the Fifteenth Americas Conference on Information Systems*, San Francisco, CA.

Mui, L. (2002). *Computational models of trust and reputation: Agents, evolutionary games, and social networks* (Unpublished doctoral dissertation). Massachusetts Institute of Technology, Cambridge, MA.

Munns, A. K. (1995). Potential influence of trust on the successful completion of a project. *International Journal of Project Management, 13*(1), 19–24. doi:10.1016/0263-7863(95)95699-E.

Murphy, R. R. (2000). Using robot competitions to promote intellectual development. *AI Magazine, 21*(1), 77–90.

Myers, J. H., & Robertson, T. S. (1972). Dimensions of opinion leadership. *JMR, Journal of Marketing Research, 9*(1), 41–46. doi:10.2307/3149604.

Myers, M. D. (2004). Hermeneutics in information systems research. In Mingers, J., & Willcocks, L. (Eds.), *Social theory and philosophy for information systems* (pp. 103–128). Chichester, UK: John Wiley & Sons.

Nahapiet, J., & Ghoshal, S. (1994). Social capital, intellectual capital, and the organizational advantage. *Academy of Management Review, 23*(2), 242–267.

Nanacherla, A. (2009). Social networking's net worth. *Training & Development*, 18–19.

Narendra, K. S., & Thathachar, M. A. L. (1989). *Learning Automata: An introduction*. Upper Saddle River, NJ: Prentice Hall.

Nasar, J. L., & Kang, J. (1989). A post-jury evaluation: The Ohio State University design competition for a center for the visual arts. *Environment and Behavior, 21*(4), 464–484. doi:10.1177/0013916589214005.

Naughton, M., Kushmerick, N., & Carthy, J. (2006). Clustering sentences for discovering events in news articles. In M. Lalmas, A. MacFarlane, S. Rüger, A. Tombros, T. Tsikrika, & A. Yavlinsky (Eds.), *Proceedings of the 28th European Conference on Advances in Information Retrieval* (LNCS 3936, pp. 535-538).

Navo, S., Navo, D., & Carmel, E. (2011). Unlocking the business potential of virtual worlds. *MIT Sloan Management Review, 52*(3), 13–17.

Newman, J. (2002). *Participatory action research*. Retrieved September 24, 2007, from http://www.goshen.edu.soan96p.htm

Neyer, A.-K., Bullinger, A. C., & Moeslein, K. M. (2009). Integrating inside and outside innovators: A sociotechnical systems perspective. *R&D Management Journal, 39*(4), 410–419. doi:10.1111/j.1467-9310.2009.00566.x.

Nielsen. (2007). *Word-of-mouth the most powerful selling tool: Nielsen global survey*. Retrieved from http://www.nielsen.com/media/2007/pr_071001.html

Nohria, N., & Eccles, R. G. (Eds.). (1992). *Problems of explanation in economic sociology, networks and organizations: Structure, form, and action*. Boston, MA: Harvard Business School.

Nolan, D. (1971). *Classifying and analyzing politico-economic systems. The Individualist*. Society for Individual Liberty.

Nonaka, I. A., & Takeuchi, H. A. (1995). *The knowledge-creating company: How Japanese companies create the dynamics of innovation*. New York, NY: Oxford University Press.

Novak, T. P., Hoffman, D. L., & Duhachek, A. (2003). The influence of goal-directed and experiential activities in online flow experiences. *Journal of Consumer Psychology*, *13*(1-2), 3–16. doi:10.1207/S15327663JCP13-1&2_01.

Novak, T. P., Hoffman, D. L., & Yung, Y. F. (2000). Measuring the customer experience in online environments: a structural modeling approach. *Marketing Science*, *19*(1), 22–42. doi:10.1287/mksc.19.1.22.15184.

Nowak, A., Szamrej, J., & Latane, B. (1990). From private attitude to public opinion: A dynamic theory of social impact. *Psychological Review*, *97*, 362. doi:10.1037/0033-295X.97.3.362.

Nowak, M. A., Tarmita, C. E., & Antal, T. (2010). Evolutionary dynamics in structured population. *Philosophical Transaction of the Royal Society B*, *365*(1537), 19–30. doi:10.1098/rstb.2009.0215.

Nunnally, J. C. (1978). *Psychometric theory*. New York, NY: McGraw-Hill.

Nwosu, B. U., & Lee, M. M. (2008). Evaluation of short and tall stature in children. *American Family Physician*, *78*(5), 597–604. PMID:18788236.

Nyblom, J., Borgatti, S., Roslakka, J., & Salo, A. M. (2003). Statistical Analysis of Network Data—An Application to Diffusion of Innovation. *Social Networks*, *25*, 175–195. doi:10.1016/S0378-8733(02)00050-3.

O'Cass, A., & Carlson, J. (2010). Examining the effects of website-induced flow in professional sporting team websites. *Internet Research*, *20*(2), 115–134. doi:10.1108/10662241011032209.

O'Reilly, T. (2005). *What is Web 2.0: Design patterns and business models for the next generation software*. Retrieved September 26, 2009, from http://oreilly.com/pub/a/oreilly/tim/news/2005/09/30/what-is-web-20.html

Ogawa, S., & Piller, F. T. (2006). Reducing the risks of new product development. *MIT Sloan Management Review*, *47*(2), 65–71.

Oh, S., Choi, J., Lee, S., & Jung, S. (2003). Toward an integrated framework for assessing website performance: Depending on presence of virtual community. In *Proceedings of the Annual Meeting of the Decision Sciences Institute* (pp. 955-960).

Oldenburg, R. (1989). *The great good place: Cafes, coffee shops, community centers, beauty parlors, general stores, bars, hang outs, and how they get you through the day*. New York, NY: Paragon House.

Oldenburg, R. (1991). *The great good place*. New York, NY: Marlow.

Oldenburg, R. (2000). *Celebrating the Third Place: Inspiring stories about the great good places at the heart of our communities*. New York, NY: Marlow.

Oliver, R. L. (1977). Effects of expectation and disconfirmation on post-exposure product evaluation: an alternative interpretation. *The Journal of Applied Psychology*, *62*(4), 480–486. doi:10.1037/0021-9010.62.4.480.

Oliver, R. L. (1980). A cognitive model of the antecedents and consequences of satisfaction decisions. *JMR, Journal of Marketing Research*, *17*(4), 460–469. doi:10.2307/3150499.

Oliver, R. L. (1997). *Satisfaction: A Behavioral Perspective on the Consumer*. New York, NY: McGraw-Hill.

O'Malley, G. (2006). MySpace vs. eBay? Site Leaps into e-commerce. *Advertising Age*, *77*(37), 6.

Opsahl, T., Agneessens, F., & Skvoretz, J. (2010). Node Centrality in Weighted Networks: Generalizing Degree and Shortest Paths. *Social Networks*, *32*(3), 245–251. doi:10.1016/j.socnet.2010.03.006.

Outrider broadens search marketing offering with addition of social media marketing practice. (2008). *Marketing Business Weekly, 28.*

Paccagnella, L. (1997). Getting the seats of your pants dirty: Strategies for ethnographic research on virtual communities. *Journal of Computer-Mediated Communication*, *3*(1).

Palmgreen, P., & Rayburn, J. D. (1982). Gratifications sought and media exposure: An expectancy value model. *Communication Research*, *9*(4), 561–580. doi:10.1177/009365082009004004.

Pandian, S. (2010). Malaysia's 12th general election: An analysis. *European Journal of Soil Science*, *14*(4), 508–523.

Panteli, N., & Duncan, E. (2004). Trust and temporary virtual teams: Alternative explanations and dramaturgical relationships. *Information Technology & People*, *17*(4), 423–441. doi:10.1108/09593840410570276.

Pan, W. (2001). Akaike's information criterion in generalized estimating equations. *Biometrics*, *57*(1), 120–125. doi:10.1111/j.0006-341X.2001.00120.x PMID:11252586.

Papacharissi, Z. (2002). The self online: The utility of personal home pages. *Journal of Broadcasting & Electronic Media*, *46*(3), 346–368. doi:10.1207/s15506878jobem4603_3.

Papacharissi, Z. (2002). The presentation of self in virtual life: Characteristics of personal home pages. *Journalism & Mass Communication Quarterly*, *79*(3), 643–660.

Parasuraman, A., Zeithaml, V. A., & Berry, L. L. (1985). A conceptual model of service quality and its implications for future research. *Journal of Marketing*, *49*(4), 41–50. doi:10.2307/1251430.

Parasuraman, A., Zeithaml, V. A., & Malhotra, A. (2005). ES-QUAL: A multiple-item scale for assessing electronic service quality. *Journal of Service Research*, *7*(3), 213. doi:10.1177/1094670504271156.

Parasuraman, A., & Zinkhan, G. M. (2002). Marketing to and serving customers through the Internet: An overview and research agenda. *Journal of the Academy of Marketing Science*, *30*(4), 286. doi:10.1177/009207002236906.

Park, N., Kee, K. F., & Valenzuela, S. (2009). Being immersed in social networking environment: Facebook groups, uses and gratifications, and social outcomes. *Cyberpsychology & Behavior*, *12*(6), 729–733. doi:10.1089/cpb.2009.0003 PMID:19619037.

Patterson, D. A. (2004). The health of research conferences and the dearth of big idea papers. *Communications of the ACM*, *47*(12), 23–24. doi:10.1145/1035134.1035153.

Patterson, L., & Shannon, P. (1993). Reflection, inquiry, action. In Patterson, L., Santa, C. M., Short, K. G., & Smith, K. (Eds.), *Teachers are researchers: Reflection and action* (pp. 7–11). Newark, DE: International Reading Association.

Pavlou, P. A., & Lin, C. (2002). What drives electronic commerce across cultures? Across-cultural empirical investigation of the theory of planned behavior. *Journal of Electronic Commerce Research*, *3*(4), 240–253.

Payne, W. (1983). A study of emotion: Developing emotional intelligence, self integration relating to fear, pain and desire. *Dissertation Abstracts International*, *47*, 203A (AAC 8605928).

Paynter, B. (2010). Five steps to social currency. *Fast Company*, *145*, 48.

Pease, J. (1967). Faculty influence and professional participation by doctorate students. *Sociological Inquiry*, *37*, 63–70. doi:10.1111/j.1475-682X.1967.tb00639.x.

Peluchette, J., & Karl, K. (2008). Social networking profiles: an examination of student attitudes regarding use and appropriateness of content. *Cyberpsychology & Behavior*, *11*(1), 95–97. doi:10.1089/cpb.2007.9927 PMID:18275320.

Pempek, T. A., Yermolayeva, Y. A., & Calvert, S. L. (2009). College students' social networking experiences on Facebook. *Journal of Applied Developmental Psychology*, *30*(3), 227–238. doi:10.1016/j.appdev.2008.12.010.

Pénard, T., & Poussing, N. (2010). Internet use and social capital: The strength of virtual ties. *Journal of Economic Issues*, *44*(3), 569–595. doi:10.2753/JEI0021-3624440301.

Perer, A., & Shneiderman, B. (2006). Balancing systematic and flexible exploration of social networks. *IEEE Transactions on Visualization and Computer Graphics*, *12*(5), 693–700. doi:10.1109/TVCG.2006.122 PMID:17080789.

Piller, F. T., & Walcher, D. (2006). Toolkits for idea competitions: A novel method to integrate users in new product development. *R & D Management*, *36*(3), 307–318. doi:10.1111/j.1467-9310.2006.00432.x.

Pitt, L. F., Watson, R. T., & Kavan, C. B. (1995). Service quality: A measure of information systems effectiveness. *Management Information Systems Quarterly*, *19*(2), 173–187. doi:10.2307/249687.

Plaisant, C., & Grinstein, G. (2007). Promoting insight based evaluation of visualizations: From contest to benchmark repository. *IEEE Transactions on Visualization and Computer Graphics*, 1–18.

Plewczyn'ski, D. (1998). Landau theory of social clustering. *Physica A, 261*, 608–617. doi:10.1016/S0378-4371(98)00349-5.

Poetz, M. K., & Schreier, M. (2009). *The value of crowdsourcing: Can users really compete with professionals in generating new product ideas?* Paper presented at the Druid Summer Conference, Copenhagen, Denmark.

Polegato, R., & Wall, M. (1980). Information seeking by fashion opinion leaders and followers. *Family and Consumer Sciences Research Journal, 8*(5), 327–338.

Pomerantz, A. M. (1984). Agreeing and disagreeing with assessment: Some features of preferred/dis-preferred turn shapes. In Atkinson, J. M., & Heritage, J. (Eds.), *Structure of social action: Studies in conversation analysis*. Cambridge, UK: Cambridge University Press.

Potvin, J. H. (1983). Planning and organizing an annual conference. *IEEE Transactions on Personal Communication, 26*(3), 123-152.

Prahalad, C. K., & Ramaswamy, V. (2004). Co-creating unique value with customers. *Strategy and Leadership, 32*(3), 4–9. doi:10.1108/10878570410699249.

Pratt, B. (2005). *The day the internet search engines stopped growing!* Retrieved November 11, 2009, from http://www.workoninternet.com/article_3691.html

Preece, J. (2000). *Online communities: Designing usability and supporting sociabilty*. New York, NY: John Wiley & Sons.

Preston, R. (2009, August 15). Down to business: Just what the IT industry needs – More regulation. *InformationWeek*. Retrieved September 26, 2009, from http://www.informationweek.com/story/showArticle/jhtml?articleID=219300149

Pyle, D. (2004). *The handbook of data mining*. Boca Raton, FL: CRC Press.

Quinton, B. (2009). *Social nets, video are sweet spots for online growth: Nielsen*. Retrieved from http://www.promotionalbuzz.com/2009/05/social-nets-video-are-sweet-spots-for-online-growth-nielsen/

Raacke, J., & Bonds-Raacke, J. (2008). MySpace and Facebook: applying the uses and gratifications theory to exploring friend networking sites. *Cyberpsychology & Behavior, 11*(2), 169–174. doi:10.1089/cpb.2007.0056 PMID:18422409.

Rahaman, S. F., Srilakhsmi, M., & Yasin, S. (2011). Quantification of social blog network using B-Rank technique and blog recommendation. *International Journal of Computer Science and Emerging Technologies, 2*(4), 455–462.

Rahm, E., & Do, H. H. (2000). Data cleaning: Problems and current approaches. *IEEE Bulletin on Data Engineering, 23*(4), 3–13.

Rajeev, S. G., Rastogi, R., & Shim, K. (1999). Rock: A robust clustering algorithm for categorical attributes. In *Proceedings of the 15th International Conference on Data Engineering* (pp. 512-521).

Ramirez, A. Jr, Walther, J. B., & Sunnafrank, M. (2002). Information-seeking strategies, uncertainty, and computer-mediated communication toward a conceptual model. *Human Communication Research, 28*(2), 213–228.

Randolph, G. B., & Owen, D. O. (2008). Attracting communities and students to IT with a community service web contest. *Information Systems*, 77–80.

Recuero, R. D. C. (2008). Information flows and social capital in weblogs: A case study in the Brazilian blogosphere. In *Proceedings of the Nineteenth ACM Conference on Hypertext and Hypermedia* (pp. 97-106).

Reichwald, R., & Piller, F. (2009). *Interaktive Wertschoepfung: Open Innovation, Individualisierung und neue Formen der Arbeitsteilung* (2nd ed.). Wiesbaden, Germany: Gabler.

Reis, D. (2010). *Quality vs. quantity: Sustainable social media strategy*. Retrieved from http://chiefmarketer.com/news/quality-vs-quantity-sustainable-social-media-strategy

Reskin, B. (1977). Scientific productivity and the reward structure of science. *American Sociological Review, 16*, 420–504.

Reskin, B. (1979). Academic sponsorship and scientific careers. *Sociology of Education*, *52*, 126–146. doi:10.2307/2112319.

Rettie, R. (2001). An exploration of flow during Internet use. *Internet Research*, *11*(2), 103–113. doi:10.1108/10662240110695070.

Richard, E. P., & Cacioppo, J. T. (1981). *Attitude and persuasion: Classic and contemporary approaches*. Dubuque, IA: William C. Brown.

Riemer, K., Richter, A., & Seltsikas, P. (2010). Enterprise Microblogging: Procrastination or productive use? In *Proceedings of the Americas Conference on Information Systems* (p. 50). Retrieved October 19, 2011, from http://aisel.aisnet.org/amcis2010/506

Rivadeneira, A. W., Gruen, D. M., Muller, M. J., & Millen, D. R. (2007). Getting our head in the clouds: Toward evaluation studies of tagclouds. In *Proceedings of the SIGCHI Conference on Human Factors in Computing Systems* (pp. 995-998).

Rogers, E. M. (1995). *Diffusion of innovations*. New York, NY: Free Press.

Rogers, E. M., & Cartano, D. G. (1962). Methods of measuring opinion leadership. *Public Opinion*, *26*(3), 435–441. doi:10.1086/267118.

Rogers, E., & Kincaid, D. L. (1981). *Communication networks: A paradigm for new research*. New York, NY: Free Press.

Rokeach, M. (1973). *The nature of human values*. New York, NY: Free Press.

Roling, N., Ascroft, J., & Wa Chege, F. (1976). Diffusion of innovations and the issue of equity in rural development. *Communication Research*, *3*(2), 155–171. doi:10.1177/009365027600300204.

Roobina, O. (1990). Construction and validation of a scale to measure celebrity endorsers' perceived expertise, trustworthiness, and attractiveness. *Journal of Advertising*, *19*(3), 39–52.

Rosenblum, D. (2007). What anyone can know: The privacy risks of social networking sites. *IEEE Security & Privacy*, *5*(3), 40–49. doi:10.1109/MSP.2007.75.

Ross, D. A. R. (2007). Backstage with the knowledge boys and girls: Goffman and distributed agency in an organic online community. *Organization Studies*, *28*(3), 307–325. doi:10.1177/0170840607076000.

Roth, A. V., & Menor, L. J. (2003). Insights into service operations management: A research agenda. *Production and Operations Management*, *12*(2), 145–164. doi:10.1111/j.1937-5956.2003.tb00498.x.

Rowley, J. (2006). An analysis of the e-service literature: Towards a research agenda. *Internet Research*, *16*(3), 339–359. doi:10.1108/10662240610673736.

Roychoudhury, R. (2005). *Brownian Gossip: Exploiting node mobility for diffusing information in wireless networks*. Paper presented at the Workshop on Stochasticity in Distributed Systems.

Roy, M. (2009). *The Bharati and the Social Mobility in the Bengal*. Kolkata, India: Aruna Prakashani.

Sahebi, S., Oroumchian, F., & Khosravi, R. (2008). An enhanced similarity measure for utilizing site structure in web personalization systems. In *Proceedings of the IEEE/WIC/ACM International Conference on Web Intelligence and Intelligent Agent Technology* (Vol. 3, pp. 82-85).

Sampson, S. E., & Froehle, C. M. (2006). Foundations and implications of a proposed unified services theory. *Production and Operations Management*, *15*(2), 329–343. doi:10.1111/j.1937-5956.2006.tb00248.x.

Sannicolas, N. (1997). Erving Goffman, dramaturgy, and on-line relationships. *Cybersociology Magazine*, *1*. Retrieved from http://www.cybersociology.com/files/1_2_sannicolas.html

Santos, J. (2003). E-service quality: A model of virtual service quality dimensions. *Managing Service Quality*, *13*(3), 233–246. doi:10.1108/09604520310476490.

Sarwate, A. D., & Dimakis, A. G. (2009). The impact of mobility on gossip algorithm. In *Proceedings of the 28th Annual International Conference on Computer Communication*, Rio de Janeiro, Brazil.

Saunders, J., Davis, J. M., & Monsees, D. M. (1974). Opinion leadership in family planning. *Journal of Health and Social Behavior*, *15*(3), 217–227. doi:10.2307/2137022 PMID:4436526.

Sawhney, M. S., & Eliashberg, J. (1996). A parsimonious model for forecasting gross box-office revenues of motion pictures. *Marketing Science, 15*(2), 113–131. doi:10.1287/mksc.15.2.113.

Sawyer, R. K. (2005). Social Emergence: *Societies as complex systems*. Cambridge, UK: Cambridge University Press.

Schegloff, E. A. (2007). *Sequence organization in interaction: a primer in Conversation Analysis* (*Vol. 1*). Cambridge, UK: Cambridge University Press. doi:10.1017/CBO9780511791208.

Schelling, T. (1971). Dynamic models of segregation. *The Journal of Mathematical Sociology, 1*, 143–186. doi:10.1080/0022250X.1971.9989794.

Schelling, T. (1972). A process of residential segregation: Neighborhood tipping. In Pascal, A. (Ed.), *Racial discrimination in economic life* (pp. 157–184). Lexington, MA: D.C. Heath.

Schepers, J., Schnell, R., & Vroom, P. (1999). From idea to business - How Siemens bridges the innovation gap. *Research-Technology Management, 42*, 26–31.

Schroder, A., & Holzle, K. (2010). Virtual communities for innovation: Influence factors and impact on company innovation. *Virtual Communities for innovation, 19*(3), 257-267.

Schroeder, L., O'Leary, R., Jones, D., & Poocharoen, O. (2004). Routes to scholarly success in public administration: Is there a right path? *Public Administration Review, 64*(1), 92–103. doi:10.1111/j.1540-6210.2004.00349.x.

Schultze, U., & Boland, R. (2000). Knowledge management technology and the reproduction of knowledge work practices. *The Journal of Strategic Information Systems, 9*(2-3), 193–212. doi:10.1016/S0963-8687(00)00043-3.

Scott, J. (1991). *Network analysis: A handbook*. Newbury Park, CA: Sage.

Sekaran, U. (1992). *Research method for business* (2nd ed.). New York, NY: John Wiley & Sons.

Sen, A. (2006). *Identity and violence: The illusion of destiny (issues of our time)*. New York, NY: W. W. Norton.

Sen, G. N. (1962). An English Kabiwala of Bengal. *Midwest Folklore, 12*(1), 27–30.

Sen, S. (1960). *History of Bengali Literature (Forwarded by Jawaharlal Nehru)*. New Delhi, India: Sahitya Academy.

Sen, S., & Lerman, D. (2007). Why are you telling me this? An examination into negative consumer reviews on the web. *Journal of Interactive Marketing, 21*(4), 76–94. doi:10.1002/dir.20090.

Seung, H. L., Sang, W. K., Sunju, P., & Joon, H. L. (2009, June 28). Determining content power users in a blog network. In *Proceedings of the 3rd SNA-KDD Workshop*, Paris, France.

Shaeffer, S. (1990). Participatory approaches to teacher training. In Rust, V., & Dalin, P. (Eds.), *Teachers and teaching in the developing world*. New York, NY. Garland.

Shafer, G. (1976). *A mathematical theory of evidence*. Princeton, NJ: Princeton University Press.

Sheng, L., Li, S., & Zhu, J. (2008). *Using the IBM innovation factory idea management solution to focus your company on innovation and ideation for strategic issues*. Armonk, NY: IBM.

Shen, Y. C., Huang, C. Y., Chu, C. H., & Liao, H. C. (2010). Virtual community loyalty: An interpersonal-interaction perspective. *International Journal of Electronic Commerce, 15*(1), 49–73. doi:10.2753/JEC1086-4415150102.

Sheykh Esmaili, K., Jamali, M., Neshati, M., Abolhassani, H., & Soltan-Zadeh, Y. (2006). *Experiments on Persian Weblogs*. Paper presented at the WWW Workshop on Web Intelligence.

Shih, H. (2004). An empirical study on predicting user acceptance of e-shopping on the Web. *Information & Management, 41*(3), 351–368. doi:10.1016/S0378-7206(03)00079-X.

Shin, D. H. (2009). Towards an understanding of the consumer acceptance of mobile wallet. *Computers in Human Behavior, 25*(6), 1343–1354. doi:10.1016/j.chb.2009.06.001.

Shin, N. (2006). Online learner's 'flow' experience: an empirical study. *British Journal of Educational Technology*, *37*(5), 705–720. doi:10.1111/j.1467-8535.2006.00641.x.

Simmel, G., & Frisby, D. (2004). *The philosophy of money*. London, UK: Routledge/Taylor & Francis Group.

Simon, H. A. (1982). *Models of bounded rationality (Vol. 2)*. Cambridge, MA: MIT Press.

Singh, V. (2008). *Pattern formation using gossip* (Unpublished master's thesis). Indian Institute of Technology, Kharagpur, India.

Smith, A., Banzaert, A., & Susnowitz, S. (2003). The MIT ideas competition: Promoting innovation for public service. In *Proceedings of the 33rd IEEE Annual Conference on Frontiers in Education* (Vol. 3).

Smith, A. (2009). *An inquiry into the nature and causes of the wealth of nations (reproduction)*. BiblioLife.

Smith, S. (2010). Social media done right. *Restaurant Business*, *109*, 20.

Soukhoroukova, A. (2007). *Produktinnovation mit Informationsmärkten*. Unpublished doctoral dissertation, University of Passau, Passau, Germany.

Speed, F. M., Hocking, R. R., & Hackney, O. P. (1978). Methods of Analysis of Linear Models with Unbalanced Data. *Journal of the American Statistical Association*, *73*(361), 105–112. doi:10.2307/2286530.

Spence, M., & Essoussi, L. H. (2010). SME brand building and management: An exploratory study. *European Journal of Marketing*, *44*(7-8), 1037–1054. doi:10.1108/03090561011047517.

Spohrer, J., Vargo, S. L., Caswell, N., & Maglio, P. P. (2008). The service system is the basic abstraction of service science. In *Proceedings of the 41st Hawaiian International Conference on Systems Sciences* (pp. 7-10).

Spohrer, J., & Maglio, P. P. (2008). The emergence of service science: Toward systematic service innovations to accelerate co-creation of value. *Production and Operations Management*, *17*(3), 238–246. doi:10.3401/poms.1080.0027.

SPSS Inc. (2006). *SPSS Advanced Models™ 15.0*. Chicago, IL: SPSS Inc..

Srinivas, M. N. (1952). *Religion and Society among the coorgs of South India*. Oxford, UK: Oxford University Press.

Starch, R. (2003). Online opinion leaders are highly influential. *Nua Internet Surveys*. Retrieved from http://www.nua.ie/surveys/?f=VS&art_id=905355852&rel=true

Stein, B., & Busch, M. (2005). Density-based cluster algorithms in low dimensional and high-dimensional application. In *Proceedings of the Second International Workshop on Text-Based Information Retrieval* (pp. 45-56).

Stoecklin-Serino, C. M., & Paradice, D. B. (2009). An examination of the impacts of brand equity, security, and personalization on trust processes in an e-commerce environment. *Journal of Organizational and End User Computing*, *21*(1), 36. doi:10.4018/joeuc.2009010101.

Stutzman, F. (2006). An evaluation of identity-sharing behavior in social network communities. *Journal of the International Digital Media and Arts Association*, *3*(1), 10–18.

Subramaniam, M., & Youndt, M. A. (2005). The influence of intellectual capital on the types of innovative capabilities. *Academy of Management Journal*, *48*(3), 450–463. doi:10.5465/AMJ.2005.17407911.

Summers, J. O. (1970). The identity of women's clothing fashion opinion leaders. *JMR, Journal of Marketing Research*, *7*(2), 178–185. doi:10.2307/3150106.

Sun, Y., & Yang, Y. (2007, June). Rust establishment in distributed networks: Analysis and modeling. In *Proceedings of the IEEE International Communications Conference*, Glasgow, UK (pp. 1266-1273).

Sunanda, S., Guan, C., & Siguaw, J. A. (2009). Virtual social networks: Toward a research agenda. *International Journal of Virtual Communities and Social Networking*, *1*(1), 1–13. doi:10.4018/jvcsn.2009010101.

Surma, J., & Furmanek, A. (2010). Improving marketing response by data mining in social network. In *Proceedings of the International Conference on Advance in Social Networks Analysis and Mining* (pp. 446-451).

Surunhanjaya Komunikasi dan Multimedia Malaysia [SKMM]. (2008). Household use of the Internet survey. *Statistical Brief, 7*(1).

Swami, S., Eliashberg, J., & Weinberg, C. B. (1999). SilverScreener: A modeling approach to movie screens management. *Marketing Science*, *18*(3), 352–272. doi:10.1287/mksc.18.3.352.

Sykes, A. T., Venkatesh, V., & Gosain, S. (2009). Model of acceptance with peer support: A social network perspective to understand employees' system use. *Management Information Systems Quarterly*, *33*(2), 371–393.

Sznajd-Weron, K., & Sznajd, J. (2000). Opinion evolution in closed community. *International Journal of Modern Physics C*, *11*, 1157–1166. doi:10.1142/S0129183100000936.

Szymanski, D. M., & Henard, D. H. (2001). Customer satisfaction: a meta-analysis of the empirical evidence. *Journal of the Academy of Marketing Science*, *29*(1), 16–35.

Tam, J. L. M. (2008). Brand familiarity: Its effects on satisfaction evaluations. *Journal of Services Marketing*, *22*(1), 3–12. doi:10.1108/08876040810851914.

Tan, P.-N., Steinbach, M., & Kumar, V. (2005). Introduction to data mining (U.S. ed.). Reading, MA: Addison-Wesley.

Tan, W., Nguyen, T. T. D., Oo Tha, K. K., & Yu, X. (2009, August 6-9). Designing groupware that fosters social capital creation: Can Facebook support global virtual teams? In *Proceedings of the Fifteenth Americas Conference on Information Systems*, San Francisco, CA.

Tauber, E. (1995). Why Do People Shop? *Marketing Management*, *4*(2), 58–60.

Tayor, J., & MacDonald, J. (2002). The effects of asynchronous computer-mediated group interaction on group processes. *Social Science Computer Review*, *20*(3), 260–274.

Technorati. (2009). *State of the Blogosphere 2009*. Retrieved October 19, 2011, from http://technorati.com/blogging/feature/state-of-the-blogosphere-2009

Tedeschi, B. (2006, September 11). Like Shopping? Social Networking? Try Social Shopping. *New York Times*, p. C6.

Teich, A. G. (2008). Using company blogs to win over decision-makers. *Publishing Research Quarterly*, *24*, 261–266. doi:10.1007/s12109-008-9090-y.

Terwiesch, C., & Ulrich, K. (2008). *Innovation tournaments: Creating, selecting, and developing exceptional opportunities*. Philadelphia, PA: The Wharton School.

Thathachar, M. A. L., & Sastry, P. S. (2004). *Networks of Learning Automata: Techniques for Online Stochastic Optimization*. Boston, MA: Kluwar Academic. doi:10.1007/978-1-4419-9052-5.

The Nielsen Company. (2009). *Global faces and networked places: A Nielsen report on social networking's new global footprint*. Retrieved August 20, 2011, from www.blog.nielsen.com/nielsenwire/wp-content/uploads/2009/03/nielsen_globalfaces_mar09.pdf

The Star. (2008). *Political tsunami*. Kuala Lumpur, Malaysia: The Star.

Thomke, S., & Von Hippel, E. (2002). Customers as innovators: A new way to create value. *Harvard Business Review*, *80*(4), 74–81.

Thorndike, R. K. (1920). Intelligent and its uses. *Harpers Magazine*, *140*, 227–335.

Tichy, M. N., Tushman, M. L., & Fombrun, C. (1979). Social network analysis for organizations. *Academy of Management Review*, *4*(4), 507–519.

Tidd, J., Bessant, J., & Pavitt, K. (1997). *Managing innovation: Integrating technological, market, and organizational change*. Chichester, UK: John Wiley & Sons.

Tong, Y., Wang, X., & Teo, H. H. (2007). Understanding the intention of information contribution to online feedback systems from social exchange and motivation crowding perspectives. In *Proceedings of the 40th Hawaii International Conference on System Sciences* (p. 28).

Trammell, K. D., & Gasser, U. (2004, May). *Deconstructing weblogs: An analytical framework for analyzing online journals*. Paper presented at the Communication and Technology Division, Internatimnal Communication Association, New Orleans, LA.

Trammell, K. D., & Keshelashvili, A. (2005). Examining the new influencers: A self-presentation study of a-list blogs. *Journalism & Mass Communication Quarterly*, *82*(4), 968–982.

Trevino, L. K., & Webster, J. (1992). Flow in computer-mediated communication: electronic mail and voice mail evaluation and impacts. *Communication Research, 19*(5), 539–573. doi:10.1177/009365092019005001.

Trusov, M., Bucklin, R., & Pauwels, K. (2009). Effects of Word-of-Mouth versus Traditional Marketing: Findings from an Internet Social Networking Site. *Journal of Marketing, 73*, 90–102. doi:10.1509/jmkg.73.5.90.

Tsai, T. M. Shih, C. C., & Chou, S. T. (2006). Personalized blog recommendation using the value, semantic, and social model. In *Proceedings of the 3rd International Conference on Innovations in Information Technology* (pp. 1-5).

Tse, A. C. (2003). Tipping behaviour: a disconfirmation of expectation perspective. *Hospital Management, 22*(4), 461–467. doi:10.1016/j.ijhm.2003.07.002.

Tufekci, Z. (2008). Grooming, gossip, Facebook and Myspace. What can we learn about these sites from those who won't assimilate? *Information Communication and Society, 11*(4), 544–564. doi:10.1080/13691180801999050.

Twitter. (2010, November). *Discovering who to follow* [Web log post]. Retrieved from http://blog.twitter.com/2010/07/discovering-who-to-follow.html

Ulicny, B., & Baclawski, K. (2007). New metrics for newsblog credibility. In *Proceedings of the International Conference on Weblogs and Social Media*, Boulder, CO.

UNESCO. (1979). *Educational reform: Experiences and prospects (Education on the Move Series)*. Paris, France: UNESCO.

Urban, G. L., Fareena, S., & William, J. Q. (2000). Placing trust at the center of your Internet strategy. *Sloan Management Review, 42*, 39–48.

Vaast, E. (2007). Playing with masks: Fragmentation and continuity in the presentation of self in an occupational online forum. *Information Technology & People, 20*(4), 334–351. doi:10.1108/09593840710839789.

Valente, T. W. (1995). *Network models of the diffusion of innovations*. Cresskill, NJ: Hampton.

Valente, T. W. (1996). Social network thresholds in the diffusion of innovations. *Social Networks, 18*(1), 69–89. doi:10.1016/0378-8733(95)00256-1.

Valente, T. W., & Davis, R. L. (1999). Accelerating the diffusion of innovations using opinion leaders. *The Annals of the American Academy of Political and Social Science, 566*(1), 55–67. doi:10.1177/0002716299566001005.

Valente, T. W., & Rogers, E. M. (1995). The origins and development of the diffusion of innovations paradigm as an example of scientific growth. *Science Communication: An Interdisciplinary Social Science Journal, 16*(3), 238–269.

Valkenburg, P. M., Peter, J., & Schouten, A. P. (2006). Friend networking sites and their relationship to adolescents' well-being and social self-esteem. *Cyberpsychology & Behavior, 9*(5), 584–590. doi:10.1089/cpb.2006.9.584 PMID:17034326.

Van de Fliert, E. (1993). *Integrated pest management: Farmer field schools generate sustainable practices. A case study in Central Java evaluating IPM training (Paper No. 93-3)*. Wageningen, The Netherlands: PUDOC, Wageningen Agricultural University.

Van den Bulte, C., & Joshi, Y. V. (2007). New product diffusion with influentials and imitators. *Marketing Science, 26*(3), 400–421. doi:10.1287/mksc.1060.0224.

van Dyke, T. P., Kappelman, L. A., & Prybutok, V. R. (1997). Measuring information systems service quality: Concerns on the use of the SERVQUAL questionnaire. *Management Information Systems Quarterly, 21*(2), 195–208. doi:10.2307/249419.

Vardi, M. Y. (2009). Conferences vs. journals in computing research. *Communications of the ACM, 52*(5). doi:10.1145/1506409.1506410 PMID:21218176.

Vargo, S. L., & Lusch, R. F. (2004). Evolving to a new dominant logic for marketing. *Journal of Marketing, 68*(1), 1–17. doi:10.1509/jmkg.68.1.1.24036.

Vega-Redondo, F. (2007). *Complex Social Networks (Econometric Society Monographs)*. Cambridge, UK: Cambridge University Press. doi:10.1017/CBO9780511804052.

Venkatesh, V., & Morris, M. G. (2000). Why don't men ever stop to ask for directions? Gender, social influence, and their role in technology acceptance and usage behavior. *Management Information Systems Quarterly, 24*(1), 115–139. doi:10.2307/3250981.

Venkatesh, V., Morris, M. G., Davis, G. B., & Davis, F. D. (2003). User acceptance of information technology: toward a unified view. *Management Information Systems Quarterly*, *27*(3), 425–478.

Vernette, E. (2004). Targeting women's clothing fashion opinion leaders in media planning: An application for magazines. *Journal of Advertising Research*, *44*, 90–107. doi:10.1017/S0021849904040061.

Vignette. (2009). *Extranet 2.0: Driving value and revenue through social media*. Retrieved from http://www.vignette.com/dafiles/docs/Downloads/WP-Extranet-2.0.pdf

Voight, J. (2007). Study Says Web Shoppers Crave 'Social' Experience. *Adweek*, *48*, 10.

Von Hayek, F. A. (1968). Der Wettbewerb als Entdeckungsverfahren. Kiel, Germany: Institut für Weltwirtschaft an der Universität Kiel.

Von Hayek, F. A. (1971). *Die verfassung der freiheit*. Tübingen, Germany: Mohr.

Von Hippel, E. (1978). Successful industrial products from customer ideas. *Journal of Marketing*, *42*(1), 39–49. doi:10.2307/1250327.

Von Hippel, E. (2005). *Democratizing innovation*. Cambridge, MA: MIT Press.

Walcher, D. (2007). *Der Ideenwettbewerb als Methode der aktiven Kundenintegration: Theorie, empirische Analyse und Implikationen fuer den Innovationsprozess*. Wiesbaden, Germany: Gabler.

Walking Around. (2004). *New York City's ethnic neighborhoods*. Retrieved April 22, 2009, from http://www.walkingaround.com

Wallmark, J. T. (1986). Innovation by contest. Innovation 83 – An Inter-Scandinavian innovation contest. *International Journal of Management Science*, *14*(3), 251–257.

Walsh, G., & Mitchell, V. W. (2001). German market mavens' decision making styles. *Journal of Euromarketing*, *10*(4), 83–108. doi:10.1300/J037v10n04_05.

Walther, J. B. (1992). Interpersonal effects in computer-mediated interaction: A relational perspective. *Communication Research*, *19*(1), 52–90. doi:10.1177/0093650 92019001003.

Walther, J. B. (1996). Computer-mediated communication: Impersonal, interpersonal, and hyperpersonal interaction. *Communication Research*, *23*(1), 3–43. doi:10.1177/009 365096023001001.

Wang, C. (2009). Linking Shopping and Social Networking: Approaches to Social Shopping. In *Proceedings of the 15th Americas Conference on Information Systems (AMCIS)*. Retrieved from http://aisel.aisnet.org/amcis2009/27

Wang, J., & Gallivan, M. (2009, August 6-9). An empirical study on the adoption of instant messaging for work purposes. In *Proceedings of the Fifteenth Americas Conference on Information Systems*, San Francisco, CA.

Wang, C., & Zhang, P. (in press). The Evolution of Social Commerce: People, Business, Technology and Information Aspects. *Communications of the Association for Information Systems*.

Wang, Y., & Fesenmaier, D. R. (2004). Towards understanding members' general participation in and active contribution to an online travel community. *Tourism Management*, *25*(6), 709–722. doi:10.1016/j.tourman.2003.09.011.

Ward, T. (2009). *Intranet 2.0: Social media becomes mainstream on the corporate Intranet. Summary of the Intranet 2.0 Global Survey*. Toronto, ON, Canada: Prescient Digital Media.

Warkentin, M. E., Sayeed, L., & Hightower, R. (1997). Virtual teams versus face-to-face teams: An exploratory study of a web-based conference system. *Decision Sciences*, *28*(4), 975–996. doi:10.1111/j.1540-5915.1997.tb01338.x.

Wasko, M. M. L., & Faraj, S. (2000). "It is what one does": Why people participate and help others in electronic communities of practice. *The Journal of Strategic Information Systems*, *9*, 155–173. doi:10.1016/S0963-8687(00)00045-7.

Wasko, M. M. L., & Faraj, S. (2005). Why should I share? Examining social capital and knowledge contribution in electronic communities of practice. *Management Information Systems Quarterly*, *29*(1), 35–57.

Wasserman, S., & Faust, K. (1994). *Social network analysis: Methods and application*. Cambridge, UK: Cambridge University Press.

Watika, K., & Tsurumi, T. (2007). Finding community structure in mega-scale social networks. In *Proceedings of the 16th International Conference on World Wide Web* (pp. 1275-1276).

Watts, D. J., & Dodds, P. S. (2007). Influentials, networks, and public opinion formation. *The Journal of Consumer Research*, *34*(4), 441–458. doi:10.1086/518527.

Watts, D. J., Doods, P. S., & Newman, M. E. J. (2002). Identity and search in social networks. *Science*, *296*, 1302–1305. doi:10.1126/science.1070120 PMID:12016312.

Webster, J., Trevino, L. K., & Ryan, L. (1993). The dimensionality and correlates of flow in human–computer interactions. *Computers in Human Behavior*, *9*(4), 411–426. doi:10.1016/0747-5632(93)90032-N.

Weimann, G. (1994). *The influentials*. Albany, NY: State University of New York Press.

Weiner, H. (2001, May 22-23). *Panel discussion*. Paper presented at the Pan-Canadian Education Research Agenda Symposium on From Theory into Practice: Teacher Education/Educator Training: Current Trends and Future Directions, Toronto, ON, Canada.

Weisband, S. P., Schneider, S. K., & Connolly, T. (1995). Computer-mediated communication and social information: Status salience and status differences. *Academy of Management Journal*, *38*(4), 1124–1995. doi:10.2307/256623.

Wei, T. T., Marthandan, G., Chong, A. Y. L., & Ooi, K. B. (2009). What drives Malaysian m-commerce adoption? An empirical analysis. *Industrial Management & Data Systems*, *109*(3), 370–388. doi:10.1108/02635570910939399.

Wellman, B., Haase, A. Q., Witte, J., & Hampton, K. (2001). Does the Internet increase, decrease, or supplement social capital? Social networks, participation, and community commitment. *The American Behavioral Scientist*, *45*(3), 436–455. doi:10.1177/00027640121957286.

Westbrook, R. A., & Reilly, M. D. (1983). Value-percept disparity: An alternative to the disconfirmation of expectations theory of consumer satisfaction. *Advances in Consumer Research. Association for Consumer Research (U. S.)*, *10*, 256–261.

White, G. C., & Bennetts, R. E. (1996). Analysis of frequency count data using the negative binomial distribution. *Ecology*, *77*(8), 2549–2557. doi:10.2307/2265753.

Wiertz, C., & de Ruyter, K. (2007). Beyond the call of duty: Why customers contribute to firm-hosted commercial online communities. *Organization Studies*, *28*(3), 347–376. doi:10.1177/0170840607076003.

Wikipedia. (2010). *DBSCAN*. Retrieved from http://en.wikipedia.org/wiki/DBSCAN

Wikipedia. (2010). *Delicious.com*. Retrieved from http://en.wikipedia.org/wiki/Delicious.com

Wikipedia. (2010). *Semantic Web*. Retrieved from http://en.wikipedia.org/wiki/Semantic_Web

Wikipedia. (2011). *Human height*. Retrieved August 20, 2011, from http://www.en.wikipedia.org/wiki/Human_height

Wikipedia. (2011). *Pareto principle*. Retrieved May 10, 2011, from http://www.en.wikipedia.org/wiki/Pareto_principle

Wikipedia. (n. d.). *Ethnic enclave*. Retrieved March 18, 2009, from http://en.wikipedia.org/wiki/New_York_City_ethnic_enclaves

Williamson, O. E. (1993). Calculativeness, trust, and economic organization. *The Journal of Law & Economics*, *36*(1), 453–486. doi:10.1086/467284.

Williams, R. L. (1999). Managing an online community. *Journal for Quality and Participation*, *22*, 54–55.

Williams, T. G., & Slama, M. E. (1995). Market mavens' purchase decision evaluative criteria: Implications for brand and store promotion efforts. *Journal of Consumer Marketing*, *12*(3), 4–21. doi:10.1108/07363769510147218.

Woodruff, S. (2009, February 19). A handful of training tools. *Impactiviti Blog*. Retrieved August 31, 2009, from http://impactiviti.wordpress.com/2009/02/19/a-handful-of-training

Woolard, C. (2011). Virtual now part of show. *B to B*, *96*(4).

Wu, B. Y., & Chao, K.-M. (2004). *Spanning trees and optimization problems*. Boca Raton, FL: Chapman and Hall/CRC Press.

Wu, J. J., & Chang, Y. S. (2005). Towards understanding members' interactivity, trust, and flow in online travel community. *Industrial Management & Data Systems*, *105*(7), 937–954. doi:10.1108/02635570510616120.

Wu, J., Chen, Y., & Chung, Y. (2010). Trust factors influencing virtual community members: A study of transaction communities. *Journal of Business Research*, *63*(9-10), 1025–1032. doi:10.1016/j.jbusres.2009.03.022.

Wynn, E., & Katz, J. E. (1997). Hyperbole over cyberspace: Self-presentation and social boundaries in internet home pages and discourse. *The Information Society*, *13*(4), 297–327. doi:10.1080/019722497129043.

Xinyi, A. G. (2008). *Who are the influentials in virtual community? Opinion leaders among participants in bulletin board systems*. Hong Kong: School of Journalism and Communication, The Chinese University of Hong Kong.

Xiong, L., & Liu, L. (2004). Peer trust: Supporting reputation-based trust for peer-to-peer electronic communities. *IEEE Transactions on Knowledge and Data Engineering*, *16*(16).

Xu, R., & Wunsch, D. (2008). Clustering (IEEE Press Series on Computational Intelligence) (illustrated ed.). Piscataway, NJ: Wiley-IEEE Press.

Xue, M., & Field, J. M. (2008). Service coproduction with information stickiness and incomplete contracts: Implications for consulting services design. *Production and Operations Management*, *17*(3), 357–372. doi:10.3401/poms.1080.0024.

Xu, J. J., & Chen, H. (2005). CrimeNet explorer: A framework for criminal network knowledge discovery. *ACM Transactions on Information Systems*, *23*(2), 201–226. doi:10.1145/1059981.1059984.

Xu, R., & Wunsch, I. (2005). Survey of clustering algorithms. *IEEE Transactions on Neural Networks*, *16*(3), 645–678. doi:10.1109/TNN.2005.845141 PMID:15940994.

Yang, Z., Cai, S., Zhou, Z., & Zhou, N. (2005). Development and validation of an instrument to measure user perceived service quality of information presenting web portals. *Information & Management*, *42*(4), 575–589. doi:10.1016/S0378-7206(04)00073-4.

Yang, Z., & Jun, M. (2002). Consumer perception of e-service quality: From internet purchaser and non-purchaser perspectives. *The Journal of Business Strategy*, *19*(1), 19–41.

Yardi, S., Golder, S., & Brzozowski, M. (2008). *The pulse of the corporate blogosphere*. Paper presented at the Conference Supplement of the Computer Supported Collaborative Works Poster Session.

Yen, H. J., & Hsu, H. Y. (2006). Consumer co-production in product-related virtual community - Does community management matter? In *Proceedings of the 11th Annual Conference of Asia Pacific Decision Sciences Institute*, Hong Kong (pp. 14-18).

Yu, H. (2008). The exploration on the BBS opinion leadership filtering model. *The Journal of Communication*, *15*, 66–75.

Zack, M. H. (1993). Interactivity and communication mode choice in ongoing management groups. *Information Systems Research*, *4*(3), 207–239. doi:10.1287/isre.4.3.207.

Zeger, S. L., Liang, K. Y., & Albert, P. S. (1988). Models for longitudinal data: A generalized estimating equation approach. *Biometrics*, *44*, 1049–1060. doi:10.2307/2531734 PMID:3233245.

Zeithaml, V. A., Parasuraman, A., & Malhotra, A. (2000). *A conceptual framework for understanding e-service quality: Implications for future research and managerial practice* (Report No. 00-115). Cambridge, MA: Marketing Science Institute.

Zeithaml, V. A. (2002). Service excellence in electronic channels. *Managing Service Quality*, *12*(3), 135–138. doi:10.1108/09604520210429187.

Zeithaml, V. A., Parasuraman, A., & Malhotra, A. (2002). Service quality delivery through web sites: A critical review of extant knowledge. *Journal of the Academy of Marketing Science*, *30*(4), 362–375. doi:10.1177/009207002236911.

Zelasity, M. (2005). Engineering emergence through gossip. In Proceedings of the Joint Symposium on Socially Inspired Computing, AISB Convention, Hatfield, UK (pp. 123-126).

Zhang, Y., Zhaoqing, W., & Xia, C. (2010, April 20-23). Identifying key users for targeted marketing by mining online social network. In *Proceedings of the 24th Conference on Advanced Information Networking and Applications Workshops*, Perth, Australia (pp. 644-649).

Zhang, X., & Prybutok, V. R. (2005). A consumer perspective of e-service quality. *IEEE Transactions on Engineering Management, 52*(4), 461–477. doi:10.1109/TEM.2005.856568.

Zhao, S., Grasmuck, S., & Martin, J. (2008). Identity construction on Facebook: Digital empowerment in anchored relationships. *Computers in Human Behavior, 24*(5), 1816–1836. doi:10.1016/j.chb.2008.02.012.

Zhou, Y., & Davis, J. (2007). Discovering web communities in the blogspace. In *Proceedings of the 40th Annual Hawaii International Conference on System Sciences* (pp. 85-85). Retrieved from http://ieeexplore.ieee.org/xpls/abs_all.jsp?arnumber=4076542

Zukerman, H. (1977). *Scientific elite: Nobel laureates in the United States*. New York, NY: Free Press.

Zuk, R. (2009). Pulse rate: Assess your social media channels regularly. *Public Relations: Tactics, 16*(11), 7.

About the Contributors

Subhasish Dasgupta is an associate professor of information systems in the School of Business, George Washington University. Dasgupta received his PhD from Baruch College, The City University of New York (CUNY). He received both his MBA and BS from the University of Calcutta (India). He has published his research in refereed journals such as *Decision Support Systems*, the *European Journal of Information System*, the *Journal of Global Information Management*, the *Electronic Markets Journal*, and the *Simulation and Gaming Journal*. Dasgupta has published two edited books, *Internet and Intranet Technologies in Organizations* and *Encyclopedia of Virtual Communities and Technologies*. He has also presented his research in major regional, national, and international conferences.

* * *

Abdollah Aghaie is an associate professor and head of the Industrial Engineering Department at K. N. Toosi University of Technology in Tehran, Iran. He received his BSc from Sharif University of Technology in Tehran, MSc from New South Wales University in Sydney and PhD from Loughborough University in UK. His main research interests are in Modeling and Simulation, Quality Management and Control, Social Networks, Knowledge Management, Risk Management, Internet Marketing and Ergonomics.

Demosthenes Akoumianakis is Professor at the Department of Applied Information Technology & Multimedia, Technological Education Institution of Crete. He is also the founder and Director of the interactive Software and Systems Engineering Laboratory (iSTLab, http://www.istl.teiher.gr/). Prof. Akoumianakis has published widely in referred archival scientific journals, international conferences and workshops and is the author/co-author of several books. He also serves as a member of the scientific committee for various established archival journals, international conferences and national/international standards bodies.

Somayeh Alizadeh is an assistant professor in the department of Industrial Engineering at K. N. Toosi University of technology, Tehran-Iran. She received her BSc from Sharif University of Technology in Tehran, MSc and PhD from IUST University in Tehran. Her main research interests are in Information Technology, Data mining and Social Network.

Yacine Atif received the PhD degree in Computer Science from Hong Kong University of Science and Technology (HKUST) in 1996. After graduation, he worked at Purdue University in the USA as a Post- Doc and then joined a faculty position at Nanyang Technological University (NTU) in Singapore. Since 1999 he is with the UAE University as faculty, then Program Chair at the College of Information Technology. Dr. Atif has made a number of research contributions particularly in the areas of Semantic Web and Learning Technology. He is also involved in the Technical Programs of several research forums.

Nana Adu-Pipim Boaduo was born in Ghana. After graduating in 1973 as a professional certificated teacher from Offinso Teacher Training College, he taught at Methodist Primary School at Eduadin in the Ashanti Region of Ghana. From October 1974 to August 1976 he studied at the University Of Cape Coast at Winneba Advanced Teacher Training College campus. From September 1976 to August 1980 he worked for the Ghana Ministry of Education at Agogo State Secondary school, Agogo. From September 1980 to December 1983, he taught at Government Girls Secondary School, Kaduna State and Uavande Girls School near Aliade in Benue State both in Nigeria. While in southern Africa, he taught in secondary and high schools in Lesotho, the former homelands of Venda and Gazankulu. He studied with the College of Preceptors in the UK (1986-1988) and obtained the ACP and LCP qualifications respectively. From 1993 to 2001, Dr. Boaduo studied with Vista University for his MEd (1996) and PhD (1998) and the University of the Free State for masters in Development Studies (MDS (2001)). From March 1992 up until December 1997 Dr. Boaduo served in different capacities at Lemana College of Education as lecturer, senior lecturer and head of department. From 1998 to 2001, he was appointed Geography subject advisor in the Soutpansberg District of the Limpopo Province of South Africa. From 1999 to 2001, he was appointed as Vista University Distance Education coordinator at the Lemana College Campus, Elim in the Limpopo Province. He joined the University of Botswana from August 2004 until February 2008. He has written and published numerous articles in hard print and on line as well as presented seminar, and conference papers and organised workshops for professional teacher development. He has published eight academic textbooks with Lambert Academic Publishing, Germany in 2011 alone. Currently, he is appointed as Senior Lecturer, Faculty of Education, School of Continuing Professional Teacher Development, Walter Sisulu University at Mthatha Campus, Eastern Cape Province of South African and also serve as Affiliated Researcher: Faculty of Economic and Management Sciences, Centre for Development Support University of the Free State (Bloemfontein Campus): South Africa.

Charlie C. Chen is an Associate Professor in the Department of Computer Information Systems in the Walker College of Business at Appalachian State University in Boone, North Carolina. He received his PhD in Management Information Systems from Claremont Graduate University in 2003. He has authored more than 50 referred articles and proceedings, and he has presented his work at many professional conferences and venues. Dr. Chen has published in journals such as *Communications of the Association for Information Systems, Behaviour and Information Technology, International Journal of Project Management, Information and Software Technology*, and *IEEE Transactions on Engineering Management*. Dr. Chen is a Project Management Professional (PMP) certified by the Project Management Institute.

Alan J. Dubinsky (PhD, University of Minnesota) is the Dillard Distinguished professor of marketing in the Dillard College of Business Administration at Midwestern State University, Director of CALIMT Learning and Innovation Research Center, and Professor Emeritus at Purdue University. Prior to entering academia, he was a territory manager for Burroughs Corporation (now Unisys). His research has appeared in the Journal of Marketing, Journal of Marketing Research, Journal of Retailing, Journal of the Academy of Marketing Science, Journal of Applied Psychology, Personnel Psychology, Academy of Management Journal, Leadership Quarterly, and Sloan Management Review, among others. He is a former editor of the Journal of Personal Selling and Sales Management.

Leila Esmaeili is a MSc student of Information Technology Engineering in field of eCommerce in University of Qom, Qom, Iran; According to her interest in social network analysis and data mining, her thesis is about recommender systems in social networks.

Kanna Al Falahi is currently a PhD student at the Faculty of Information Technology (FIT) in the United Arab Emirates University. She works on analyzing Online Social Networks. She published original contributions in Web Recommender Systems as well as Social Influence Maximization in Web based social networks.

Saad Harous obtained his PhD in computer science from Case Western Reserve University, Cleveland, OH, USA in 1991. He has more than 20 years of experience in teaching and research in 3 different countries: USA, Oman and UAE. He is currently an Associate Professor at the Faculty of Information Technology, in United Arab Emirates University. His teaching interests include programming, data structures, design and analysis of algorithms, operating systems and network. His research interests include Parallel and Distributed Computing, and the Use of Computers in Education and processing Arabic language. He has published more than 60 journal and conference papers. He is an IEEE senior member.

Nor Laily Hashim is a senior lecturer in the School of Computing, College of Arts and Science, UUM. She obtained a PhD in Information Technology (Monash University, Melbourne), MSc Info. Tech (Carnegie Mellon University) and Bach. Information Technology (Hons.) (Universiti Utara Malaysia). Her research interests are in software testing, software architecture, software engineering, healthcare mobile application, and social media.

Shahizan Hassan, a PhD degree holder from the University of Newcastle upon Tyne, United Kingdom, is an associate professor in information systems and PhD programme Director at the Othman Yeop Abdullah Graduate school of Business, Universiti Utara Malaysia. He is very active in research projects in the area of information systems evaluation, Web design and evaluation, knowledge management, electronic government, and wireless applications. He had published three books, seventeen articles in national and international journals, and more than 30 articles in seminar and conferences.

Ching-Cha Hsieh received her PhD degree from National Chiao-Tung University, Taiwan. Currently, she is an Associate Professor at Department of Information Management, National Taiwan University. She has a longstanding interest in qualitative research method and has written on a range of topics in IT in organization transformation and human behavior in IT society.

Chia-Lin Hsu is currently a PhD candidate in the department of business administration, National Taiwan University of Science and Technology. His research interests include consumer behavior, electronic commerce and service marketing.

Nikolas Karadimitriou is an undergraduate at the Department of Applied Information Technology & Multimedia of the Technological Education Institution of Crete and currently is in his final year of studies. Since 2011, he is a member of the Interactive Software and Systems Engineering Laboratory (iSTLab, http://www.istl.teiher.gr/) and got involved with research on visualization and social networks.

Purnendu Karmakar was born in Kolkata, West Bengal, India. He obtained his bachelor of electronics and communication engineering degree with 1st class from Kalyani Govt. Engineering College, University of Kalyani, West Bengal, India in 2002. He got his M. Tech degree in E and ECE from IIT, Kharagpur, India in 2008. Since, 2003 he worked as a lecturer in Birbhum Institute of Engineering and Technology, Suri, India. He also served as visiting lecturer in Jalpaiguri Govt. Engineering College, West Bengal, India. He is now pursuing PhD in GSSST, IIT Kharagpur. His area of interest is computer communication and networking, Wireless networks, Internet algorithms.

Lynn B. Keane is an instructor in the Integrated Information Technology program in the College of Hospitality, Retail, and Sport Management at the University of South Carolina. She teaches computer applications and IT training courses. Her research interests focus on learning in community, service and experiential learning, and new technologies to support learning and collaboration. Dr. Keane has a BS and MS from Pace University and a PhD from New York University.

Giorgos Ktistakis holds a BSc degree in Computer Science from the University of Crete and he is currently MSc student at the Department of Applied Information Technology & Multimedia, Technological Institution of Crete. He has participated in various research and development programs both National and European, as member of the interactive Software Technologies & System Engineering Laboratory (iSTLab, http://www.istl.teiher.gr/). He has a wide range of skills in programming and his research interests are: eLearning, public APIs, social networking and human-computer interaction.

Mikko O. J. Laine is a doctoral student at the Department of Industrial Engineering and Management at Aalto University School of Science, where he has also received his M.Sc. degree. His doctoral research examines open innovation in the online media. His other areas of research interest include entrepreneurship and organizational behavior. He has been a visiting scholar at Stanford University and University of California, Berkeley, and has presented his work in various international conferences. Currently, he is also working as a project manager and researcher at BIT Research Centre at Aalto University. Previously he has worked in the telecommunications and mobile software industries in various roles including project manager.

Chien-nai Lin received her PhD degree from department of information management, National Taiwan University. Before engaging in the academic filed, she had worked at IBM as a System Engineer and at Chunghwa Telecom, Taiwan as an IT researcher. She holds MS/MIS degree from Boston University, bachelor's degree in MIS from National Sun Yat-Sen University, Taiwan. She is currently an independent researcher. She focuses her interests on human behavior in virtual world, especially Internet addiction in adolescents and Internet isolation in aged people.

Yu-Tzu Lin is the instructor of International Business Administration Program (IBAP) at International Trade Institute (ITI) in Taiwan. Prior to her appointment at ITI, she received her PhD from the Information Management department at the National Taiwan University. Her research focuses on applying qualitative research method to understand how the adoption and diffusion of IT innovation within organizations shapes and it shaped over time by its changing institutional and technological contexts. She is the recipient of the Best Thesis Award from Taiwan Information Management Doctoral Consortium in 2011. Her PhD thesis addresses the importance of discourse in shaping the interpretation and understanding of IT innovation in financial industry. Her research work has appeared in a variety of journals and conferences, including Journal of Information Management, ICIS, PACIS, HICSS, and AOM.

Kamna Malik, PhD, is associate professor of IT Management at U21Global Graduate School, Singapore. She has handled diverse roles in software and IT infrastructure projects, management education, research and consulting. Her broad teaching and research focus lies in enabling better use of IT for improved business value. Her work has appeared in international publications including Emerald, IEEE, IGI Global, McGraw-Hill, MIT, and Springer. She consistently volunteers as a conference organizer and also as a guest editor and reviewer for refereed international journals.

B. Dawn Medlin is Professor and Chair of the Department of Computer Information Systems and the Co-Director of the Center for Advanced Research on Emerging Technologies, John A. Walker College of Business, at Appalachian State University in Boone, NC. She has published in journals such as *The Journal of Information Systems Security*, *Information Systems Security*, *International Journal of Electronic Marketing and Retailing*, and the *International Journal of Healthcare Information Systems and Informatics*. Dr. Medlin's academic profile includes Université d'Angers and Addis Ababa University in Ethiopia.

Giannis Milolidakis holds a BSc degree (in Applied Information Technology & Multimedia) from the Technological Education Institution of Crete in 2007. Since 2008, he is a PhD student in Euromed Marseille Ecole de Management, France. His research is broadly related to practice-based theory and its implications for information systems. Currently is an affiliated researcher of the Interactive Software and Systems Engineering Laboratory (iSTLab, http://www.istl.teiher.gr/) and has become involved in various national and European Research and Development projects.

Behrouz Minaei-Bidgoli obtained his PhD degree from Michigan State University, East Lansing, Michigan, USA, in the field of Data Mining and Web-Based Educational Systems in Computer Science and Engineering Department. He is working as an assistant professor in Computer Engineering Department of Iran University of Science & Technology, Tehran, Iran. He is also leading at a Data and Text Mining research group in Computer Research Center of Islamic Sciences, NOOR co. Qom, Iran, developing large scale NLP and Text Mining projects for Farsi and Arabic languages.

Niyoosha Jafari Momtaz earned a bachelor's degree in computer engineering from Bu-Ali Sina University, Hamedan-Iran. She received her master's degree in Information Technology from K. N. Toosi University of Technology, Tehran-Iran. Her research has focused on social network analysis in marketing activities. She is also interested in the fields of consumer behavior in electronic commerce, data mining and metaheuristic algorithms.

Mahdi Nasiri is a PhD student in the Department of Computer Engineering in Iran University of Science & Technology, Tehran, Iran. He has worked on data mining and link analysis.

Karen P. Patton is an assistant professor in the Integrated Information Technology program at the University of South Carolina, Columbia, SC. She teaches IT project management, telecommunications, and networking. Her research interests include executive IT management issues, mobility technology management, and IT curriculum development. She has a BS from Purdue University, an MS from the University of Minnesota, and a PhD from the New Jersey Institute of Technology. She is the author of *Data Networking Made Easy* for small business owners and has published articles in *Communications of the Association for Computing Machinery, Communications of the Association for Information Systems, Cutter IT Journal,* and the *International Journal of Computers, Systems and Signals.*

Juhana Peltonen is a doctoral student at the Department of industrial engineering and management at Aalto University School of Science. In his doctoral research, he examines the performance of small entrepreneurial firms in recession. Mr. Peltonen holds a MS degree in software engineering from Tampere University of Technology. Prior to his doctoral studies, he worked as a project manager in the software industry specializing in mobile infrastructure and applications, and managed research projects at Aalto University. He has also been a visiting scholar at Stanford University and presented his work at the Academy of Management Meeting, Strategic Management Society Conference, and the Babson College Entrepreneurship Research Conference.

Rajarshi Roy was born in Kolkata, West Bengal, India. He obtained his BE degree in electronics and telecommunication with 1st class (Hons.) from Jadavpur University, Kolkata, West Bengal, India in 1992. He got his MS (Engg.) degree in ECE from IISc, Bangalore, India in 1995. He got his PhD in electrical engineering from Polytechnic University, Brooklyn, NY, USA in 2001. He is now serving department of E and ECE, IIT, Kharagpur, India as an associate professor. His area of interest is communication networks, internet algorithms, information systems, queuing and optimization.

Mohd Samsu Sajat is a lecturer at Universiti Utara Malaysia (UUM). He has a Bachelor Degree in Information Studies majoring in Information System Management from Universiti Teknologi MARA (UiTM) and Master of Science in Information Technology from UUM. He is certified as Cisco Network Associates (CCNA), Cisco Certified Network Professional (CCNP) and EC-Council Certified Security Specialist (ECSS). He is actively doing research in networking including grid computing and Wi-Fi security and currently involves in social media research.

Mohd Fo'ad Sakdan, a PhD degree holder from the University of Hull, United Kingdom, is an Associate Professor in Conflict Management at School of Law, Governance and International Studies, Universiti Utara Malaysia (UUM). He is very active in research projects in the area of conflict management and election. To date, he had completed thirteen research projects funded by various agencies. He has vast teaching experiences in Conflict management.

Norshuhada Shiratuddin is a professor in IT specializing in Design Research. She obtained her PhD in Computer and Information Sciences (Uni. of Strathclyde, Glasgow), MSc IT (Uni. of Nottingham, UK) and BSc (Hons) Maths, Stats and Computing (Uni. of Manchester, UK). Her research interests are in multimedia development, social media usage, mobile advances and e-learning. She has published in more than 30 journals. Currently, she is the Dean of the School of Multimedia Technology and Communication, Uni. Utara Malaysia (UUM).

Yong Tan is a professor of information systems and Evert McCabe faculty fellow at the Michael G. Foster School of Business, University of Washington. His research interests include electronic and social commerce, economics of information systems, social and economic networks, and software engineering. He has published in Management Science, Information Systems Research, Operations Research, Management Information Systems Quarterly, Journal of Management Information Systems, INFORMS Journal on Computing, IEEE/ACM Transactions on Networking, IEEE Transactions on Software Engineering, IEEE Transactions on Knowledge and Data Engineering, IIE Transactions, European Journal on Operations Research, and Decision Support Systems. He served as an associate editor of Information Systems Research and is an associate editor of Management Science.

Aku Valtakoski is a post-doc researcher at the BIT Research Centre of Aalto University School of Science. His research interests include understanding the impact of service provision on organizational learning, firm performance and industry evolution. Currently, he is working in a research project studying the provision of knowledge-intensive services by manufacturing firms. He has presented his work at international management conferences, including Academy of Management meetings and European Academy of Management conferences. He gained his PhD degree from Aalto University, and also holds M.Sc. and M.Soc.Sc. degrees from University of Helsinki.

Sandra A. Vannoy is an Assistant Professor in the Department of Computer Information Systems in the Walker College of Business at Appalachian State University in Boone, North Carolina. She received her PhD in Information Systems from the University of North Carolina at Greensboro in 2010. Her research has appeared in such journals as *Information Systems Research* and *Communications of the ACM*, among others. Dr. Vannoy has presented her research at international conferences including the International Conference on Information Systems (ICIS), Americas Conference on Information Systems (AMCIS), and the Institute for Operations Research and the Management Sciences (INFORMS). She serves as a Co-Editor of the *International Journal of Dependable and Trustworthy Information Systems*.

George Vlachakis holds a BSc degree in Applied Information Technology from the Technological Education Institution of Crete in 2011 and he is currently MSc student at the Department of Applied Information Technology & Multimedia of the Technological Institution of Crete. Since 2011, he is a member of the Interactive Software and Systems Engineering Laboratory (iSTLab, http://www.istl.teiher.gr/).

Chingning Wang is an assistant professor at the National Sun Yat-Sen University. She earned her PhD at the Syracuse University in the United States. Her current research interests include social commerce, organizational communication, media management and IT professional management.

Cou-Chen Wu is professor of business administration at National Taiwan University of Science and Technology. He received his PhD in management science and operations research from the University of California, Berkeley. Her research interests are brand management, high-tech marketing, strategic marketing, consumer behavior, and electronic commerce. His work has appeared in journals such as *European Journal of Marketing, European Journal of Operational Research, African Journal of Business Management, Journal of Product & Brand Management, Journal of Consumer Behaviour, The Scientific World Journal, and Journal of Operational Research Society*.

Guoying Zhang is an assistant professor of management information systems at the Dillard College of Business Administration, Midwestern State University. She received her PhD in information systems from the University of Washington. Her research interests include information security, social networks, and economics of information systems. She has published in Decision Support Systems, International Journal of Networking and Virtual Organisations, Journal of International Technology and Information Management, Journal of Selling and Major Account Management, Southwestern Business Administration Journal.

Index